WESTON CAGE & NICOLAS CAGE'S

VOODOO CHILD ™

WESTON CAGE & NICOLAS CAGE'S
VOODOO CHILD ™

created by
WESTON CAGE &
NICOLAS CAGE

story by
WESTON CAGE
NICOLAS CAGE
& MIKE CAREY

script
MIKE CAREY

Art
DEAN RUBEN HYRAPIET

COLOR
S. SUNDARAKANNAN

cover Art
BEN TEMPLESMITH

Additional covers
BEN TEMPLESMITH
JONATHAN HICKMAN
DEAN RUBEN HYRAPIET with
R. GAVASKAR &
S. SUNDARAKANNAN

COLOR CONSULTANT
LAURA MARTIN

Letters
NiLesh S. Mahadik
Rakesh B. Mahadik
SUDHIR B. PISAL
NiLesh P. KudaLe

project manager
REUBEN THOMAS

coLLected editions
project Manager
SANDEEP NAIR

coLLected editions Editor
SANA AMANAT

Assistant Editor
CHARLIE BECKERMAN

Editor
MACKENZIE CADENHEAD

special thanks to
NORM GOLIGHTLY

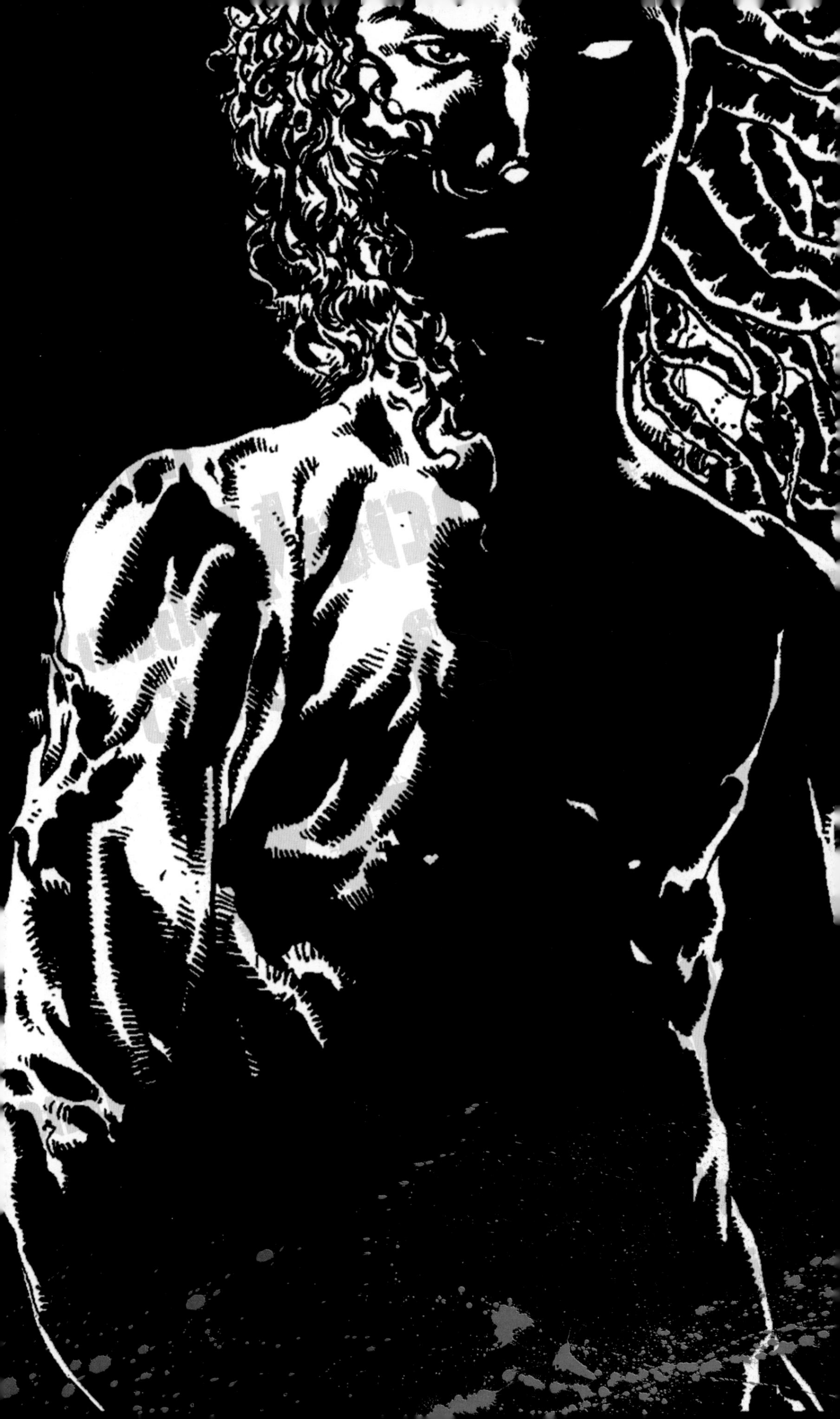

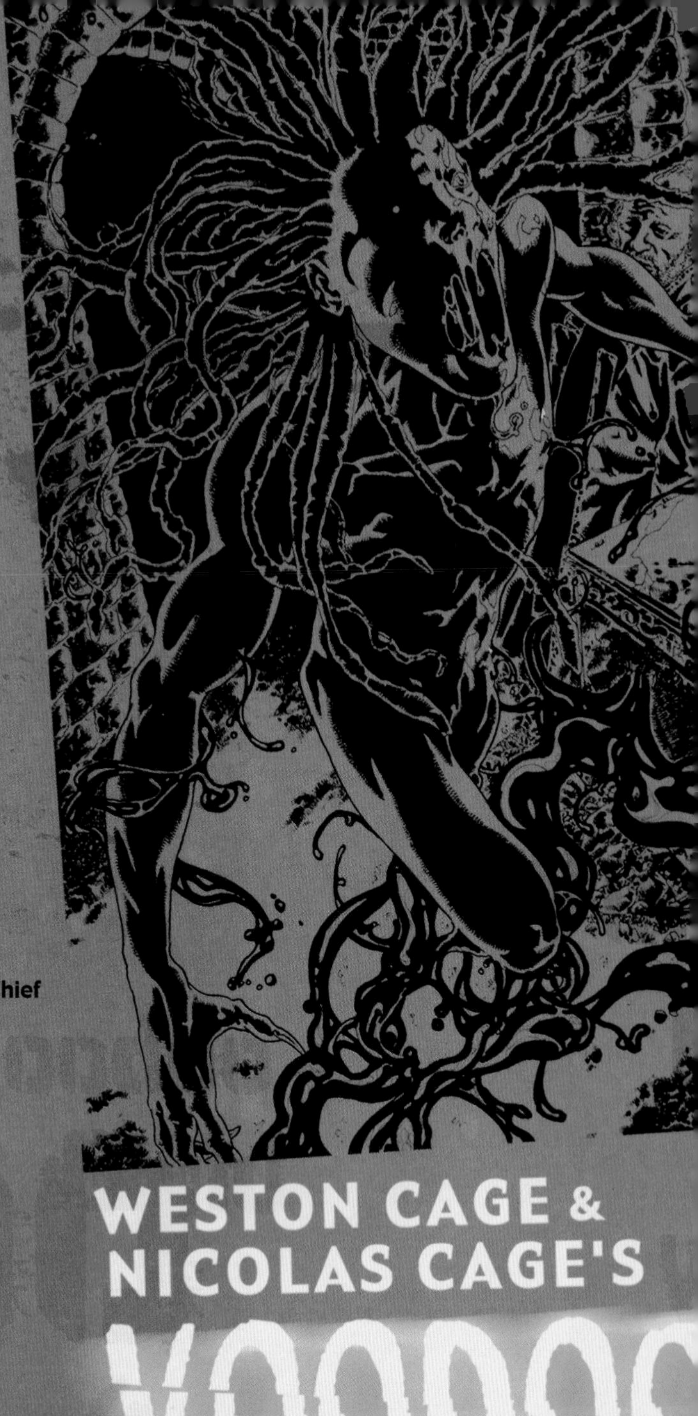

WESTON CAGE & NICOLAS CAGE'S

VOODOO CHILD™

VIRGIN COMICS

Chief Executive Officer and Publisher
SHARAD DEVARAJAN

Chief Creative Officer and Editor-in-Chief
GOTHAM CHOPRA

President and Studio Chief
SURESH SEETHARAMAN

Chief Marketing Officer
LARRY LIEBERMAN

SRVP - Studio
JEEVAN KANG

VP - Operations
ALAGAPPAN KANNAN

Director of Development
MACKENZIE CADENHEAD

Chief Visionaries
DEEPAK CHOPRA,
SHEKHAR KAPUR,
SIR RICHARD BRANSON

Special Thanks to:
Frances Farrow, Dan Porter, Christopher Linen, Peter Feldman, Raju Puthukarai, Mallika Chopra and Jonathan Peachey

VOODOO CHILD Vol. 1, January 2008 published by VIRGIN COMICS L.L.C. OFFICE OF PUBLICATION: 594 Broadway, New York, NY 10012.

For advertising, licensing and sales info please contact:
info@virgincomics.com or (212) 584-4040.
www.virgincomics.com

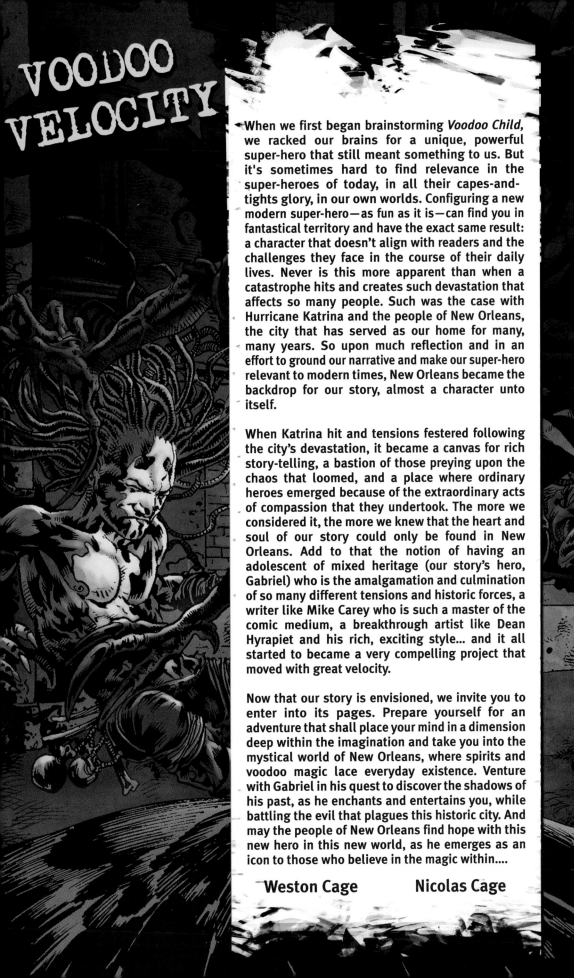

VOODOO VELOCITY

When we first began brainstorming *Voodoo Child*, we racked our brains for a unique, powerful super-hero that still meant something to us. But it's sometimes hard to find relevance in the super-heroes of today, in all their capes-and-tights glory, in our own worlds. Configuring a new modern super-hero—as fun as it is—can find you in fantastical territory and have the exact same result: a character that doesn't align with readers and the challenges they face in the course of their daily lives. Never is this more apparent than when a catastrophe hits and creates such devastation that affects so many people. Such was the case with Hurricane Katrina and the people of New Orleans, the city that has served as our home for many, many years. So upon much reflection and in an effort to ground our narrative and make our super-hero relevant to modern times, New Orleans became the backdrop for our story, almost a character unto itself.

When Katrina hit and tensions festered following the city's devastation, it became a canvas for rich story-telling, a bastion of those preying upon the chaos that loomed, and a place where ordinary heroes emerged because of the extraordinary acts of compassion that they undertook. The more we considered it, the more we knew that the heart and soul of our story could only be found in New Orleans. Add to that the notion of having an adolescent of mixed heritage (our story's hero, Gabriel) who is the amalgamation and culmination of so many different tensions and historic forces, a writer like Mike Carey who is such a master of the comic medium, a breakthrough artist like Dean Hyrapiet and his rich, exciting style... and it all started to became a very compelling project that moved with great velocity.

Now that our story is envisioned, we invite you to enter into its pages. Prepare yourself for an adventure that shall place your mind in a dimension deep within the imagination and take you into the mystical world of New Orleans, where spirits and voodoo magic lace everyday existence. Venture with Gabriel in his quest to discover the shadows of his past, as he enchants and entertains you, while battling the evil that plagues this historic city. And may the people of New Orleans find hope with this new hero in this new world, as he emerges as an icon to those who believe in the magic within....

Weston Cage   **Nicolas Cage**

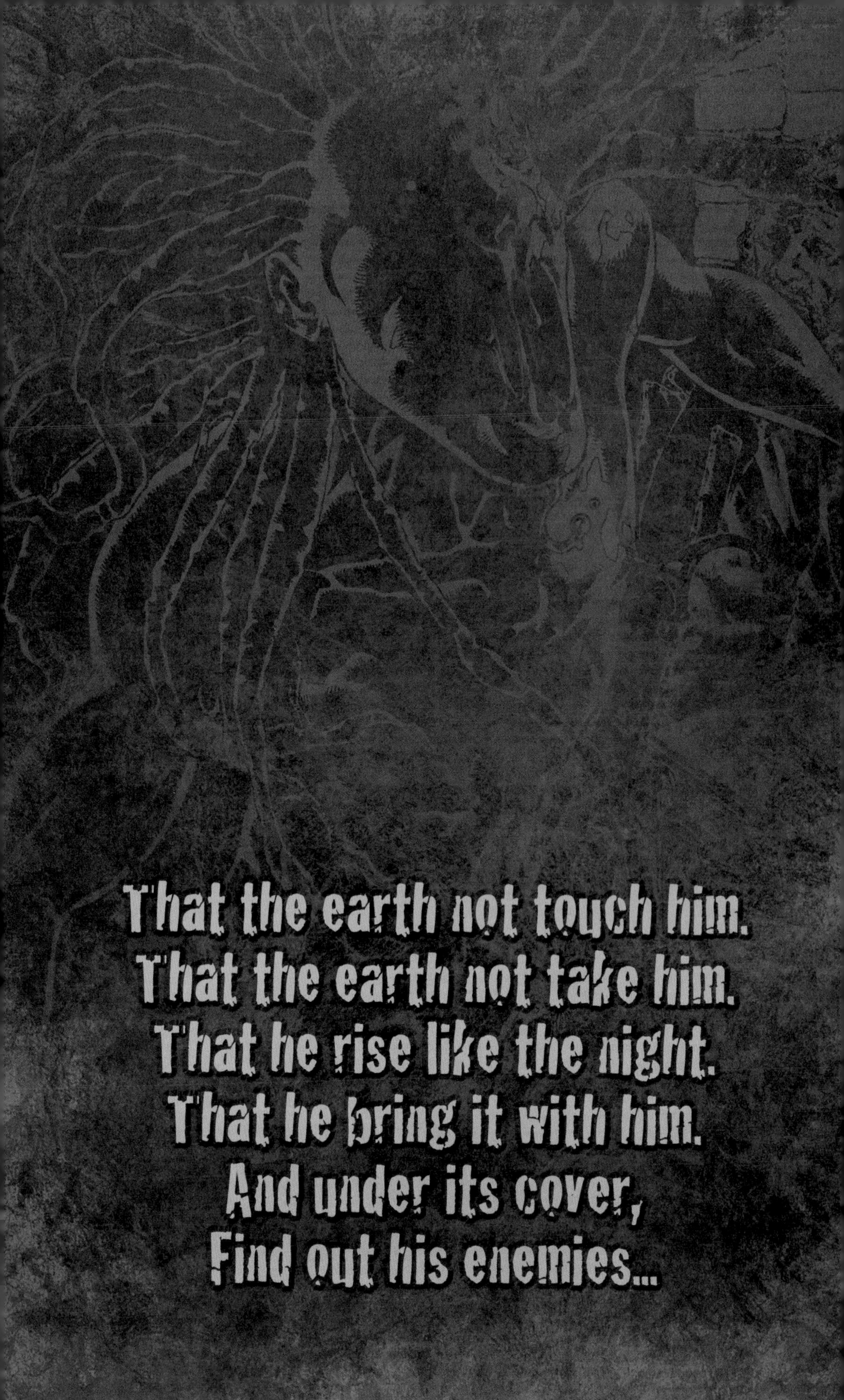

That the earth not touch him.
That the earth not take him.
That he rise like the night.
That he bring it with him.
And under its cover,
Find out his enemies...

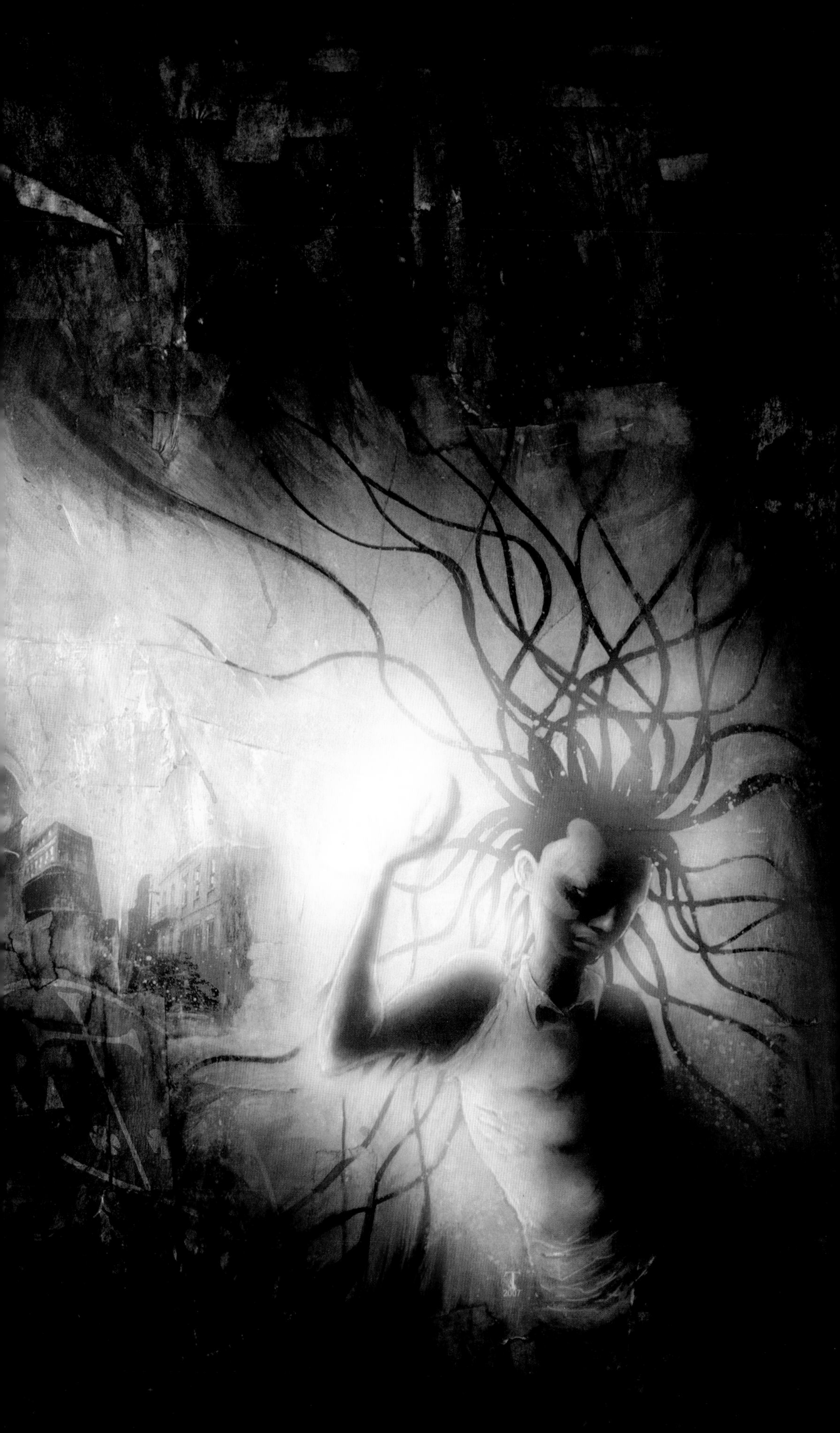

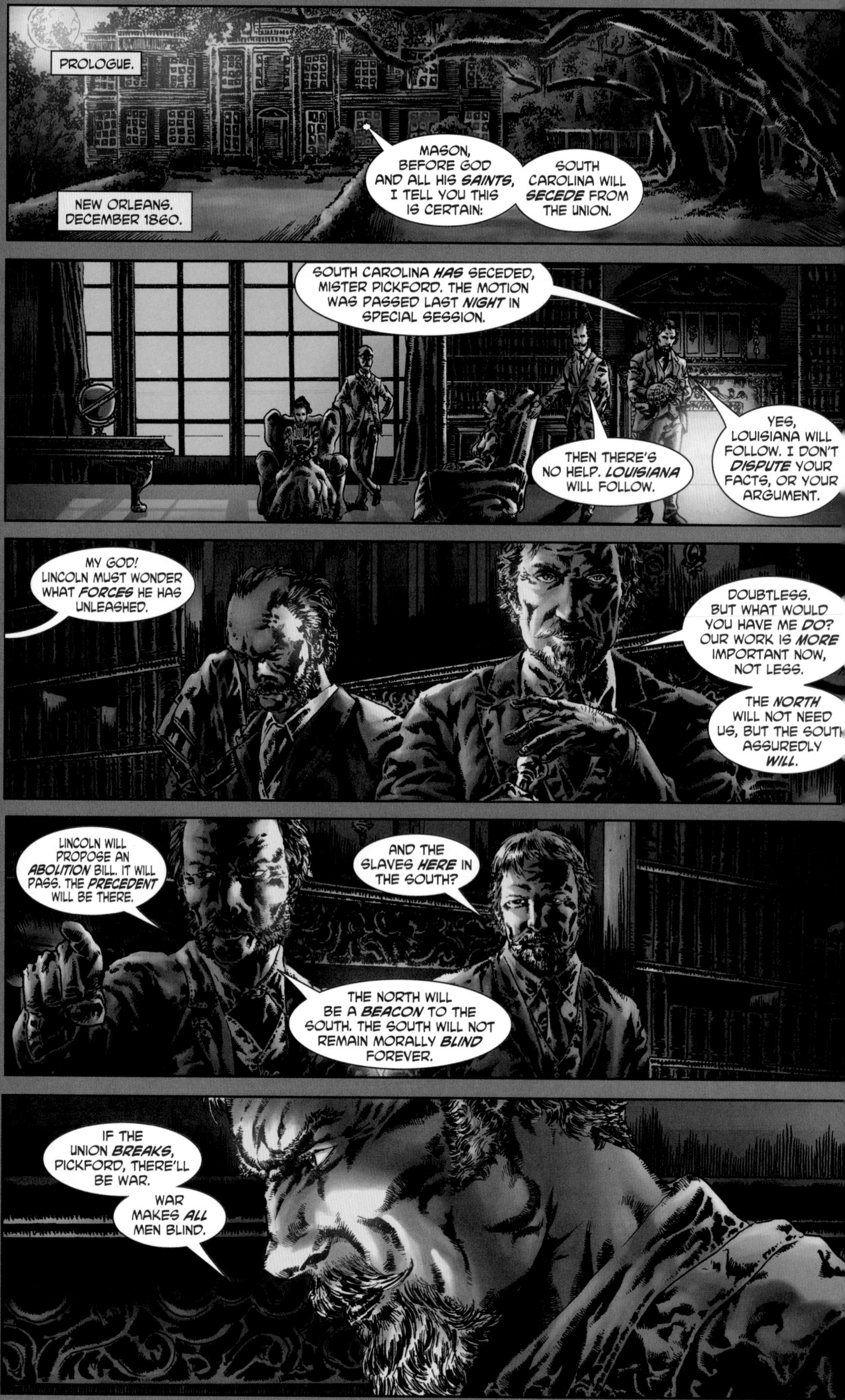
PROLOGUE.
NEW ORLEANS. DECEMBER 1860.
MASON, BEFORE GOD AND ALL HIS SAINTS, I TELL YOU THIS IS CERTAIN:
SOUTH CAROLINA WILL SECEDE FROM THE UNION.
SOUTH CAROLINA HAS SECEDED, MISTER PICKFORD. THE MOTION WAS PASSED LAST NIGHT IN SPECIAL SESSION.
THEN THERE'S NO HELP. LOUISIANA WILL FOLLOW.
YES, LOUISIANA WILL FOLLOW. I DON'T DISPUTE YOUR FACTS, OR YOUR ARGUMENT.
MY GOD! LINCOLN MUST WONDER WHAT FORCES HE HAS UNLEASHED.
DOUBTLESS. BUT WHAT WOULD YOU HAVE ME DO? OUR WORK IS MORE IMPORTANT NOW, NOT LESS.
THE NORTH WILL NOT NEED US, BUT THE SOUTH ASSUREDLY WILL.
LINCOLN WILL PROPOSE AN ABOLITION BILL. IT WILL PASS. THE PRECEDENT WILL BE THERE.
AND THE SLAVES HERE IN THE SOUTH?
THE NORTH WILL BE A BEACON TO THE SOUTH. THE SOUTH WILL NOT REMAIN MORALLY BLIND FOREVER.
IF THE UNION BREAKS, PICKFORD, THERE'LL BE WAR.
WAR MAKES ALL MEN BLIND.

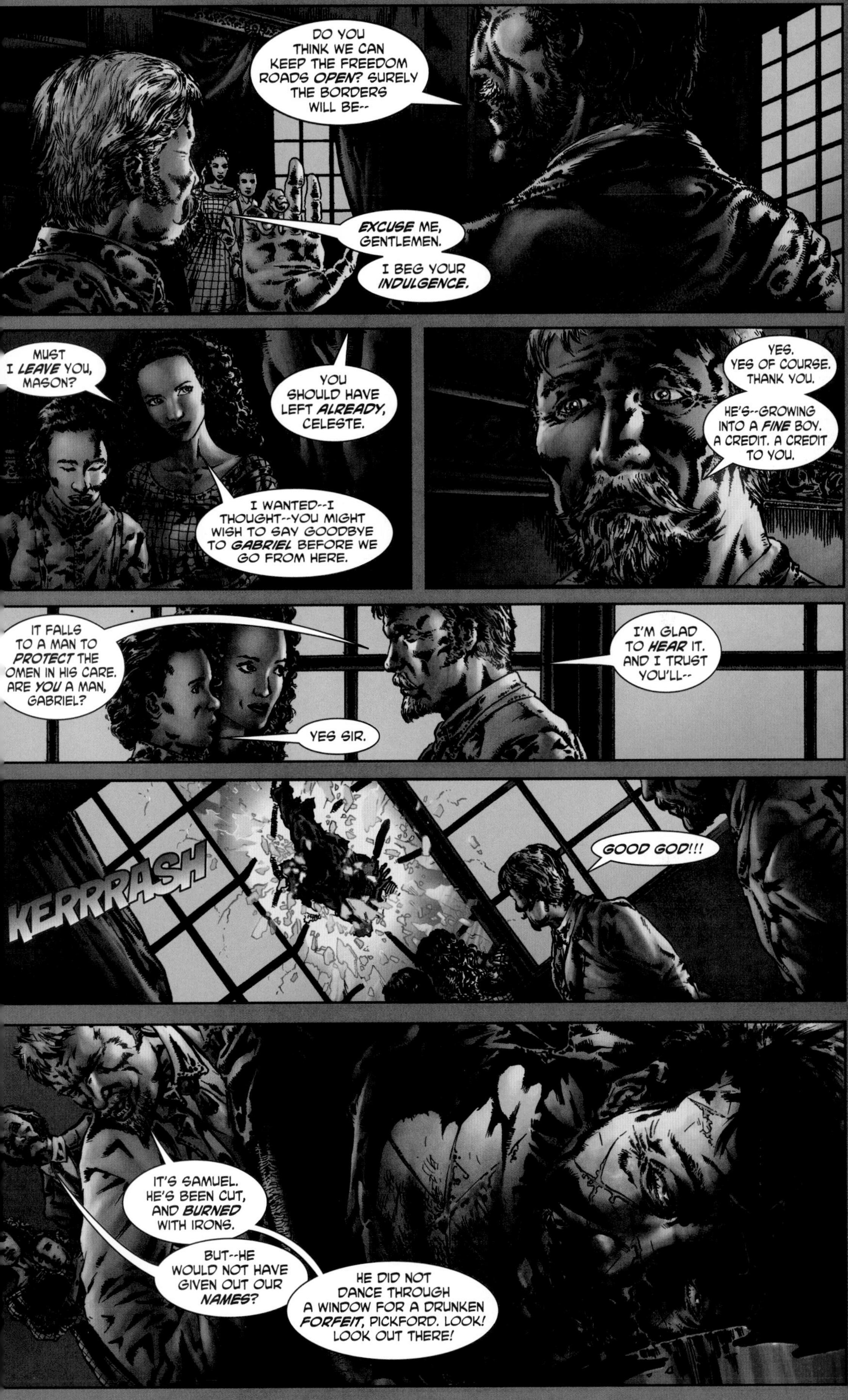
DO YOU THINK WE CAN KEEP THE FREEDOM ROADS OPEN? SURELY THE BORDERS WILL BE--
EXCUSE ME, GENTLEMEN.
I BEG YOUR INDULGENCE.
MUST I LEAVE YOU, MASON?
YOU SHOULD HAVE LEFT ALREADY, CELESTE.
I WANTED--I THOUGHT--YOU MIGHT WISH TO SAY GOODBYE TO GABRIEL BEFORE WE GO FROM HERE.
YES. YES OF COURSE. THANK YOU.
HE'S--GROWING INTO A FINE BOY. A CREDIT. A CREDIT TO YOU.
IT FALLS TO A MAN TO PROTECT THE OMEN IN HIS CARE. ARE YOU A MAN, GABRIEL?
YES SIR.
I'M GLAD TO HEAR IT. AND I TRUST YOU'LL--
KERRRASH
GOOD GOD!!!
IT'S SAMUEL. HE'S BEEN CUT, AND BURNED WITH IRONS.
BUT--HE WOULD NOT HAVE GIVEN OUT OUR NAMES?
HE DID NOT DANCE THROUGH A WINDOW FOR A DRUNKEN FORFEIT, PICKFORD. LOOK! LOOK OUT THERE!

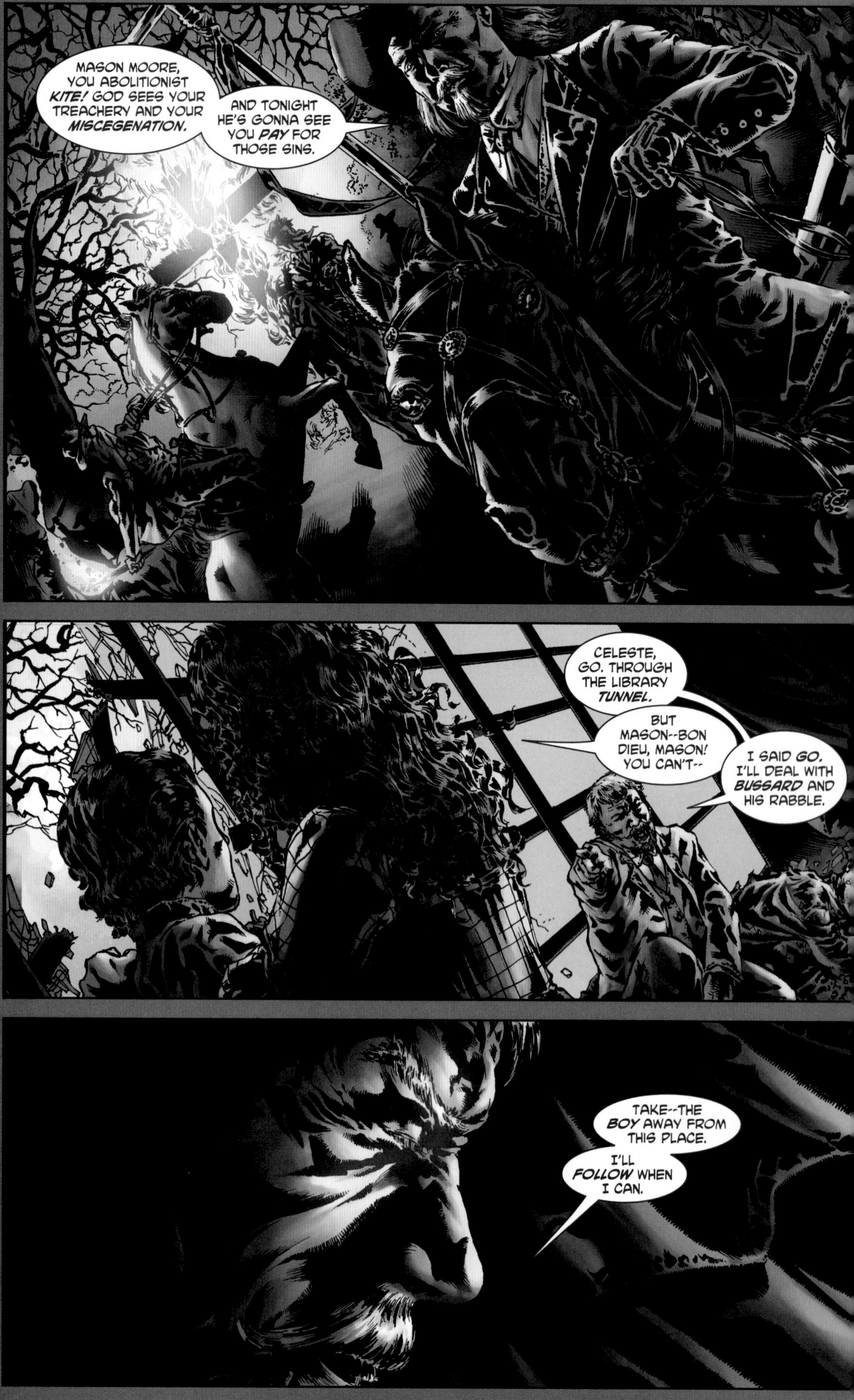
MASON MOORE, YOU ABOLITIONIST KITE! GOD SEES YOUR TREACHERY AND YOUR MISCEGENATION.
AND TONIGHT HE'S GONNA SEE YOU PAY FOR THOSE SINS.
CELESTE, GO. THROUGH THE LIBRARY TUNNEL.
BUT MASON--BON DIEU, MASON! YOU CAN'T--
I SAID GO. I'LL DEAL WITH BUSSARD AND HIS RABBLE.
TAKE--THE BOY AWAY FROM THIS PLACE.
I'LL FOLLOW WHEN I CAN.

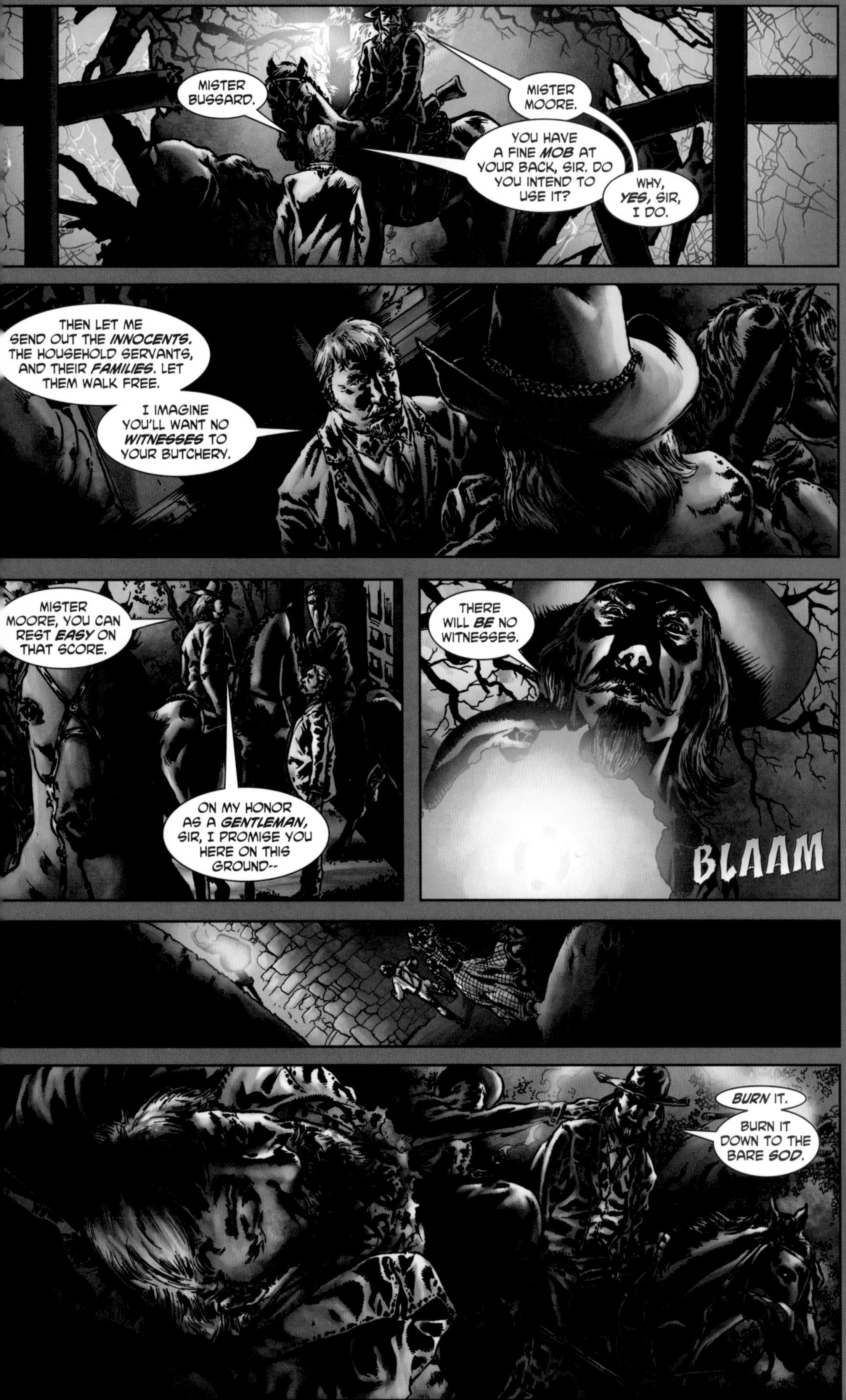
MISTER BUSSARD.
MISTER MOORE.
YOU HAVE A FINE MOB AT YOUR BACK, SIR. DO YOU INTEND TO USE IT?
WHY, YES, SIR, I DO.
THEN LET ME SEND OUT THE INNOCENTS. THE HOUSEHOLD SERVANTS, AND THEIR FAMILIES. LET THEM WALK FREE.
I IMAGINE YOU'LL WANT NO WITNESSES TO YOUR BUTCHERY.
MISTER MOORE, YOU CAN REST EASY ON THAT SCORE.
ON MY HONOR AS A GENTLEMAN, SIR, I PROMISE YOU HERE ON THIS GROUND--
THERE WILL BE NO WITNESSES.
BLAAM
BURN IT.
BURN IT DOWN TO THE BARE SOD.

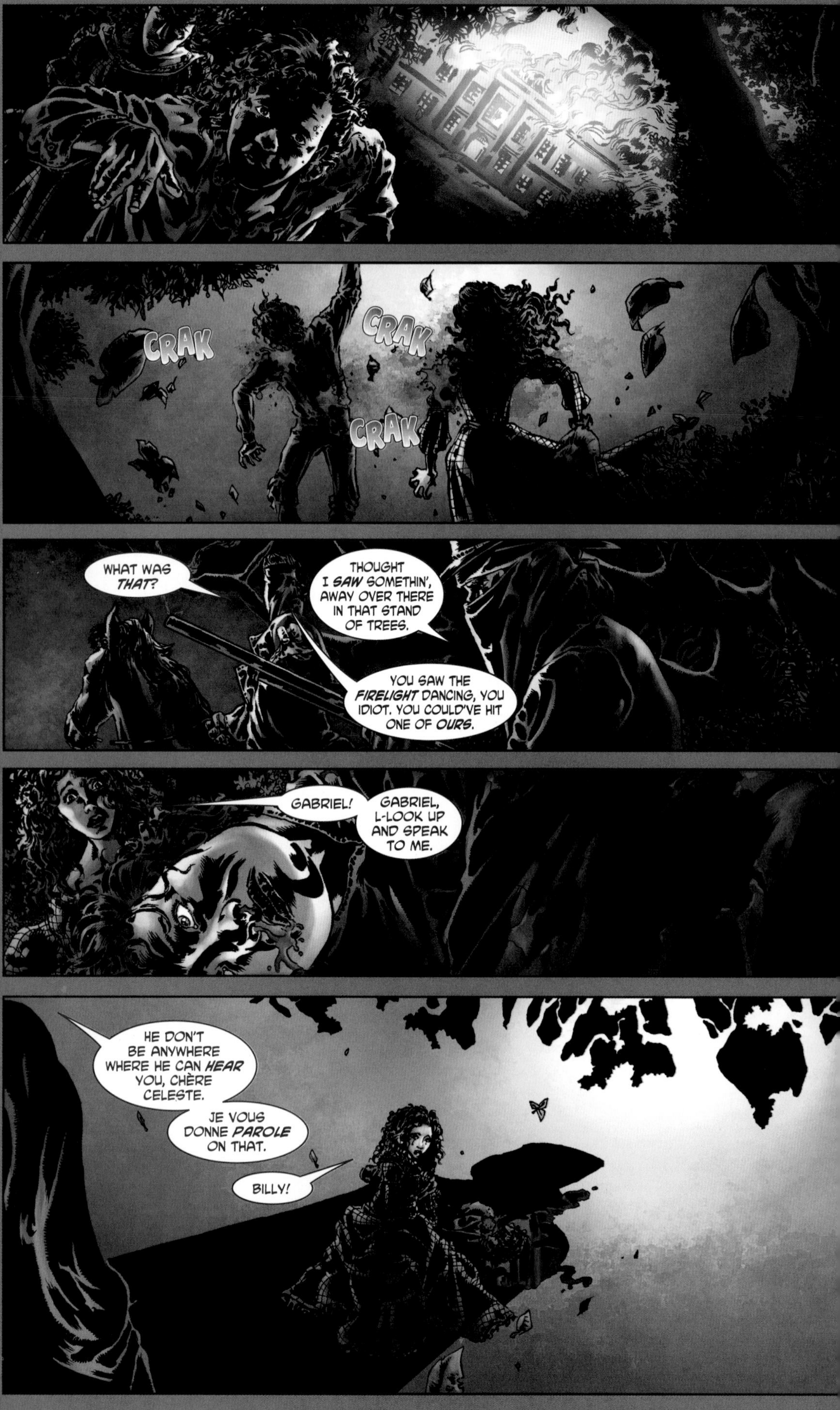
CRAK
CRAK
CRAK
WHAT WAS THAT?
THOUGHT I SAW SOMETHIN', AWAY OVER THERE IN THAT STAND OF TREES.
YOU SAW THE FIRELIGHT DANCING, YOU IDIOT. YOU COULD'VE HIT ONE OF OURS.
GABRIEL!
GABRIEL, L-LOOK UP AND SPEAK TO ME.
HE DON'T BE ANYWHERE WHERE HE CAN HEAR YOU, CHÈRE CELESTE.
JE VOUS DONNE PAROLE ON THAT.
BILLY!

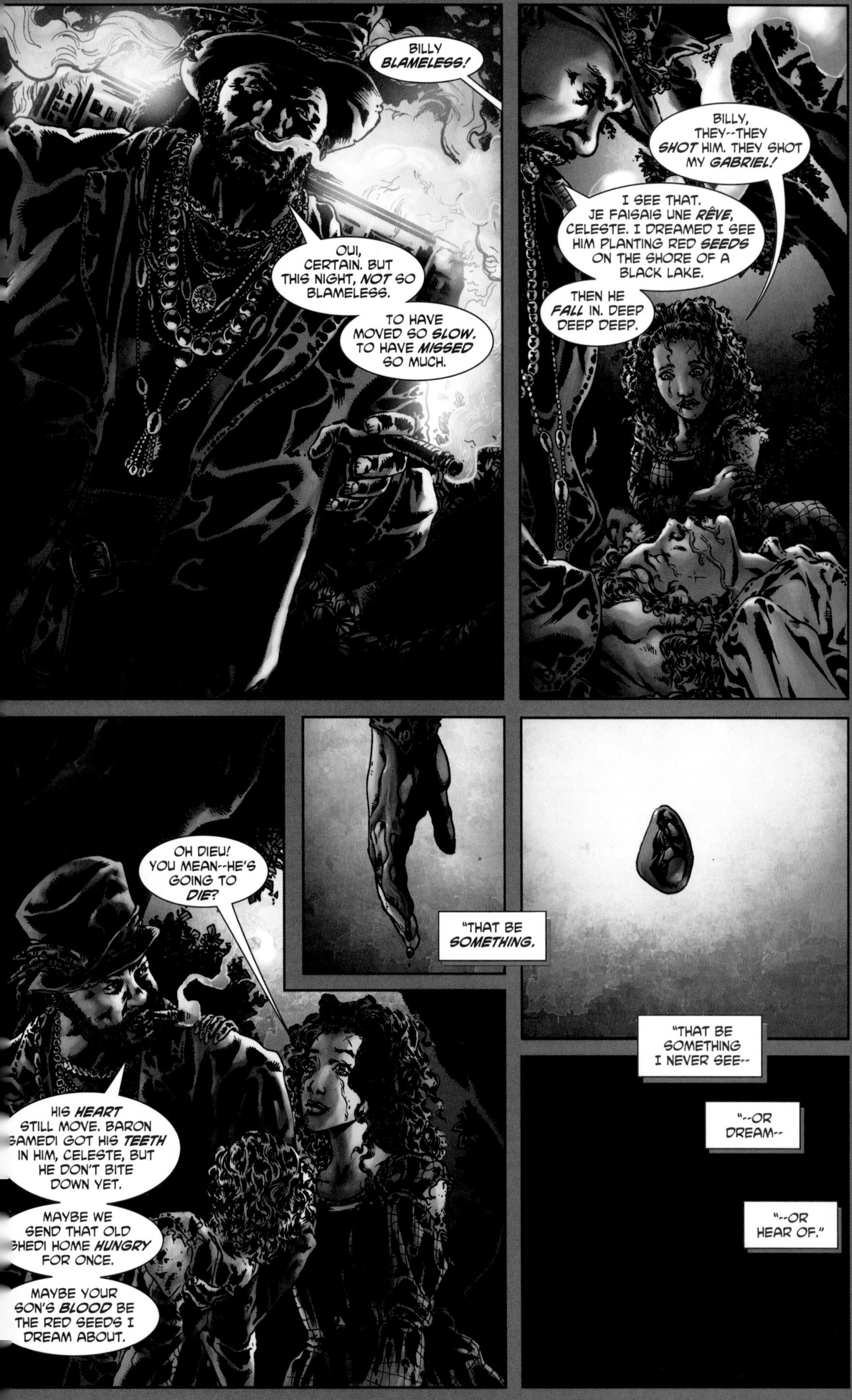
BILLY BLAMELESS!
OUI, CERTAIN. BUT THIS NIGHT, NOT SO BLAMELESS.
TO HAVE MOVED SO SLOW. TO HAVE MISSED SO MUCH.
BILLY, THEY--THEY SHOT HIM. THEY SHOT MY GABRIEL!
I SEE THAT. JE FAISAIS UNE RÊVE, CELESTE. I DREAMED I SEE HIM PLANTING RED SEEDS ON THE SHORE OF A BLACK LAKE.
THEN HE FALL IN. DEEP DEEP DEEP.
OH DIEU! YOU MEAN--HE'S GOING TO DIE?
HIS HEART STILL MOVE. BARON SAMEDI GOT HIS TEETH IN HIM, CELESTE, BUT HE DON'T BITE DOWN YET.
MAYBE WE SEND THAT OLD SHEDI HOME HUNGRY FOR ONCE.
MAYBE YOUR SON'S BLOOD BE THE RED SEEDS I DREAM ABOUT.
"THAT BE SOMETHING.
"THAT BE SOMETHING I NEVER SEE--
"--OR DREAM--
"--OR HEAR OF."

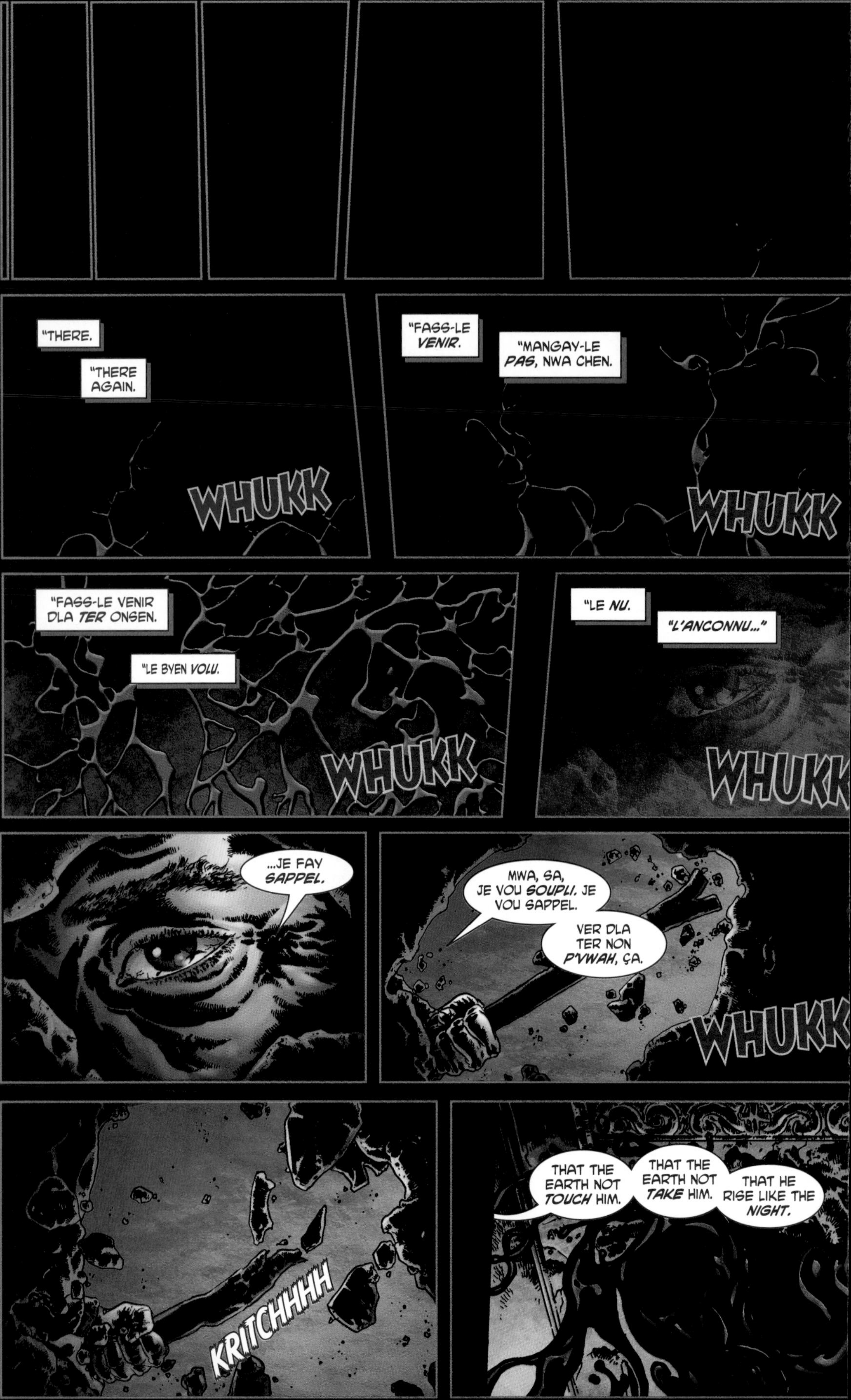

"THERE.
"THERE AGAIN.
WHUKK
"FASS-LE *VENIR*.
"MANGAY-LE *PAS*, NWA CHEN.
WHUKK
"FASS-LE VENIR DLA *TER* ONSEN.
"LE BYEN *VOLU*.
WHUKK
"LE *NU*.
"*L'ANCONNU...*"
WHUKK
...JE FAY *SAPPEL*.
MWA, SA, JE VOU *SOUPLI*. JE VOU SAPPEL.
VER DLA TER NON *P'VWAH*, ÇA.
WHUKK
KRITCHHHH
THAT THE EARTH NOT *TOUCH* HIM.
THAT THE EARTH NOT *TAKE* HIM.
THAT HE RISE LIKE THE *NIGHT*.

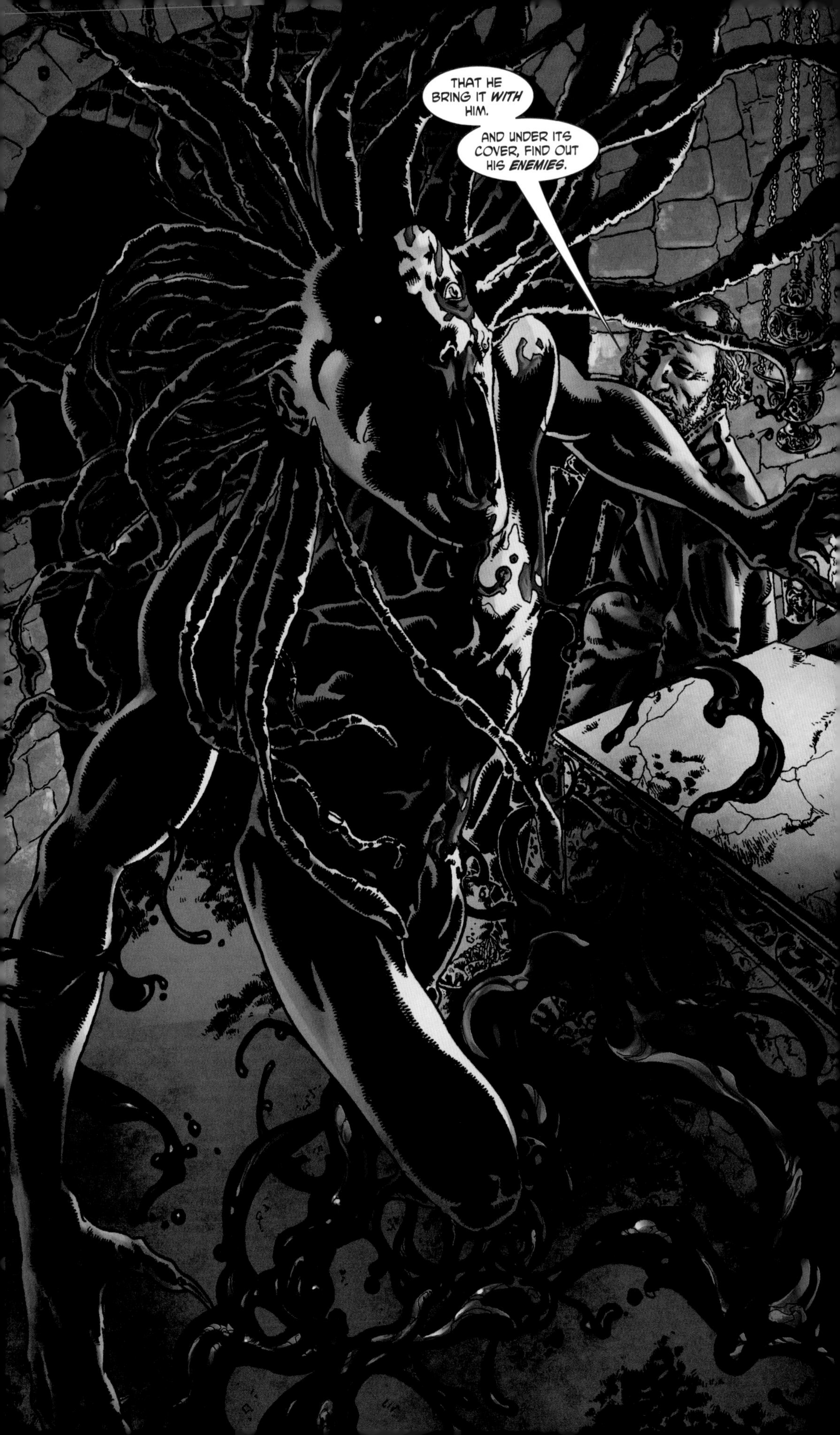
THAT HE BRING IT *WITH* HIM.
AND UNDER ITS COVER, FIND OUT HIS *ENEMIES*.

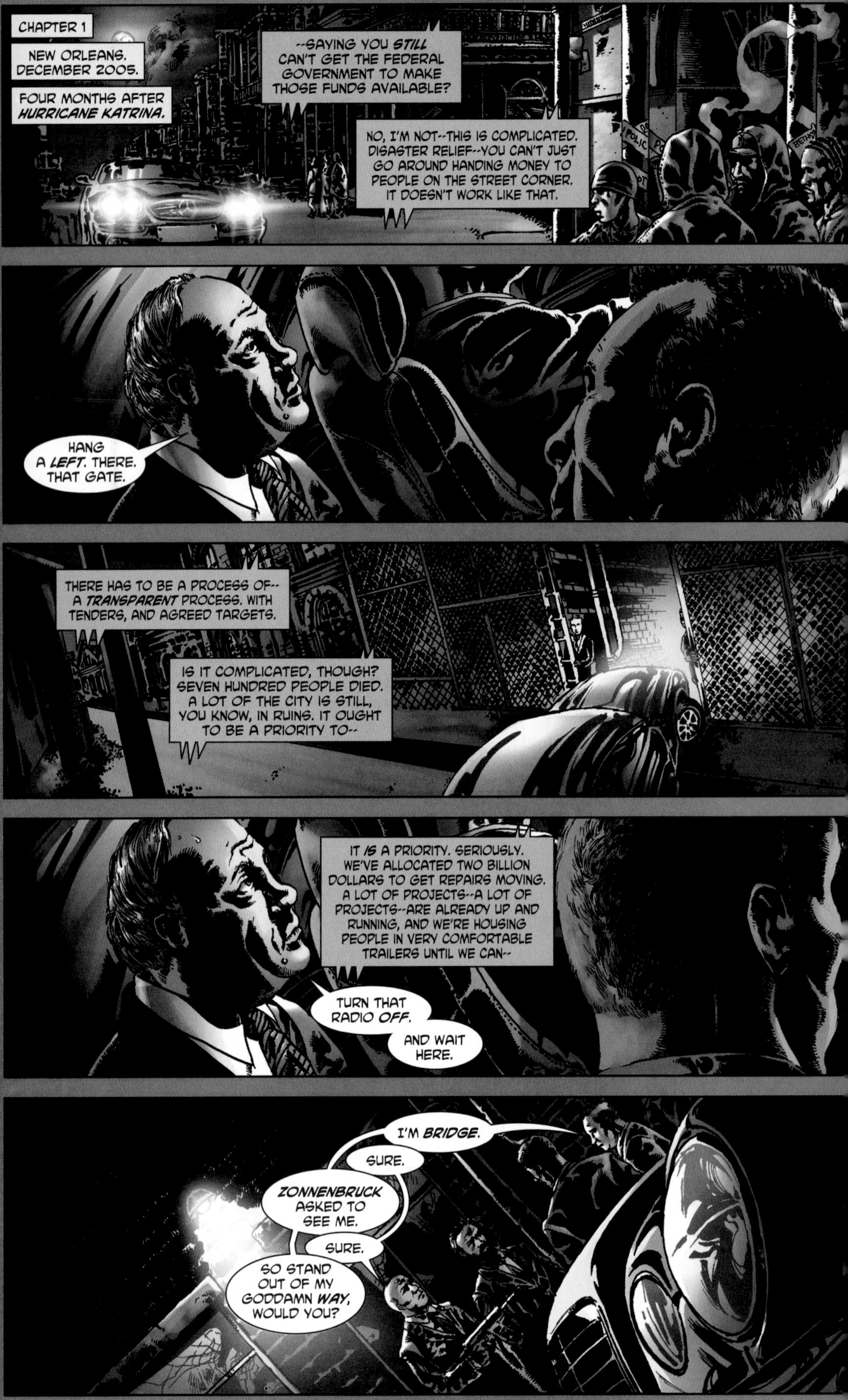
CHAPTER 1
NEW ORLEANS. DECEMBER 2005.
FOUR MONTHS AFTER *HURRICANE KATRINA.*
--SAYING YOU *STILL* CAN'T GET THE FEDERAL GOVERNMENT TO MAKE THOSE FUNDS AVAILABLE?
NO, I'M NOT--THIS IS COMPLICATED. DISASTER RELIEF--YOU CAN'T JUST GO AROUND HANDING MONEY TO PEOPLE ON THE STREET CORNER. IT DOESN'T WORK LIKE THAT.
HANG A *LEFT*. THERE. THAT GATE.
THERE HAS TO BE A PROCESS OF--A *TRANSPARENT* PROCESS. WITH TENDERS, AND AGREED TARGETS.
IS IT COMPLICATED, THOUGH? SEVEN HUNDRED PEOPLE DIED. A LOT OF THE CITY IS STILL, YOU KNOW, IN RUINS. IT OUGHT TO BE A PRIORITY TO--
IT *IS* A PRIORITY. SERIOUSLY. WE'VE ALLOCATED TWO BILLION DOLLARS TO GET REPAIRS MOVING. A LOT OF PROJECTS--A LOT OF PROJECTS--ARE ALREADY UP AND RUNNING, AND WE'RE HOUSING PEOPLE IN VERY COMFORTABLE TRAILERS UNTIL WE CAN--
TURN THAT RADIO *OFF*.
AND WAIT HERE.
I'M *BRIDGE*.
SURE.
ZONNENBRUCK ASKED TO SEE ME.
SURE.
SO STAND OUT OF MY GODDAMN *WAY*, WOULD YOU?

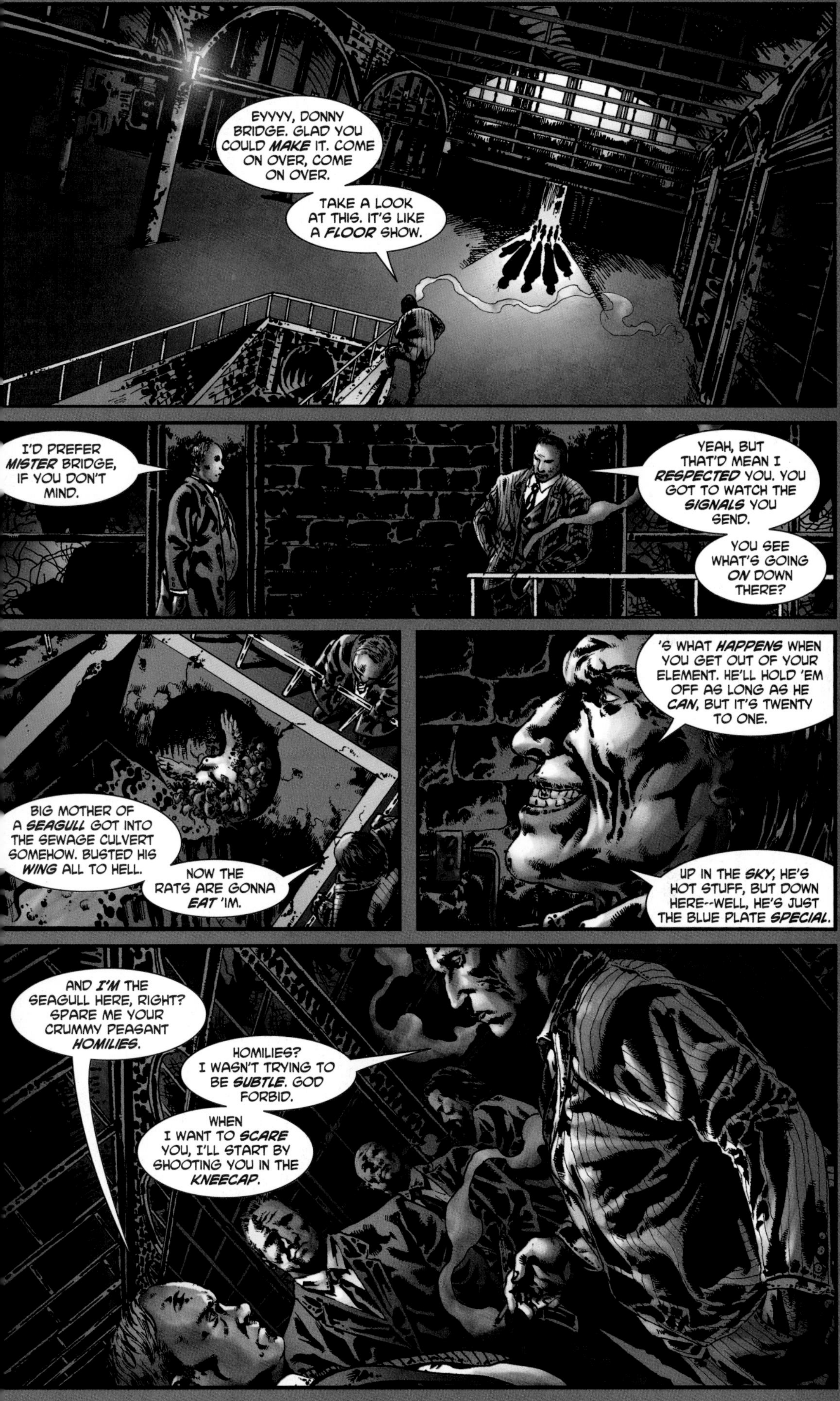
EYYYY, DONNY BRIDGE. GLAD YOU COULD MAKE IT. COME ON OVER, COME ON OVER.
TAKE A LOOK AT THIS. IT'S LIKE A FLOOR SHOW.
I'D PREFER MISTER BRIDGE, IF YOU DON'T MIND.
YEAH, BUT THAT'D MEAN I RESPECTED YOU. YOU GOT TO WATCH THE SIGNALS YOU SEND.
YOU SEE WHAT'S GOING ON DOWN THERE?
BIG MOTHER OF A SEAGULL GOT INTO THE SEWAGE CULVERT SOMEHOW. BUSTED HIS WING ALL TO HELL.
NOW THE RATS ARE GONNA EAT 'IM.
'S WHAT HAPPENS WHEN YOU GET OUT OF YOUR ELEMENT. HE'LL HOLD 'EM OFF AS LONG AS HE CAN, BUT IT'S TWENTY TO ONE.
UP IN THE SKY, HE'S HOT STUFF, BUT DOWN HERE--WELL, HE'S JUST THE BLUE PLATE SPECIAL.
AND I'M THE SEAGULL HERE, RIGHT? SPARE ME YOUR CRUMMY PEASANT HOMILIES.
HOMILIES? I WASN'T TRYING TO BE SUBTLE. GOD FORBID.
WHEN I WANT TO SCARE YOU, I'LL START BY SHOOTING YOU IN THE KNEECAP.

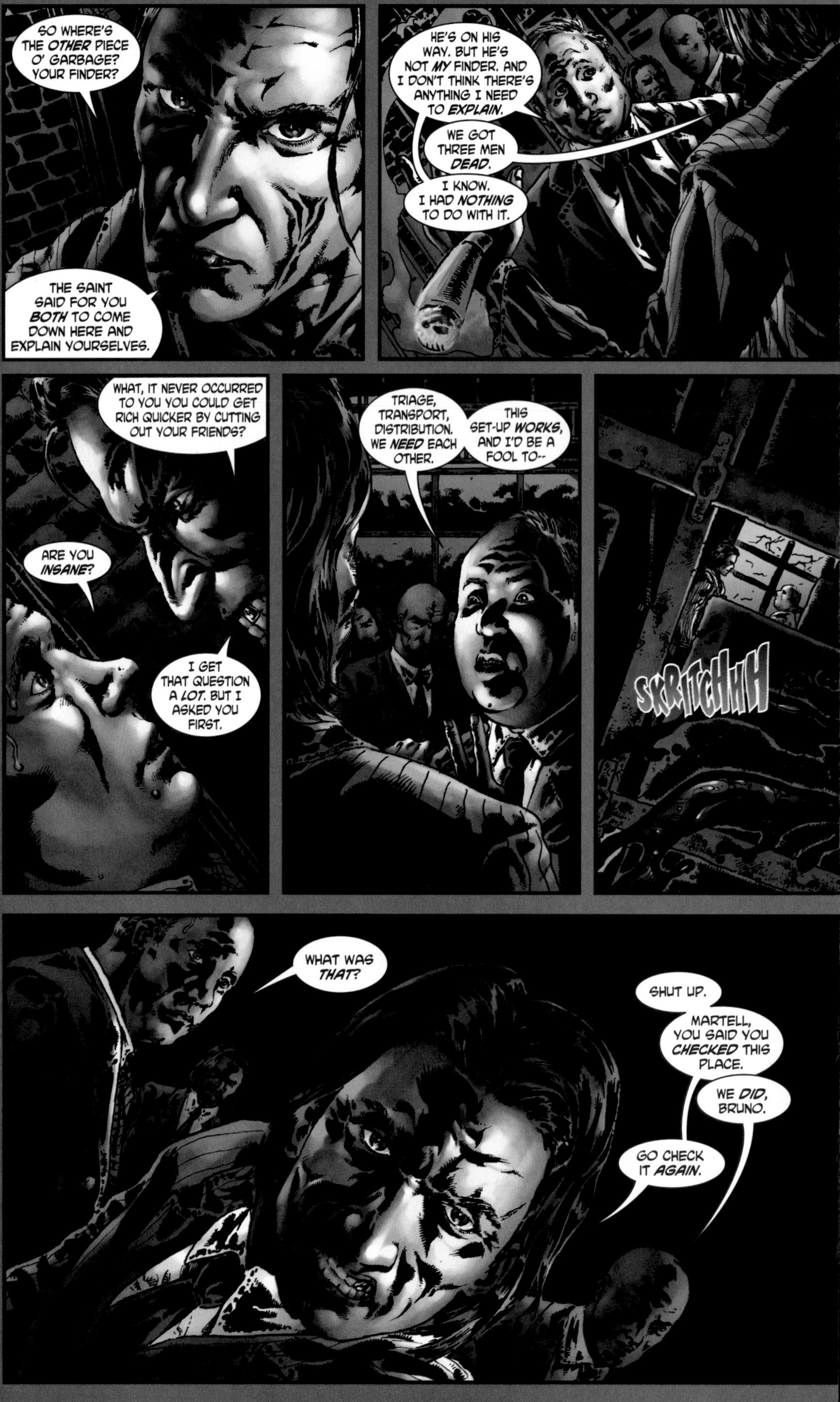
SO WHERE'S THE OTHER PIECE O' GARBAGE? YOUR FINDER?
THE SAINT SAID FOR YOU BOTH TO COME DOWN HERE AND EXPLAIN YOURSELVES.
HE'S ON HIS WAY. BUT HE'S NOT MY FINDER. AND I DON'T THINK THERE'S ANYTHING I NEED TO EXPLAIN.
WE GOT THREE MEN DEAD.
I KNOW. I HAD NOTHING TO DO WITH IT.
WHAT, IT NEVER OCCURRED TO YOU YOU COULD GET RICH QUICKER BY CUTTING OUT YOUR FRIENDS?
ARE YOU INSANE?
I GET THAT QUESTION A LOT. BUT I ASKED YOU FIRST.
TRIAGE, TRANSPORT, DISTRIBUTION. WE NEED EACH OTHER.
THIS SET-UP WORKS, AND I'D BE A FOOL TO--
SKRITCHHH
WHAT WAS THAT?
SHUT UP.
MARTELL, YOU SAID YOU CHECKED THIS PLACE.
WE DID, BRUNO.
GO CHECK IT AGAIN.

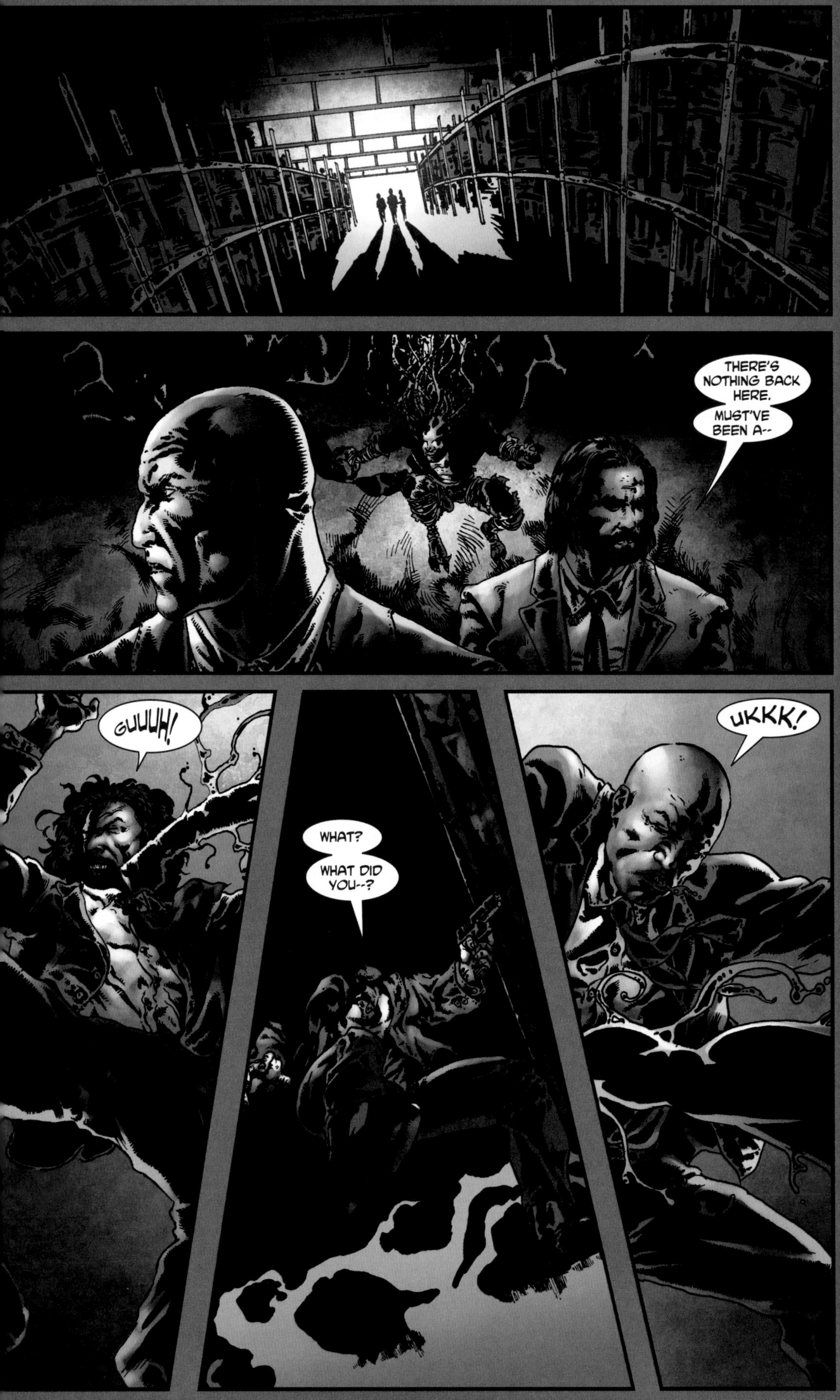
THERE'S NOTHING BACK HERE.
MUST'VE BEEN A--
GUUUH!
WHAT?
WHAT DID YOU--?
UKKK!

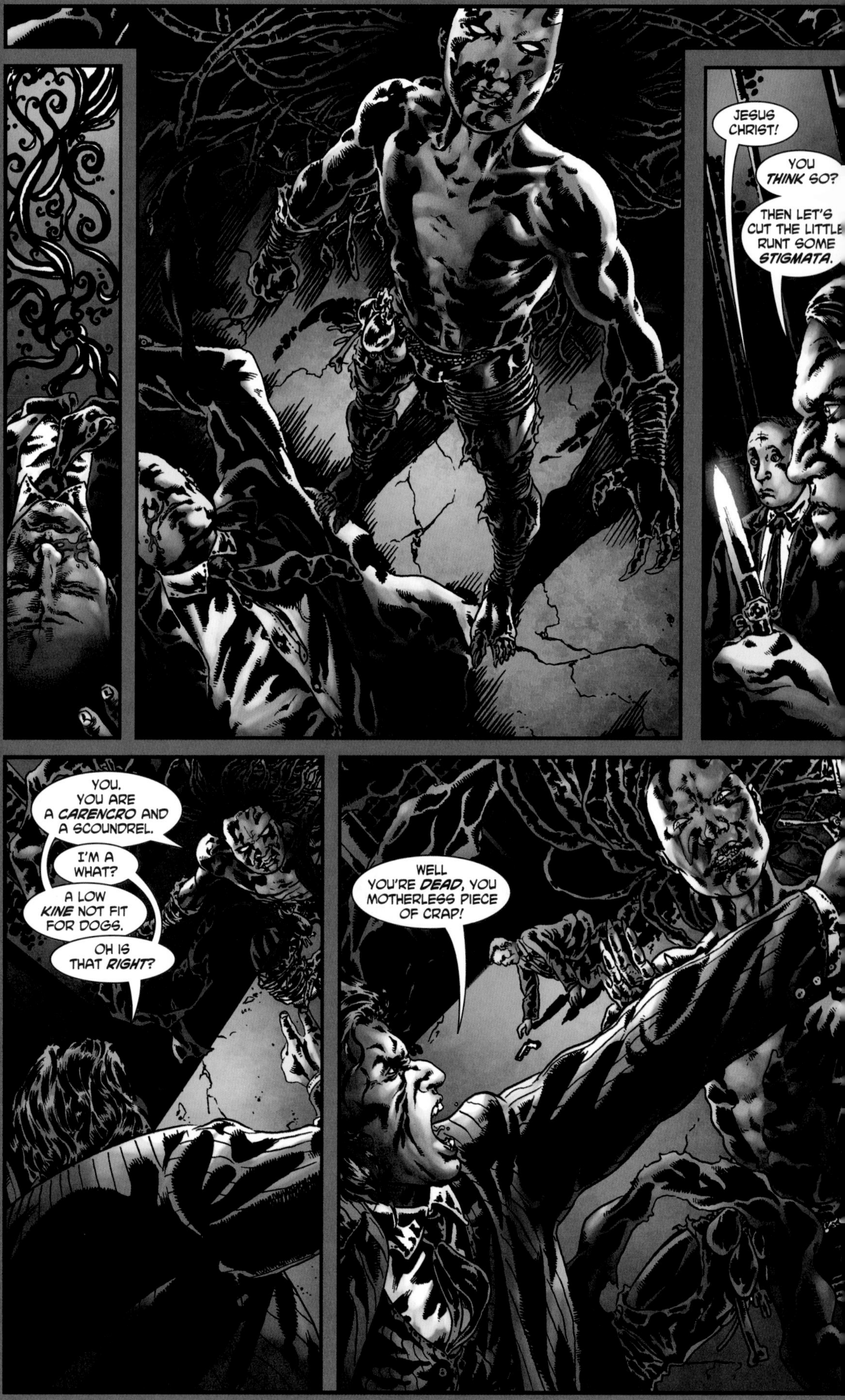
JESUS CHRIST!
YOU THINK SO?
THEN LET'S CUT THE LITTLE RUNT SOME STIGMATA.
YOU. YOU ARE A CARENCRO AND A SCOUNDREL.
I'M A WHAT?
A LOW KINE NOT FIT FOR DOGS.
OH IS THAT RIGHT?
WELL YOU'RE DEAD, YOU MOTHERLESS PIECE OF CRAP!

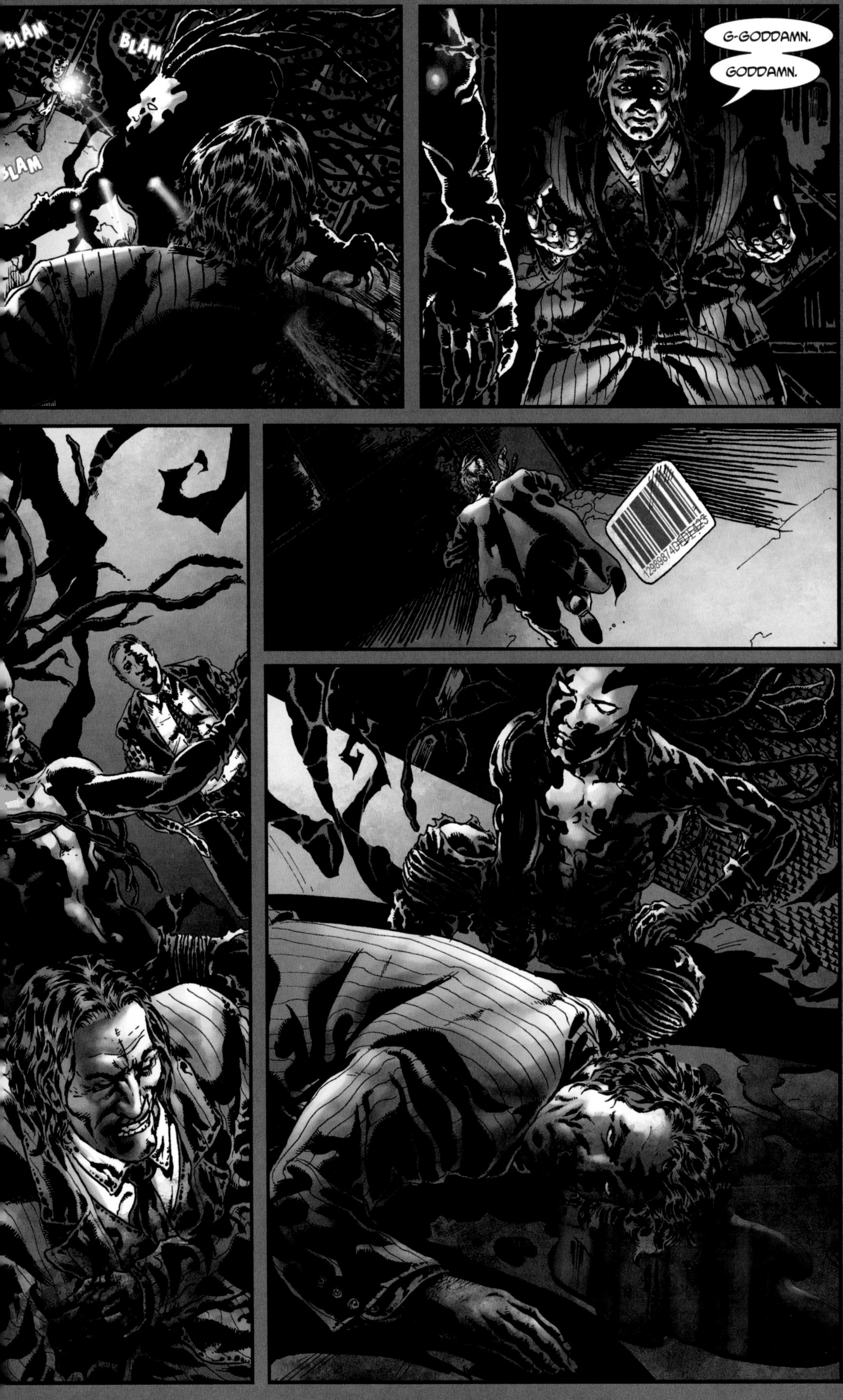
BLAM
BLAM
BLAM
G-GODDAMN.
GODDAMN.

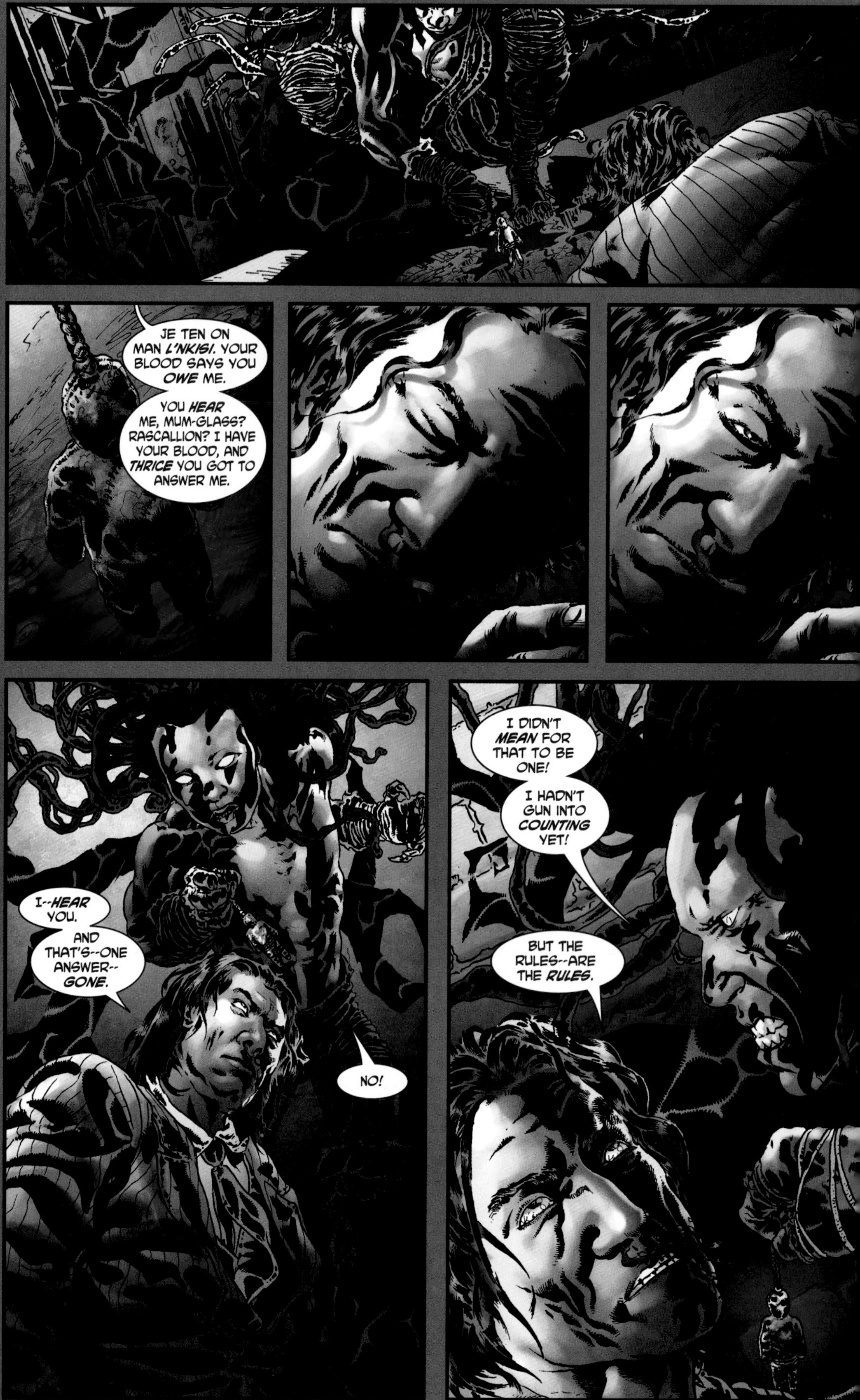
JE TEN ON MAN L'NKISI. YOUR BLOOD SAYS YOU OWE ME.
YOU HEAR ME, MUM-GLASS? RASCALLION? I HAVE YOUR BLOOD, AND THRICE YOU GOT TO ANSWER ME.
I--HEAR YOU.
AND THAT'S--ONE ANSWER--GONE.
NO!
I DIDN'T MEAN FOR THAT TO BE ONE!
I HADN'T GUN INTO COUNTING YET!
BUT THE RULES--ARE THE RULES.

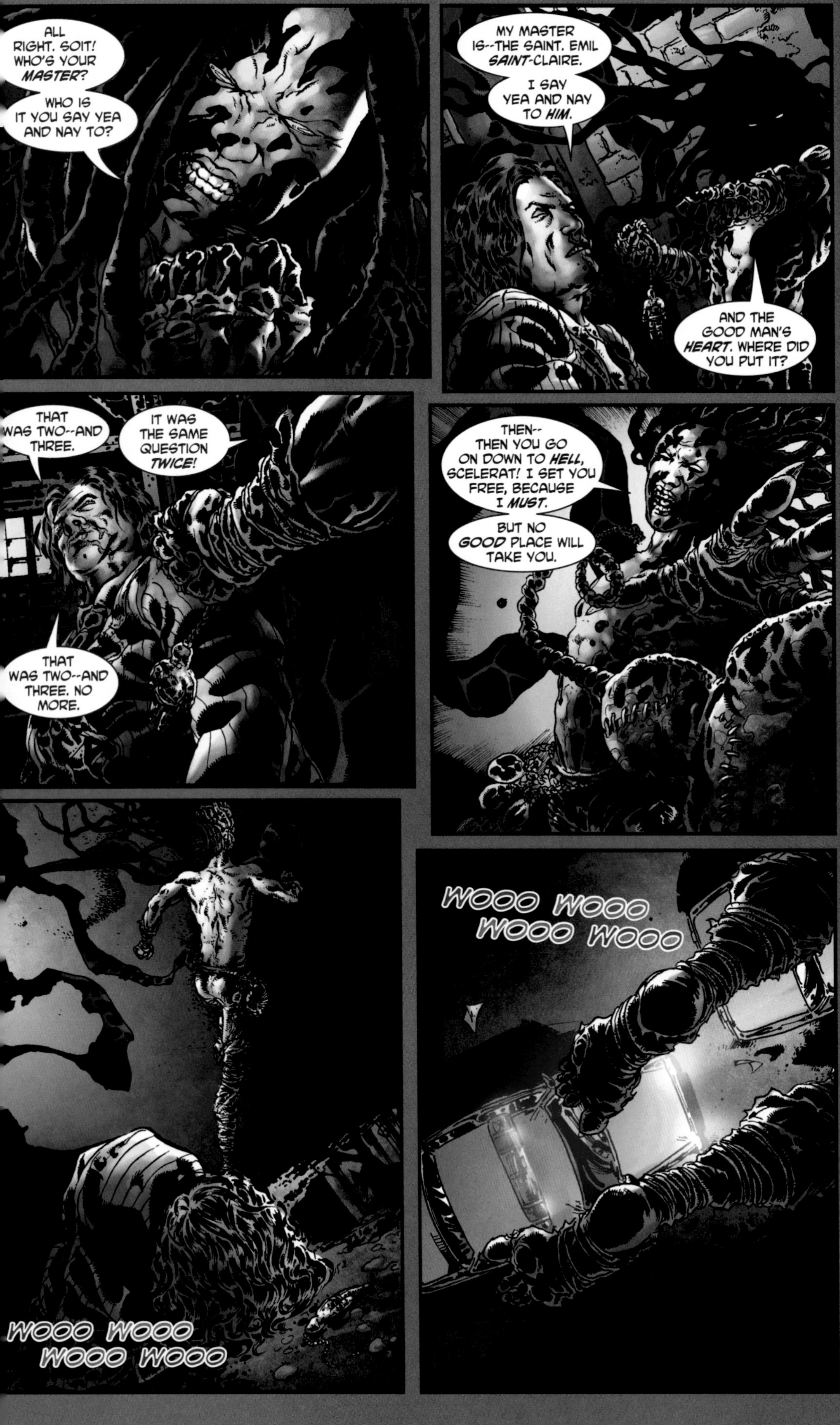
ALL RIGHT. SOIT! WHO'S YOUR MASTER?
WHO IS IT YOU SAY YEA AND NAY TO?
MY MASTER IS--THE SAINT. EMIL SAINT-CLAIRE.
I SAY YEA AND NAY TO HIM.
AND THE GOOD MAN'S HEART. WHERE DID YOU PUT IT?
THAT WAS TWO--AND THREE.
IT WAS THE SAME QUESTION TWICE!
THAT WAS TWO--AND THREE. NO MORE.
THEN-- THEN YOU GO ON DOWN TO HELL, SCELERAT! I SET YOU FREE, BECAUSE I MUST.
BUT NO GOOD PLACE WILL TAKE YOU.
WOOO WOOO WOOO WOOO
WOOO WOOO WOOO WOOO

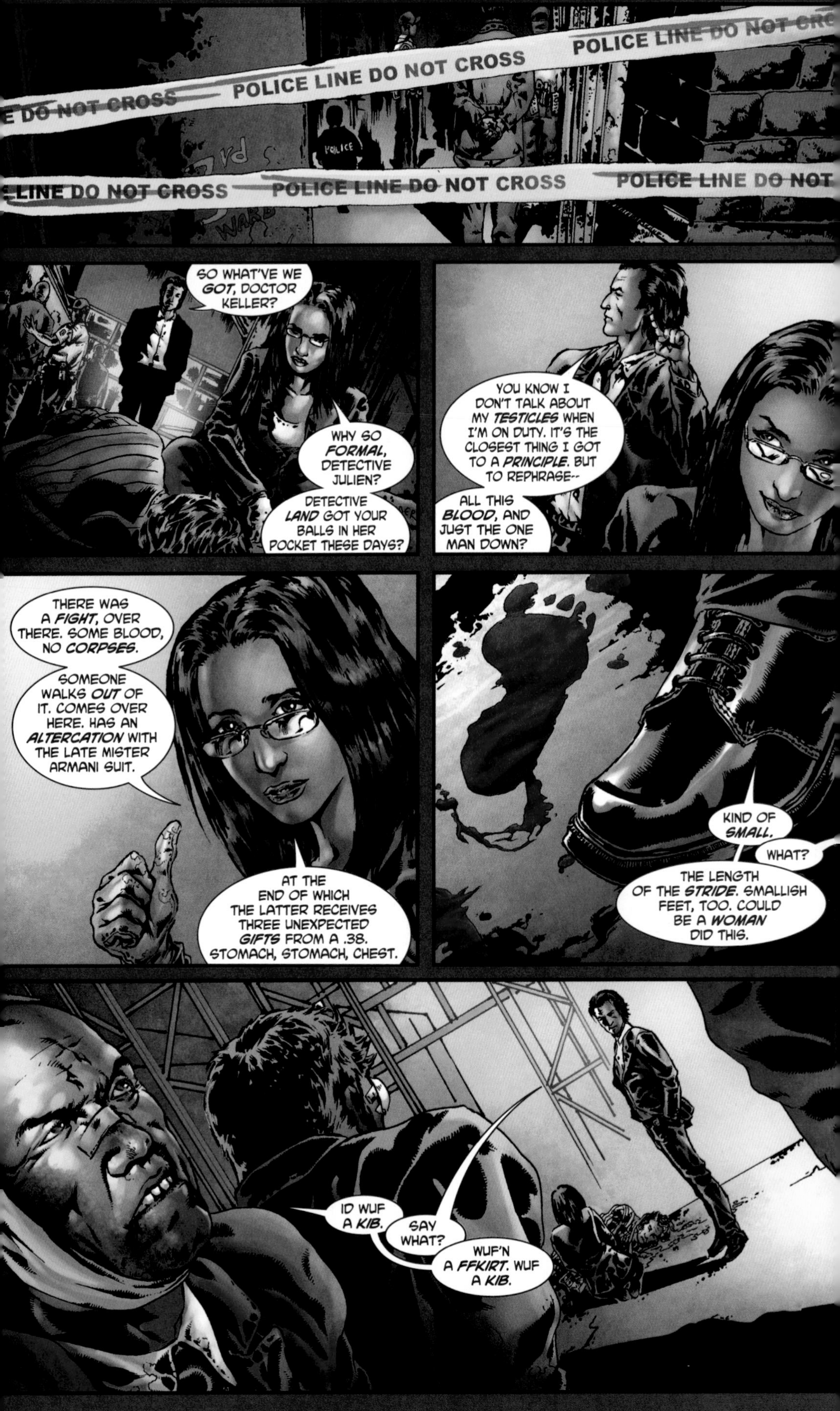
POLICE LINE DO NOT CROSS
SO WHAT'VE WE GOT, DOCTOR KELLER?
WHY SO FORMAL, DETECTIVE JULIEN?
DETECTIVE LAND GOT YOUR BALLS IN HER POCKET THESE DAYS?
YOU KNOW I DON'T TALK ABOUT MY TESTICLES WHEN I'M ON DUTY. IT'S THE CLOSEST THING I GOT TO A PRINCIPLE. BUT TO REPHRASE--
ALL THIS BLOOD, AND JUST THE ONE MAN DOWN?
THERE WAS A FIGHT, OVER THERE. SOME BLOOD, NO CORPSES.
SOMEONE WALKS OUT OF IT. COMES OVER HERE. HAS AN ALTERCATION WITH THE LATE MISTER ARMANI SUIT.
AT THE END OF WHICH THE LATTER RECEIVES THREE UNEXPECTED GIFTS FROM A .38. STOMACH, STOMACH, CHEST.
KIND OF SMALL.
WHAT?
THE LENGTH OF THE STRIDE. SMALLISH FEET, TOO. COULD BE A WOMAN DID THIS.
ID WUF A KIB.
SAY WHAT?
WUF'N A FFKIRT. WUF A KIB.

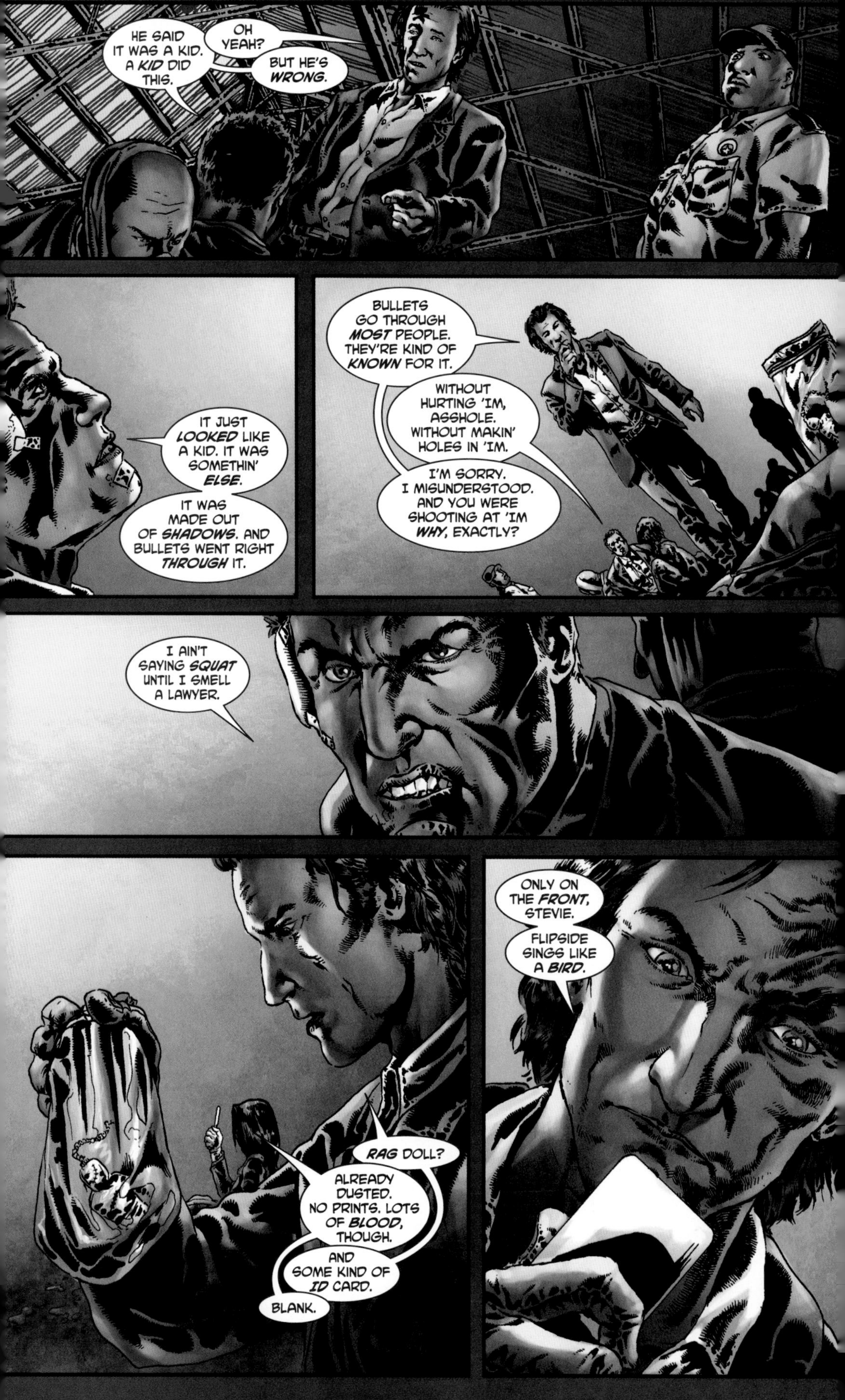

HE SAID IT WAS A KID. A KID DID THIS.
OH YEAH?
BUT HE'S WRONG.
IT JUST LOOKED LIKE A KID. IT WAS SOMETHIN' ELSE.
IT WAS MADE OUT OF SHADOWS. AND BULLETS WENT RIGHT THROUGH IT.
BULLETS GO THROUGH MOST PEOPLE. THEY'RE KIND OF KNOWN FOR IT.
WITHOUT HURTING 'IM, ASSHOLE. WITHOUT MAKIN' HOLES IN 'IM.
I'M SORRY. I MISUNDERSTOOD. AND YOU WERE SHOOTING AT 'IM WHY, EXACTLY?
I AIN'T SAYING SQUAT UNTIL I SMELL A LAWYER.
RAG DOLL?
ALREADY DUSTED. NO PRINTS. LOTS OF BLOOD, THOUGH.
AND SOME KIND OF ID CARD.
BLANK.
ONLY ON THE FRONT, STEVIE.
FLIPSIDE SINGS LIKE A BIRD.

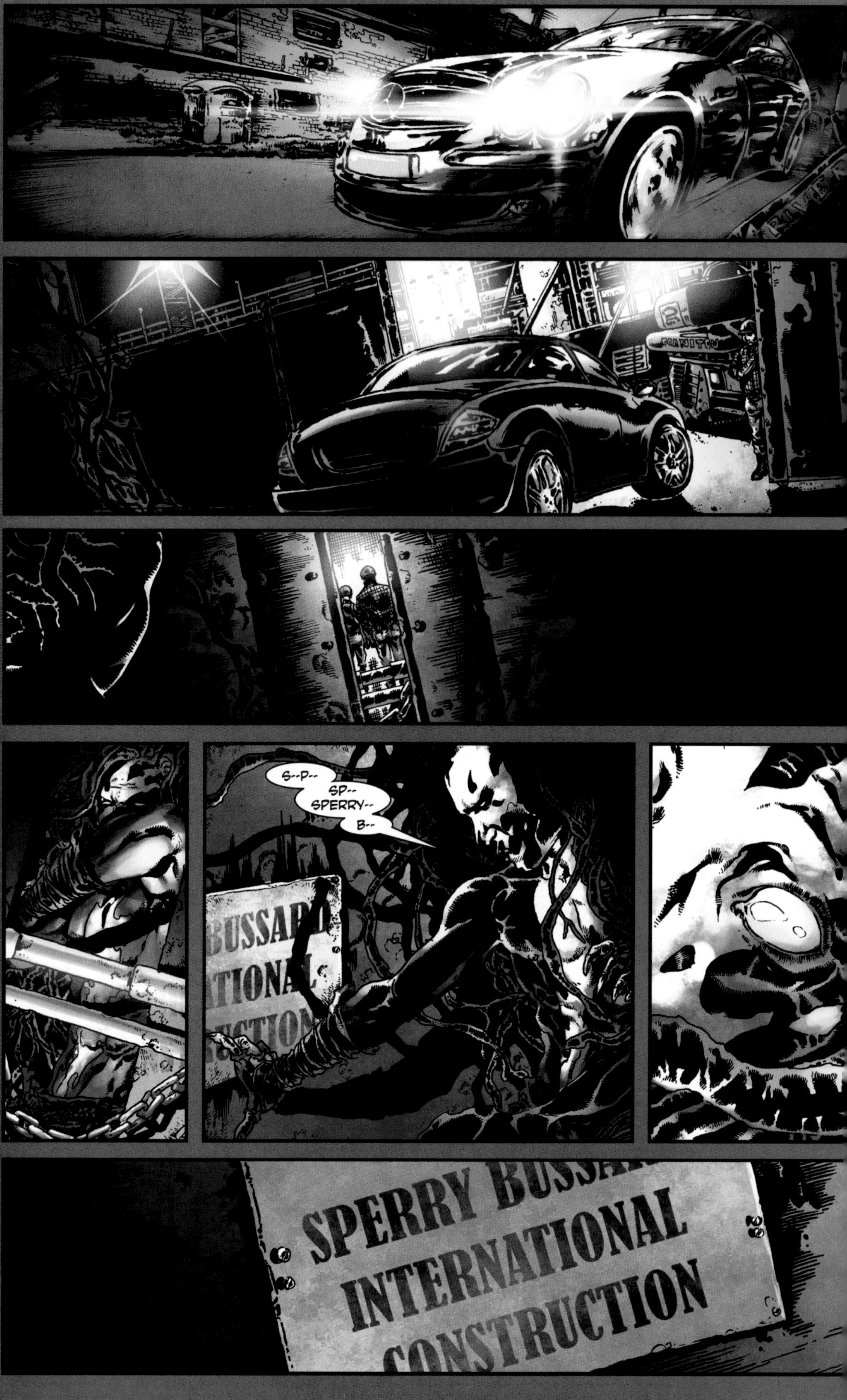

S--P--
SP--
SPERRY--
B--
BUSSARD
SPERRY
INTERNATIONAL
CONSTRUCTION

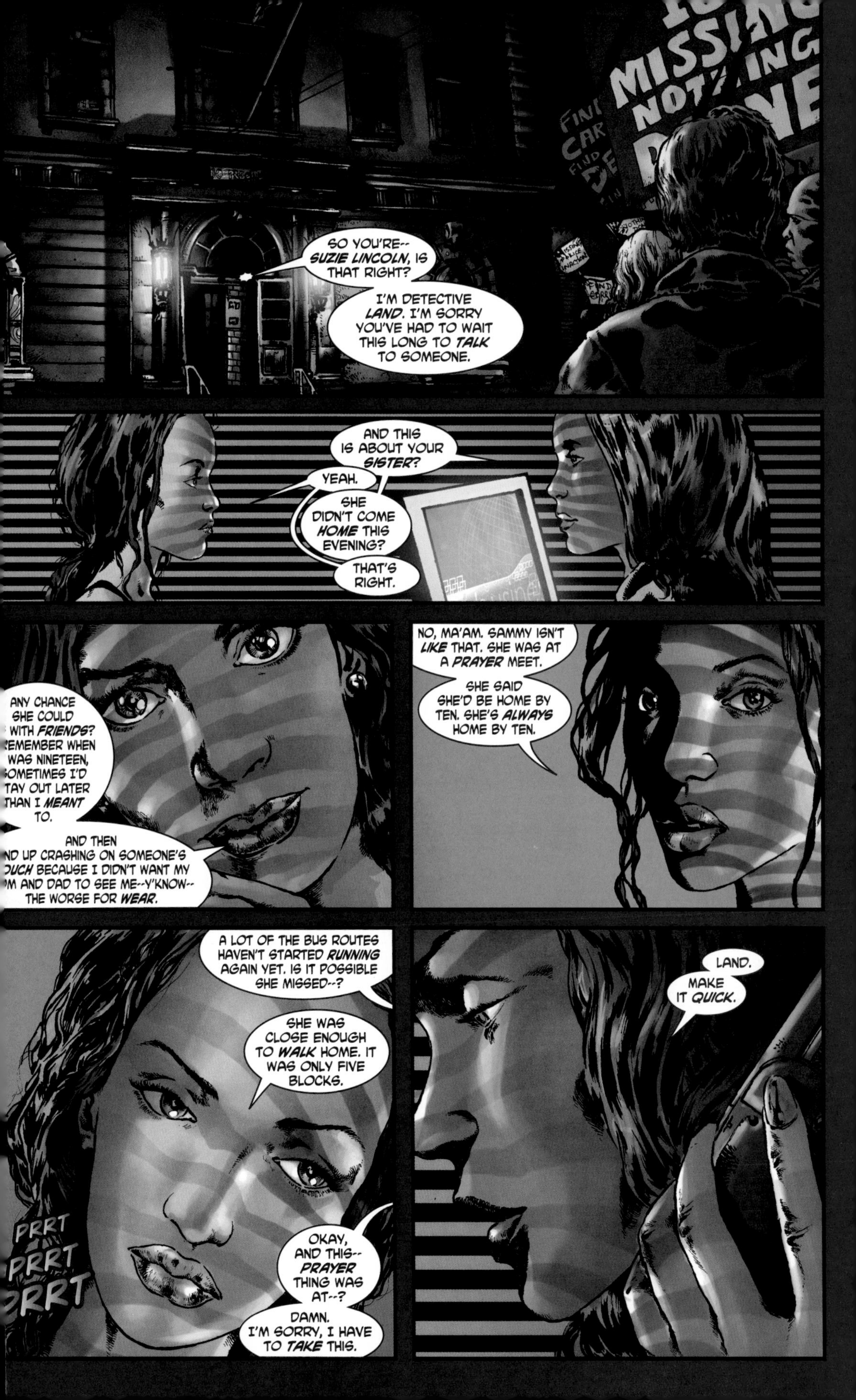

MISSING
SO YOU'RE-- SUZIE LINCOLN, IS THAT RIGHT?
I'M DETECTIVE LAND. I'M SORRY YOU'VE HAD TO WAIT THIS LONG TO TALK TO SOMEONE.
AND THIS IS ABOUT YOUR SISTER?
YEAH.
SHE DIDN'T COME HOME THIS EVENING?
THAT'S RIGHT.
ANY CHANCE SHE COULD WITH FRIENDS? REMEMBER WHEN WAS NINETEEN, OMETIMES I'D TAY OUT LATER THAN I MEANT TO.
AND THEN ND UP CRASHING ON SOMEONE'S OUCH BECAUSE I DIDN'T WANT MY M AND DAD TO SEE ME--Y'KNOW-- THE WORSE FOR WEAR.
NO, MA'AM. SAMMY ISN'T LIKE THAT. SHE WAS AT A PRAYER MEET.
SHE SAID SHE'D BE HOME BY TEN. SHE'S ALWAYS HOME BY TEN.
A LOT OF THE BUS ROUTES HAVEN'T STARTED RUNNING AGAIN YET. IS IT POSSIBLE SHE MISSED--?
SHE WAS CLOSE ENOUGH TO WALK HOME. IT WAS ONLY FIVE BLOCKS.
PRRT PRRT RRT
OKAY, AND THIS-- PRAYER THING WAS AT--?
DAMN. I'M SORRY, I HAVE TO TAKE THIS.
LAND. MAKE IT QUICK.

WE GOT ANOTHER DEAD *GANGSTER*.

YEAH?

YEAH. NOBODY I'VE *MET* BEFORE, BUT IT'S ALL PART OF THE SAME TURF WAR. I'D BET *MONEY* ON IT.

TURF WAR'S JUST A *THEORY*, REMEMBER.

FITS THE *FACTS*, THOUGH. EVERYTHING UP IN THE AIR. GUYS TRYING TO CUT THEMSELVES A BIGGER SLICE OF THE *PIE*.

WHAT GUYS, JULIEN? UNTIL YOU'VE GOT A *NAME*, IT'S JUST MOONDUST.

WELL THAT'S WHERE YOU CAN HELP ME, WHEN YOU GET A MOMENT FREE FROM YOUR MISSING *PERSONS* THING.

DEAD GUY HAD A *CELL*. HOW'D YOU LIKE TO SNAG THE RECORDS FROM THE *PHONE* COMPANY?

OH, I'D JUST *LOVE* TO. I'M ONLY HAPPY WHEN I'M HELPING *YOU*.

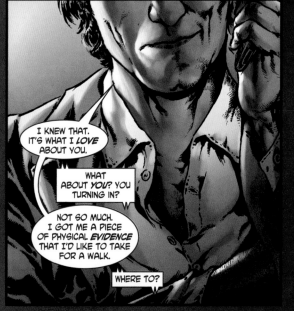

I KNEW THAT. IT'S WHAT I *LOVE* ABOUT YOU.

WHAT ABOUT *YOU*? YOU TURNING IN?

NOT SO MUCH. I GOT ME A PIECE OF PHYSICAL *EVIDENCE* THAT I'D LIKE TO TAKE FOR A WALK.

WHERE TO?

WELL THAT'S THE FUNNY *THING*, REBECCA.

YOU SITTING *DOWN*?

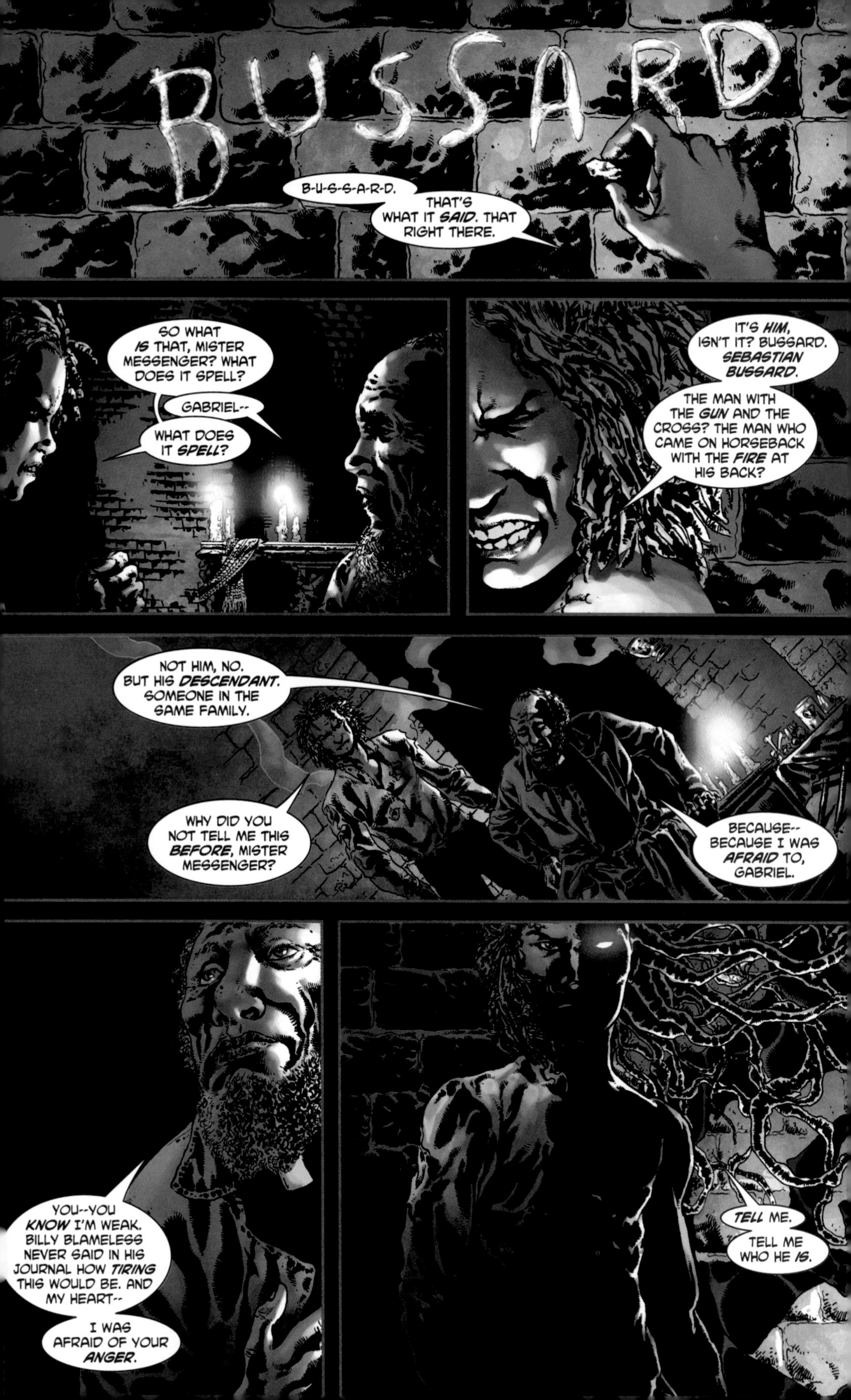
BUSSARD
B-U-S-S-A-R-D.
THAT'S WHAT IT SAID. THAT RIGHT THERE.
SO WHAT IS THAT, MISTER MESSENGER? WHAT DOES IT SPELL?
GABRIEL--
WHAT DOES IT SPELL?
IT'S HIM, ISN'T IT? BUSSARD. SEBASTIAN BUSSARD.
THE MAN WITH THE GUN AND THE CROSS? THE MAN WHO CAME ON HORSEBACK WITH THE FIRE AT HIS BACK?
NOT HIM, NO. BUT HIS DESCENDANT. SOMEONE IN THE SAME FAMILY.
WHY DID YOU NOT TELL ME THIS BEFORE, MISTER MESSENGER?
BECAUSE--BECAUSE I WAS AFRAID TO, GABRIEL.
YOU--YOU KNOW I'M WEAK. BILLY BLAMELESS NEVER SAID IN HIS JOURNAL HOW TIRING THIS WOULD BE. AND MY HEART--
I WAS AFRAID OF YOUR ANGER.
TELL ME.
TELL ME WHO HE IS.

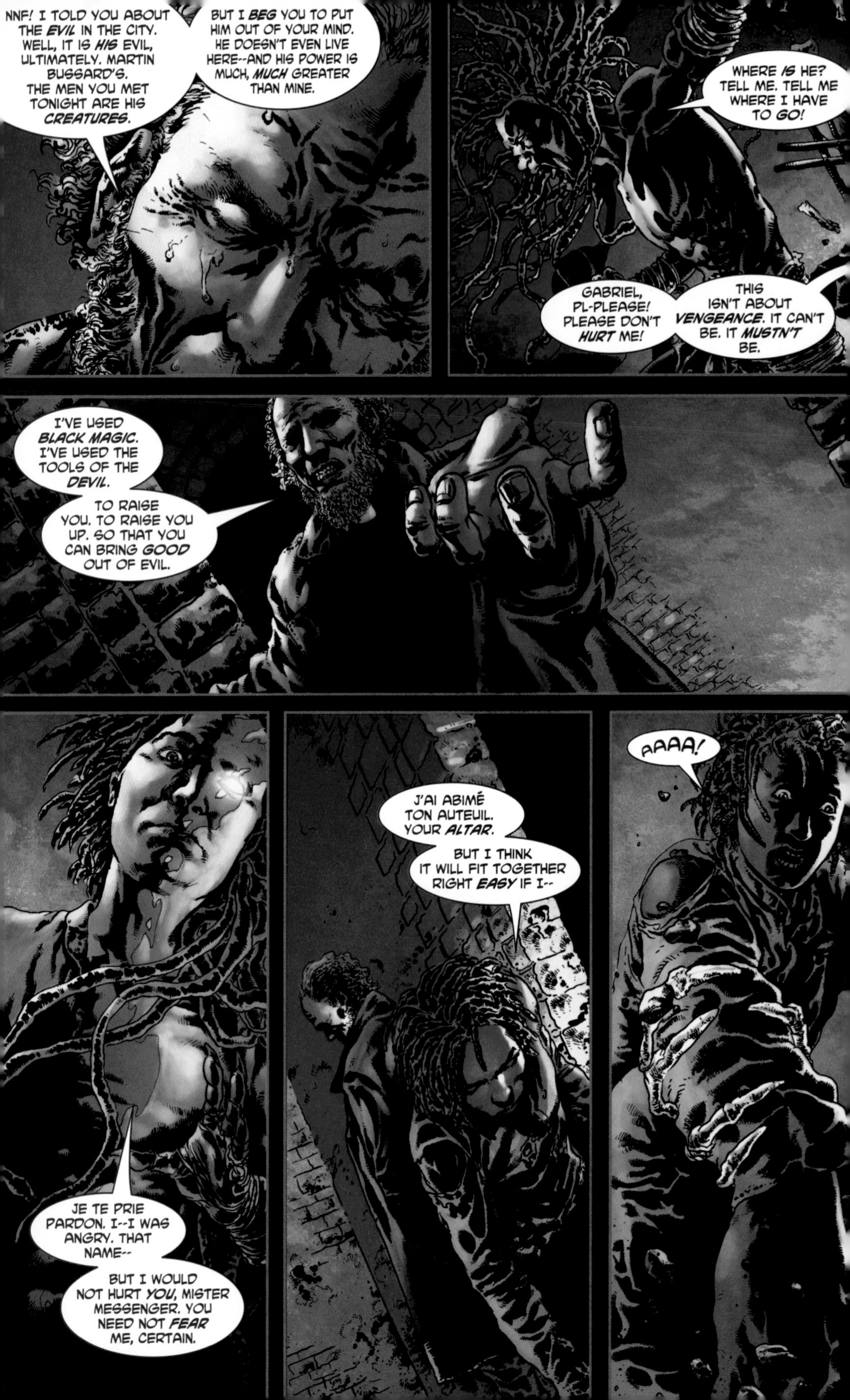
NNF! I TOLD YOU ABOUT THE EVIL IN THE CITY. WELL, IT IS HIS EVIL, ULTIMATELY. MARTIN BUSSARD'S. THE MEN YOU MET TONIGHT ARE HIS CREATURES.
BUT I BEG YOU TO PUT HIM OUT OF YOUR MIND. HE DOESN'T EVEN LIVE HERE--AND HIS POWER IS MUCH, MUCH GREATER THAN MINE.
WHERE IS HE? TELL ME. TELL ME WHERE I HAVE TO GO!
GABRIEL, PL-PLEASE! PLEASE DON'T HURT ME!
THIS ISN'T ABOUT VENGEANCE. IT CAN'T BE. IT MUSTN'T BE.
I'VE USED BLACK MAGIC. I'VE USED THE TOOLS OF THE DEVIL.
TO RAISE YOU. TO RAISE YOU UP. SO THAT YOU CAN BRING GOOD OUT OF EVIL.
JE TE PRIE PARDON. I--I WAS ANGRY. THAT NAME--
BUT I WOULD NOT HURT YOU, MISTER MESSENGER. YOU NEED NOT FEAR ME, CERTAIN.
J'AI ABIMÉ TON AUTEUIL. YOUR ALTAR.
BUT I THINK IT WILL FIT TOGETHER RIGHT EASY IF I--
AAAA!

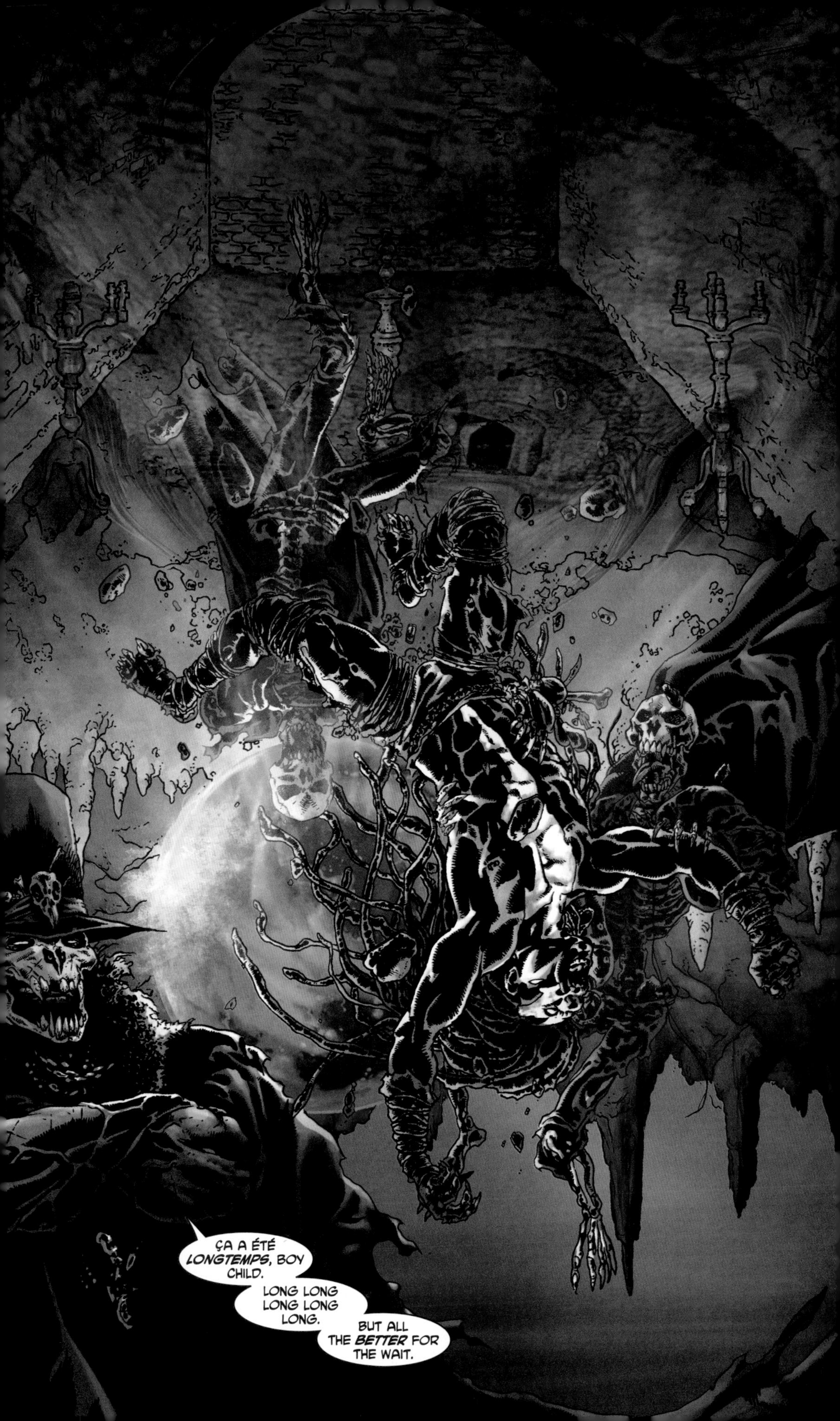
ÇA A ÉTÉ *LONGTEMPS*, BOY CHILD.
LONG LONG LONG LONG LONG.
BUT ALL THE *BETTER* FOR THE WAIT.

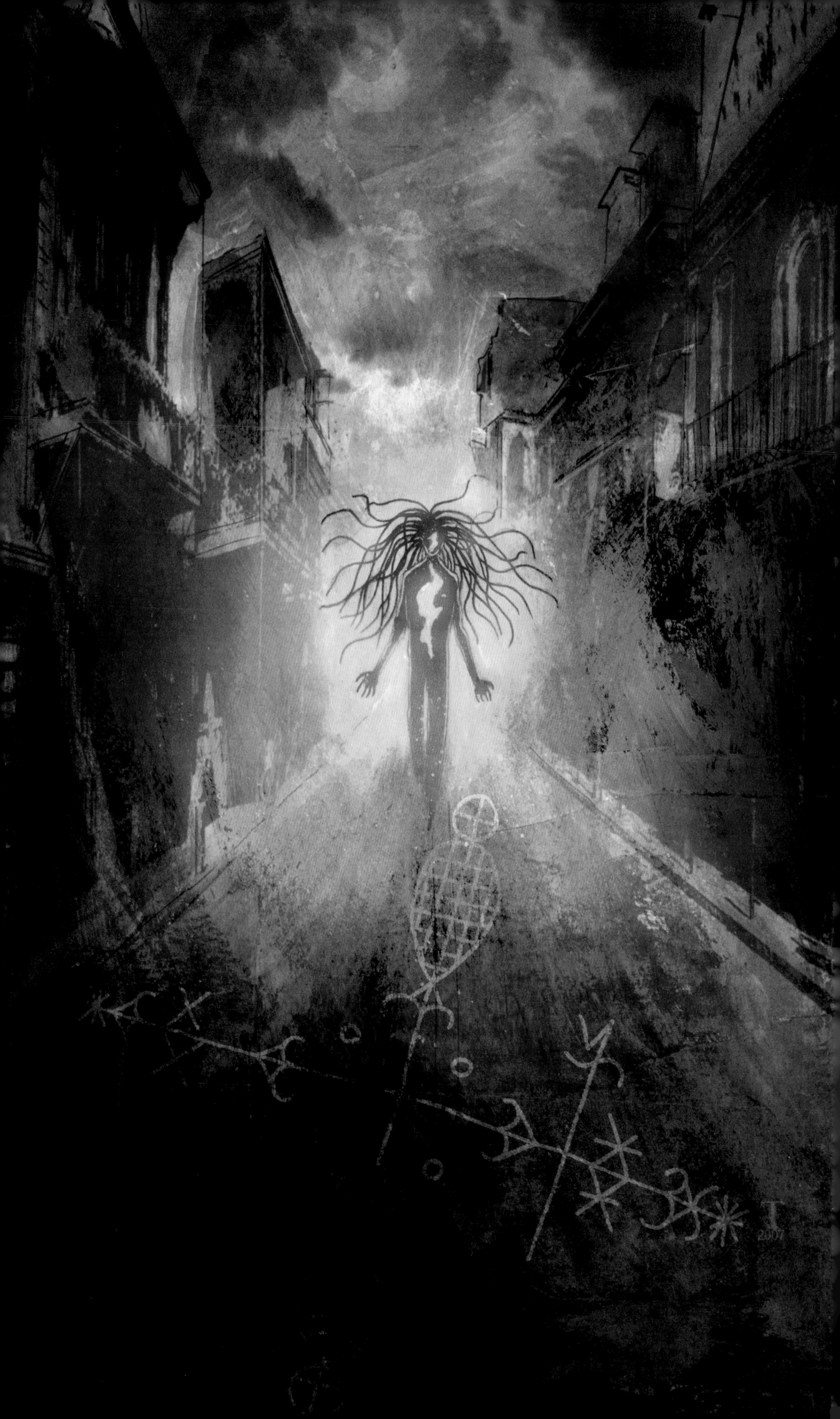
2007

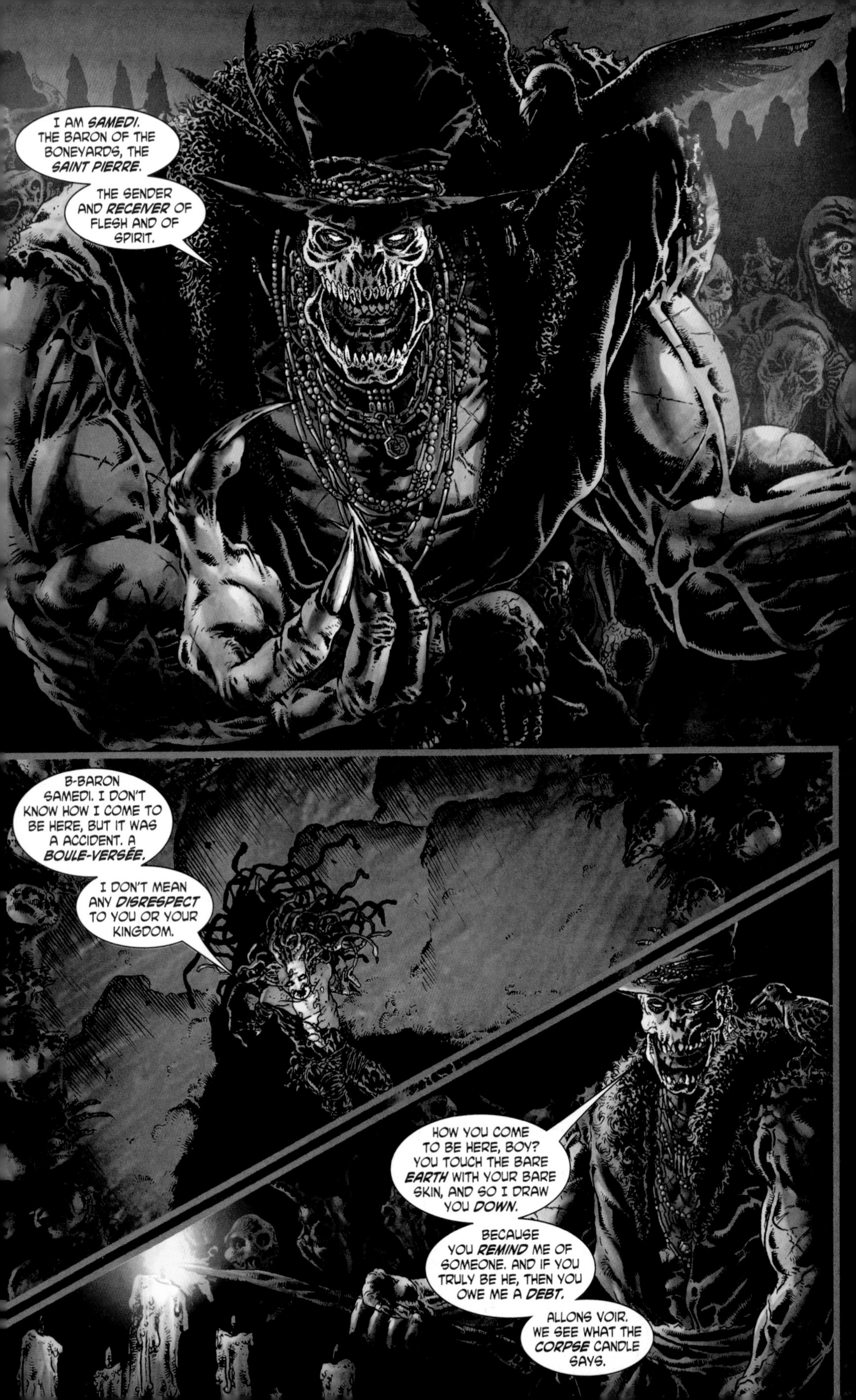
I AM *SAMEDI*. THE BARON OF THE BONEYARDS, THE *SAINT PIERRE*.
THE SENDER AND *RECEIVER* OF FLESH AND OF SPIRIT.
B-BARON SAMEDI. I DON'T KNOW HOW I COME TO BE HERE, BUT IT WAS A ACCIDENT. A *BOULE-VERSÉE*.
I DON'T MEAN ANY *DISRESPECT* TO YOU OR YOUR KINGDOM.
HOW YOU COME TO BE HERE, BOY? YOU TOUCH THE BARE *EARTH* WITH YOUR BARE SKIN, AND SO I DRAW YOU *DOWN*.
BECAUSE YOU *REMIND* ME OF SOMEONE. AND IF YOU TRULY BE HE, THEN YOU OWE ME A *DEBT*.
ALLONS VOIR. WE SEE WHAT THE *CORPSE* CANDLE SAYS.

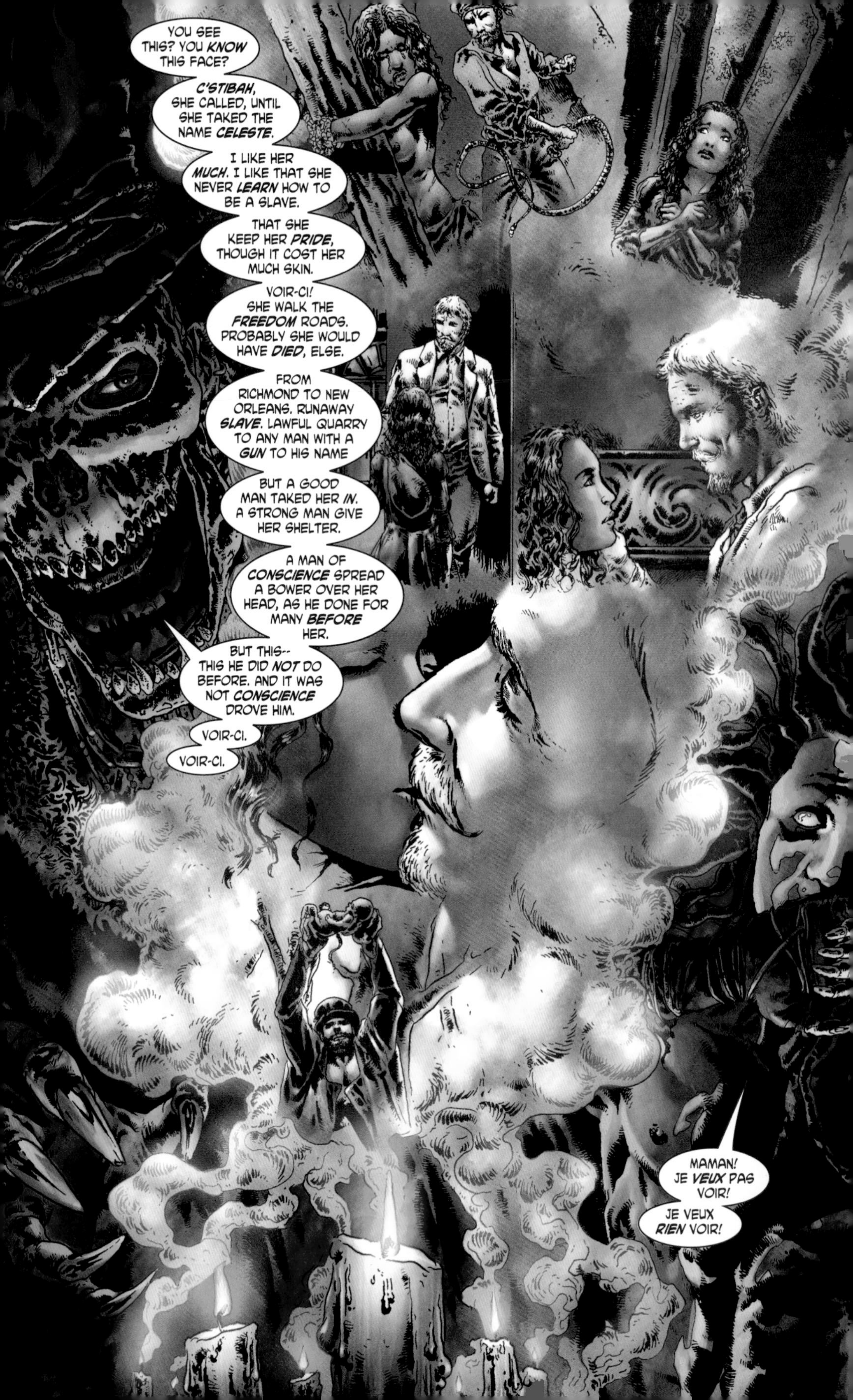
YOU SEE THIS? YOU KNOW THIS FACE?
C'STIBAH, SHE CALLED, UNTIL SHE TAKED THE NAME CELESTE.
I LIKE HER MUCH. I LIKE THAT SHE NEVER LEARN HOW TO BE A SLAVE.
THAT SHE KEEP HER PRIDE, THOUGH IT COST HER MUCH SKIN.
VOIR-CI! SHE WALK THE FREEDOM ROADS. PROBABLY SHE WOULD HAVE DIED, ELSE.
FROM RICHMOND TO NEW ORLEANS. RUNAWAY SLAVE. LAWFUL QUARRY TO ANY MAN WITH A GUN TO HIS NAME
BUT A GOOD MAN TAKED HER IN. A STRONG MAN GIVE HER SHELTER.
A MAN OF CONSCIENCE SPREAD A BOWER OVER HER HEAD, AS HE DONE FOR MANY BEFORE HER.
BUT THIS-- THIS HE DID NOT DO BEFORE. AND IT WAS NOT CONSCIENCE DROVE HIM.
VOIR-CI.
VOIR-CI.
MAMAN! JE VEUX PAS VOIR!
JE VEUX RIEN VOIR!

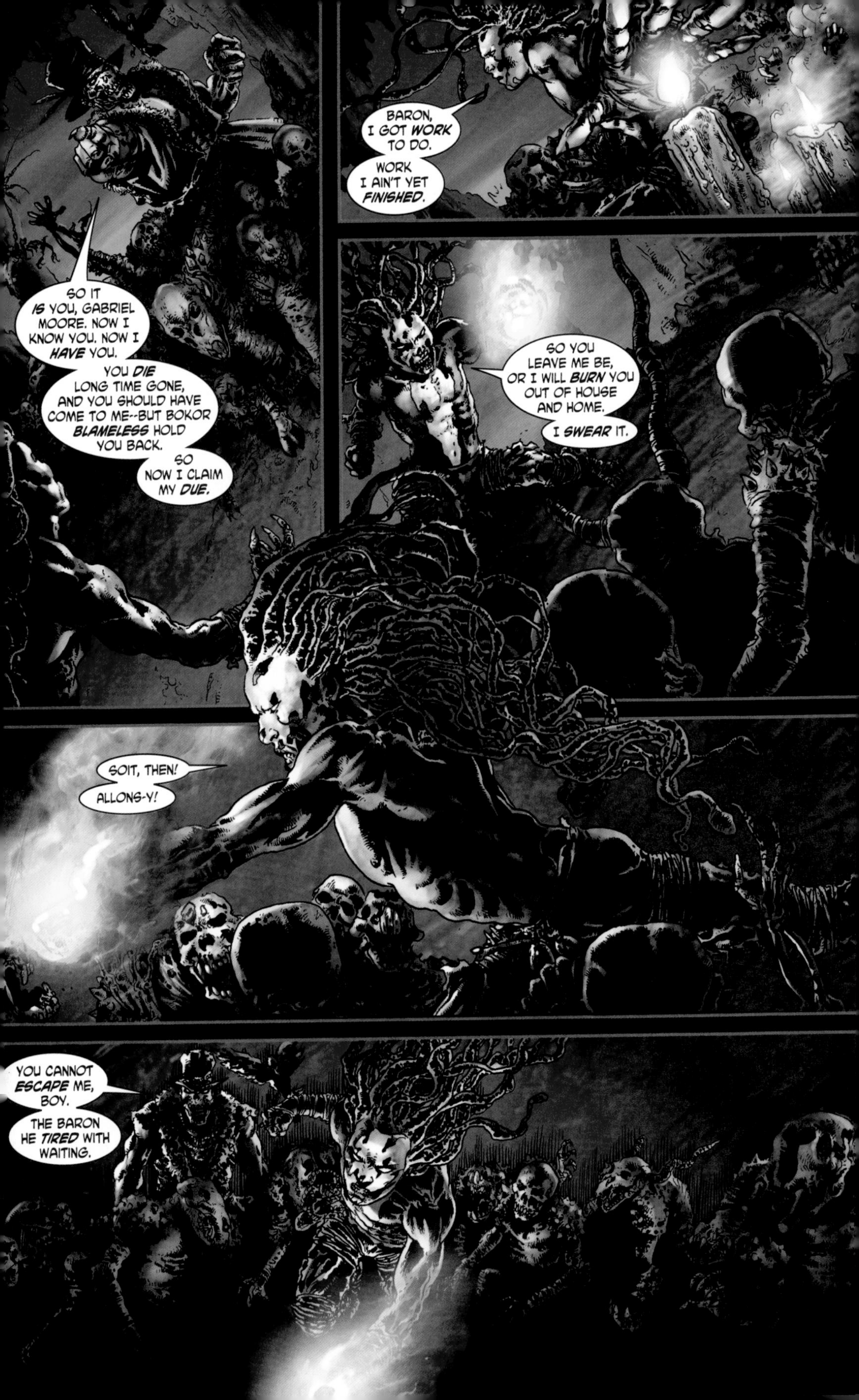
BARON, I GOT WORK TO DO.
WORK I AIN'T YET FINISHED.
SO IT IS YOU, GABRIEL MOORE. NOW I KNOW YOU. NOW I HAVE YOU.
YOU DIE LONG TIME GONE, AND YOU SHOULD HAVE COME TO ME--BUT BOKOR BLAMELESS HOLD YOU BACK.
SO NOW I CLAIM MY DUE.
SO YOU LEAVE ME BE, OR I WILL BURN YOU OUT OF HOUSE AND HOME.
I SWEAR IT.
SOIT, THEN!
ALLONS-Y!
YOU CANNOT ESCAPE ME, BOY.
THE BARON HE TIRED WITH WAITING.

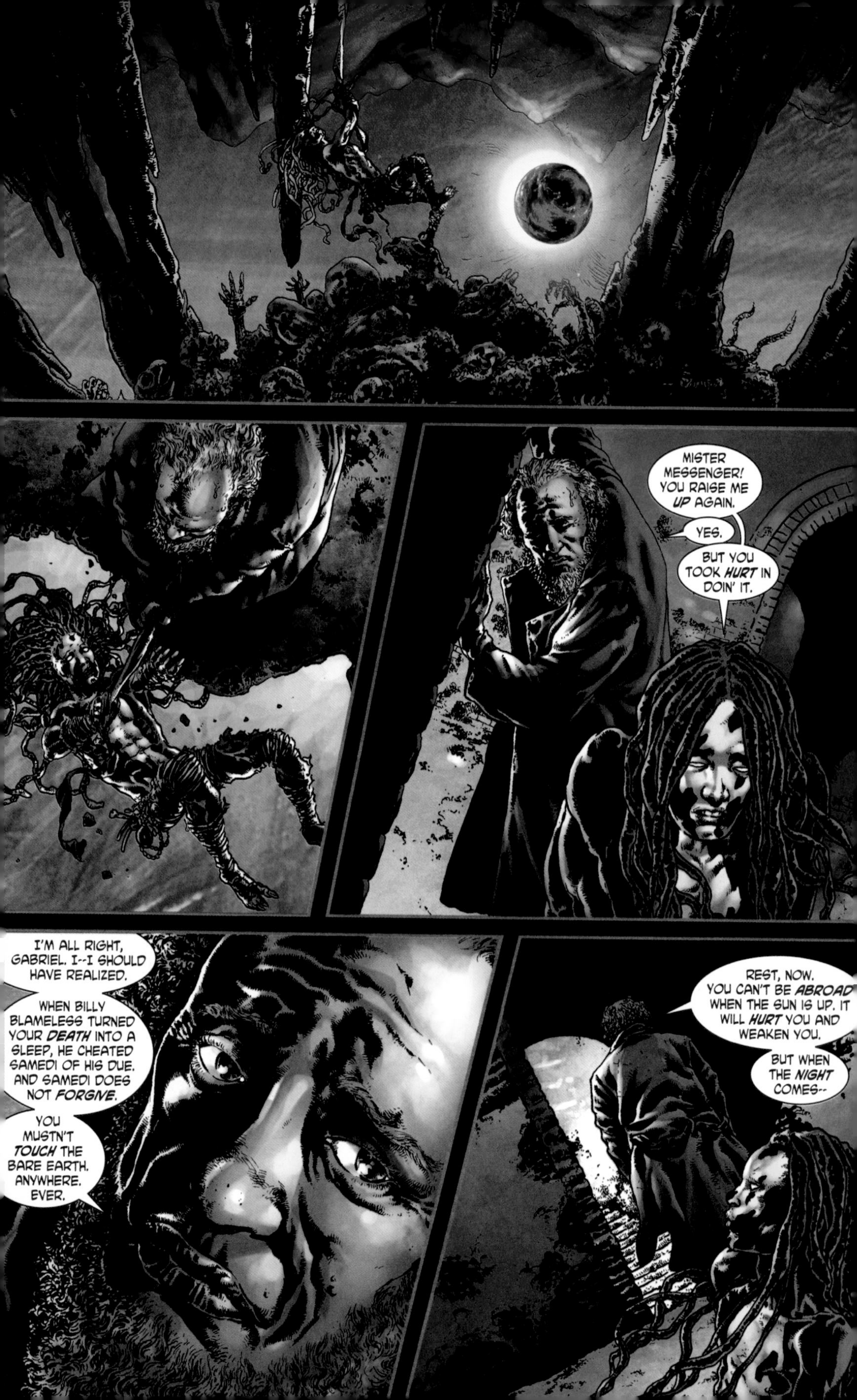
MISTER MESSENGER! YOU RAISE ME UP AGAIN.
YES.
BUT YOU TOOK HURT IN DOIN' IT.
I'M ALL RIGHT, GABRIEL. I--I SHOULD HAVE REALIZED.
WHEN BILLY BLAMELESS TURNED YOUR DEATH INTO A SLEEP, HE CHEATED SAMEDI OF HIS DUE. AND SAMEDI DOES NOT FORGIVE.
YOU MUSTN'T TOUCH THE BARE EARTH. ANYWHERE. EVER.
REST, NOW. YOU CAN'T BE ABROAD WHEN THE SUN IS UP. IT WILL HURT YOU AND WEAKEN YOU.
BUT WHEN THE NIGHT COMES--

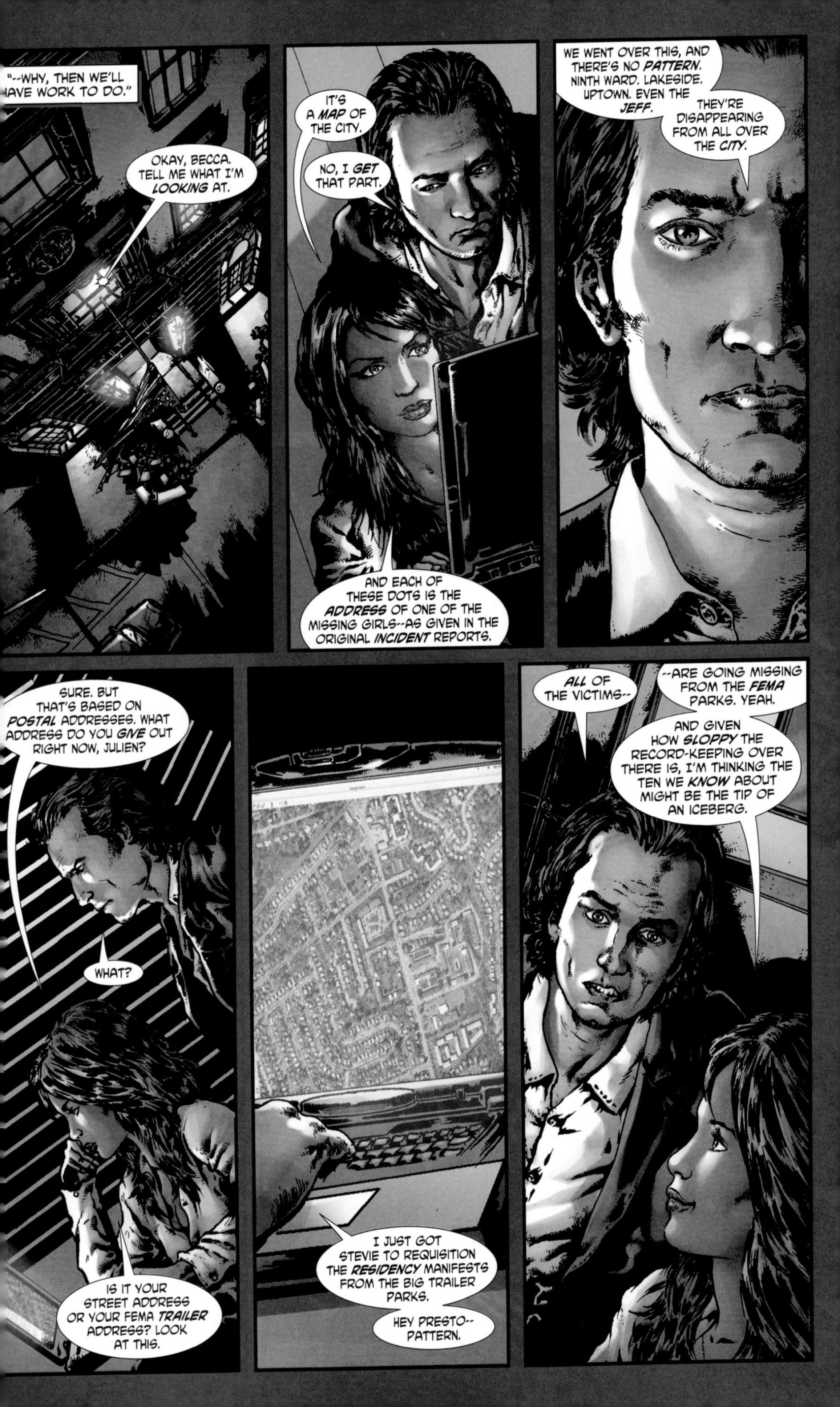
"--WHY, THEN WE'LL HAVE WORK TO DO."
OKAY, BECCA. TELL ME WHAT I'M LOOKING AT.
IT'S A MAP OF THE CITY.
NO, I GET THAT PART.
AND EACH OF THESE DOTS IS THE ADDRESS OF ONE OF THE MISSING GIRLS--AS GIVEN IN THE ORIGINAL INCIDENT REPORTS.
WE WENT OVER THIS, AND THERE'S NO PATTERN. NINTH WARD. LAKESIDE. UPTOWN. EVEN THE JEFF.
THEY'RE DISAPPEARING FROM ALL OVER THE CITY.
SURE. BUT THAT'S BASED ON POSTAL ADDRESSES. WHAT ADDRESS DO YOU GIVE OUT RIGHT NOW, JULIEN?
WHAT?
IS IT YOUR STREET ADDRESS OR YOUR FEMA TRAILER ADDRESS? LOOK AT THIS.
I JUST GOT STEVIE TO REQUISITION THE RESIDENCY MANIFESTS FROM THE BIG TRAILER PARKS.
HEY PRESTO--PATTERN.
ALL OF THE VICTIMS--
--ARE GOING MISSING FROM THE FEMA PARKS. YEAH.
AND GIVEN HOW SLOPPY THE RECORD-KEEPING OVER THERE IS, I'M THINKING THE TEN WE KNOW ABOUT MIGHT BE THE TIP OF AN ICEBERG.

SO. YOU'RE GONNA GO *OUT* THERE AND TURN OVER SOME STONES?

YEAH. YOU GONNA COME WITH ME?

NOPE.

POURQUOI?

THE GANG-WAR THING. I GOT AN APPOINTMENT WITH A BIG WHEEL AT SPERRY-BUSSARD. GUY NAME OF BRIDGE.

I WANT TO SEE IF I CAN FIND ANYTHING OUT ABOUT THIS BLANK *ID CARD* I FOUND NEXT TO THE LATEST BODY.

SO YOU'RE NOT GOING TO WATCH MY *BACK?*

ONLY AS YOU WALK OUT OF THE ROOM. I NEVER MISS *THAT* VIEW.

AND NAGIN CANCELLED *MARDI GRAS.* TODAY SUCKS.

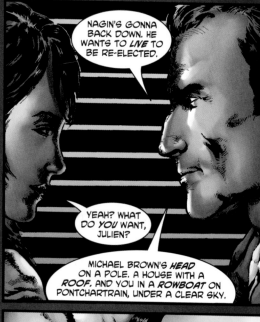

NAGIN'S GONNA BACK DOWN. HE WANTS TO *LIVE* TO BE RE-ELECTED.

YEAH? WHAT DO *YOU* WANT, JULIEN?

MICHAEL BROWN'S *HEAD* ON A POLE. A HOUSE WITH A *ROOF.* AND YOU IN A *ROWBOAT* ON PONTCHARTRAIN, UNDER A CLEAR SKY.

NEXT TIME, YOU PUT ME *BEFORE* THE ROOF--

--OR I'LL BITE.

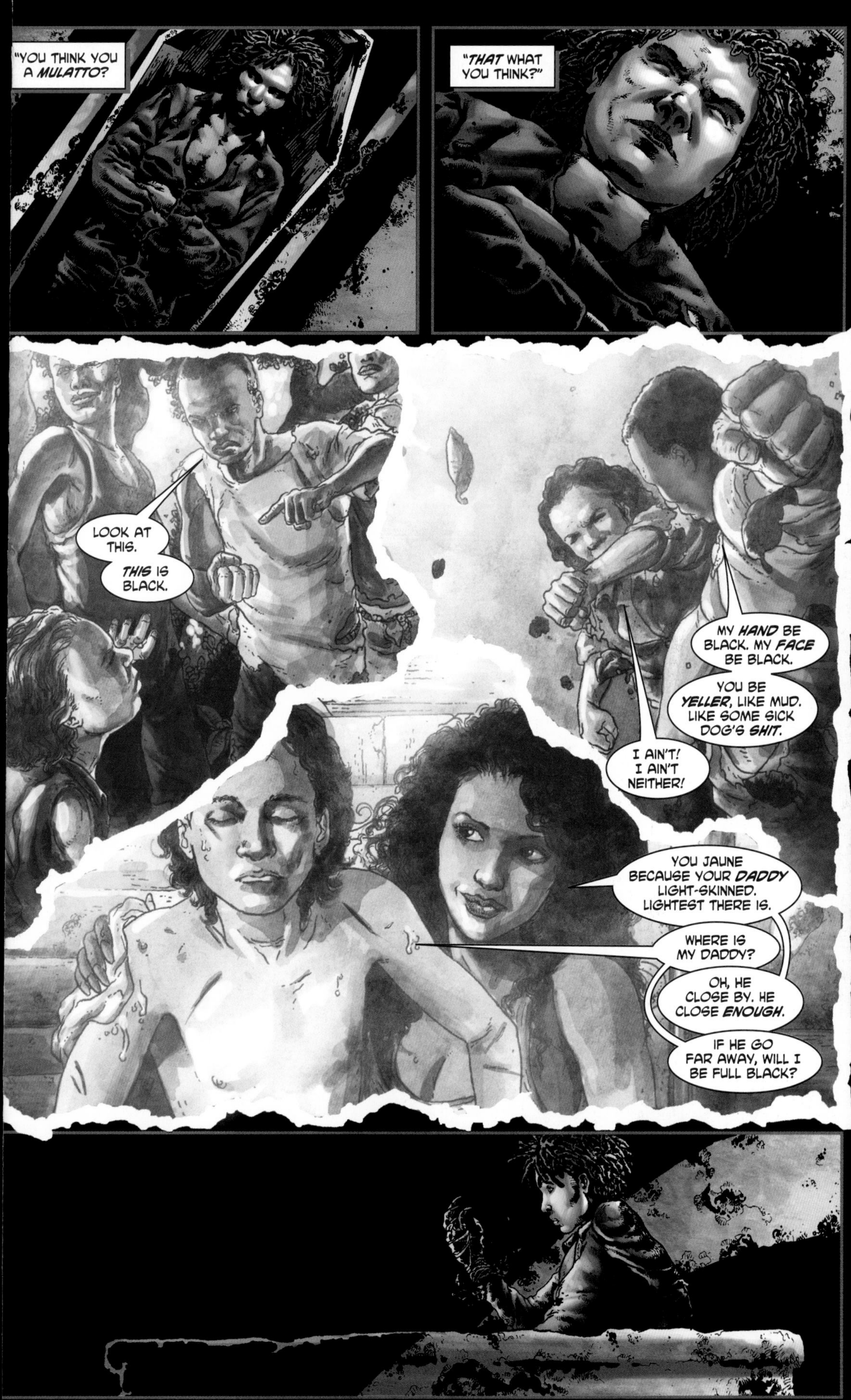
"YOU THINK YOU A *MULATTO*?
"*THAT* WHAT YOU THINK?"
LOOK AT THIS.
THIS IS BLACK.
MY *HAND* BE BLACK. MY *FACE* BE BLACK.
YOU BE *YELLER*, LIKE MUD. LIKE SOME SICK DOG'S *SHIT*.
I AIN'T! I AIN'T NEITHER!
YOU JAUNE BECAUSE YOUR *DADDY* LIGHT-SKINNED. LIGHTEST THERE IS.
WHERE IS MY DADDY?
OH, HE CLOSE BY. HE CLOSE *ENOUGH*.
IF HE GO FAR AWAY, WILL I BE FULL BLACK?

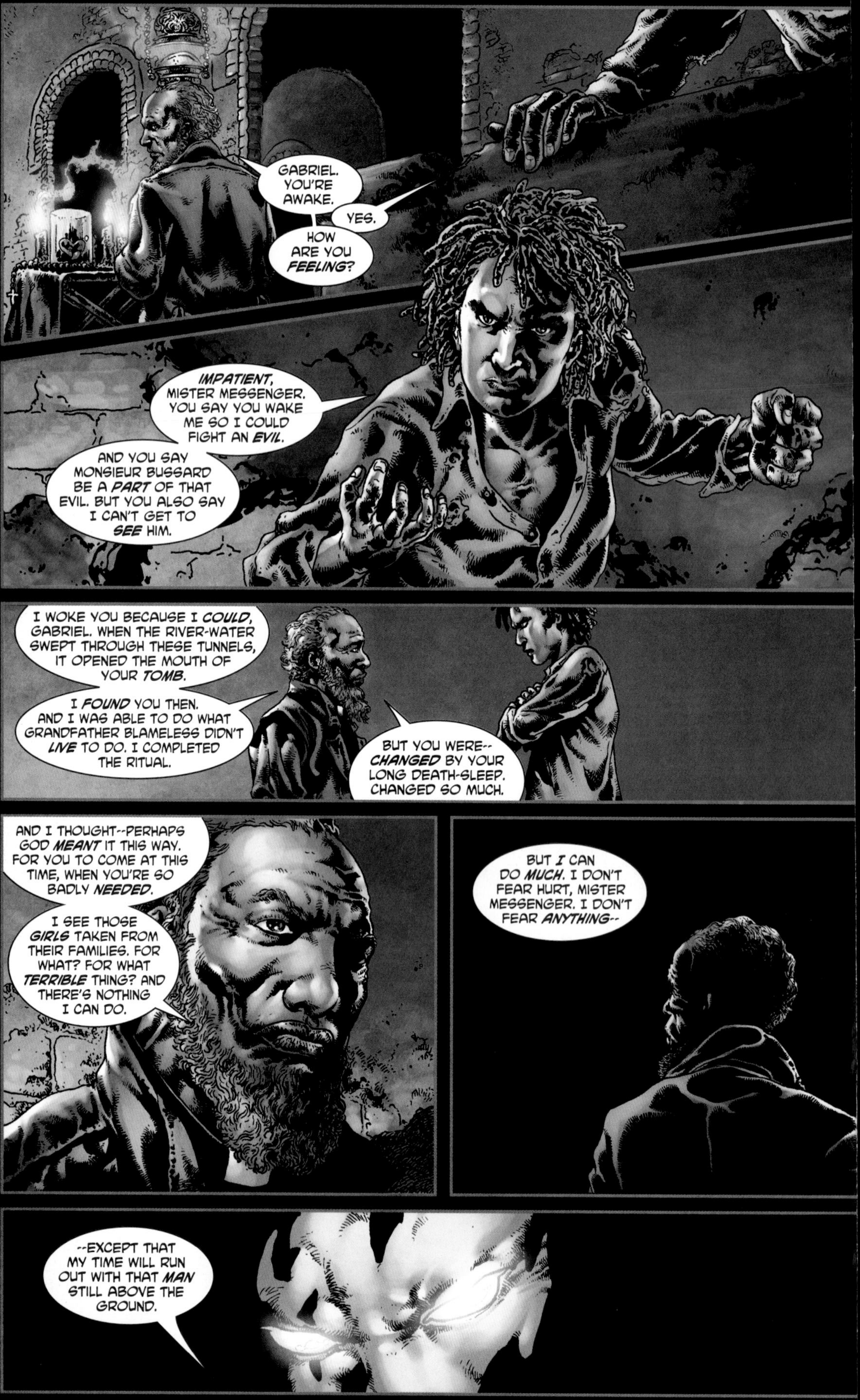
GABRIEL. YOU'RE AWAKE.
YES.
HOW ARE YOU FEELING?
IMPATIENT, MISTER MESSENGER. YOU SAY YOU WAKE ME SO I COULD FIGHT AN EVIL.
AND YOU SAY MONSIEUR BUSSARD BE A PART OF THAT EVIL. BUT YOU ALSO SAY I CAN'T GET TO SEE HIM.
I WOKE YOU BECAUSE I COULD, GABRIEL. WHEN THE RIVER-WATER SWEPT THROUGH THESE TUNNELS, IT OPENED THE MOUTH OF YOUR TOMB.
I FOUND YOU THEN. AND I WAS ABLE TO DO WHAT GRANDFATHER BLAMELESS DIDN'T LIVE TO DO. I COMPLETED THE RITUAL.
BUT YOU WERE-- CHANGED BY YOUR LONG DEATH-SLEEP. CHANGED SO MUCH.
AND I THOUGHT--PERHAPS GOD MEANT IT THIS WAY. FOR YOU TO COME AT THIS TIME, WHEN YOU'RE SO BADLY NEEDED.
I SEE THOSE GIRLS TAKEN FROM THEIR FAMILIES. FOR WHAT? FOR WHAT TERRIBLE THING? AND THERE'S NOTHING I CAN DO.
BUT I CAN DO MUCH. I DON'T FEAR HURT, MISTER MESSENGER. I DON'T FEAR ANYTHING--
--EXCEPT THAT MY TIME WILL RUN OUT WITH THAT MAN STILL ABOVE THE GROUND.

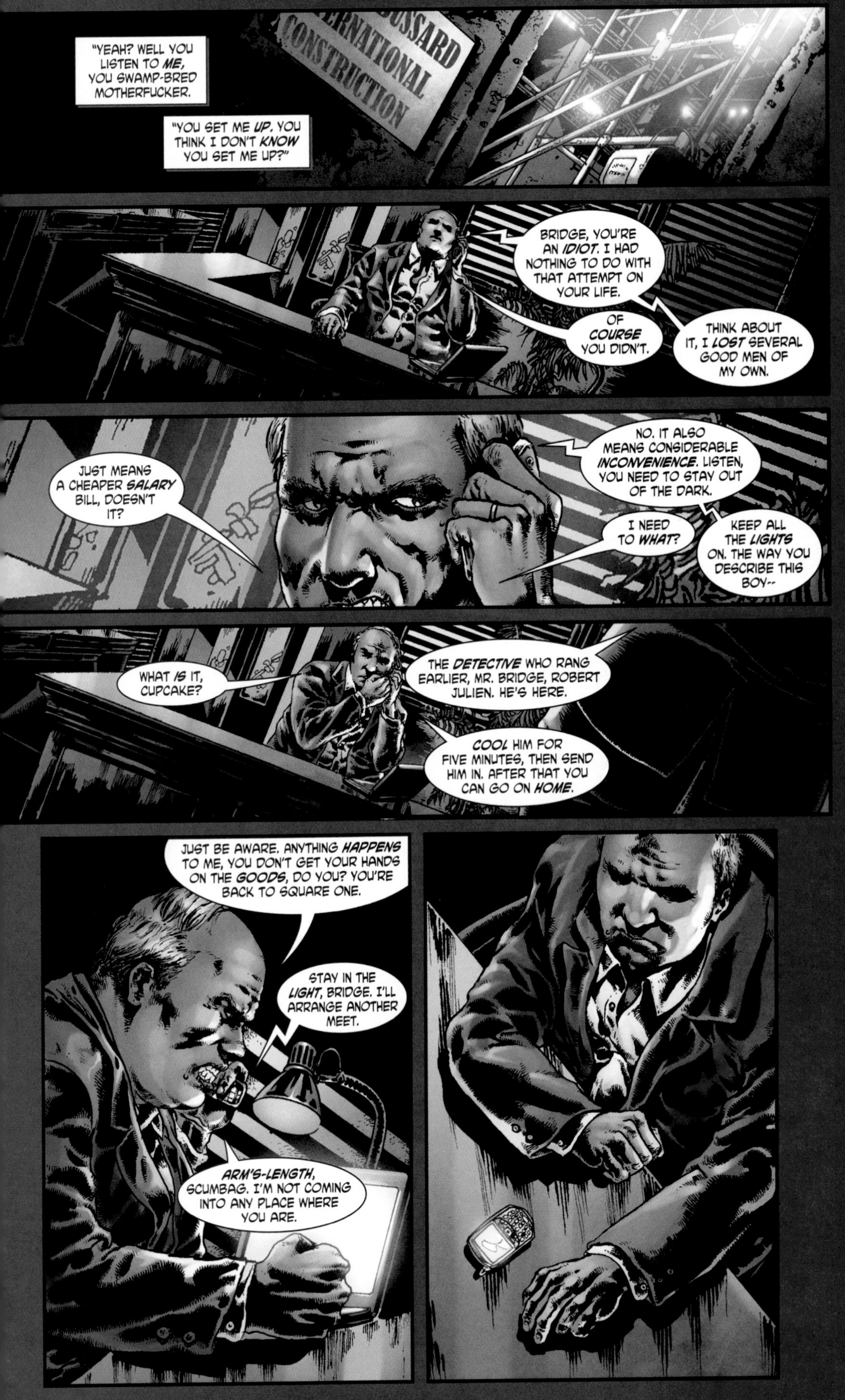

"YEAH? WELL YOU LISTEN TO ME, YOU SWAMP-BRED MOTHERFUCKER.
"YOU SET ME UP. YOU THINK I DON'T KNOW YOU SET ME UP?"
INTERNATIONAL CONSTRUCTION
BRIDGE, YOU'RE AN IDIOT. I HAD NOTHING TO DO WITH THAT ATTEMPT ON YOUR LIFE.
OF COURSE YOU DIDN'T.
THINK ABOUT IT, I LOST SEVERAL GOOD MEN OF MY OWN.
JUST MEANS A CHEAPER SALARY BILL, DOESN'T IT?
NO. IT ALSO MEANS CONSIDERABLE INCONVENIENCE. LISTEN, YOU NEED TO STAY OUT OF THE DARK.
I NEED TO WHAT?
KEEP ALL THE LIGHTS ON. THE WAY YOU DESCRIBE THIS BOY--
WHAT IS IT, CUPCAKE?
THE DETECTIVE WHO RANG EARLIER, MR. BRIDGE, ROBERT JULIEN. HE'S HERE.
COOL HIM FOR FIVE MINUTES, THEN SEND HIM IN. AFTER THAT YOU CAN GO ON HOME.
JUST BE AWARE. ANYTHING HAPPENS TO ME, YOU DON'T GET YOUR HANDS ON THE GOODS, DO YOU? YOU'RE BACK TO SQUARE ONE.
STAY IN THE LIGHT, BRIDGE. I'LL ARRANGE ANOTHER MEET.
ARM'S-LENGTH, SCUMBAG. I'M NOT COMING INTO ANY PLACE WHERE YOU ARE.

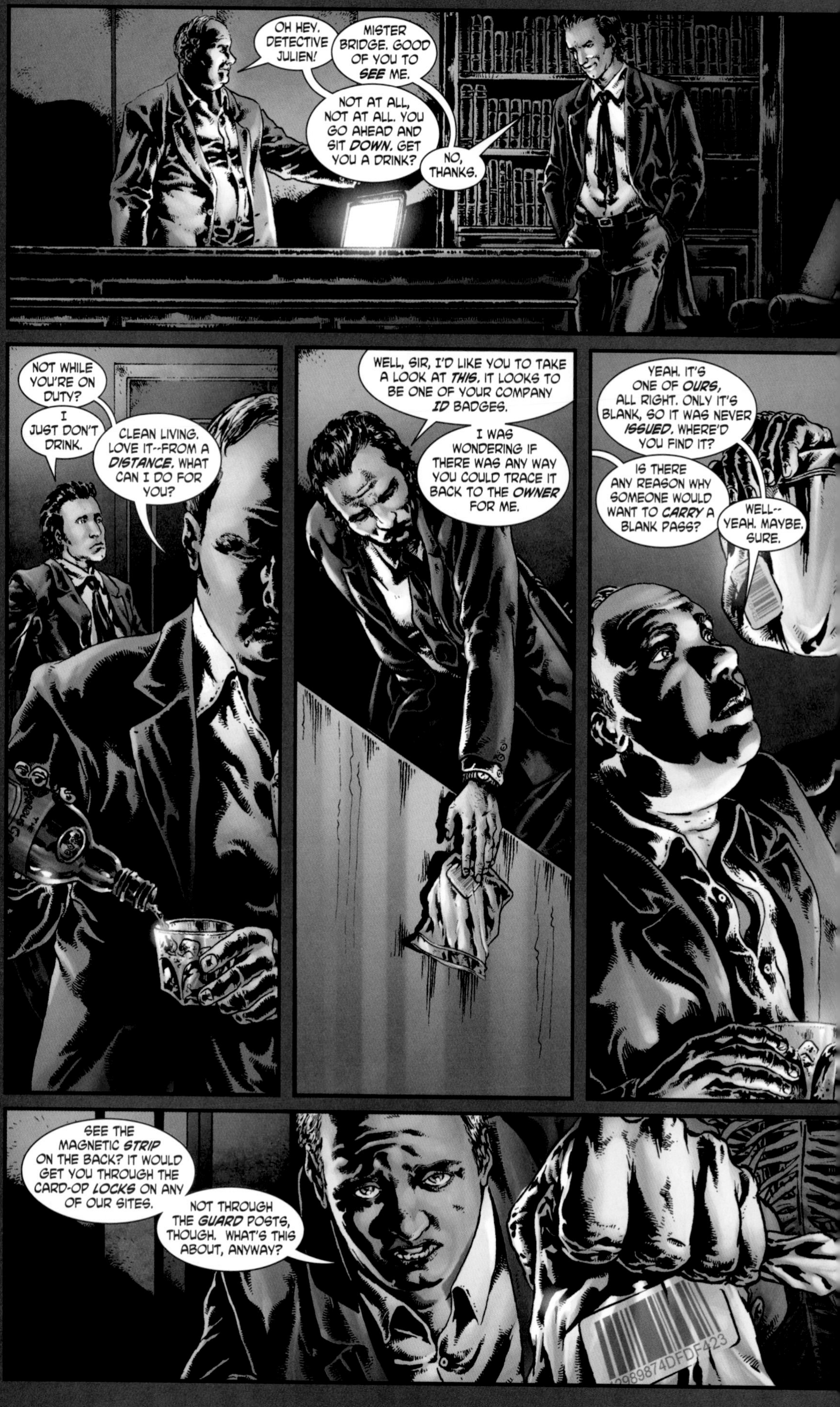
OH HEY. DETECTIVE JULIEN!
MISTER BRIDGE. GOOD OF YOU TO SEE ME.
NOT AT ALL, NOT AT ALL. YOU GO AHEAD AND SIT DOWN. GET YOU A DRINK?
NO, THANKS.
NOT WHILE YOU'RE ON DUTY?
I JUST DON'T DRINK.
CLEAN LIVING. LOVE IT--FROM A DISTANCE. WHAT CAN I DO FOR YOU?
WELL, SIR, I'D LIKE YOU TO TAKE A LOOK AT THIS. IT LOOKS TO BE ONE OF YOUR COMPANY ID BADGES.
I WAS WONDERING IF THERE WAS ANY WAY YOU COULD TRACE IT BACK TO THE OWNER FOR ME.
YEAH. IT'S ONE OF OURS, ALL RIGHT. ONLY IT'S BLANK, SO IT WAS NEVER ISSUED. WHERE'D YOU FIND IT?
IS THERE ANY REASON WHY SOMEONE WOULD WANT TO CARRY A BLANK PASS?
WELL-- YEAH. MAYBE. SURE.
SEE THE MAGNETIC STRIP ON THE BACK? IT WOULD GET YOU THROUGH THE CARD-OP LOCKS ON ANY OF OUR SITES.
NOT THROUGH THE GUARD POSTS, THOUGH. WHAT'S THIS ABOUT, ANYWAY?
2989874DFDF423

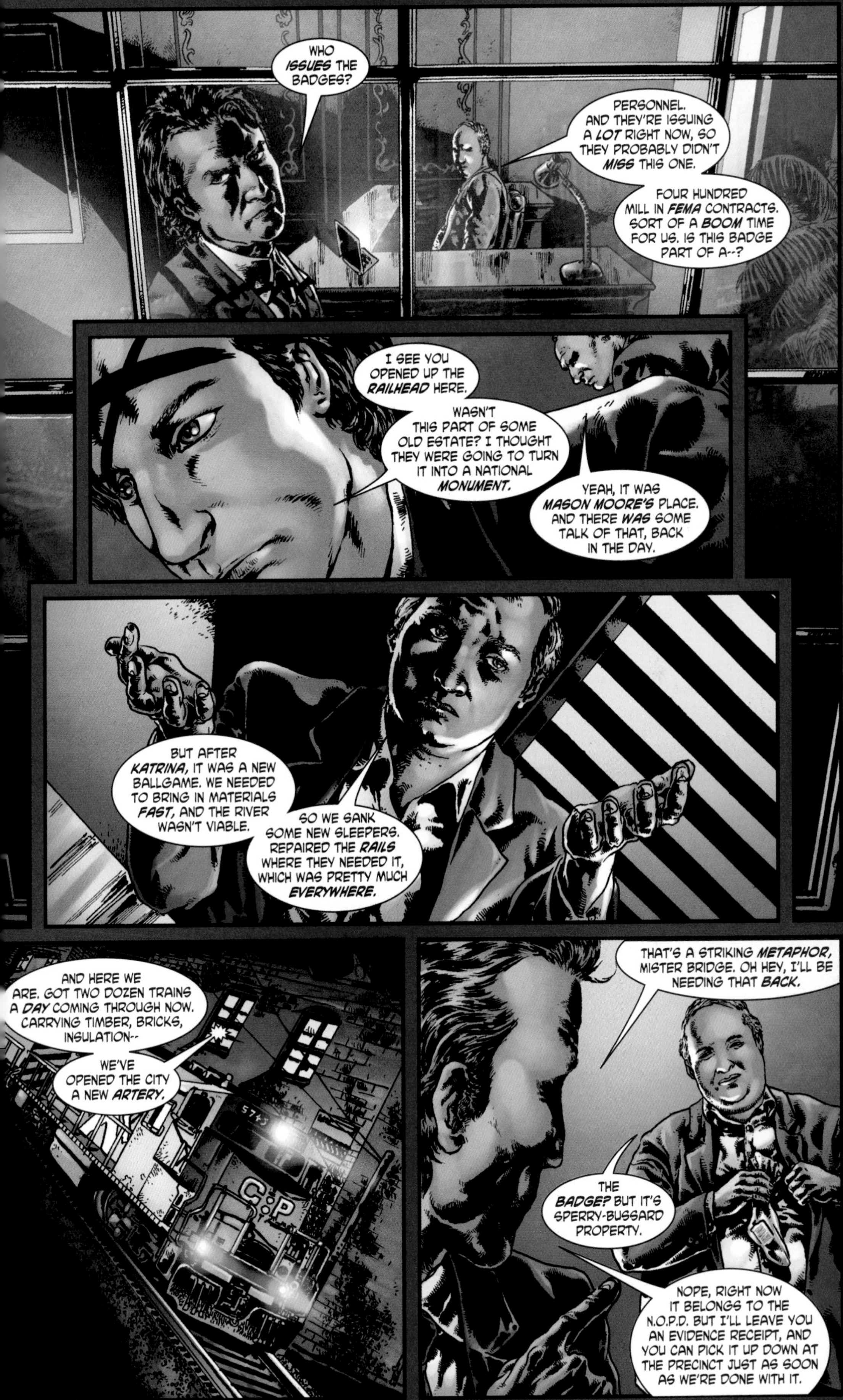
WHO ISSUES THE BADGES?
PERSONNEL. AND THEY'RE ISSUING A LOT RIGHT NOW, SO THEY PROBABLY DIDN'T MISS THIS ONE.
FOUR HUNDRED MILL IN FEMA CONTRACTS. SORT OF A BOOM TIME FOR US. IS THIS BADGE PART OF A--?
I SEE YOU OPENED UP THE RAILHEAD HERE.
WASN'T THIS PART OF SOME OLD ESTATE? I THOUGHT THEY WERE GOING TO TURN IT INTO A NATIONAL MONUMENT.
YEAH, IT WAS MASON MOORE'S PLACE. AND THERE WAS SOME TALK OF THAT, BACK IN THE DAY.
BUT AFTER KATRINA, IT WAS A NEW BALLGAME. WE NEEDED TO BRING IN MATERIALS FAST, AND THE RIVER WASN'T VIABLE.
SO WE SANK SOME NEW SLEEPERS. REPAIRED THE RAILS WHERE THEY NEEDED IT, WHICH WAS PRETTY MUCH EVERYWHERE.
AND HERE WE ARE. GOT TWO DOZEN TRAINS A DAY COMING THROUGH NOW. CARRYING TIMBER, BRICKS, INSULATION--
WE'VE OPENED THE CITY A NEW ARTERY.
5743
C&P
THAT'S A STRIKING METAPHOR, MISTER BRIDGE. OH HEY, I'LL BE NEEDING THAT BACK.
THE BADGE? BUT IT'S SPERRY-BUSSARD PROPERTY.
NOPE, RIGHT NOW IT BELONGS TO THE N.O.P.D. BUT I'LL LEAVE YOU AN EVIDENCE RECEIPT, AND YOU CAN PICK IT UP DOWN AT THE PRECINCT JUST AS SOON AS WE'RE DONE WITH IT.

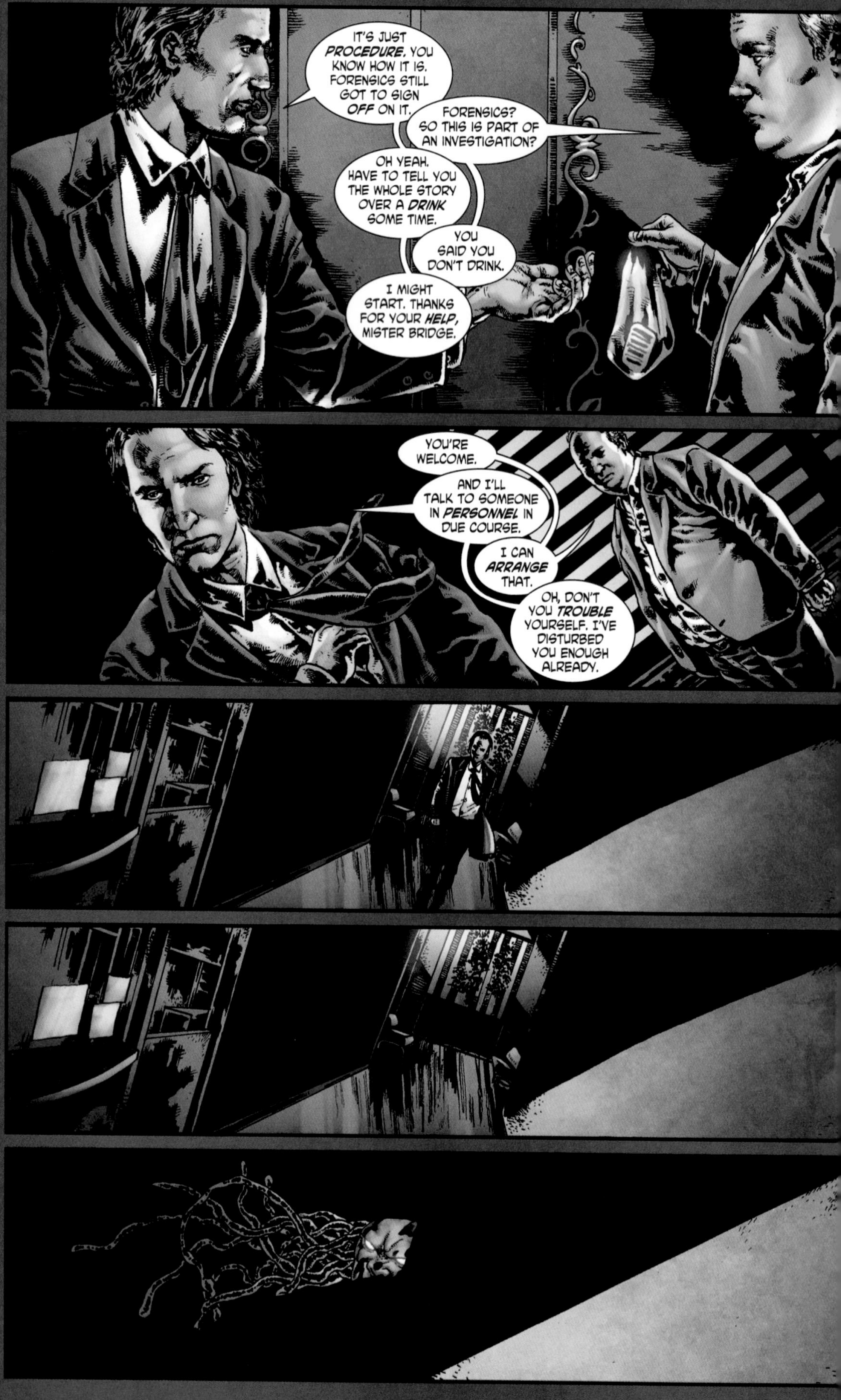
IT'S JUST PROCEDURE. YOU KNOW HOW IT IS. FORENSICS STILL GOT TO SIGN OFF ON IT.
FORENSICS? SO THIS IS PART OF AN INVESTIGATION?
OH YEAH. HAVE TO TELL YOU THE WHOLE STORY OVER A DRINK SOME TIME.
YOU SAID YOU DON'T DRINK.
I MIGHT START. THANKS FOR YOUR HELP, MISTER BRIDGE.
YOU'RE WELCOME.
AND I'LL TALK TO SOMEONE IN PERSONNEL IN DUE COURSE.
I CAN ARRANGE THAT.
OH, DON'T YOU TROUBLE YOURSELF. I'VE DISTURBED YOU ENOUGH ALREADY.

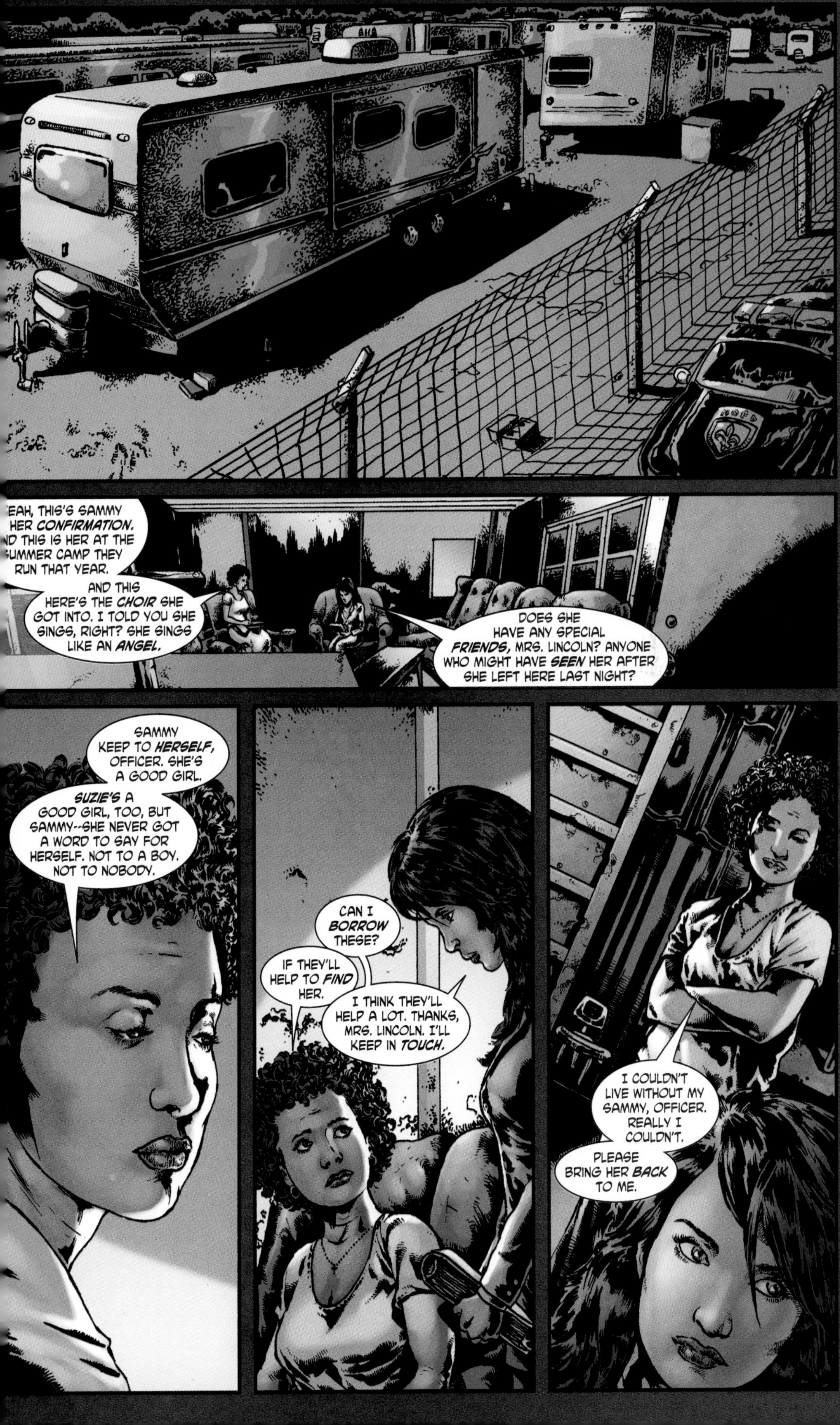
EAH, THIS'S SAMMY
HER CONFIRMATION.
ND THIS IS HER AT THE
SUMMER CAMP THEY
RUN THAT YEAR.
AND THIS HERE'S THE CHOIR SHE GOT INTO. I TOLD YOU SHE SINGS, RIGHT? SHE SINGS LIKE AN ANGEL.
DOES SHE HAVE ANY SPECIAL FRIENDS, MRS. LINCOLN? ANYONE WHO MIGHT HAVE SEEN HER AFTER SHE LEFT HERE LAST NIGHT?
SAMMY KEEP TO HERSELF, OFFICER. SHE'S A GOOD GIRL.
SUZIE'S A GOOD GIRL, TOO, BUT SAMMY--SHE NEVER GOT A WORD TO SAY FOR HERSELF. NOT TO A BOY. NOT TO NOBODY.
CAN I BORROW THESE?
IF THEY'LL HELP TO FIND HER.
I THINK THEY'LL HELP A LOT. THANKS, MRS. LINCOLN. I'LL KEEP IN TOUCH.
I COULDN'T LIVE WITHOUT MY SAMMY, OFFICER. REALLY I COULDN'T.
PLEASE BRING HER BACK TO ME.

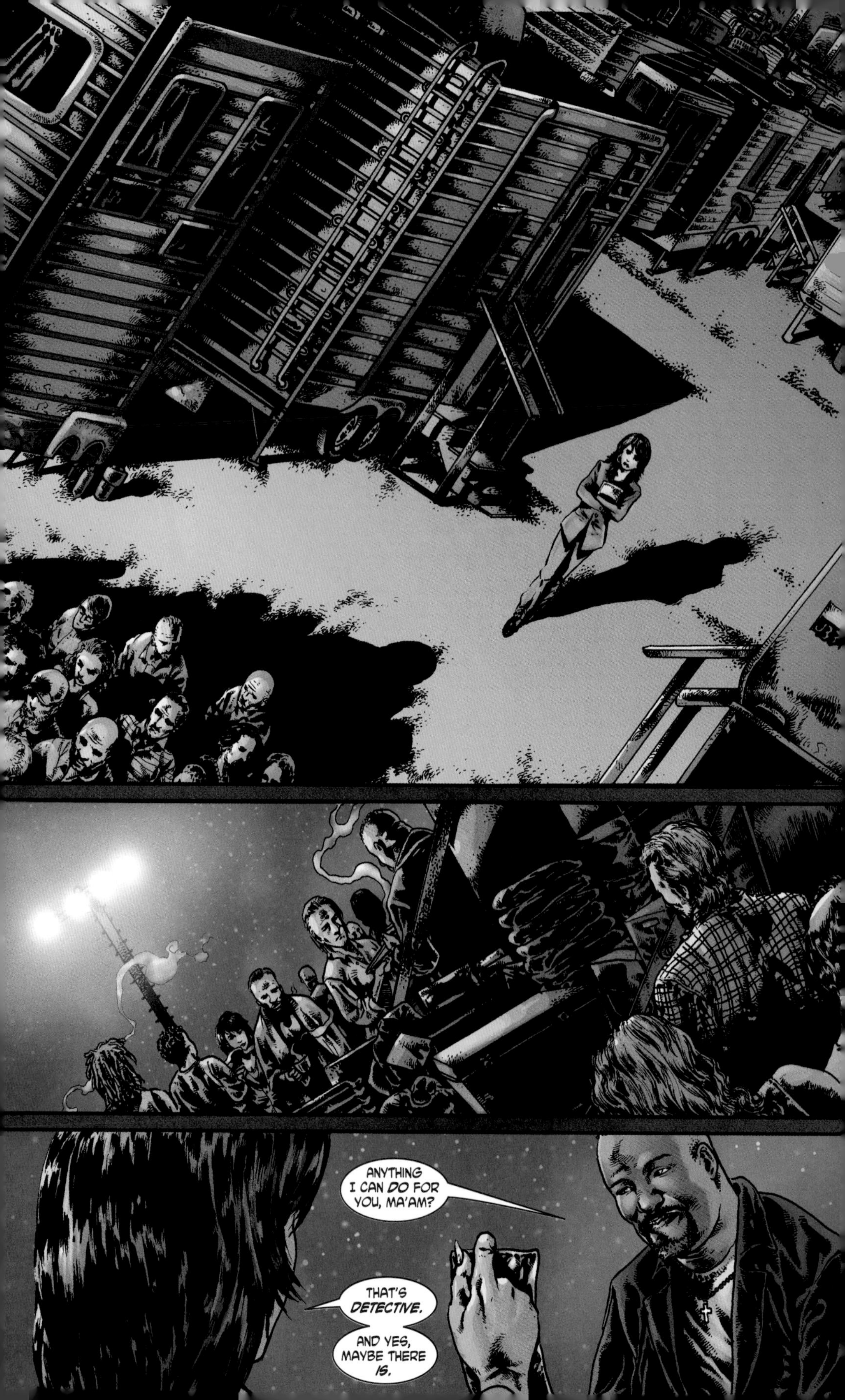
ANYTHING I CAN DO FOR YOU, MA'AM?
THAT'S DETECTIVE.
AND YES, MAYBE THERE IS.

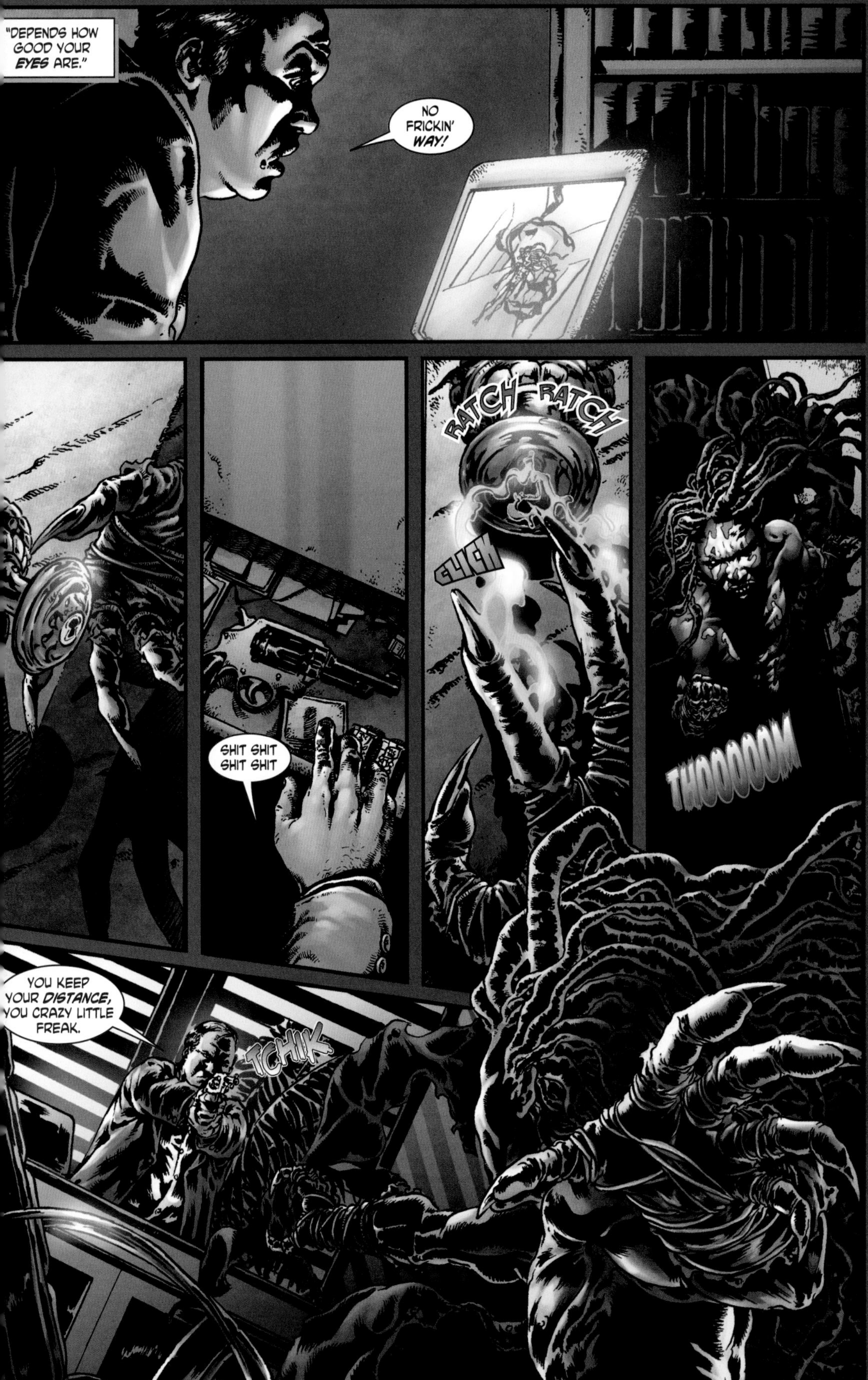
"DEPENDS HOW GOOD YOUR EYES ARE."
NO FRICKIN' WAY!
SHIT SHIT SHIT SHIT
RATCH RATCH
CLICK
THOOOOOM
YOU KEEP YOUR DISTANCE, YOU CRAZY LITTLE FREAK.
TCHIK

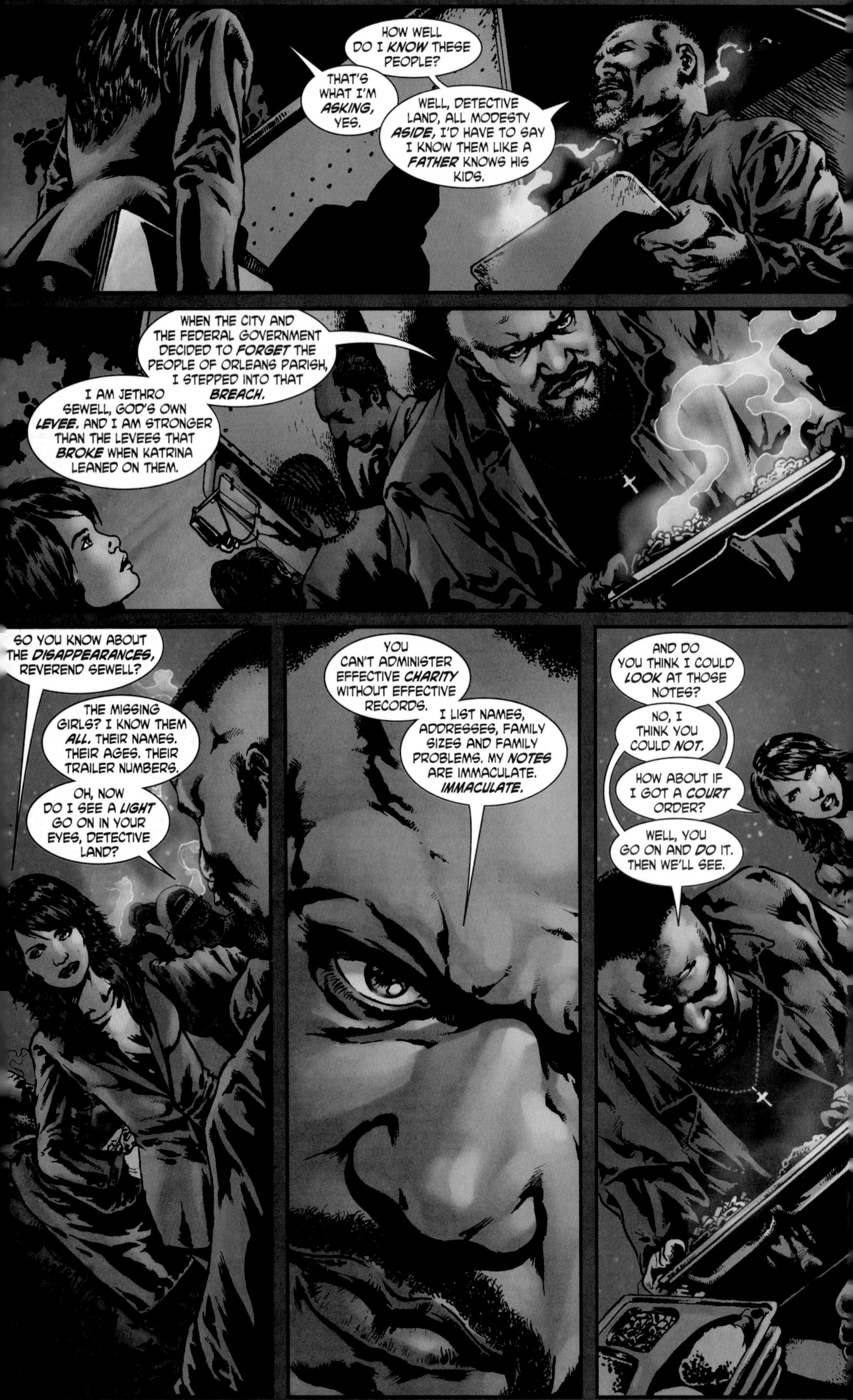
HOW WELL DO I KNOW THESE PEOPLE?
THAT'S WHAT I'M ASKING, YES.
WELL, DETECTIVE LAND, ALL MODESTY ASIDE, I'D HAVE TO SAY I KNOW THEM LIKE A FATHER KNOWS HIS KIDS.
WHEN THE CITY AND THE FEDERAL GOVERNMENT DECIDED TO FORGET THE PEOPLE OF ORLEANS PARISH, I STEPPED INTO THAT BREACH.
I AM JETHRO SEWELL, GOD'S OWN LEVEE. AND I AM STRONGER THAN THE LEVEES THAT BROKE WHEN KATRINA LEANED ON THEM.
SO YOU KNOW ABOUT THE DISAPPEARANCES, REVEREND SEWELL?
THE MISSING GIRLS? I KNOW THEM ALL. THEIR NAMES. THEIR AGES. THEIR TRAILER NUMBERS.
OH, NOW DO I SEE A LIGHT GO ON IN YOUR EYES, DETECTIVE LAND?
YOU CAN'T ADMINISTER EFFECTIVE CHARITY WITHOUT EFFECTIVE RECORDS.
I LIST NAMES, ADDRESSES, FAMILY SIZES AND FAMILY PROBLEMS. MY NOTES ARE IMMACULATE. IMMACULATE.
AND DO YOU THINK I COULD LOOK AT THOSE NOTES?
NO, I THINK YOU COULD NOT.
HOW ABOUT IF I GOT A COURT ORDER?
WELL, YOU GO ON AND DO IT. THEN WE'LL SEE.

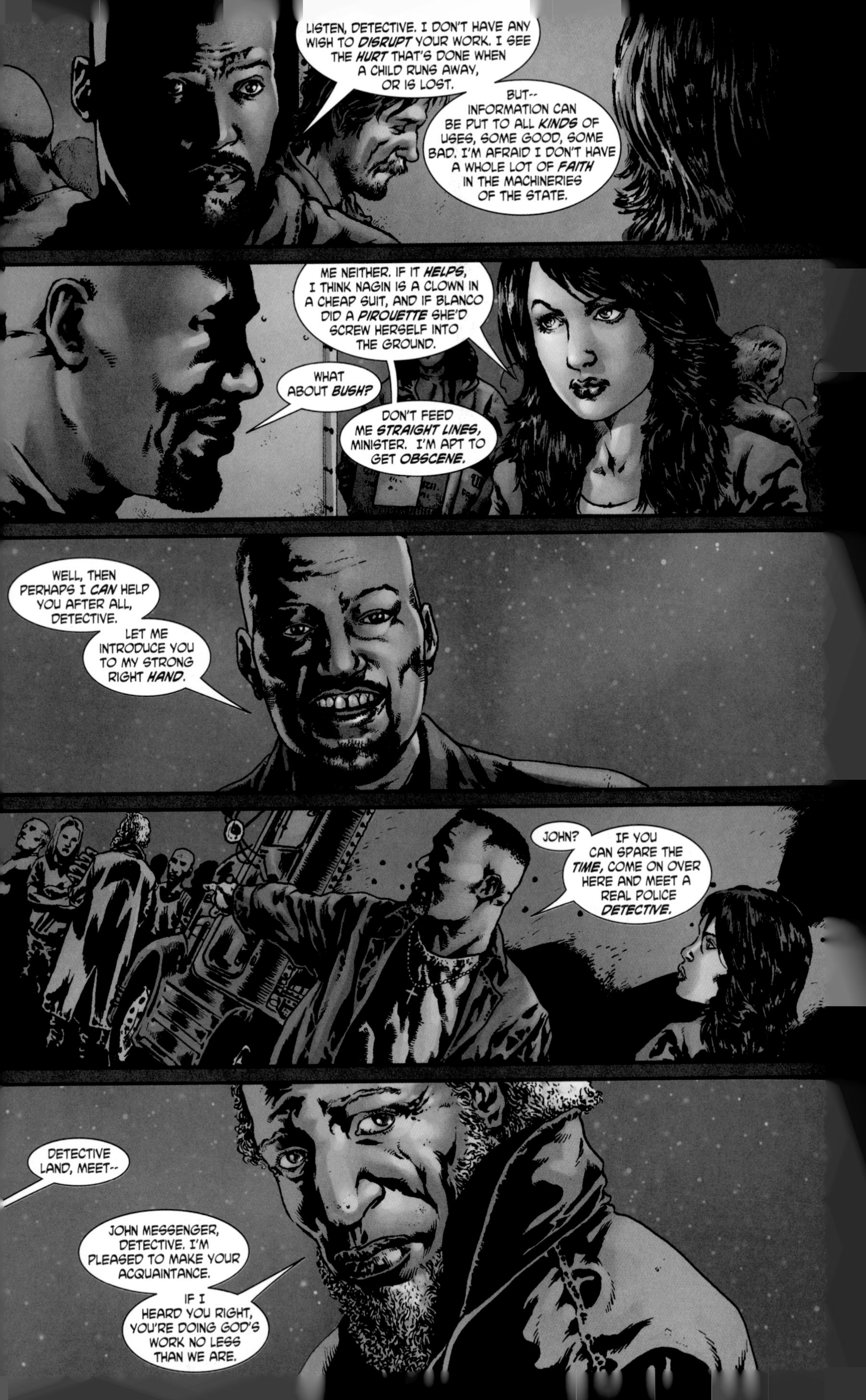
LISTEN, DETECTIVE. I DON'T HAVE ANY WISH TO DISRUPT YOUR WORK. I SEE THE HURT THAT'S DONE WHEN A CHILD RUNS AWAY, OR IS LOST.
BUT-- INFORMATION CAN BE PUT TO ALL KINDS OF USES, SOME GOOD, SOME BAD. I'M AFRAID I DON'T HAVE A WHOLE LOT OF FAITH IN THE MACHINERIES OF THE STATE.
ME NEITHER. IF IT HELPS, I THINK NAGIN IS A CLOWN IN A CHEAP SUIT, AND IF BLANCO DID A PIROUETTE SHE'D SCREW HERSELF INTO THE GROUND.
WHAT ABOUT BUSH?
DON'T FEED ME STRAIGHT LINES, MINISTER. I'M APT TO GET OBSCENE.
WELL, THEN PERHAPS I CAN HELP YOU AFTER ALL, DETECTIVE.
LET ME INTRODUCE YOU TO MY STRONG RIGHT HAND.
JOHN?
IF YOU CAN SPARE THE TIME, COME ON OVER HERE AND MEET A REAL POLICE DETECTIVE.
DETECTIVE LAND, MEET--
JOHN MESSENGER, DETECTIVE. I'M PLEASED TO MAKE YOUR ACQUAINTANCE.
IF I HEARD YOU RIGHT, YOU'RE DOING GOD'S WORK NO LESS THAN WE ARE.

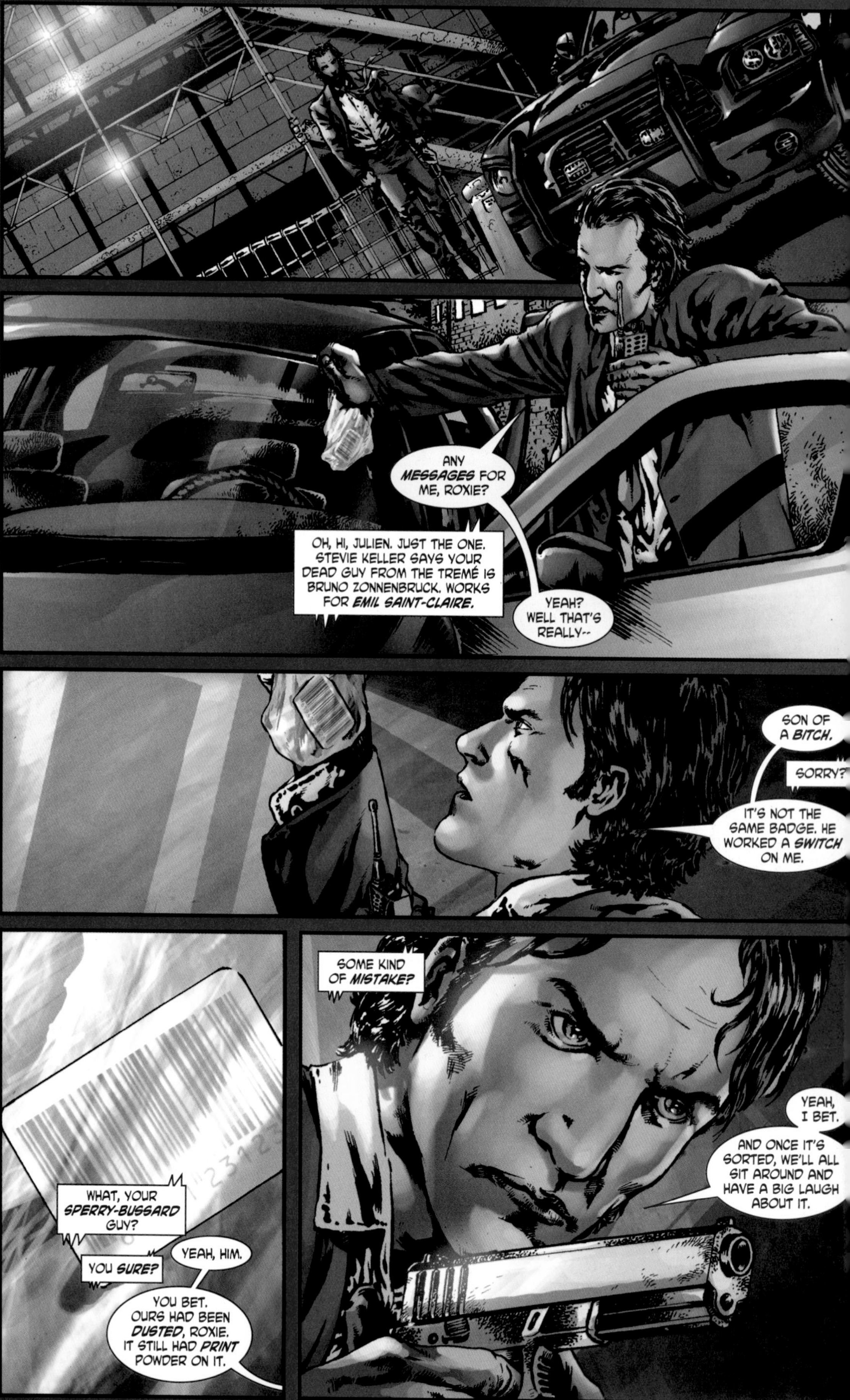
ANY MESSAGES FOR ME, ROXIE?
OH, HI, JULIEN. JUST THE ONE. STEVIE KELLER SAYS YOUR DEAD GUY FROM THE TREMÉ IS BRUNO ZONNENBRUCK. WORKS FOR EMIL SAINT-CLAIRE.
YEAH? WELL THAT'S REALLY--
SON OF A BITCH.
SORRY?
IT'S NOT THE SAME BADGE. HE WORKED A SWITCH ON ME.
WHAT, YOUR SPERRY-BUSSARD GUY?
YEAH, HIM.
YOU SURE?
YOU BET. OURS HAD BEEN DUSTED, ROXIE. IT STILL HAD PRINT POWDER ON IT.
SOME KIND OF MISTAKE?
YEAH, I BET.
AND ONCE IT'S SORTED, WE'LL ALL SIT AROUND AND HAVE A BIG LAUGH ABOUT IT.

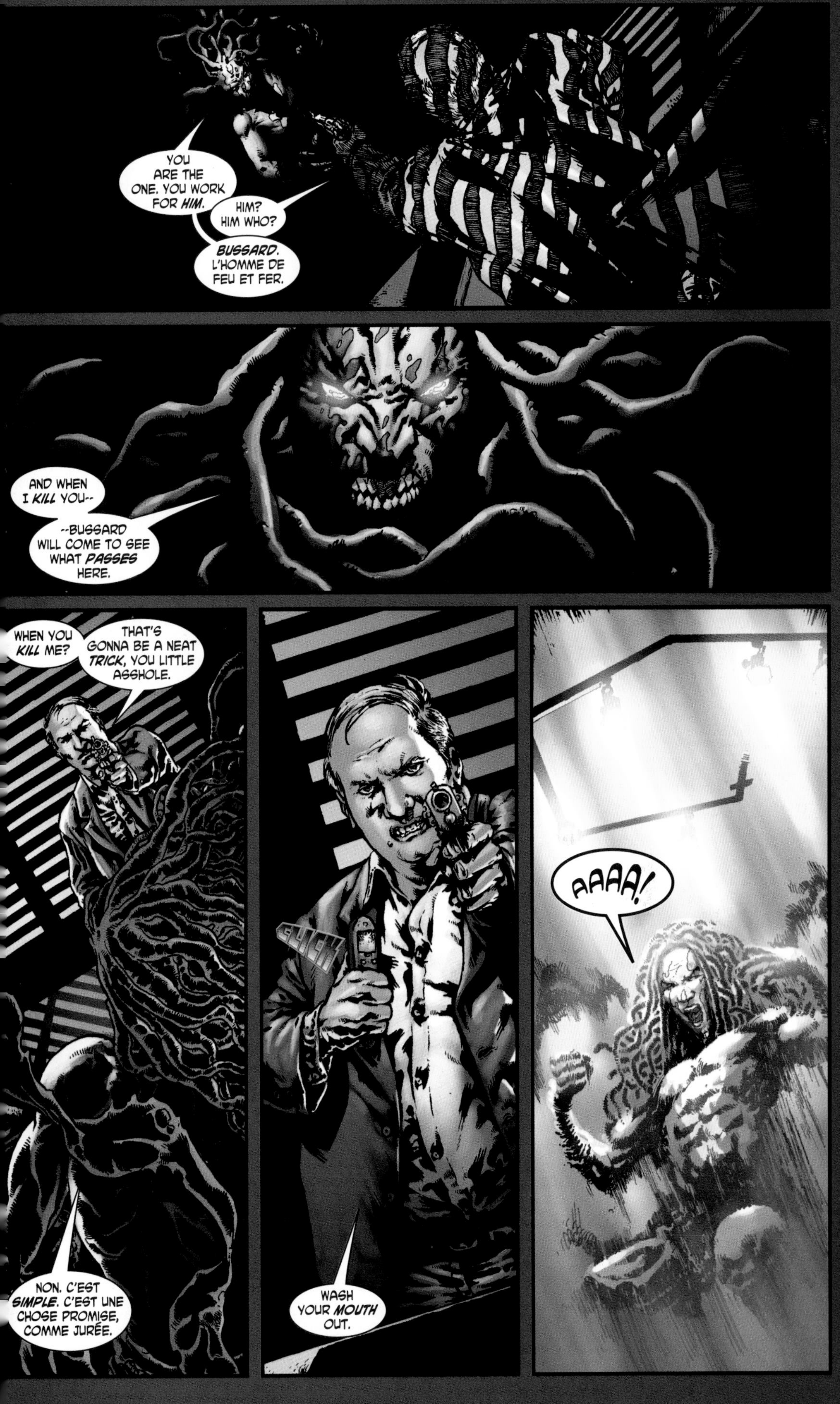
YOU ARE THE ONE. YOU WORK FOR *HIM*.
HIM? HIM WHO?
BUSSARD. L'HOMME DE FEU ET FER.
AND WHEN I *KILL* YOU--
--BUSSARD WILL COME TO SEE WHAT *PASSES* HERE.
WHEN YOU *KILL* ME?
THAT'S GONNA BE A NEAT *TRICK*, YOU LITTLE ASSHOLE.
NON. C'EST *SIMPLE*. C'EST UNE CHOSE PROMISE, COMME JURÉE.
WASH YOUR *MOUTH* OUT.
AAAA!

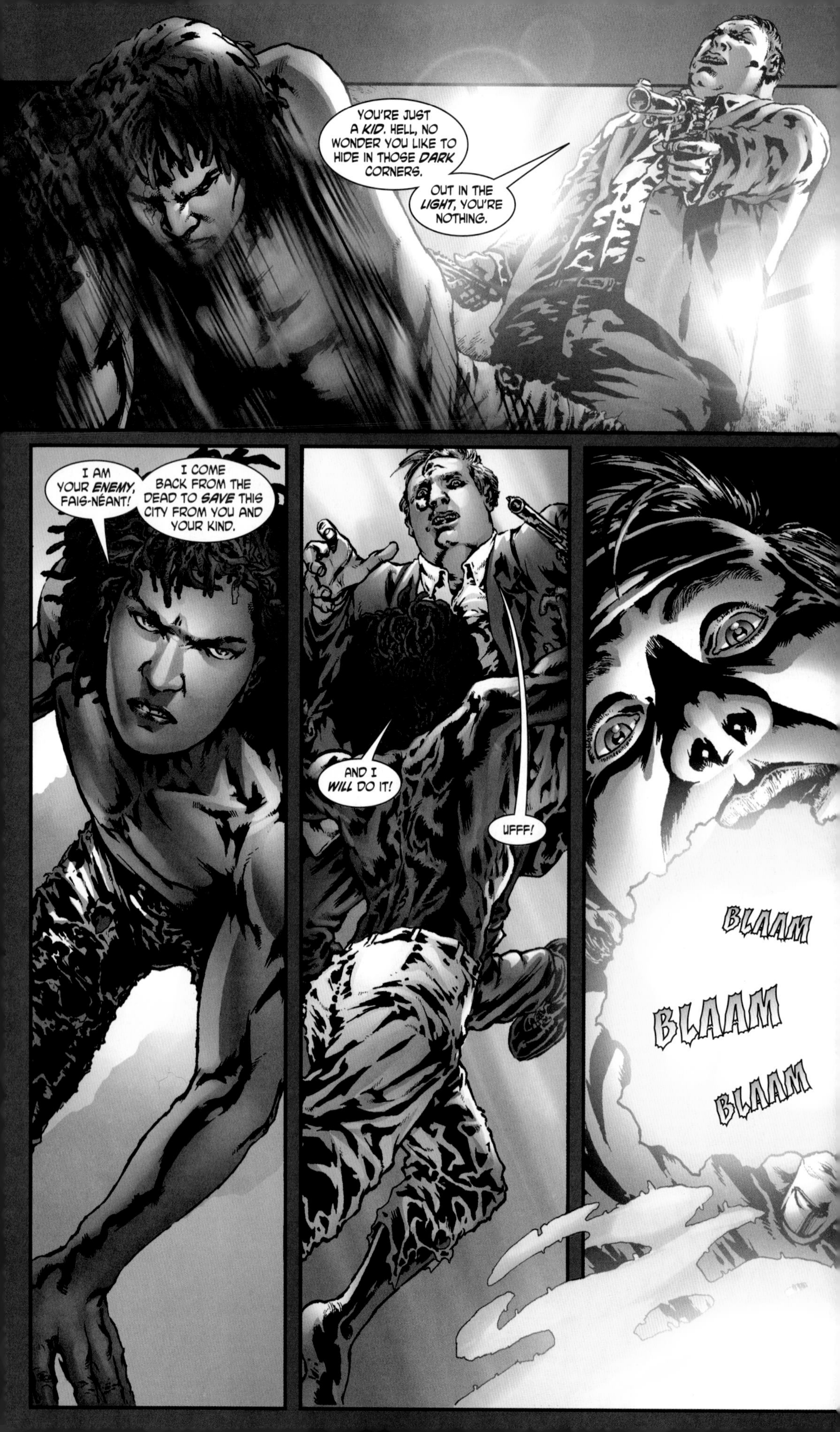
YOU'RE JUST A KID. HELL, NO WONDER YOU LIKE TO HIDE IN THOSE DARK CORNERS.
OUT IN THE LIGHT, YOU'RE NOTHING.
I AM YOUR ENEMY, FAIS-NÉANT!
I COME BACK FROM THE DEAD TO SAVE THIS CITY FROM YOU AND YOUR KIND.
AND I WILL DO IT!
UFFF!
BLAAM
BLAAM
BLAAM

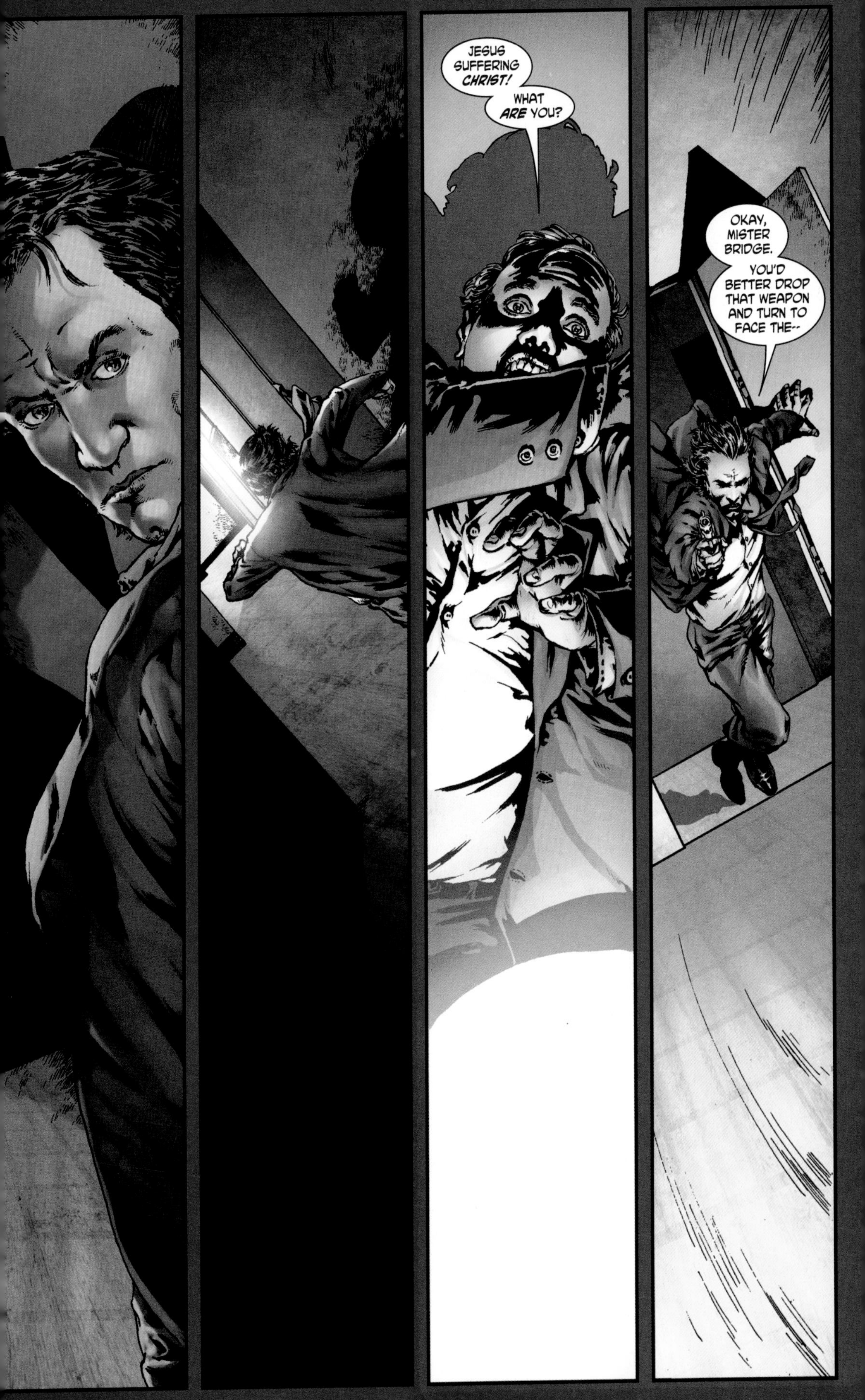
JESUS SUFFERING *CHRIST!*
WHAT *ARE* YOU?
OKAY, MISTER BRIDGE.
YOU'D BETTER DROP THAT WEAPON AND TURN TO FACE THE--

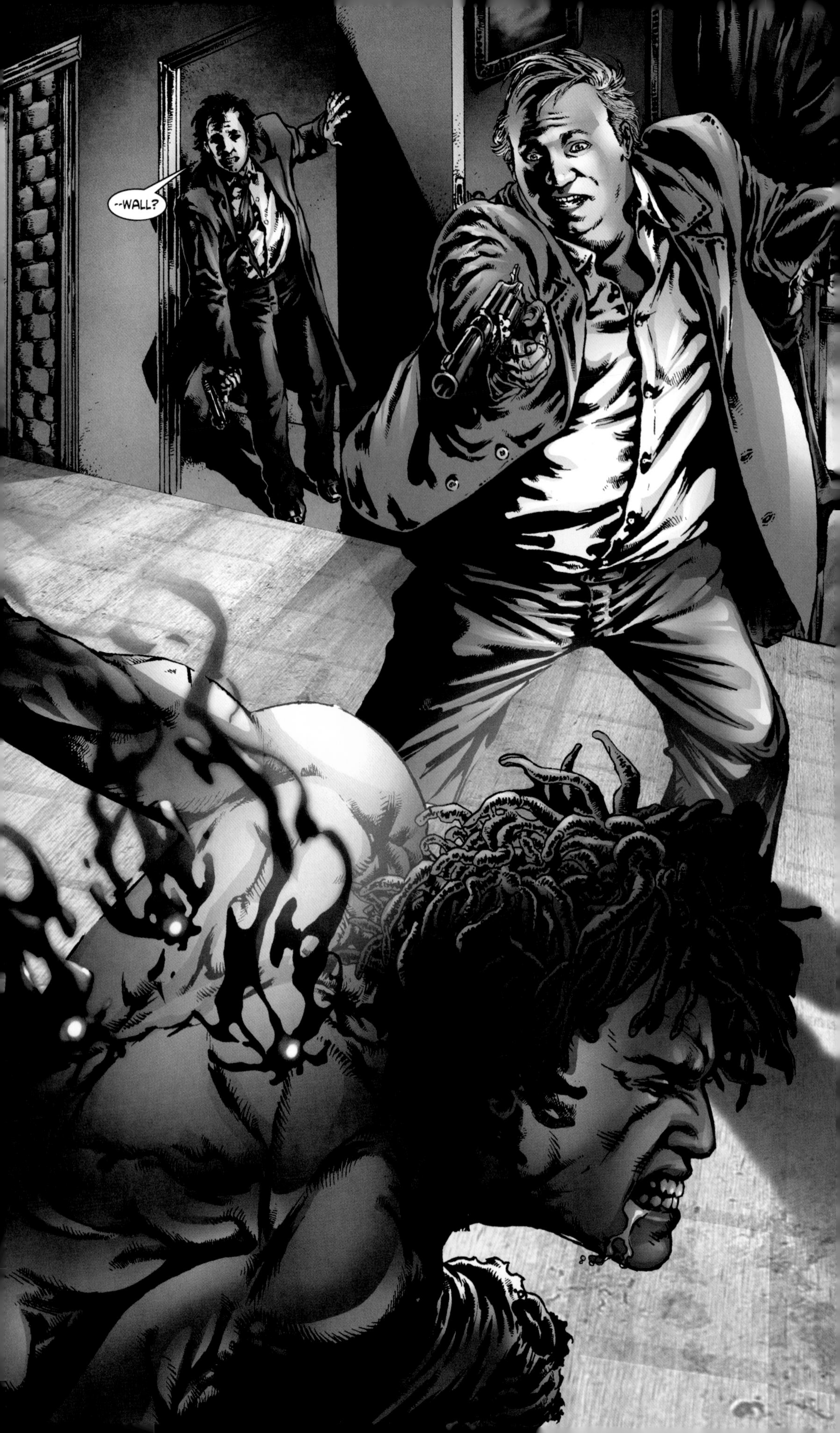
--WALL?

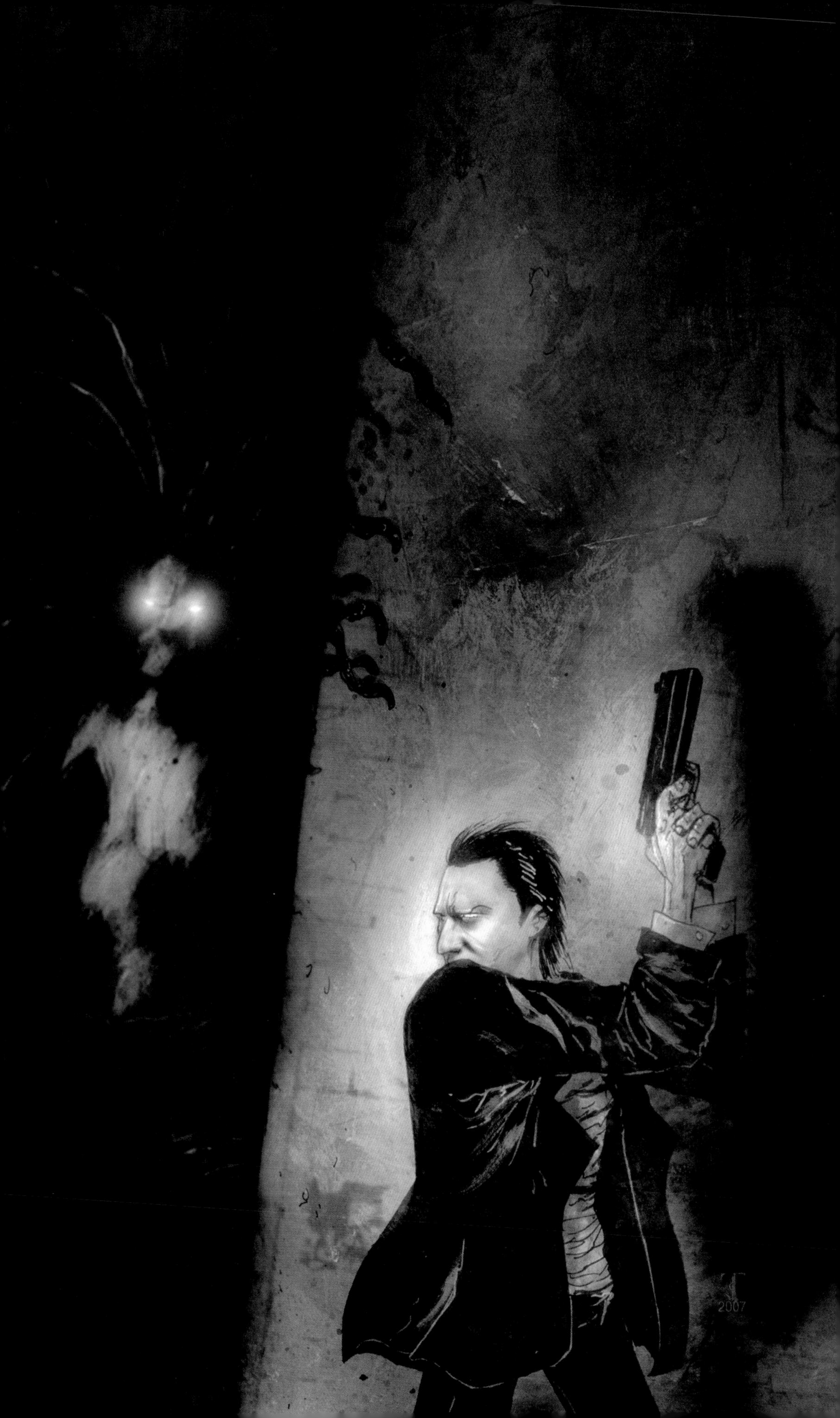
2007

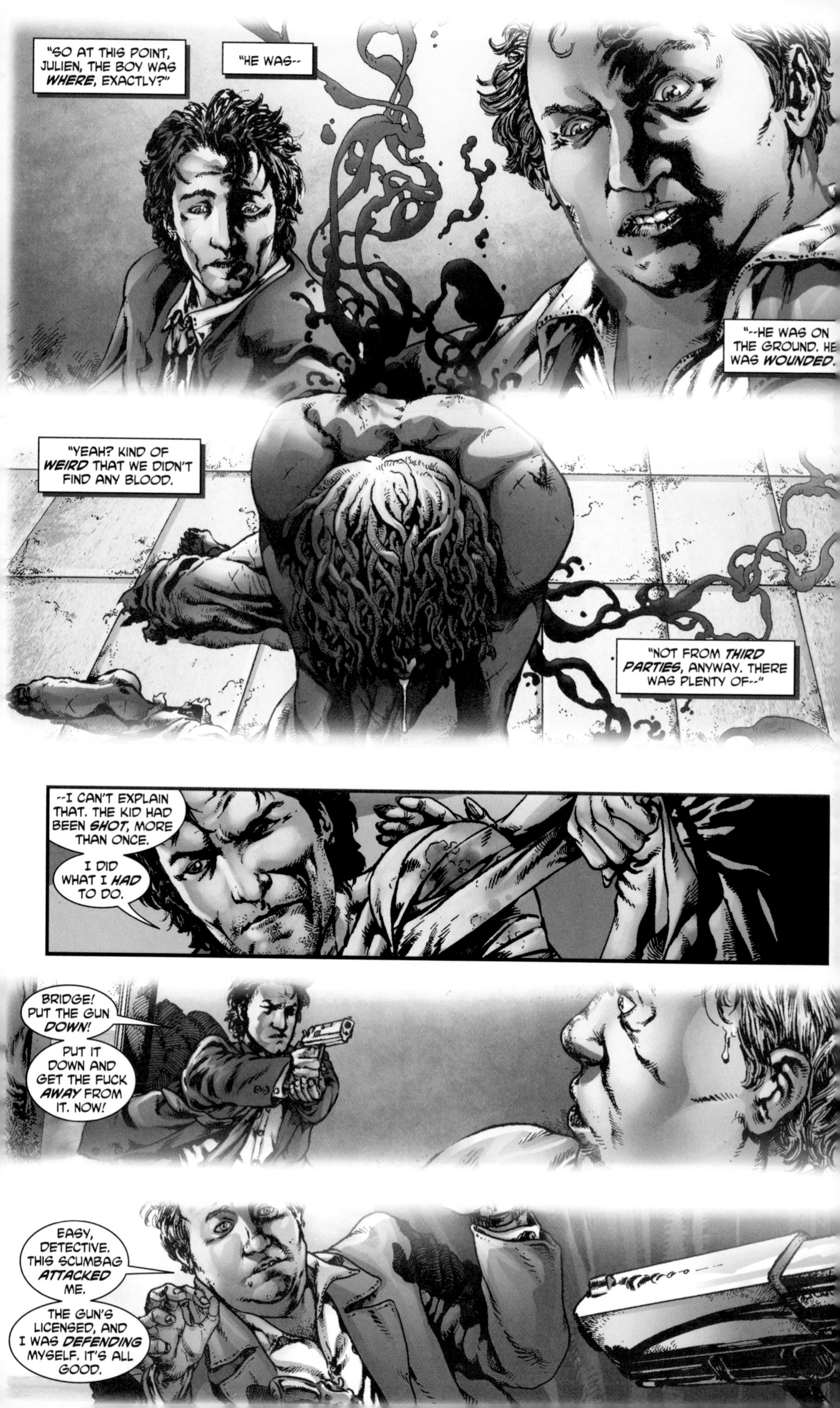
"SO AT THIS POINT, JULIEN, THE BOY WAS *WHERE*, EXACTLY?"
"HE WAS--
"--HE WAS ON THE GROUND. HE WAS *WOUNDED*.
"YEAH? KIND OF *WEIRD* THAT WE DIDN'T FIND ANY BLOOD.
"NOT FROM *THIRD PARTIES*, ANYWAY. THERE WAS PLENTY OF--"
--I CAN'T EXPLAIN THAT. THE KID HAD BEEN *SHOT*, MORE THAN ONCE.
I DID WHAT I *HAD* TO DO.
BRIDGE! PUT THE GUN *DOWN*!
PUT IT DOWN AND GET THE FUCK *AWAY* FROM IT. NOW!
EASY, DETECTIVE. THIS SCUMBAG *ATTACKED* ME.
THE GUN'S LICENSED, AND I WAS *DEFENDING* MYSELF. IT'S ALL GOOD.

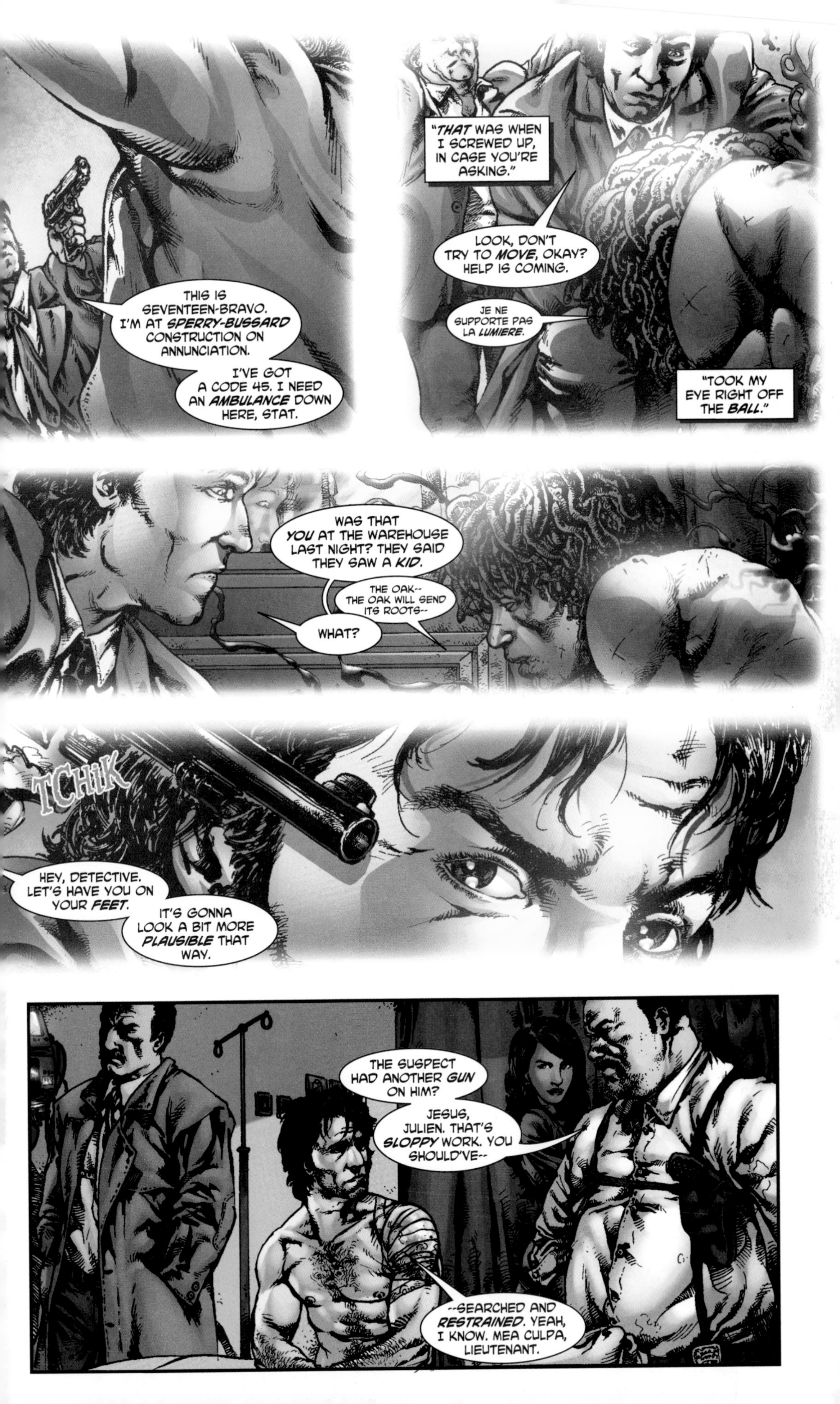

THIS IS SEVENTEEN-BRAVO. I'M AT SPERRY-BUSSARD CONSTRUCTION ON ANNUNCIATION.
I'VE GOT A CODE 45. I NEED AN AMBULANCE DOWN HERE, STAT.
"THAT WAS WHEN I SCREWED UP, IN CASE YOU'RE ASKING."
LOOK, DON'T TRY TO MOVE, OKAY? HELP IS COMING.
JE NE SUPPORTE PAS LA LUMIERE.
"TOOK MY EYE RIGHT OFF THE BALL."
WAS THAT YOU AT THE WAREHOUSE LAST NIGHT? THEY SAID THEY SAW A KID.
THE OAK-- THE OAK WILL SEND ITS ROOTS--
WHAT?
TCHIK
HEY, DETECTIVE. LET'S HAVE YOU ON YOUR FEET.
IT'S GONNA LOOK A BIT MORE PLAUSIBLE THAT WAY.
THE SUSPECT HAD ANOTHER GUN ON HIM?
JESUS, JULIEN. THAT'S SLOPPY WORK. YOU SHOULD'VE--
--SEARCHED AND RESTRAINED. YEAH, I KNOW. MEA CULPA, LIEUTENANT.

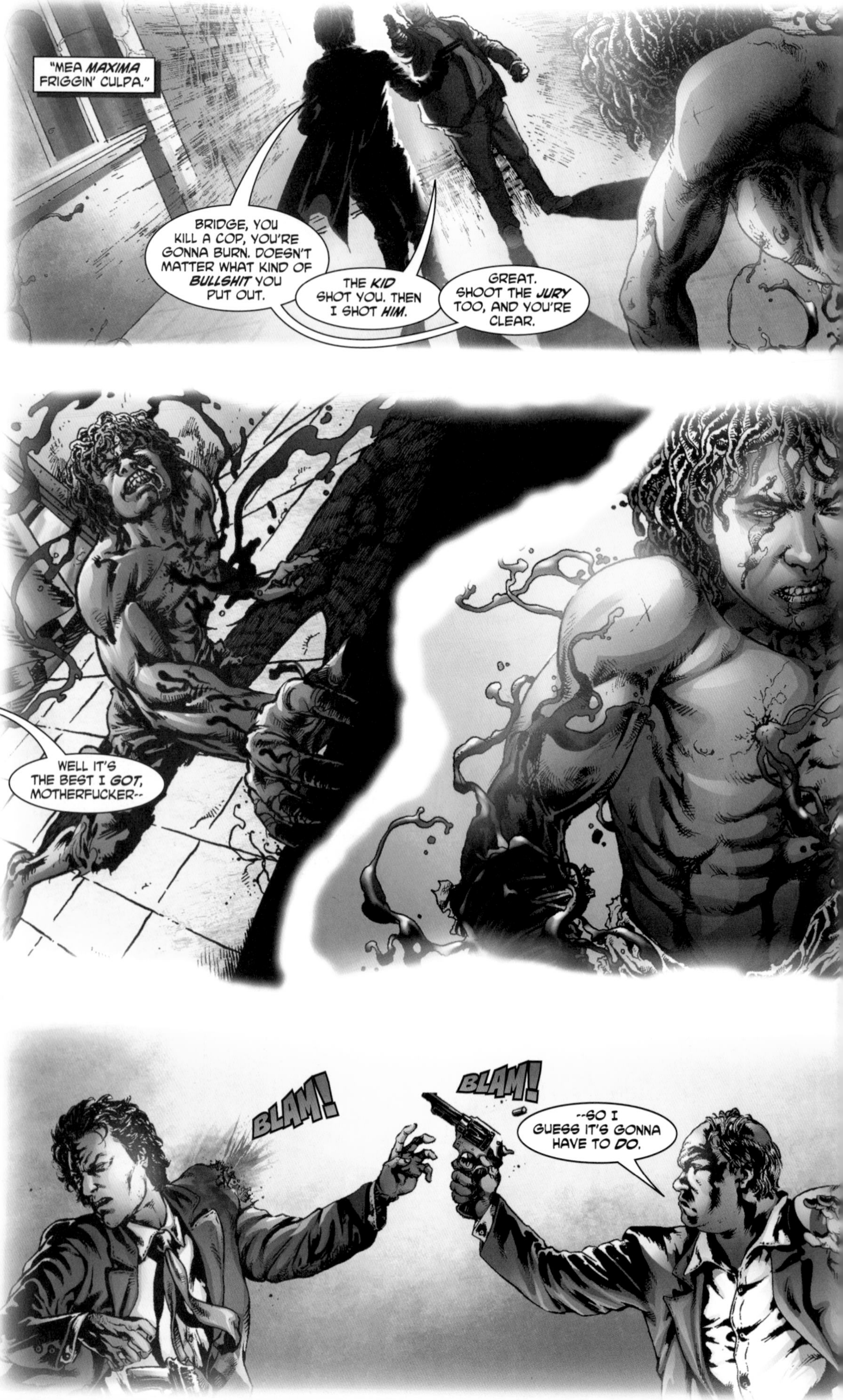
"MEA MAXIMA FRIGGIN' CULPA."
BRIDGE, YOU KILL A COP, YOU'RE GONNA BURN. DOESN'T MATTER WHAT KIND OF BULLSHIT YOU PUT OUT.
THE KID SHOT YOU. THEN I SHOT HIM.
GREAT. SHOOT THE JURY TOO, AND YOU'RE CLEAR.
WELL IT'S THE BEST I GOT, MOTHERFUCKER--
BLAM!
BLAM!
--SO I GUESS IT'S GONNA HAVE TO DO.

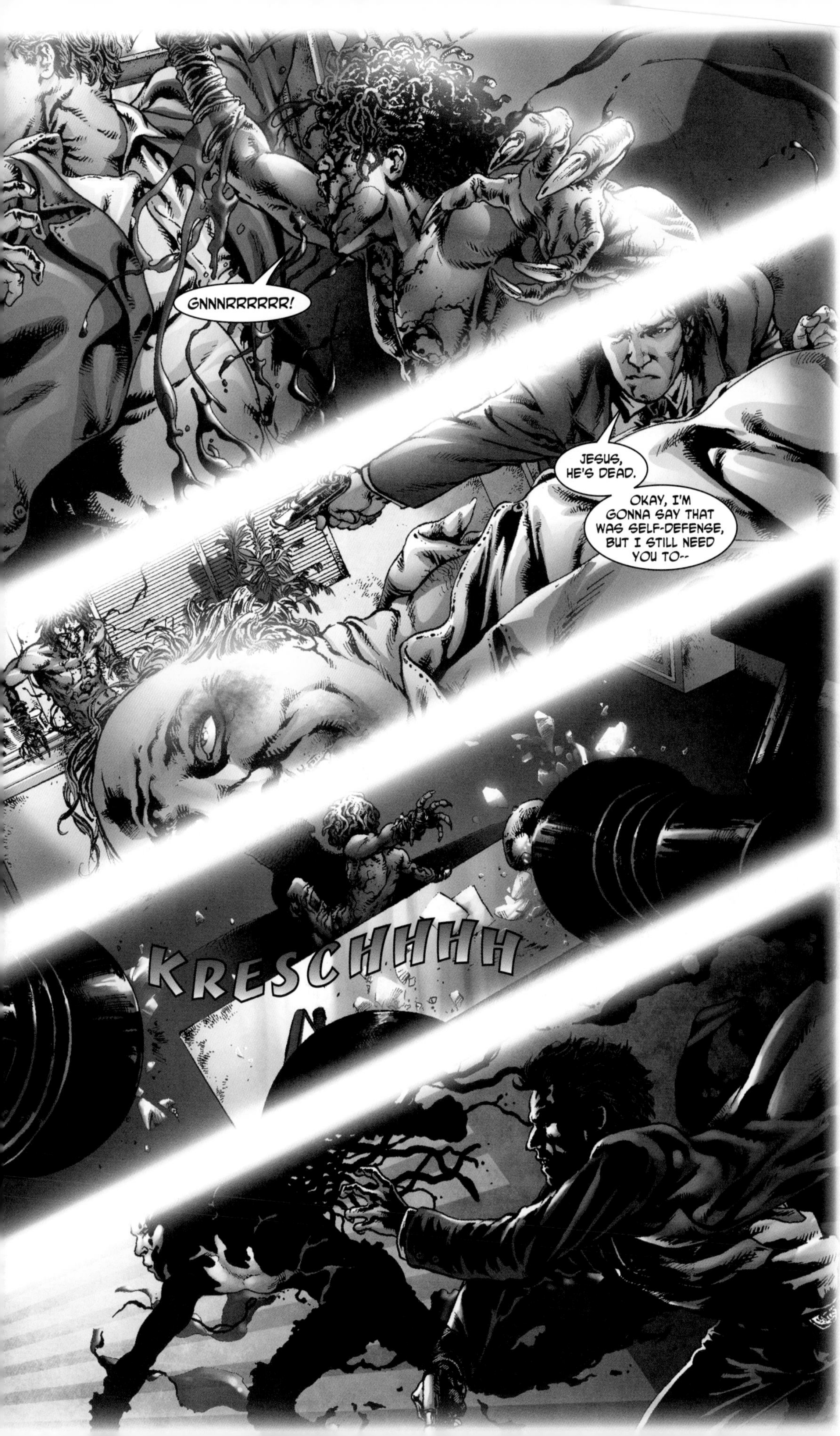
GNNNRRRRRR!
JESUS, HE'S DEAD.
OKAY, I'M GONNA SAY THAT WAS SELF-DEFENSE, BUT I STILL NEED YOU TO--
KRESCHHHHH

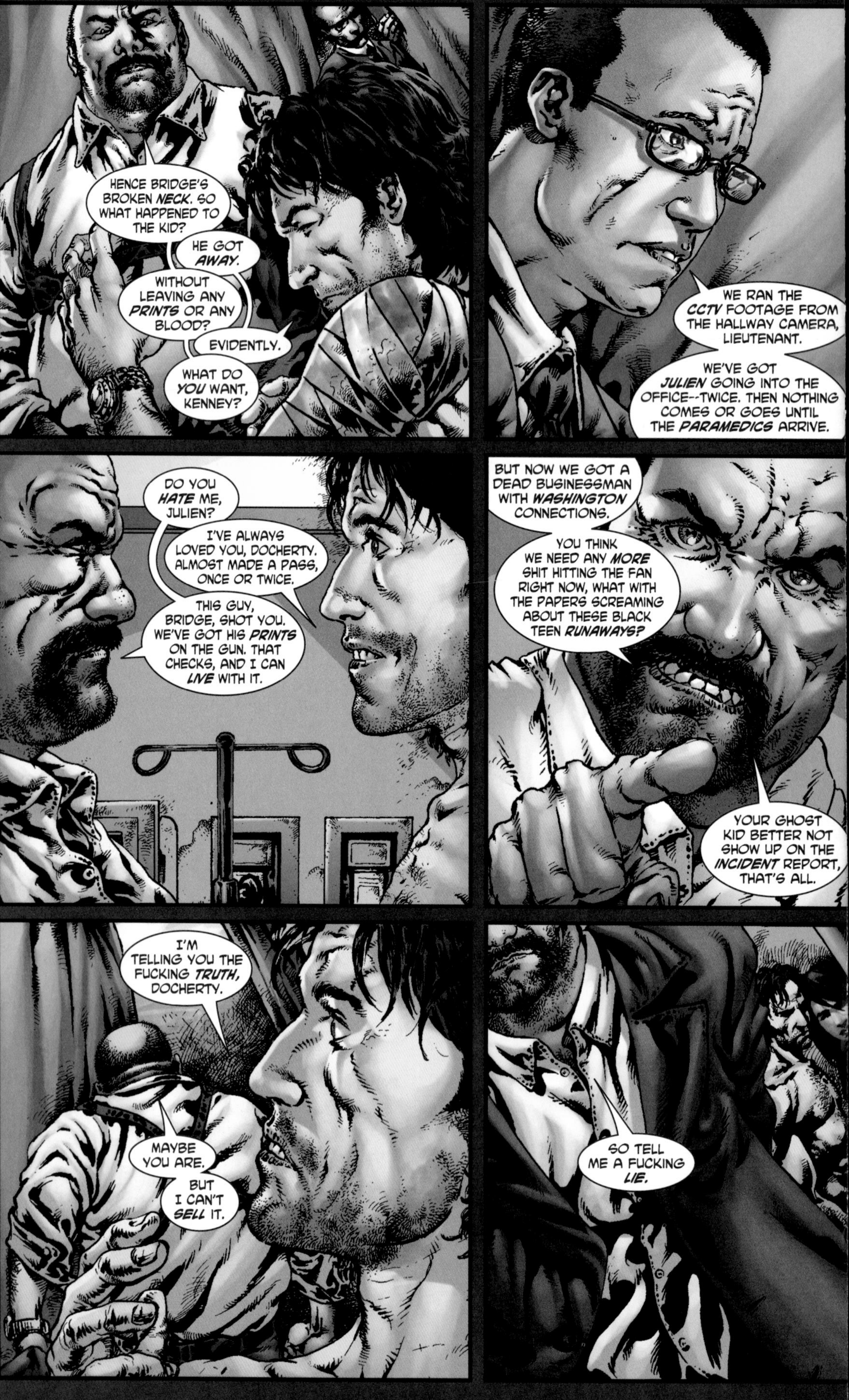
HENCE BRIDGE'S BROKEN NECK. SO WHAT HAPPENED TO THE KID?
HE GOT AWAY.
WITHOUT LEAVING ANY PRINTS OR ANY BLOOD?
EVIDENTLY.
WHAT DO YOU WANT, KENNEY?
WE RAN THE CCTV FOOTAGE FROM THE HALLWAY CAMERA, LIEUTENANT.
WE'VE GOT JULIEN GOING INTO THE OFFICE--TWICE. THEN NOTHING COMES OR GOES UNTIL THE PARAMEDICS ARRIVE.
DO YOU HATE ME, JULIEN?
I'VE ALWAYS LOVED YOU, DOCHERTY. ALMOST MADE A PASS, ONCE OR TWICE.
THIS GUY, BRIDGE, SHOT YOU. WE'VE GOT HIS PRINTS ON THE GUN. THAT CHECKS, AND I CAN LIVE WITH IT.
BUT NOW WE GOT A DEAD BUSINESSMAN WITH WASHINGTON CONNECTIONS.
YOU THINK WE NEED ANY MORE SHIT HITTING THE FAN RIGHT NOW, WHAT WITH THE PAPERS SCREAMING ABOUT THESE BLACK TEEN RUNAWAYS?
YOUR GHOST KID BETTER NOT SHOW UP ON THE INCIDENT REPORT, THAT'S ALL.
I'M TELLING YOU THE FUCKING TRUTH, DOCHERTY.
MAYBE YOU ARE.
BUT I CAN'T SELL IT.
SO TELL ME A FUCKING LIE.

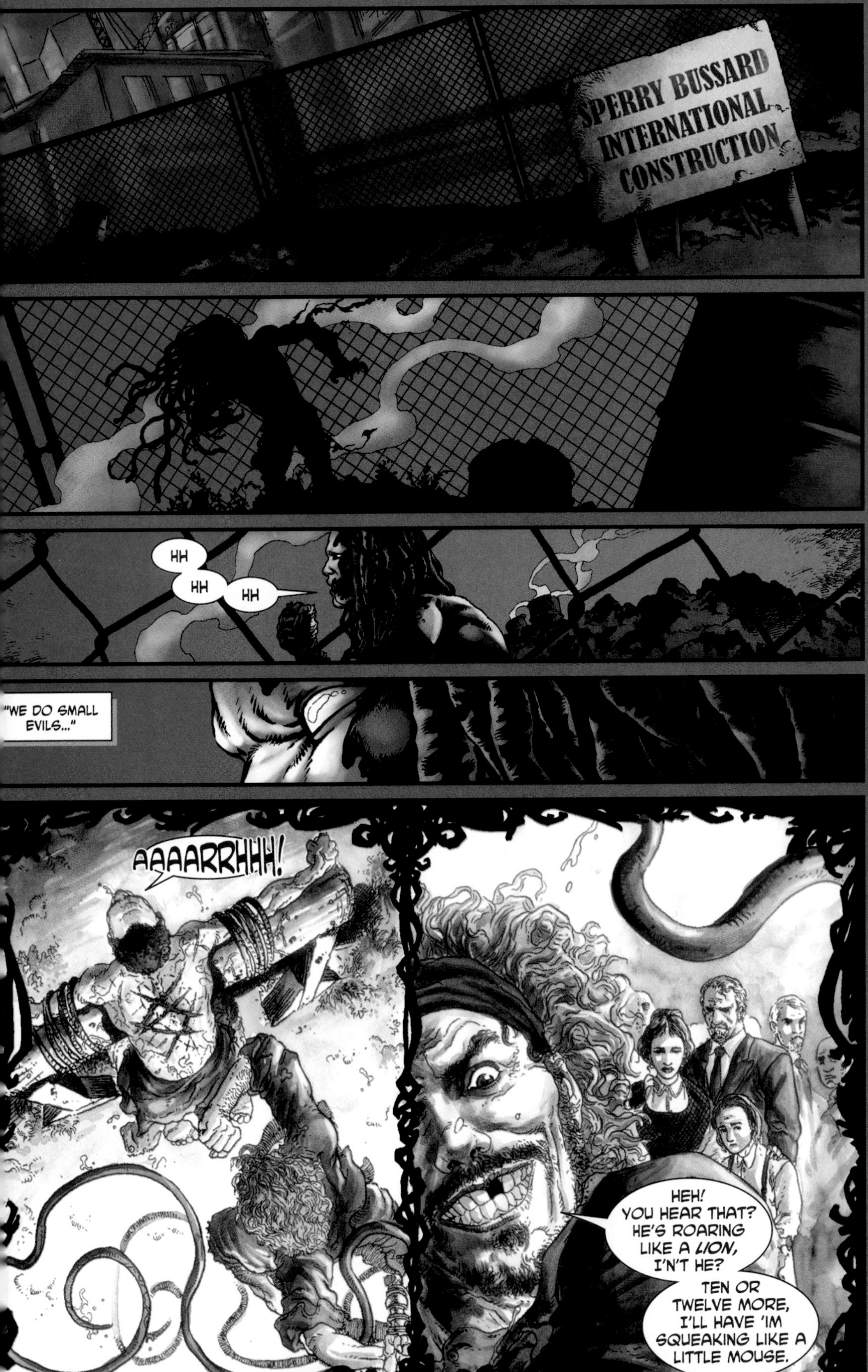
SPERRY BUSSARD INTERNATIONAL CONSTRUCTION
HH
HH
HH
"WE DO SMALL EVILS..."
AAAARRHHH!
HEH! YOU HEAR THAT? HE'S ROARING LIKE A *LION*, I'N'T HE?
TEN OR TWELVE MORE, I'LL HAVE 'IM SQUEAKING LIKE A LITTLE MOUSE.

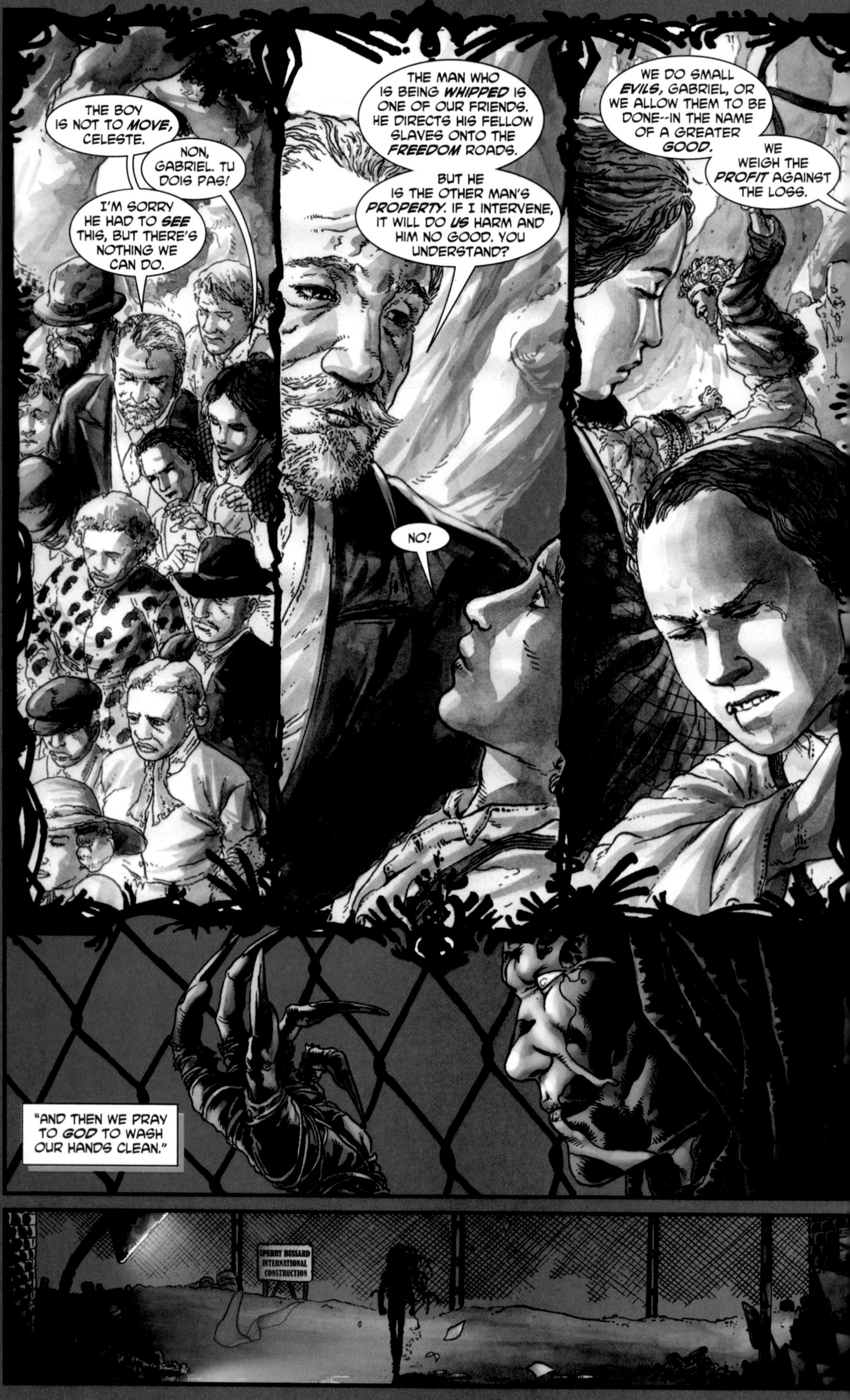
THE BOY IS NOT TO *MOVE,* CELESTE.
NON, GABRIEL. TU DOIS PAS!
I'M SORRY HE HAD TO *SEE* THIS, BUT THERE'S NOTHING WE CAN DO.
THE MAN WHO IS BEING *WHIPPED* IS ONE OF OUR FRIENDS. HE DIRECTS HIS FELLOW SLAVES ONTO THE *FREEDOM* ROADS.
BUT HE IS THE OTHER MAN'S *PROPERTY*. IF I INTERVENE, IT WILL DO *US* HARM AND HIM NO GOOD. YOU UNDERSTAND?
NO!
WE DO SMALL *EVILS,* GABRIEL, OR WE ALLOW THEM TO BE DONE--IN THE NAME OF A GREATER *GOOD.*
WE WEIGH THE *PROFIT* AGAINST THE LOSS.
"AND THEN WE PRAY TO *GOD* TO WASH OUR HANDS CLEAN."
SPERRY BUSSARD INTERNATIONAL CONSTRUCTION

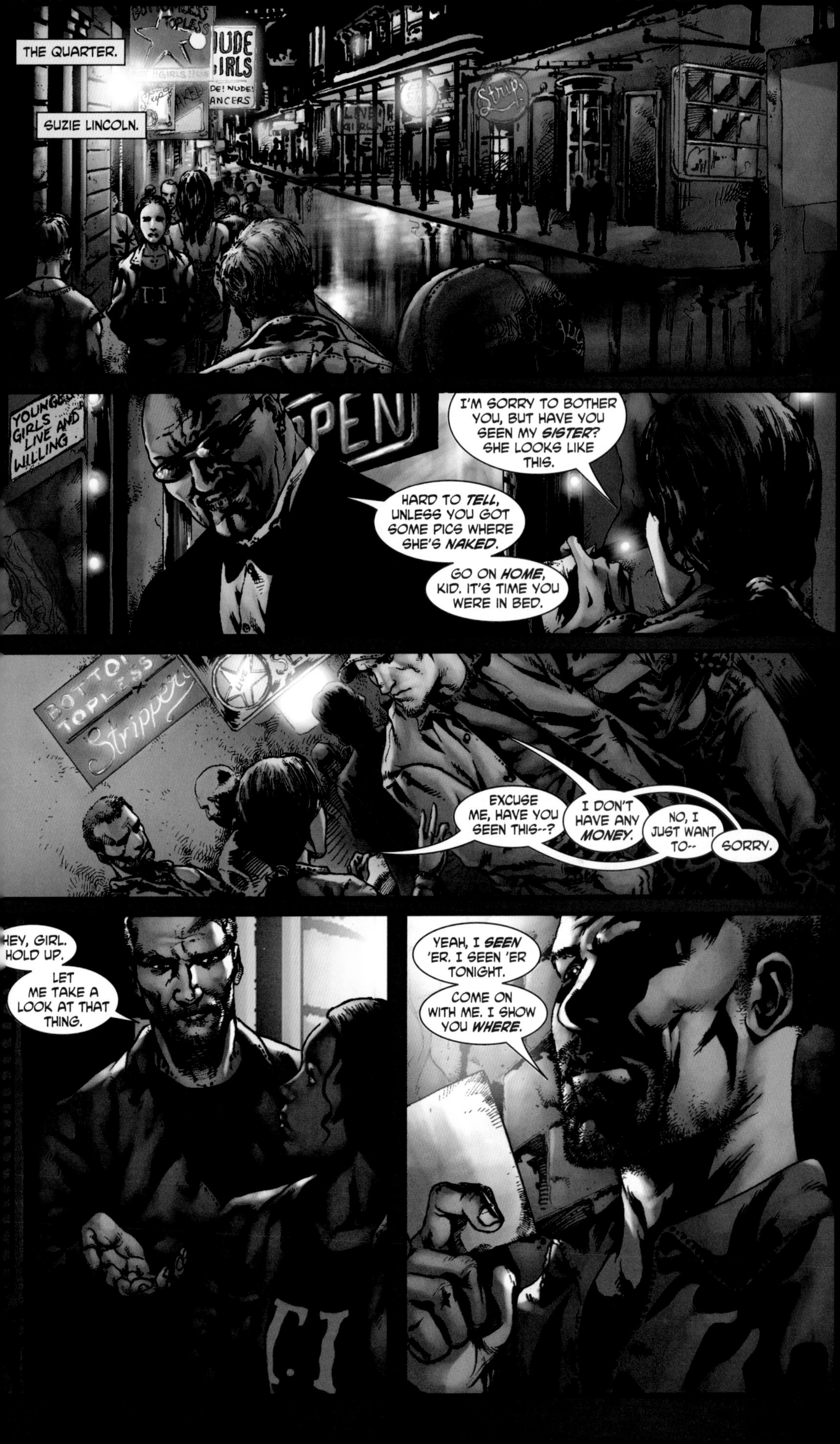
THE QUARTER.
SUZIE LINCOLN.
NUDE GIRLS
DE! NUDE! ANCERS
Strip
I'M SORRY TO BOTHER YOU, BUT HAVE YOU SEEN MY SISTER? SHE LOOKS LIKE THIS.
HARD TO TELL, UNLESS YOU GOT SOME PICS WHERE SHE'S NAKED.
GO ON HOME, KID. IT'S TIME YOU WERE IN BED.
GIRLS LIVE AND WILLING
OPEN
TOPLESS
Stripper
EXCUSE ME, HAVE YOU SEEN THIS--?
I DON'T HAVE ANY MONEY.
NO, I JUST WANT TO--
SORRY.
HEY, GIRL. HOLD UP.
LET ME TAKE A LOOK AT THAT THING.
YEAH, I SEEN 'ER. I SEEN 'ER TONIGHT.
COME ON WITH ME. I SHOW YOU WHERE.

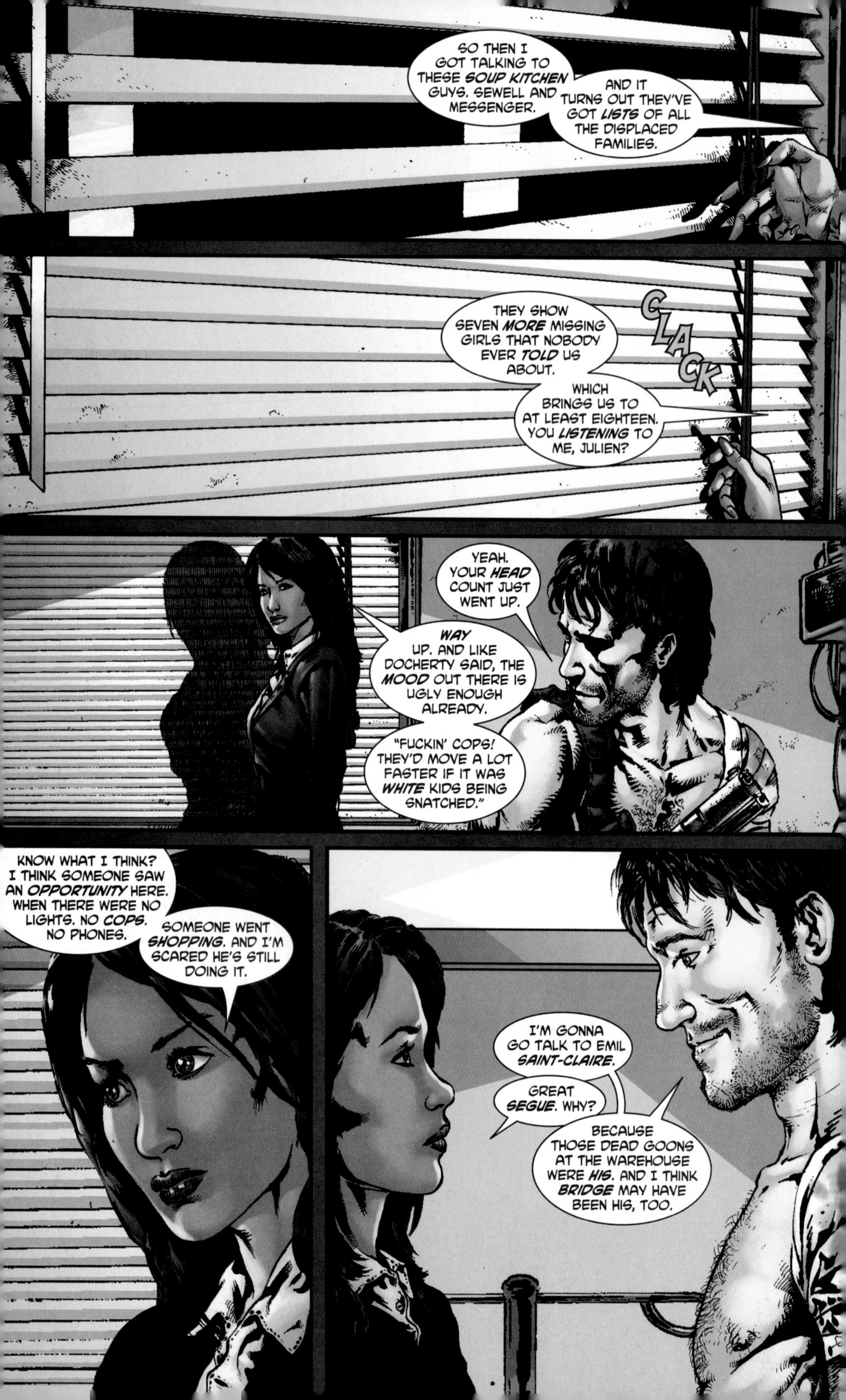
SO THEN I GOT TALKING TO THESE SOUP KITCHEN GUYS. SEWELL AND MESSENGER.
AND IT TURNS OUT THEY'VE GOT LISTS OF ALL THE DISPLACED FAMILIES.
CLACK
THEY SHOW SEVEN MORE MISSING GIRLS THAT NOBODY EVER TOLD US ABOUT.
WHICH BRINGS US TO AT LEAST EIGHTEEN. YOU LISTENING TO ME, JULIEN?
YEAH. YOUR HEAD COUNT JUST WENT UP.
WAY UP. AND LIKE DOCHERTY SAID, THE MOOD OUT THERE IS UGLY ENOUGH ALREADY.
"FUCKIN' COPS! THEY'D MOVE A LOT FASTER IF IT WAS WHITE KIDS BEING SNATCHED."
KNOW WHAT I THINK? I THINK SOMEONE SAW AN OPPORTUNITY HERE. WHEN THERE WERE NO LIGHTS. NO COPS. NO PHONES.
SOMEONE WENT SHOPPING. AND I'M SCARED HE'S STILL DOING IT.
I'M GONNA GO TALK TO EMIL SAINT-CLAIRE.
GREAT SEGUE. WHY?
BECAUSE THOSE DEAD GOONS AT THE WAREHOUSE WERE HIS. AND I THINK BRIDGE MAY HAVE BEEN HIS, TOO.

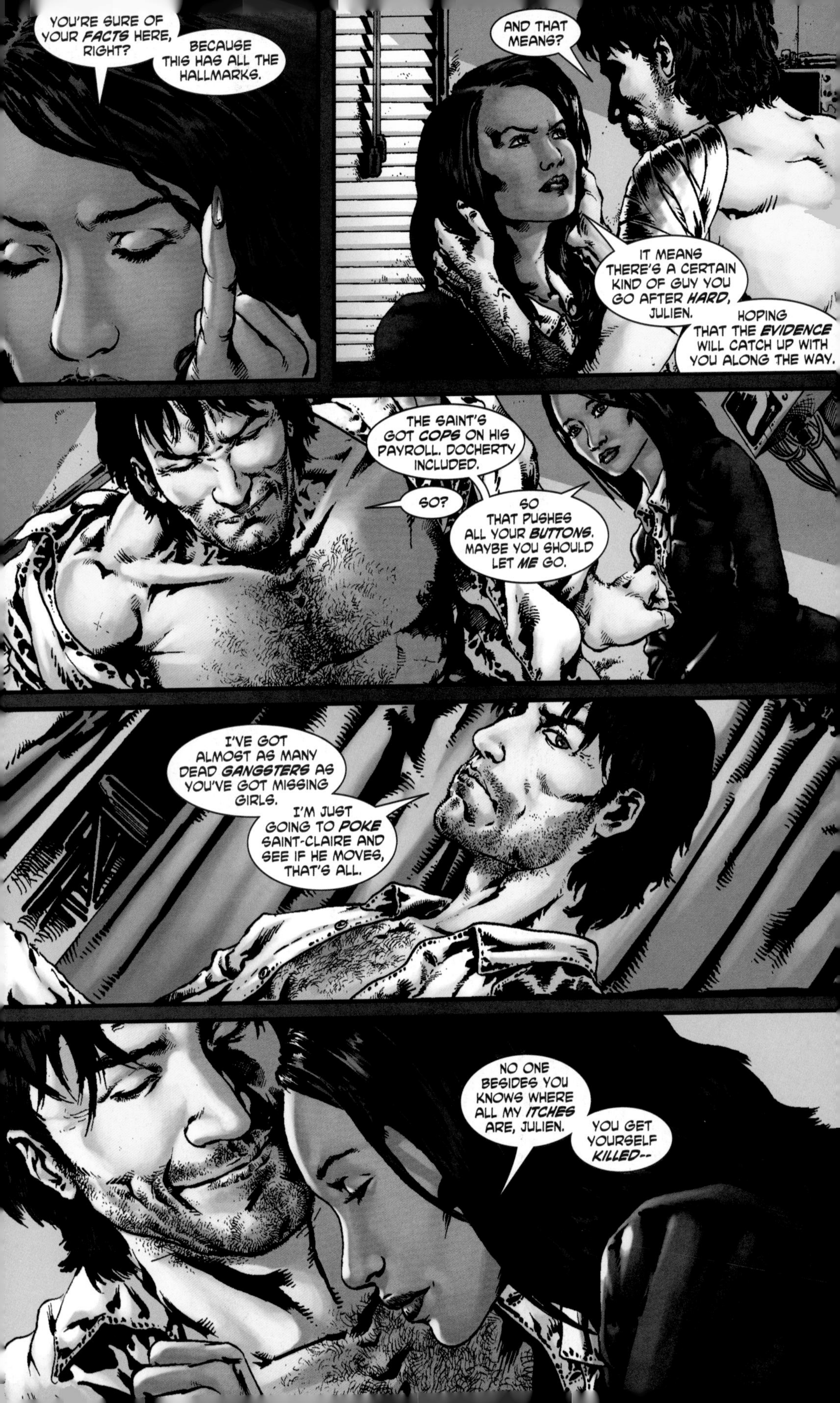
YOU'RE SURE OF YOUR FACTS HERE, RIGHT?
BECAUSE THIS HAS ALL THE HALLMARKS.
AND THAT MEANS?
IT MEANS THERE'S A CERTAIN KIND OF GUY YOU GO AFTER HARD, JULIEN.
HOPING THAT THE EVIDENCE WILL CATCH UP WITH YOU ALONG THE WAY.
THE SAINT'S GOT COPS ON HIS PAYROLL. DOCHERTY INCLUDED.
SO?
SO THAT PUSHES ALL YOUR BUTTONS. MAYBE YOU SHOULD LET ME GO.
I'VE GOT ALMOST AS MANY DEAD GANGSTERS AS YOU'VE GOT MISSING GIRLS.
I'M JUST GOING TO POKE SAINT-CLAIRE AND SEE IF HE MOVES, THAT'S ALL.
NO ONE BESIDES YOU KNOWS WHERE ALL MY ITCHES ARE, JULIEN.
YOU GET YOURSELF KILLED--

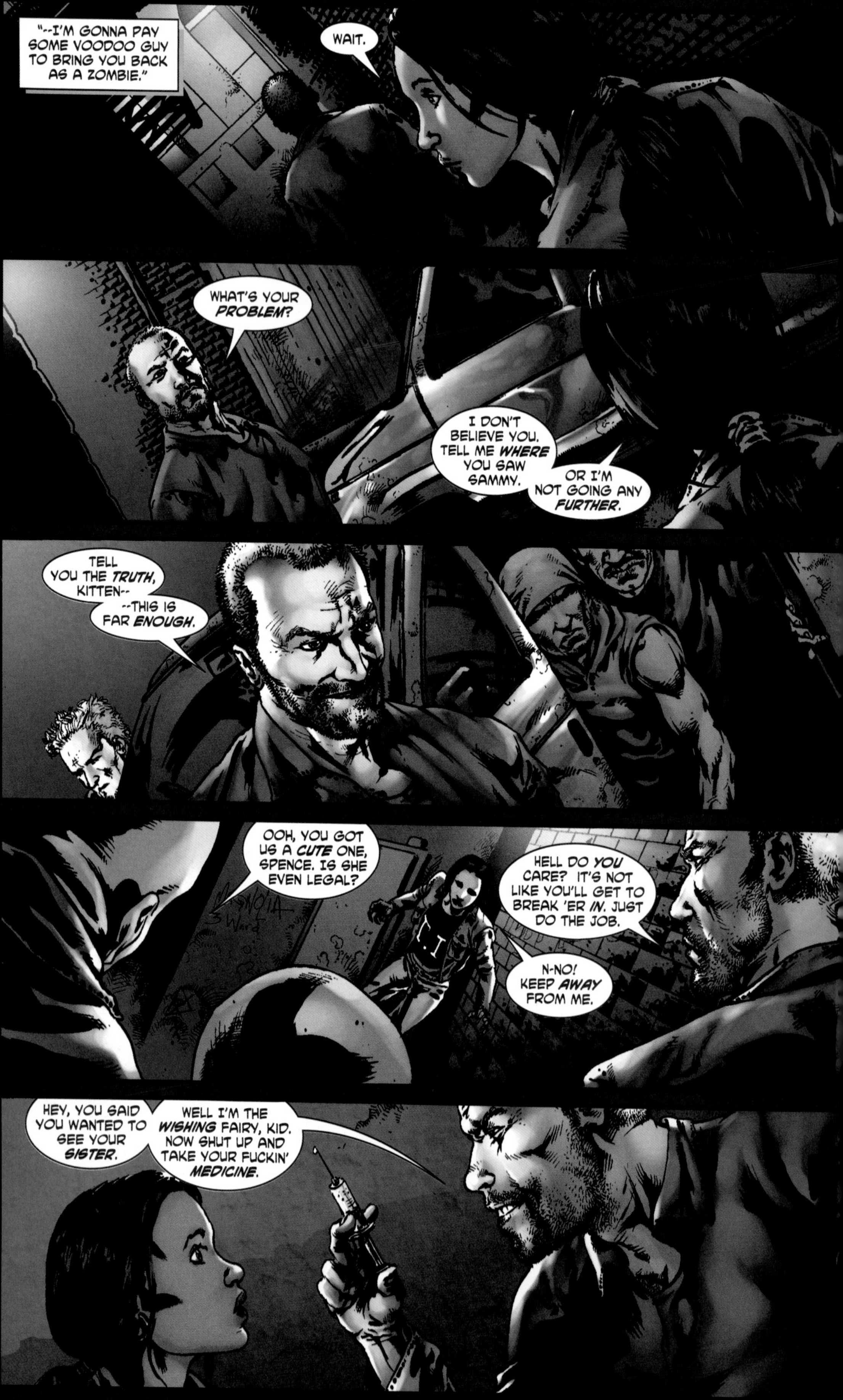
"--I'M GONNA PAY SOME VOODOO GUY TO BRING YOU BACK AS A ZOMBIE."
WAIT.
WHAT'S YOUR PROBLEM?
I DON'T BELIEVE YOU. TELL ME WHERE YOU SAW SAMMY.
OR I'M NOT GOING ANY FURTHER.
TELL YOU THE TRUTH, KITTEN--
--THIS IS FAR ENOUGH.
OOH, YOU GOT US A CUTE ONE, SPENCE. IS SHE EVEN LEGAL?
HELL DO YOU CARE? IT'S NOT LIKE YOU'LL GET TO BREAK 'ER IN. JUST DO THE JOB.
N-NO! KEEP AWAY FROM ME.
HEY, YOU SAID YOU WANTED TO SEE YOUR SISTER.
WELL I'M THE WISHING FAIRY, KID. NOW SHUT UP AND TAKE YOUR FUCKIN' MEDICINE.

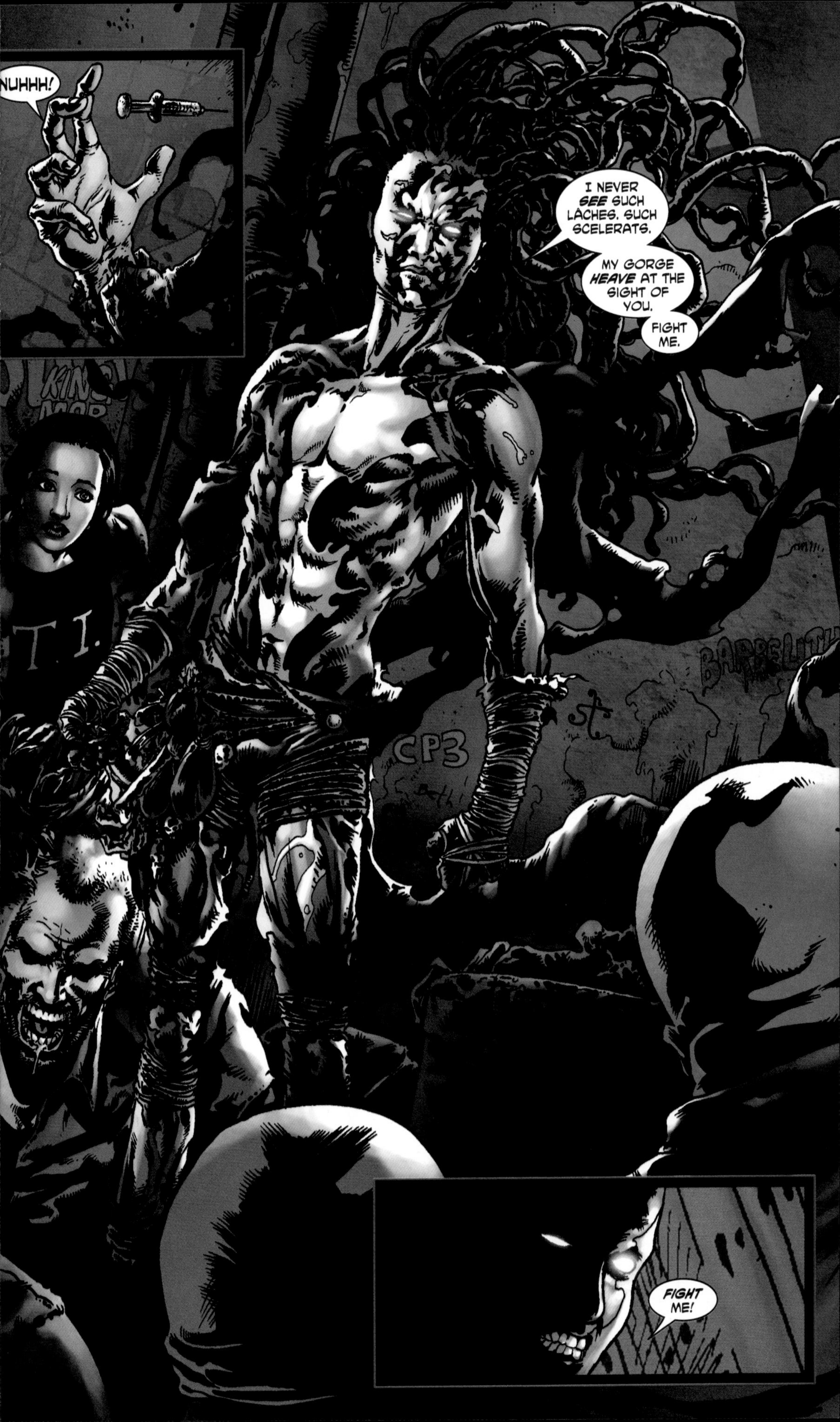
NUHHH!
I NEVER SEE SUCH LÂCHES, SUCH SCELERATS.
MY GORGE HEAVE AT THE SIGHT OF YOU.
FIGHT ME.
FIGHT ME!

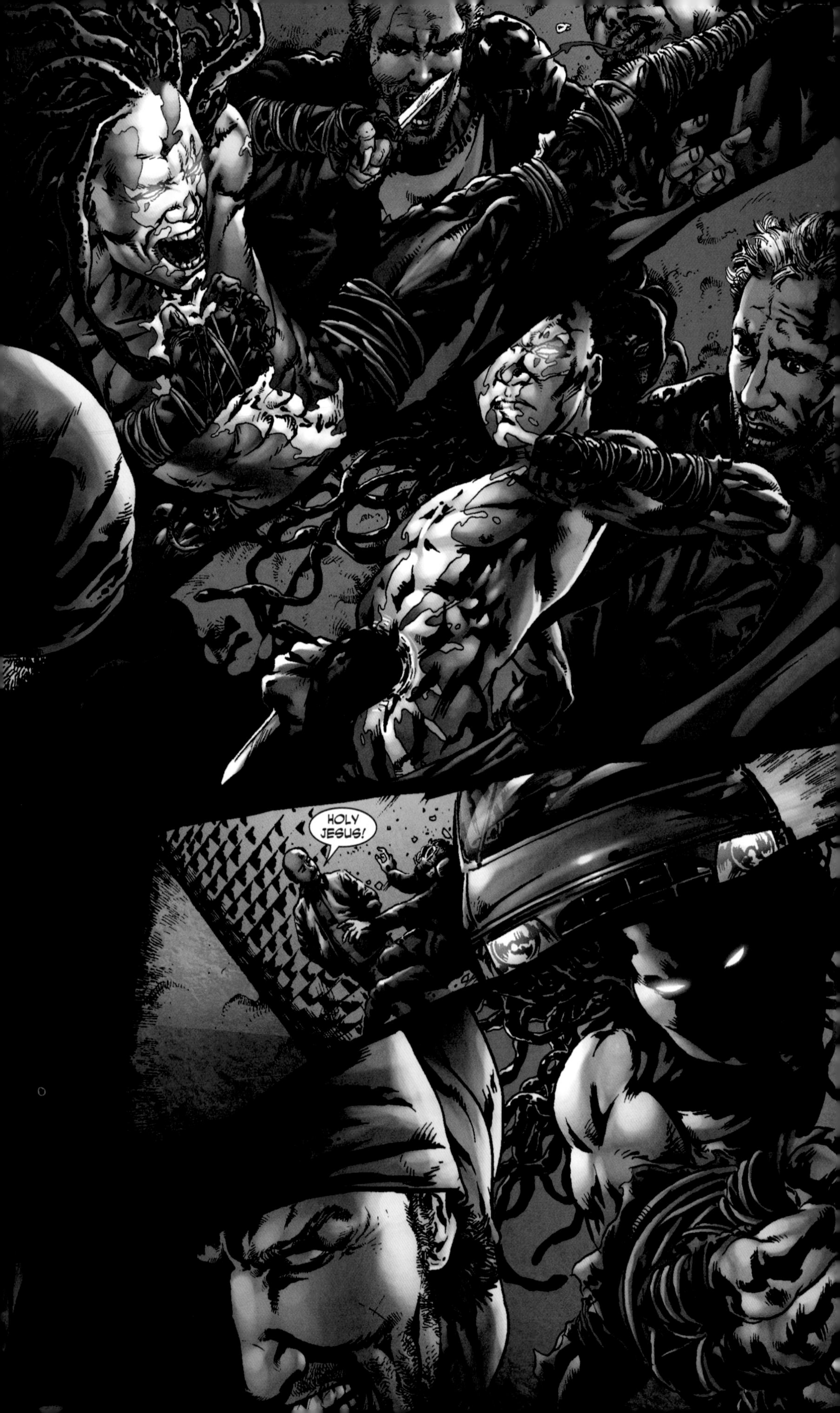
HOLY JESUS!

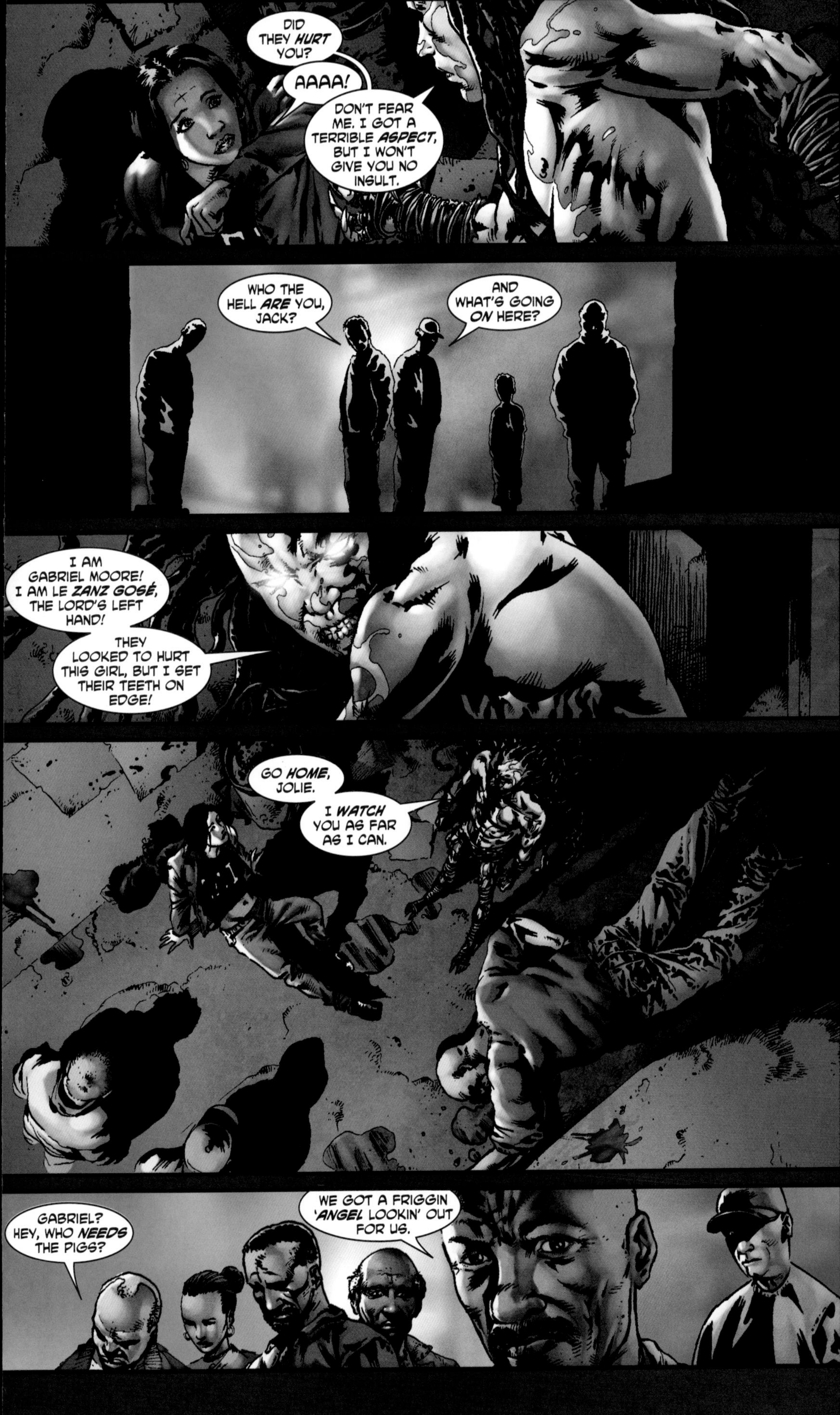
DID THEY *HURT* YOU?
AAAA!
DON'T FEAR ME. I GOT A TERRIBLE *ASPECT*, BUT I WON'T GIVE YOU NO INSULT.
WHO THE HELL *ARE* YOU, JACK?
AND WHAT'S GOING *ON* HERE?
I AM GABRIEL MOORE! I AM LE *ZANZ GOSÉ*, THE LORD'S LEFT HAND!
THEY LOOKED TO HURT THIS GIRL, BUT I SET THEIR TEETH ON EDGE!
GO *HOME*, JOLIE.
I *WATCH* YOU AS FAR AS I CAN.
GABRIEL? HEY, WHO *NEEDS* THE PIGS?
WE GOT A FRIGGIN '*ANGEL* LOOKIN' OUT FOR US.

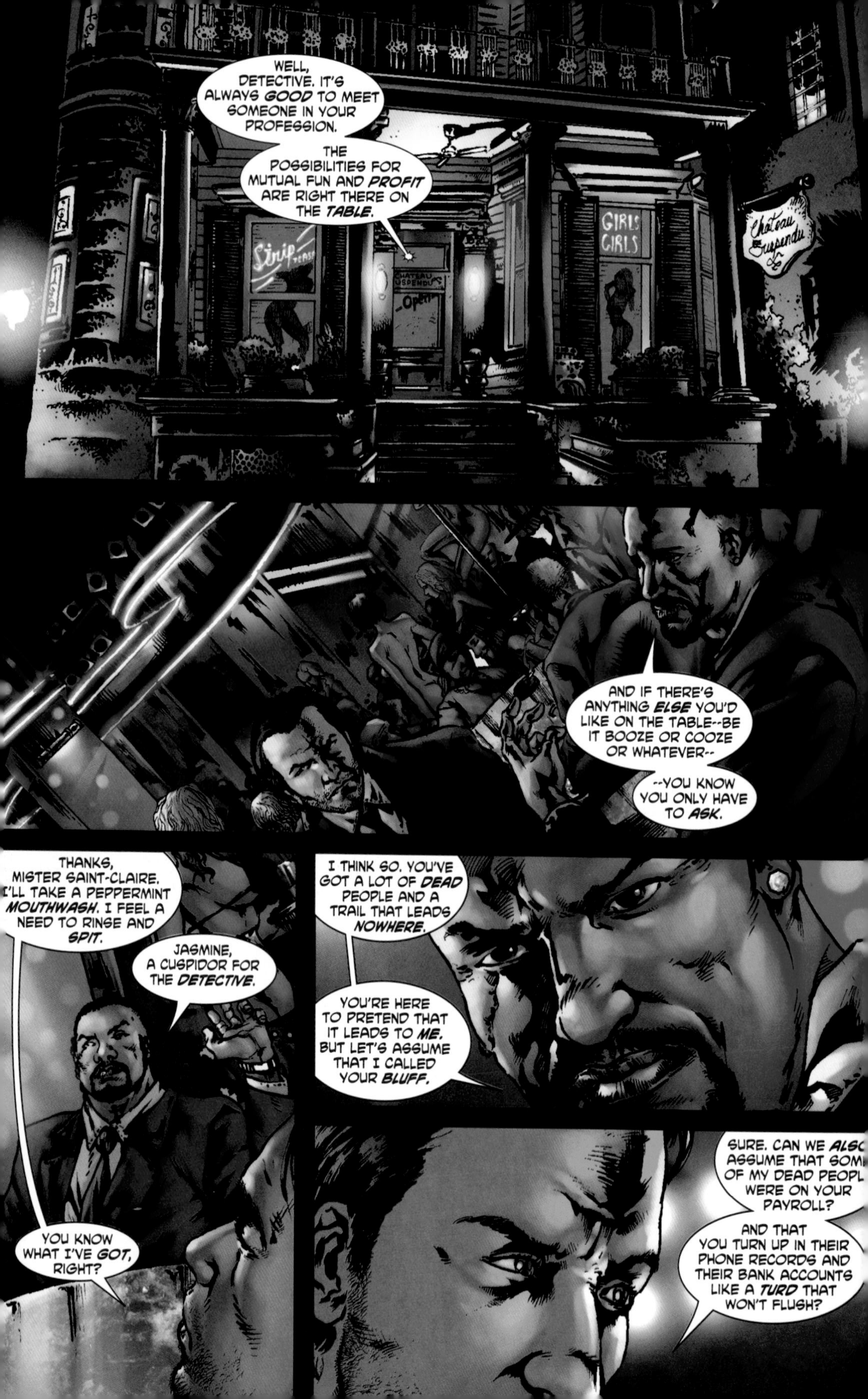

WELL, DETECTIVE. IT'S ALWAYS GOOD TO MEET SOMEONE IN YOUR PROFESSION.
THE POSSIBILITIES FOR MUTUAL FUN AND PROFIT ARE RIGHT THERE ON THE TABLE.
Strip TEASE
CHATEAU SUSPENDU
Open
GIRLS GIRLS
Chateau Suspendu
AND IF THERE'S ANYTHING ELSE YOU'D LIKE ON THE TABLE--BE IT BOOZE OR COOZE OR WHATEVER--
--YOU KNOW YOU ONLY HAVE TO ASK.
THANKS, MISTER SAINT-CLAIRE. I'LL TAKE A PEPPERMINT MOUTHWASH. I FEEL A NEED TO RINSE AND SPIT.
JASMINE, A CUSPIDOR FOR THE DETECTIVE.
YOU KNOW WHAT I'VE GOT, RIGHT?
I THINK SO. YOU'VE GOT A LOT OF DEAD PEOPLE AND A TRAIL THAT LEADS NOWHERE.
YOU'RE HERE TO PRETEND THAT IT LEADS TO ME. BUT LET'S ASSUME THAT I CALLED YOUR BLUFF.
SURE. CAN WE ALSO ASSUME THAT SOME OF MY DEAD PEOPLE WERE ON YOUR PAYROLL?
AND THAT YOU TURN UP IN THEIR PHONE RECORDS AND THEIR BANK ACCOUNTS LIKE A TURD THAT WON'T FLUSH?

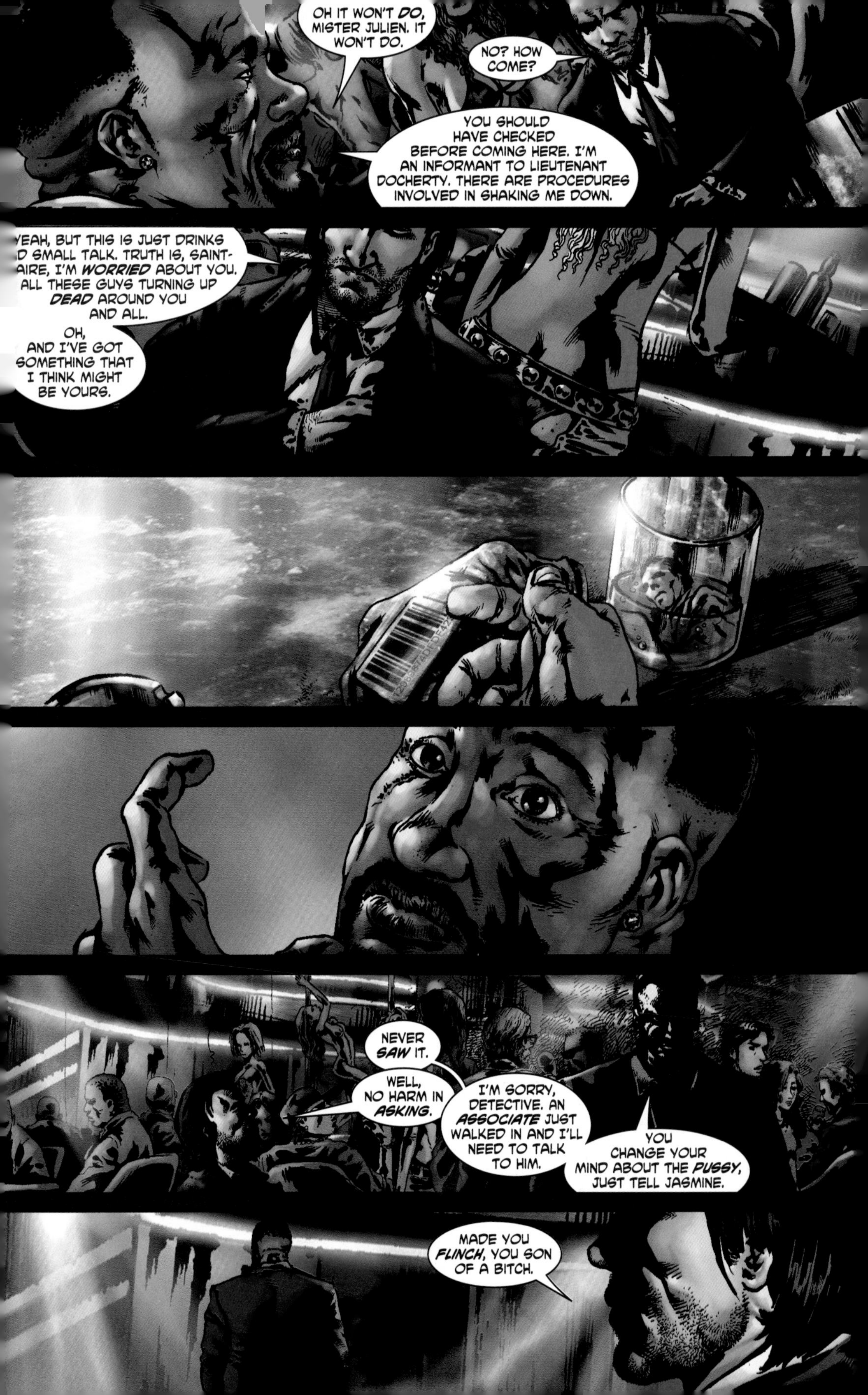
OH IT WON'T *DO*, MISTER JULIEN. IT WON'T DO.
NO? HOW COME?
YOU SHOULD HAVE CHECKED BEFORE COMING HERE. I'M AN INFORMANT TO LIEUTENANT DOCHERTY. THERE ARE PROCEDURES INVOLVED IN SHAKING ME DOWN.
YEAH, BUT THIS IS JUST DRINKS D SMALL TALK. TRUTH IS, SAINT-AIRE, I'M *WORRIED* ABOUT YOU. ALL THESE GUYS TURNING UP *DEAD* AROUND YOU AND ALL.
OH, AND I'VE GOT SOMETHING THAT I THINK MIGHT BE YOURS.
NEVER *SAW* IT.
WELL, NO HARM IN *ASKING*.
I'M SORRY, DETECTIVE. AN *ASSOCIATE* JUST WALKED IN AND I'LL NEED TO TALK TO HIM.
YOU CHANGE YOUR MIND ABOUT THE *PUSSY*, JUST TELL JASMINE.
MADE YOU *FLINCH*, YOU SON OF A BITCH.

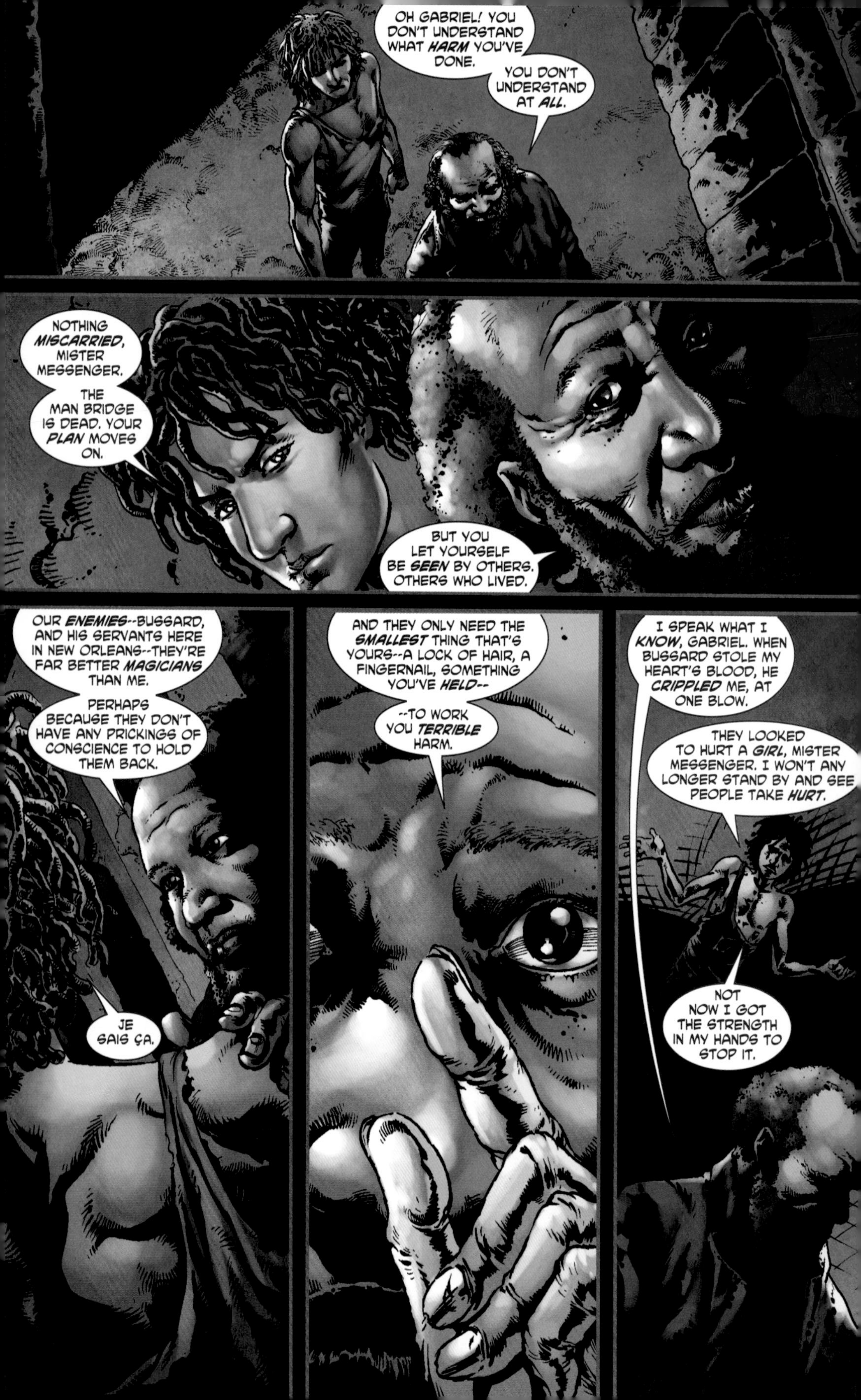
OH GABRIEL! YOU DON'T UNDERSTAND WHAT HARM YOU'VE DONE.
YOU DON'T UNDERSTAND AT ALL.
NOTHING MISCARRIED, MISTER MESSENGER.
THE MAN BRIDGE IS DEAD. YOUR PLAN MOVES ON.
BUT YOU LET YOURSELF BE SEEN BY OTHERS. OTHERS WHO LIVED.
OUR ENEMIES--BUSSARD, AND HIS SERVANTS HERE IN NEW ORLEANS--THEY'RE FAR BETTER MAGICIANS THAN ME.
PERHAPS BECAUSE THEY DON'T HAVE ANY PRICKINGS OF CONSCIENCE TO HOLD THEM BACK.
JE SAIS ÇA.
AND THEY ONLY NEED THE SMALLEST THING THAT'S YOURS--A LOCK OF HAIR, A FINGERNAIL, SOMETHING YOU'VE HELD--
--TO WORK YOU TERRIBLE HARM.
I SPEAK WHAT I KNOW, GABRIEL. WHEN BUSSARD STOLE MY HEART'S BLOOD, HE CRIPPLED ME, AT ONE BLOW.
THEY LOOKED TO HURT A GIRL, MISTER MESSENGER. I WON'T ANY LONGER STAND BY AND SEE PEOPLE TAKE HURT.
NOT NOW I GOT THE STRENGTH IN MY HANDS TO STOP IT.

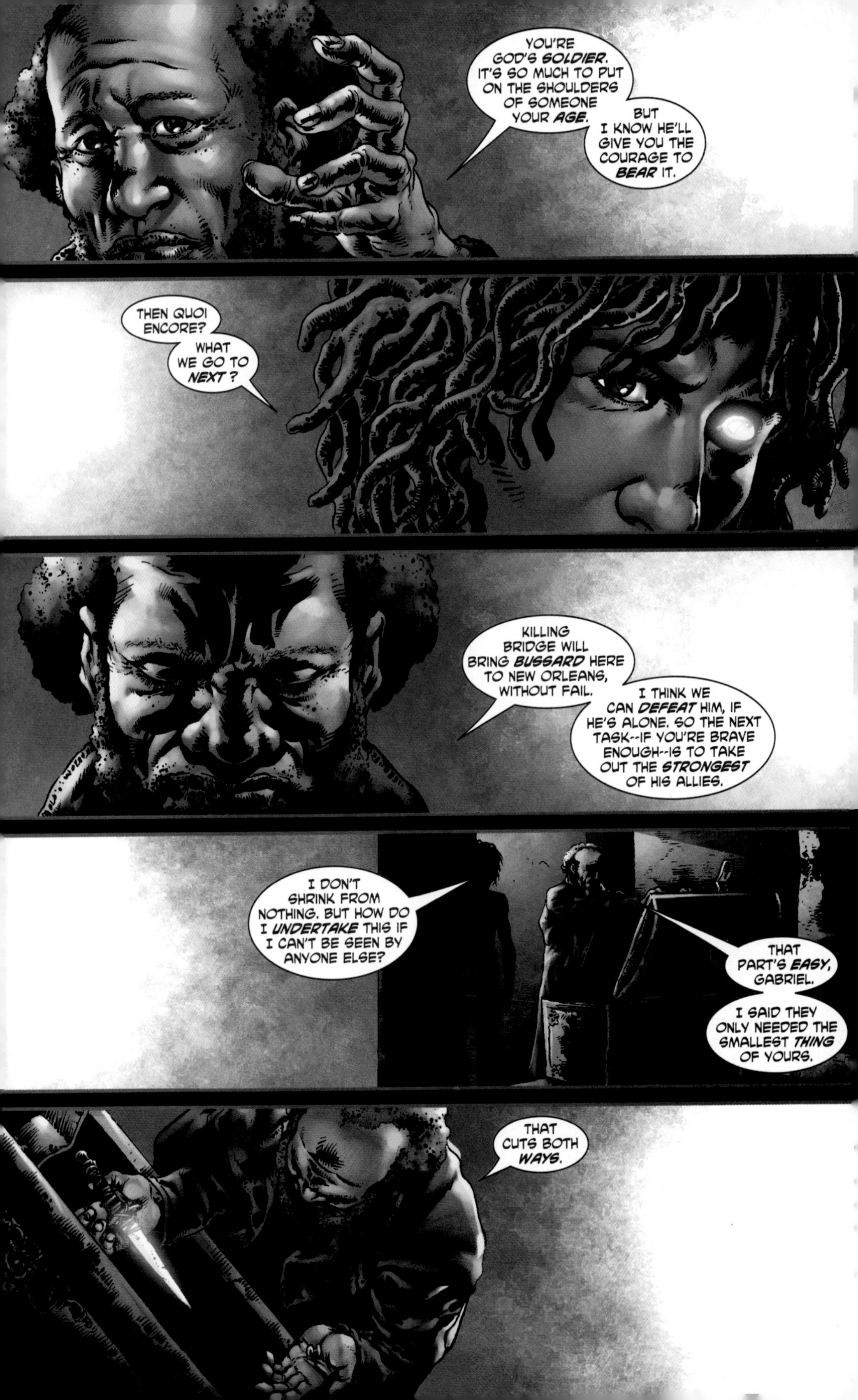
YOU'RE GOD'S SOLDIER. IT'S SO MUCH TO PUT ON THE SHOULDERS OF SOMEONE YOUR AGE.
BUT I KNOW HE'LL GIVE YOU THE COURAGE TO BEAR IT.
THEN QUOI ENCORE?
WHAT WE GO TO NEXT?
KILLING BRIDGE WILL BRING BUSSARD HERE TO NEW ORLEANS, WITHOUT FAIL.
I THINK WE CAN DEFEAT HIM, IF HE'S ALONE. SO THE NEXT TASK--IF YOU'RE BRAVE ENOUGH--IS TO TAKE OUT THE STRONGEST OF HIS ALLIES.
I DON'T SHRINK FROM NOTHING. BUT HOW DO I UNDERTAKE THIS IF I CAN'T BE SEEN BY ANYONE ELSE?
THAT PART'S EASY, GABRIEL.
I SAID THEY ONLY NEEDED THE SMALLEST THING OF YOURS.
THAT CUTS BOTH WAYS.

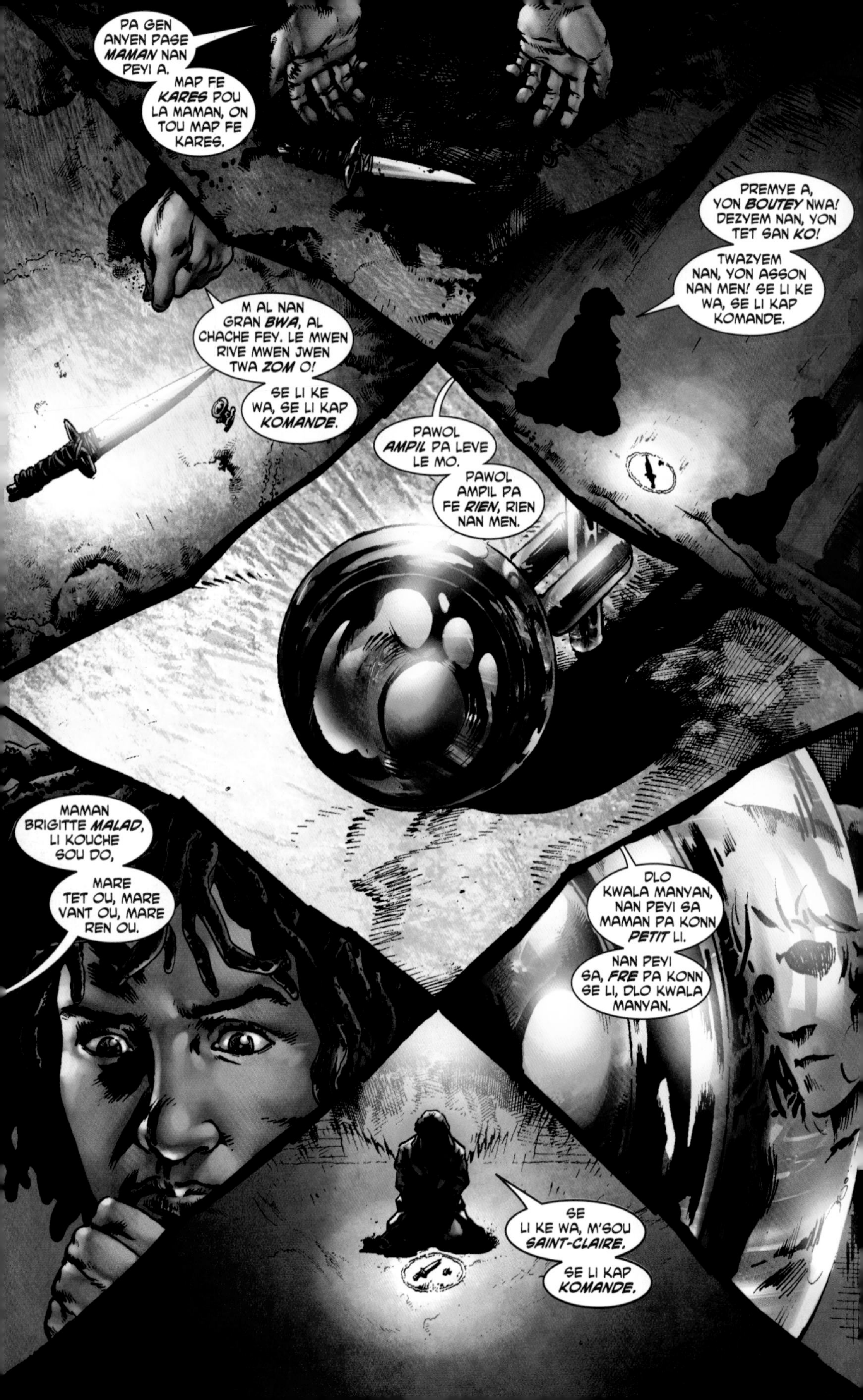
PA GEN ANYEN PASE MAMAN NAN PEYI A.
MAP FE KARES POU LA MAMAN, ON TOU MAP FE KARES.
PREMYE A, YON BOUTEY NWA! DEZYEM NAN, YON TET SAN KO!
TWAZYEM NAN, YON ASSON NAN MEN! SE LI KE WA, SE LI KAP KOMANDE.
M AL NAN GRAN BWA, AL CHACHE FEY. LE MWEN RIVE MWEN JWEN TWA ZOM O!
SE LI KE WA, SE LI KAP KOMANDE.
PAWOL AMPIL PA LEVE LE MO.
PAWOL AMPIL PA FE RIEN, RIEN NAN MEN.
MAMAN BRIGITTE MALAD, LI KOUCHE SOU DO,
MARE TET OU, MARE VANT OU, MARE REN OU.
DLO KWALA MANYAN, NAN PEYI SA MAMAN PA KONN PETIT LI.
NAN PEYI SA, FRE PA KONN SE LI, DLO KWALA MANYAN.
SE LI KE WA, M'SOU SAINT-CLAIRE.
SE LI KAP KOMANDE.

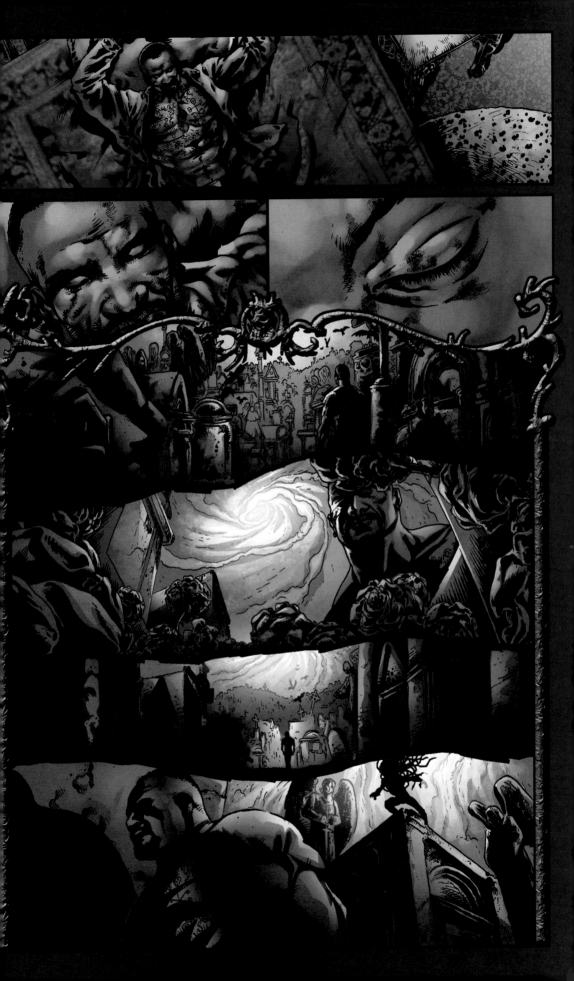

THE HOUR IS COME FOR YOU, CARENCRO!
AS IT COME FOR ALL LIKE YOU.
AND WHERE THE FUCK DID YOU SPRING FROM? OUT OF THE BOURBON, OR OUT OF THE DOPE?
YOU ARE BUSSARD'S MAN.
WAS IT YOU STOLE THE GOODMAN'S HEART BLOOD? WAS IT?
HEY, IT'S MY DREAM, MOTHERFUCKER.
GO PISS UP A ROPE.
I WARN YOU. THE GOOD MAN GIVE ME A WEAPON THAT CAN CUT YOU IN YOUR DREAM.
UFFF!
YOU FEEL THIS EDGE. AND YOU ANSWER MY ASKING.
YEAH, THAT'S--OW, THAT'S SHARP ALL RIGHT.
YOU GOT A GOOD BOKOR. I'LL GIVE YOU THAT.
LET'S SEE IF HE'S AS GOOD AS ME.

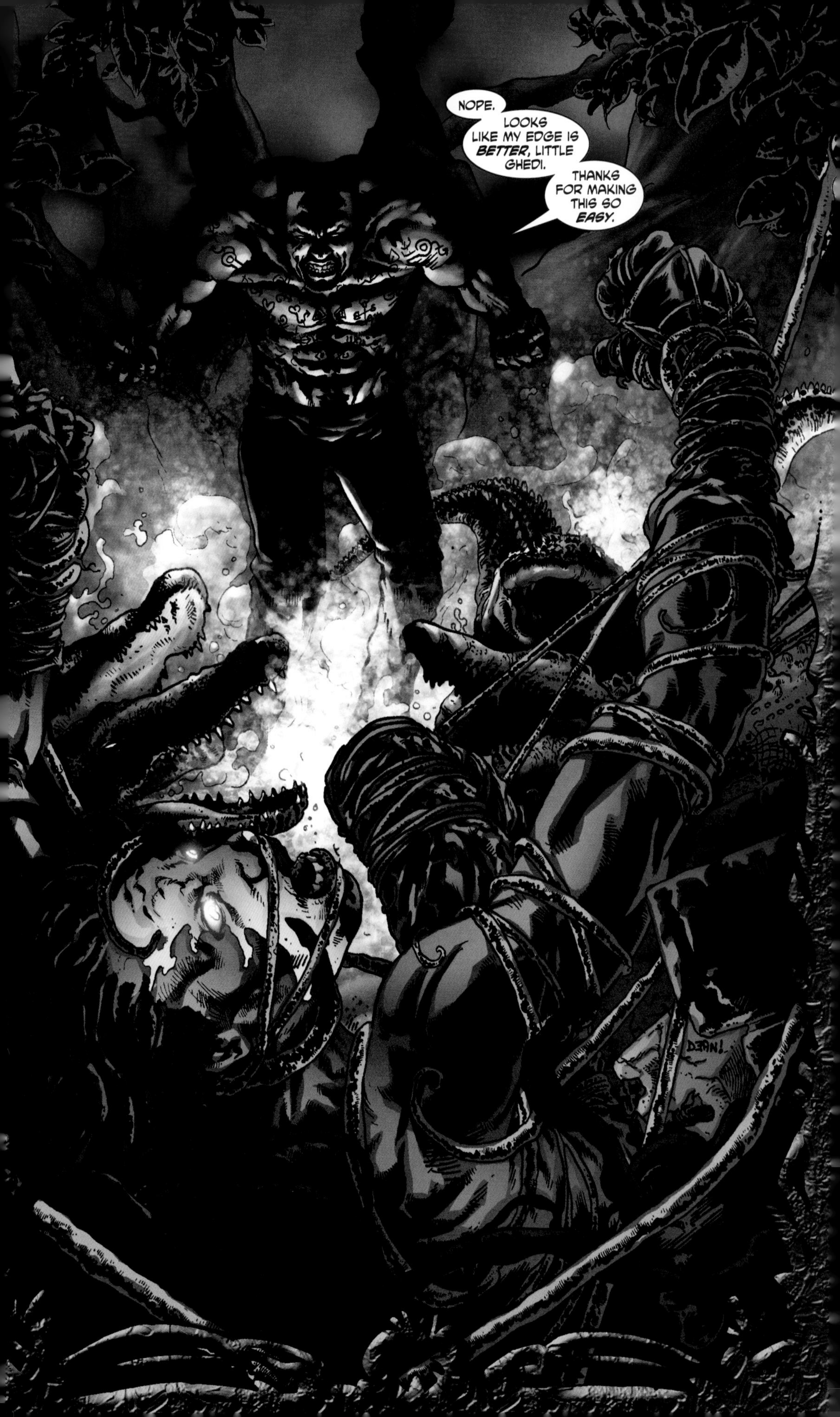
NOPE.
LOOKS LIKE MY EDGE IS *BETTER*, LITTLE GHEDI.
THANKS FOR MAKING THIS SO *EASY*.

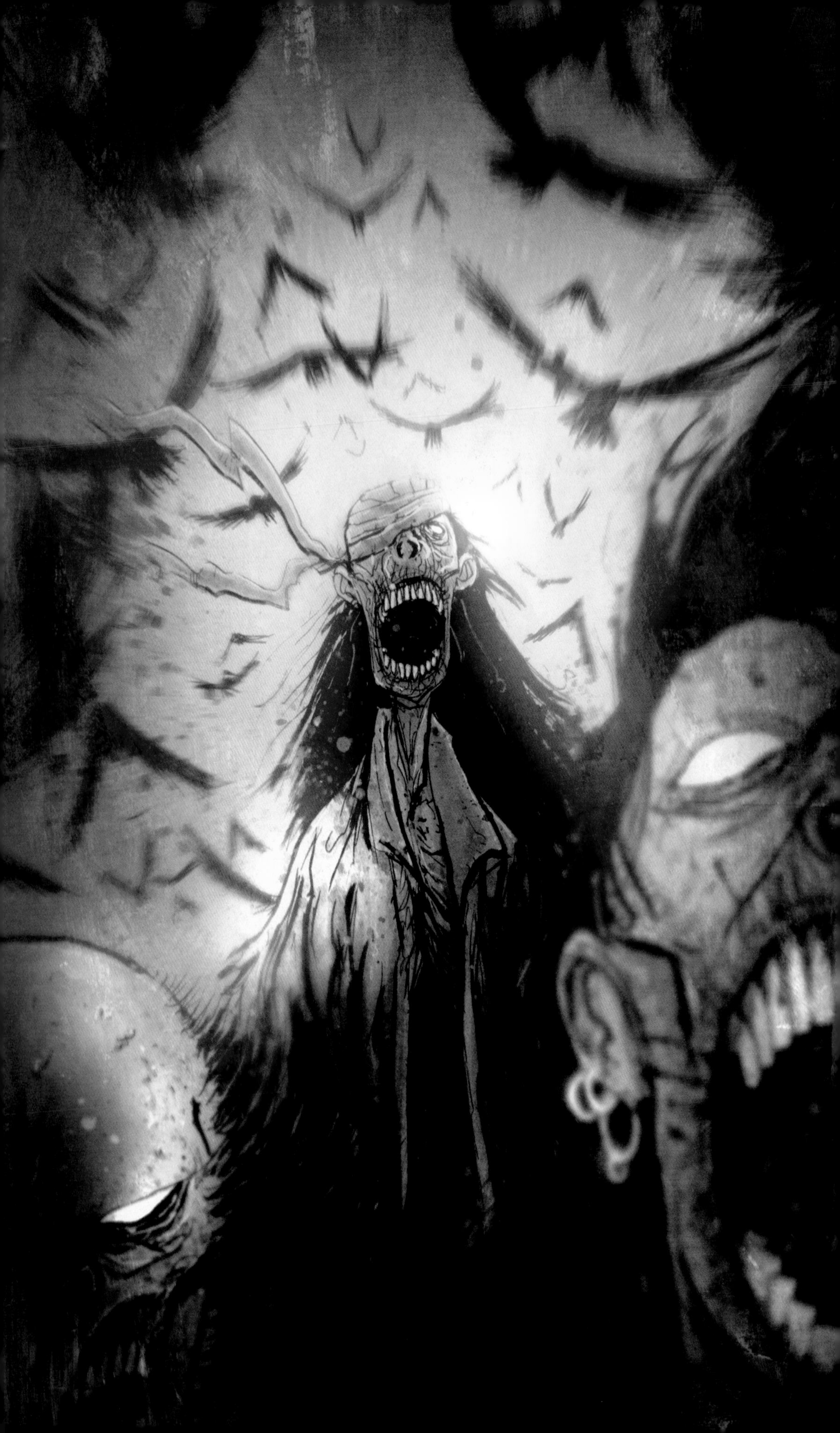

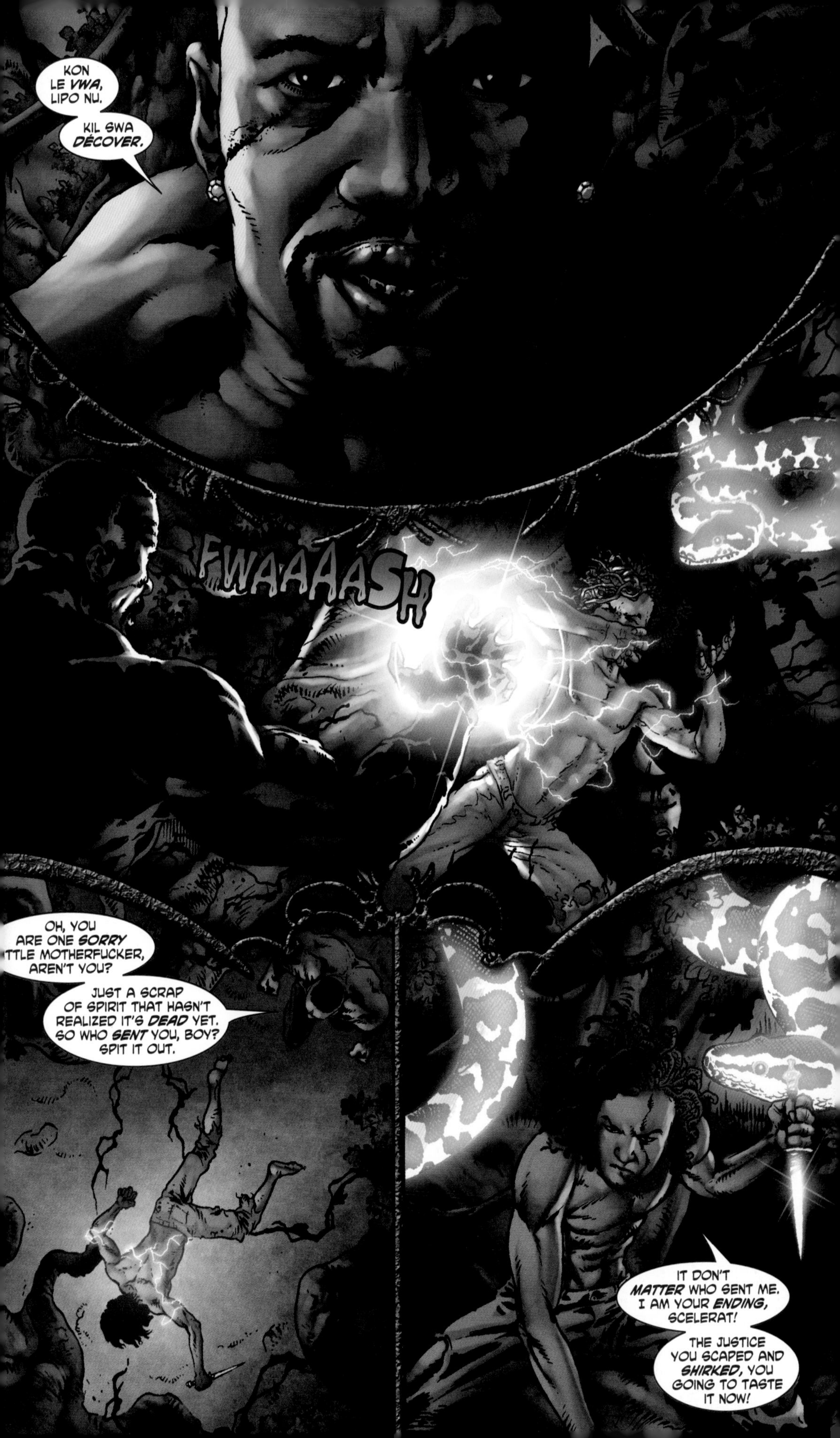
KON LE VWA, LIPO NU.
KIL SWA DÉCOVER.
FWAAAASH
OH, YOU ARE ONE SORRY ...TTLE MOTHERFUCKER, AREN'T YOU?
JUST A SCRAP OF SPIRIT THAT HASN'T REALIZED IT'S DEAD YET. SO WHO SENT YOU, BOY? SPIT IT OUT.
IT DON'T MATTER WHO SENT ME. I AM YOUR ENDING, SCELERAT!
THE JUSTICE YOU SCAPED AND SHIRKED, YOU GOING TO TASTE IT NOW!

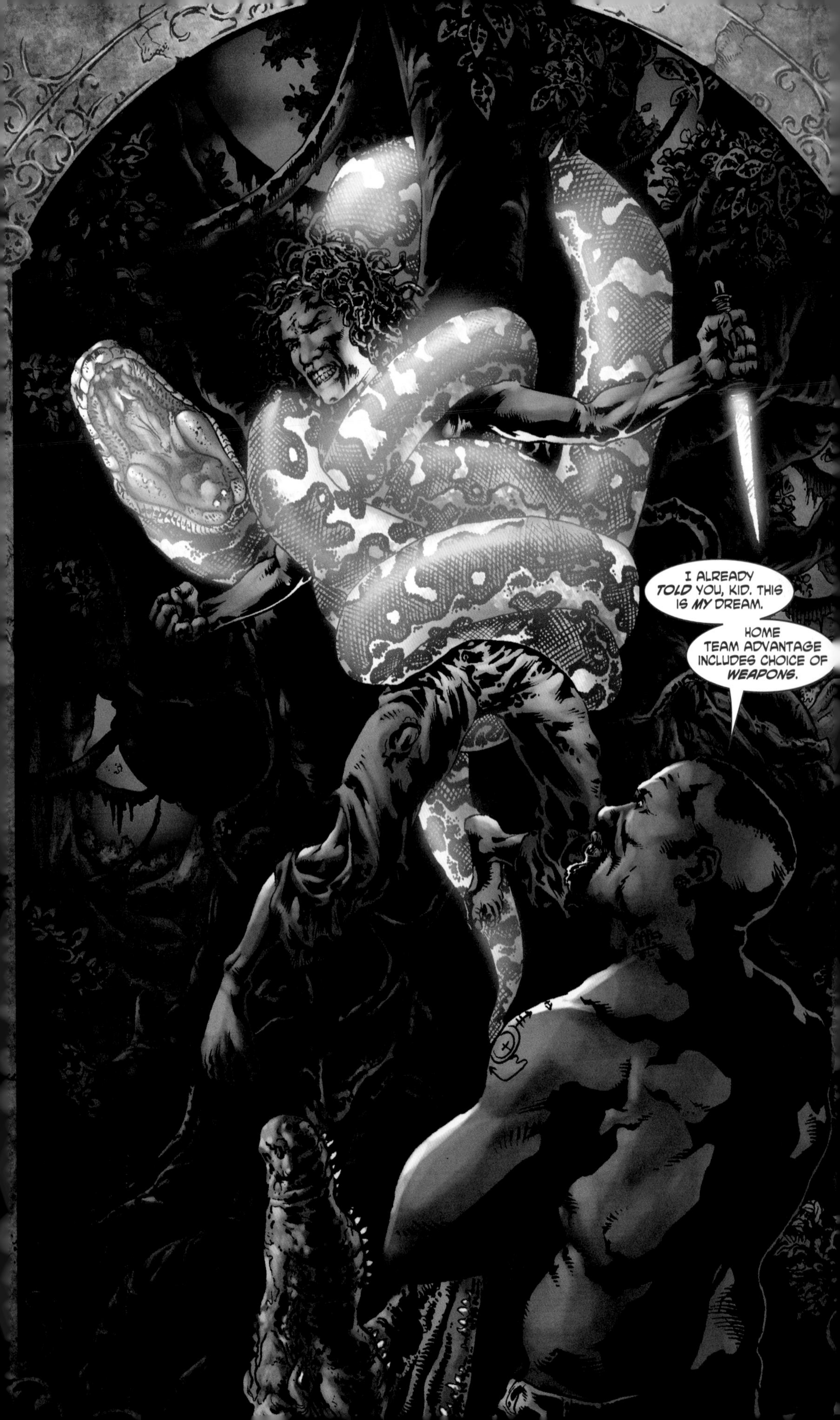
I ALREADY *TOLD* YOU, KID. THIS IS *MY* DREAM.
HOME TEAM ADVANTAGE INCLUDES CHOICE OF *WEAPONS*.

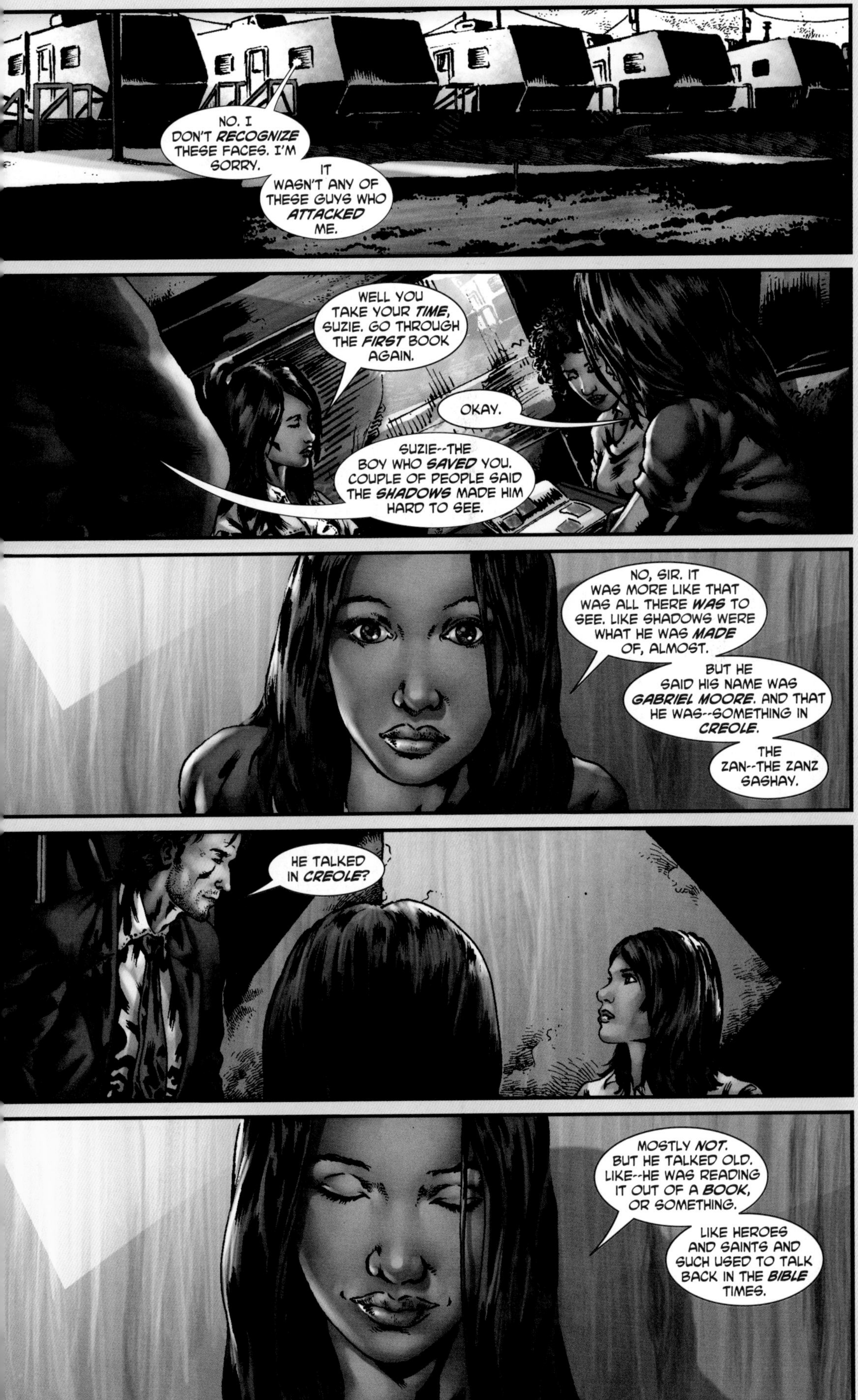
NO. I DON'T RECOGNIZE THESE FACES. I'M SORRY.
IT WASN'T ANY OF THESE GUYS WHO ATTACKED ME.
WELL YOU TAKE YOUR TIME, SUZIE. GO THROUGH THE FIRST BOOK AGAIN.
OKAY.
SUZIE--THE BOY WHO SAVED YOU. COUPLE OF PEOPLE SAID THE SHADOWS MADE HIM HARD TO SEE.
NO, SIR. IT WAS MORE LIKE THAT WAS ALL THERE WAS TO SEE. LIKE SHADOWS WERE WHAT HE WAS MADE OF, ALMOST.
BUT HE SAID HIS NAME WAS GABRIEL MOORE. AND THAT HE WAS--SOMETHING IN CREOLE.
THE ZAN--THE ZANZ SASHAY.
HE TALKED IN CREOLE?
MOSTLY NOT. BUT HE TALKED OLD. LIKE--HE WAS READING IT OUT OF A BOOK, OR SOMETHING.
LIKE HEROES AND SAINTS AND SUCH USED TO TALK BACK IN THE BIBLE TIMES.

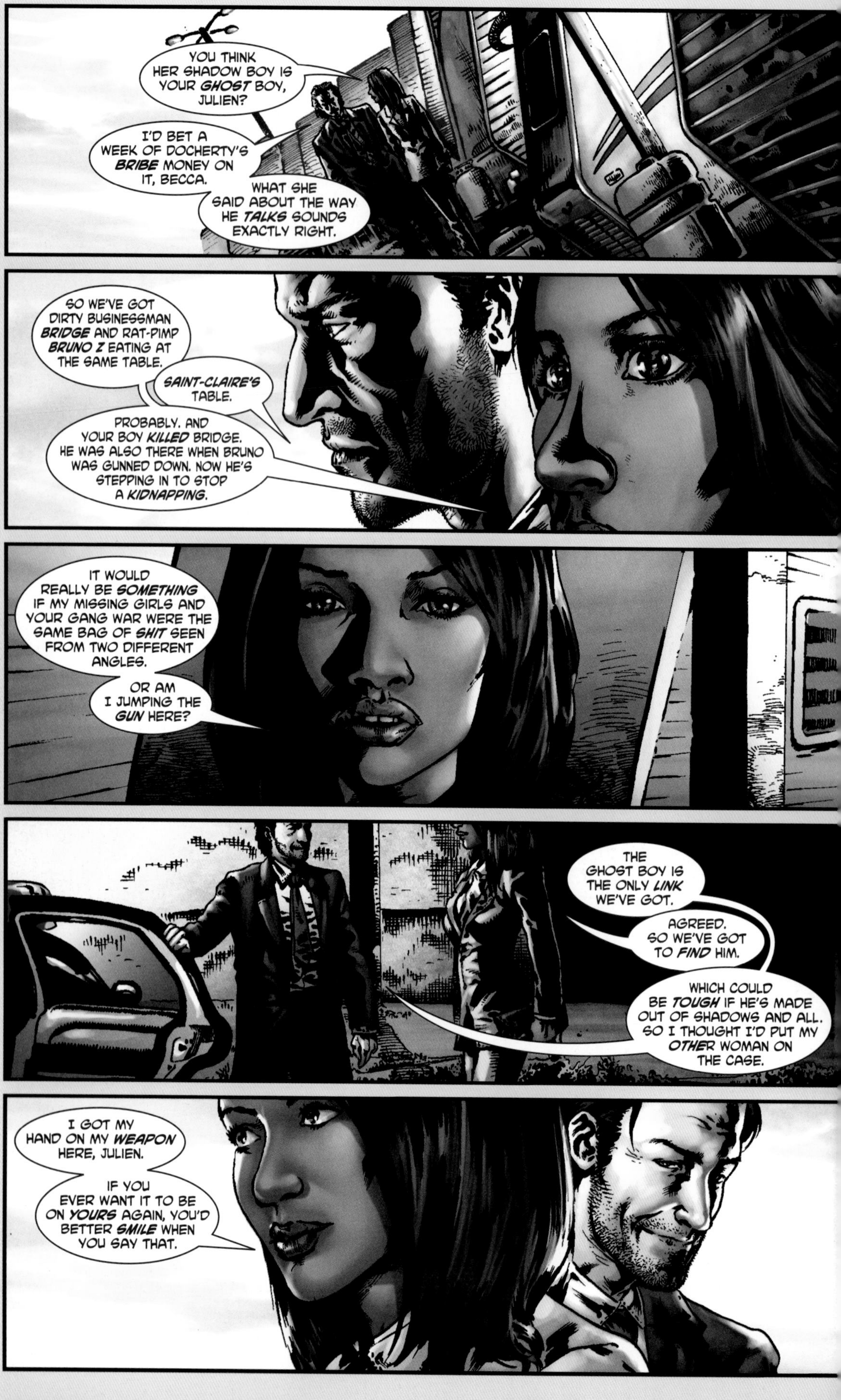

YOU THINK HER SHADOW BOY IS YOUR GHOST BOY, JULIEN?
I'D BET A WEEK OF DOCHERTY'S BRIBE MONEY ON IT, BECCA.
WHAT SHE SAID ABOUT THE WAY HE TALKS SOUNDS EXACTLY RIGHT.
SO WE'VE GOT DIRTY BUSINESSMAN BRIDGE AND RAT-PIMP BRUNO Z EATING AT THE SAME TABLE.
SAINT-CLAIRE'S TABLE.
PROBABLY. AND YOUR BOY KILLED BRIDGE. HE WAS ALSO THERE WHEN BRUNO WAS GUNNED DOWN. NOW HE'S STEPPING IN TO STOP A KIDNAPPING.
IT WOULD REALLY BE SOMETHING IF MY MISSING GIRLS AND YOUR GANG WAR WERE THE SAME BAG OF SHIT SEEN FROM TWO DIFFERENT ANGLES.
OR AM I JUMPING THE GUN HERE?
THE GHOST BOY IS THE ONLY LINK WE'VE GOT.
AGREED. SO WE'VE GOT TO FIND HIM.
WHICH COULD BE TOUGH IF HE'S MADE OUT OF SHADOWS AND ALL. SO I THOUGHT I'D PUT MY OTHER WOMAN ON THE CASE.
I GOT MY HAND ON MY WEAPON HERE, JULIEN.
IF YOU EVER WANT IT TO BE ON YOURS AGAIN, YOU'D BETTER SMILE WHEN YOU SAY THAT.

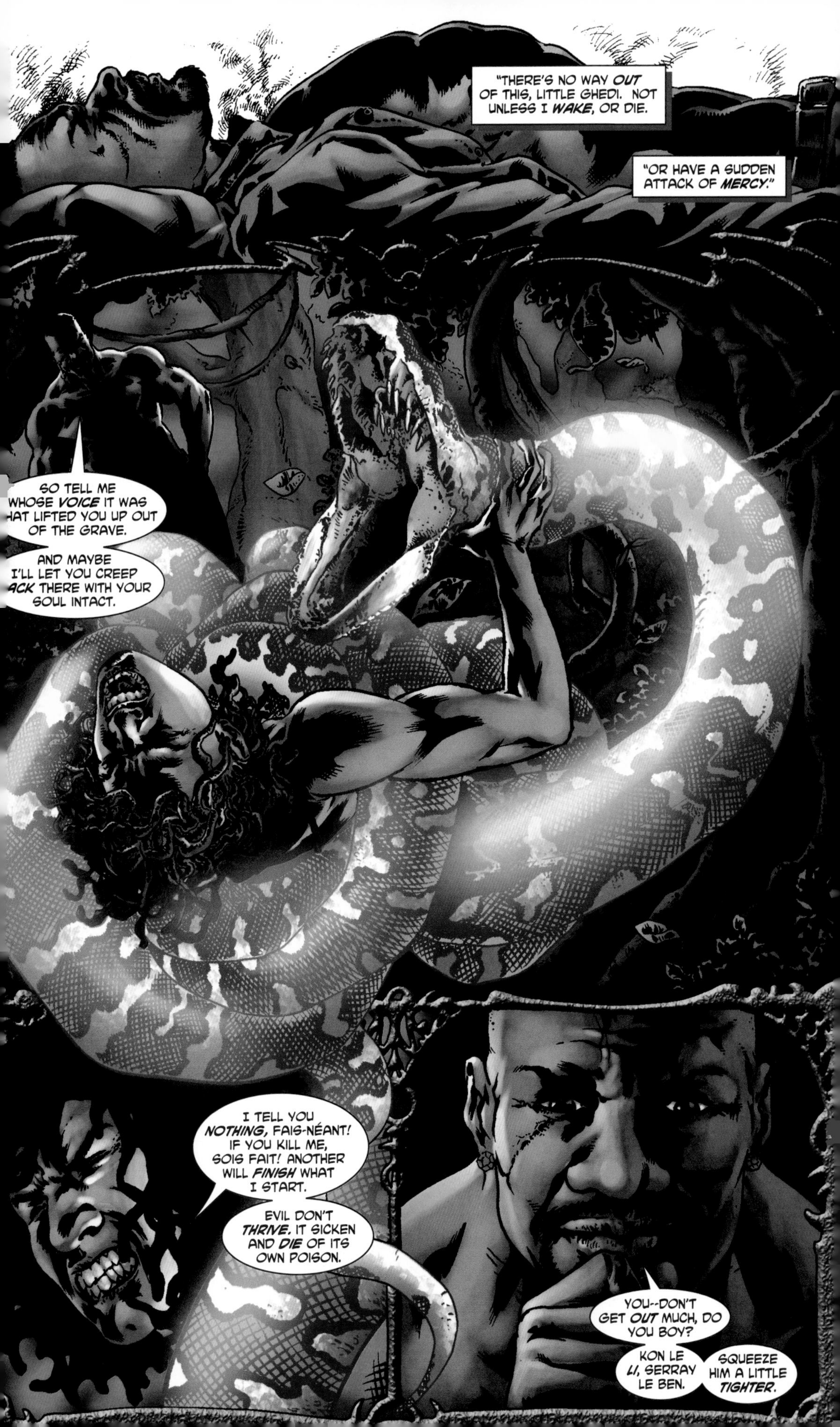
"THERE'S NO WAY OUT OF THIS, LITTLE GHEDI. NOT UNLESS I WAKE, OR DIE.
"OR HAVE A SUDDEN ATTACK OF MERCY."
SO TELL ME WHOSE VOICE IT WAS HAT LIFTED YOU UP OUT OF THE GRAVE.
AND MAYBE I'LL LET YOU CREEP ACK THERE WITH YOUR SOUL INTACT.
I TELL YOU NOTHING, FAIS-NÉANT! IF YOU KILL ME, SOIS FAIT! ANOTHER WILL FINISH WHAT I START.
EVIL DON'T THRIVE. IT SICKEN AND DIE OF ITS OWN POISON.
YOU--DON'T GET OUT MUCH, DO YOU BOY?
KON LE LI, SERRAY LE BEN.
SQUEEZE HIM A LITTLE TIGHTER.

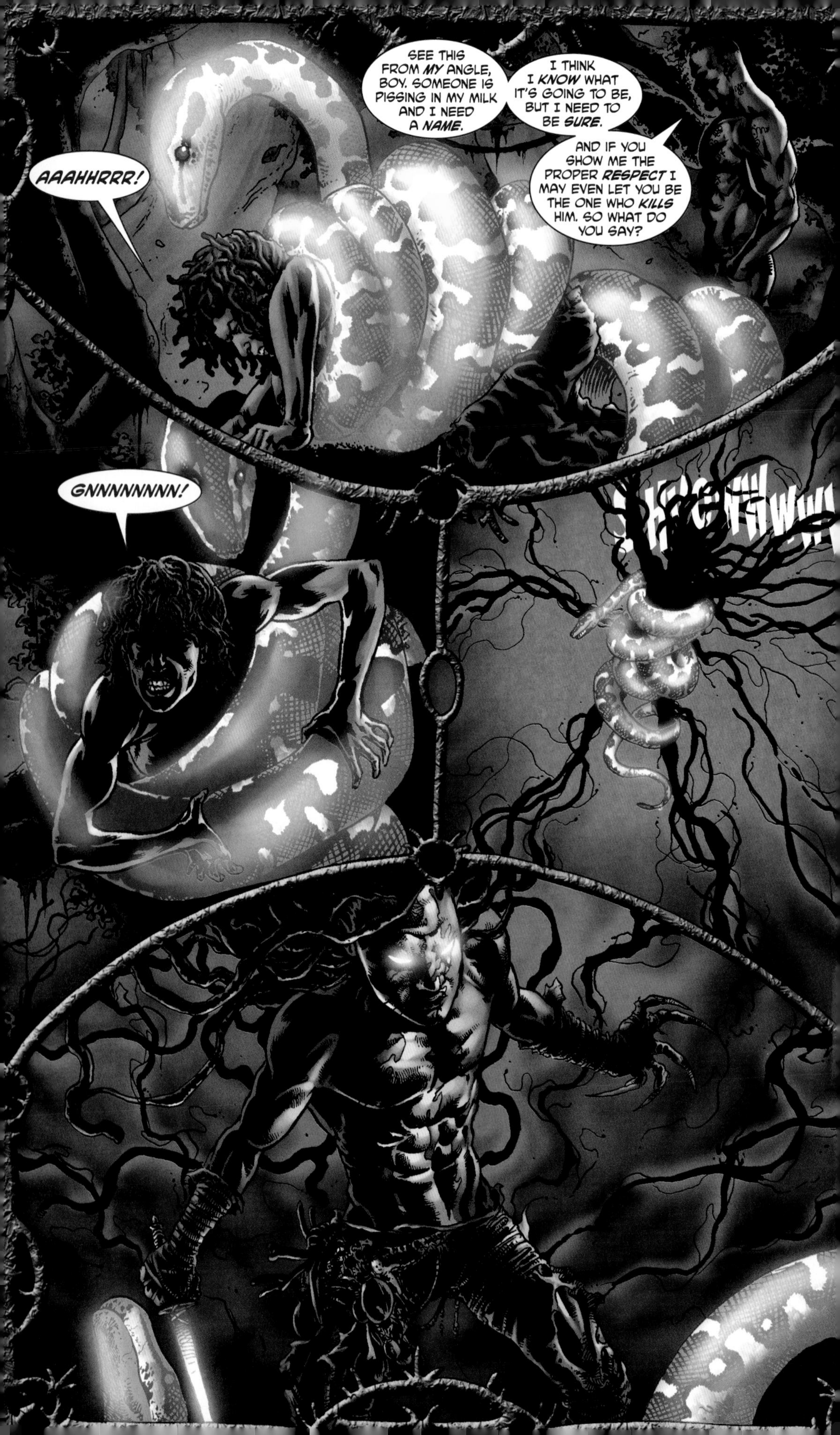
AAAHHRRR!
SEE THIS FROM MY ANGLE, BOY. SOMEONE IS PISSING IN MY MILK AND I NEED A NAME.
I THINK I KNOW WHAT IT'S GOING TO BE, BUT I NEED TO BE SURE.
AND IF YOU SHOW ME THE PROPER RESPECT I MAY EVEN LET YOU BE THE ONE WHO KILLS HIM. SO WHAT DO YOU SAY?
GNNNNNNNN!

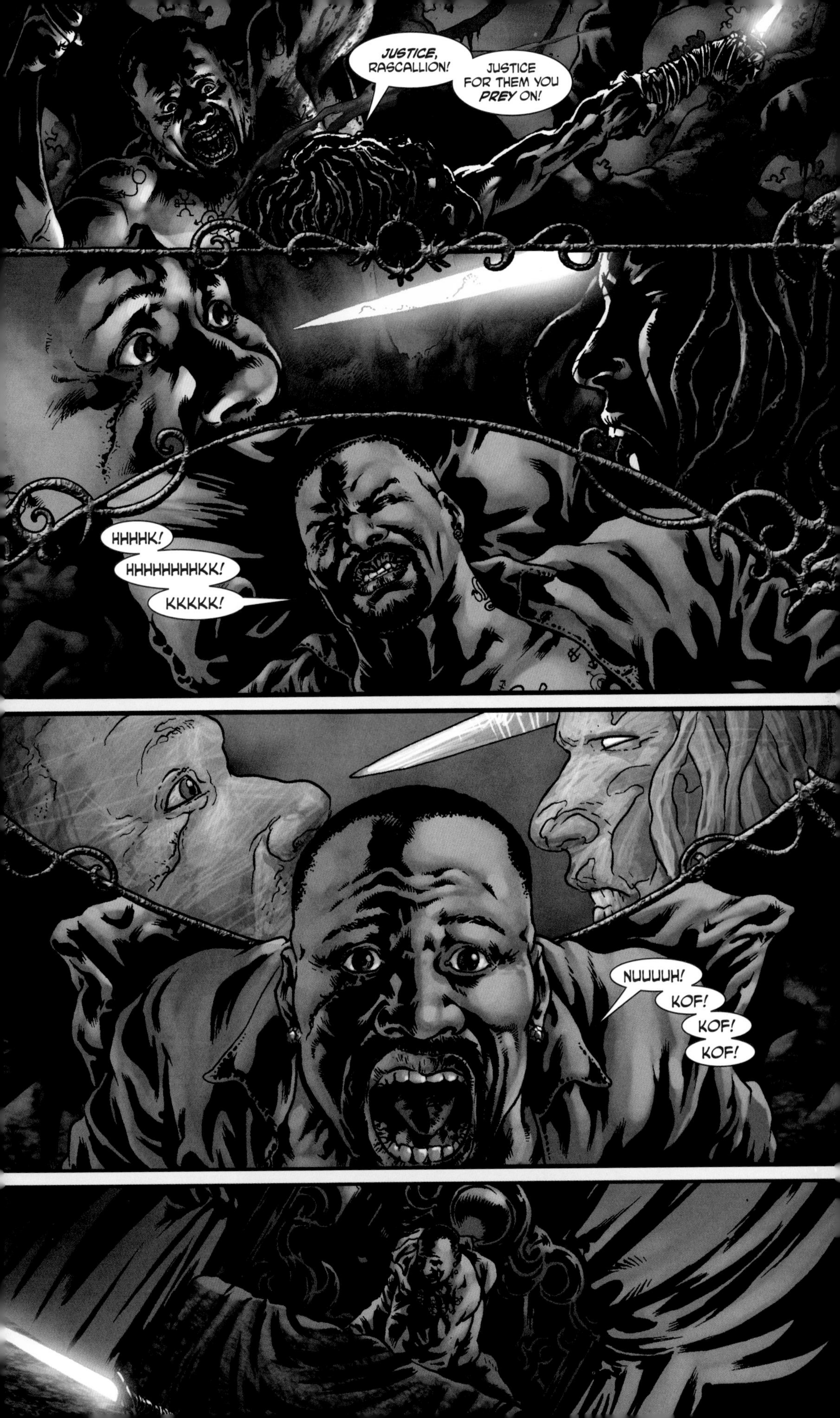
JUSTICE, RASCALLION!
JUSTICE FOR THEM YOU PREY ON!
HHHHK!
HHHHHHHHKK!
KKKKK!
NUUUUH!
KOF!
KOF!
KOF!

KRAKOOOM

GABRIEL! OH GOOD GOD, ARE YOU ALL RIGHT?

I--I *BREATHE*, MISTER MESSENGER.

I BREATHE *YET*.

AND *SAINT-CLAIRE*?

J'AI--J'AI RATÉ LE COUP. I *FAIL* YOU.

HE FEND ME OFF. AND I LEFT THE *DAGGER* BEHIND ME.

THE DAGGER?

THAT'S BAD. *VERY* BAD.

SAINT-CLAIRE COULD USE IT *AGAINST* US. HE COULD--

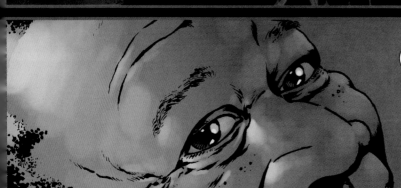

BUT NO. I'M *PANICKING* WITHOUT REASON. WE'RE STILL SAFE.

BEFORE HE COULD DO *ANYTHING* TO HURT YOU--

--HE'D NEED TO KNOW YOUR *NAME*.

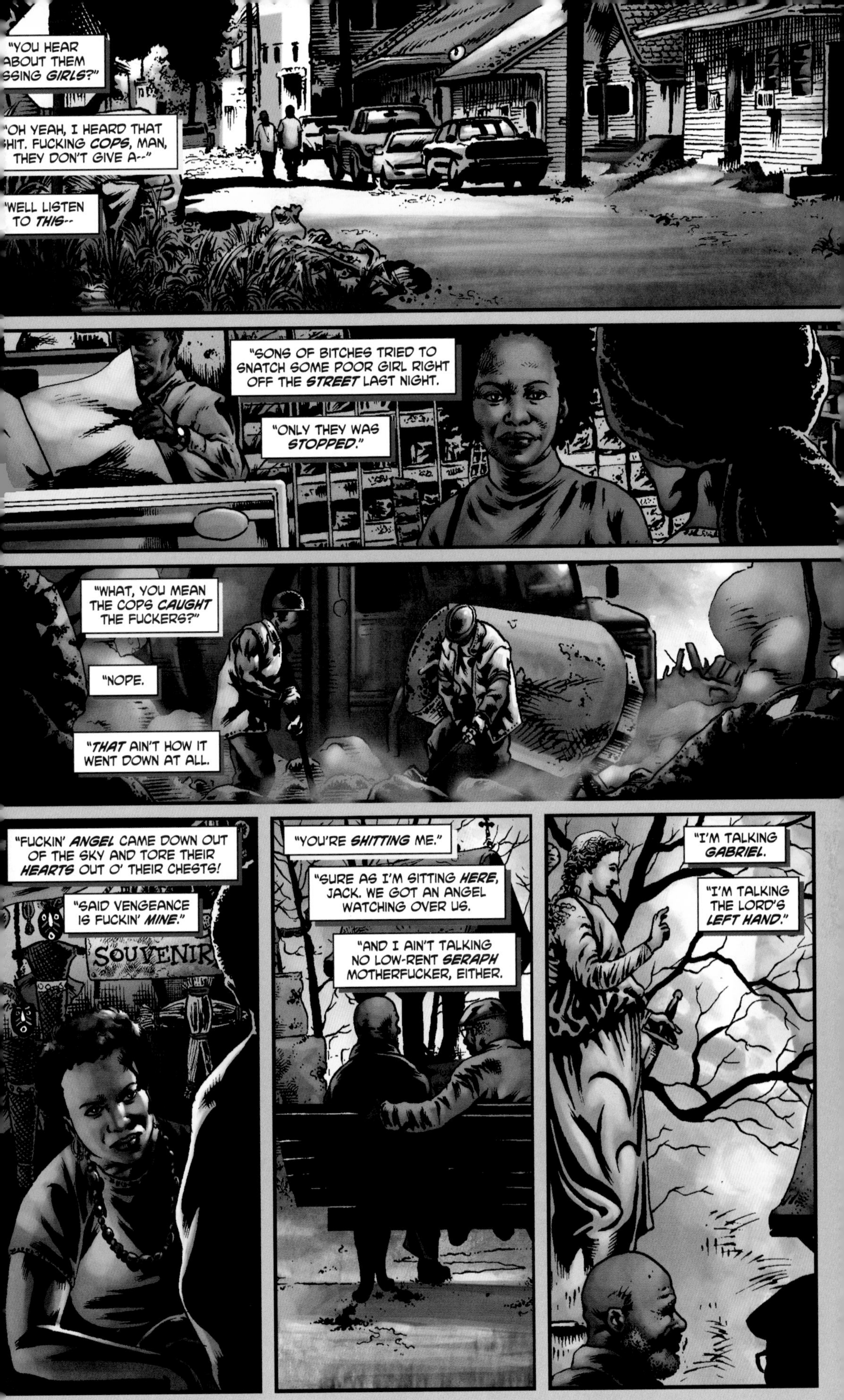
"YOU HEAR ABOUT THEM SSING GIRLS?"
"OH YEAH, I HEARD THAT HIT. FUCKING COPS, MAN, THEY DON'T GIVE A--"
"WELL LISTEN TO THIS--
"SONS OF BITCHES TRIED TO SNATCH SOME POOR GIRL RIGHT OFF THE STREET LAST NIGHT.
"ONLY THEY WAS STOPPED."
"WHAT, YOU MEAN THE COPS CAUGHT THE FUCKERS?"
"NOPE.
"THAT AIN'T HOW IT WENT DOWN AT ALL.
"FUCKIN' ANGEL CAME DOWN OUT OF THE SKY AND TORE THEIR HEARTS OUT O' THEIR CHESTS!
"SAID VENGEANCE IS FUCKIN' MINE."
SOUVENIR
"YOU'RE SHITTING ME."
"SURE AS I'M SITTING HERE, JACK. WE GOT AN ANGEL WATCHING OVER US.
"AND I AIN'T TALKING NO LOW-RENT SERAPH MOTHERFUCKER, EITHER.
"I'M TALKING GABRIEL.
"I'M TALKING THE LORD'S LEFT HAND."

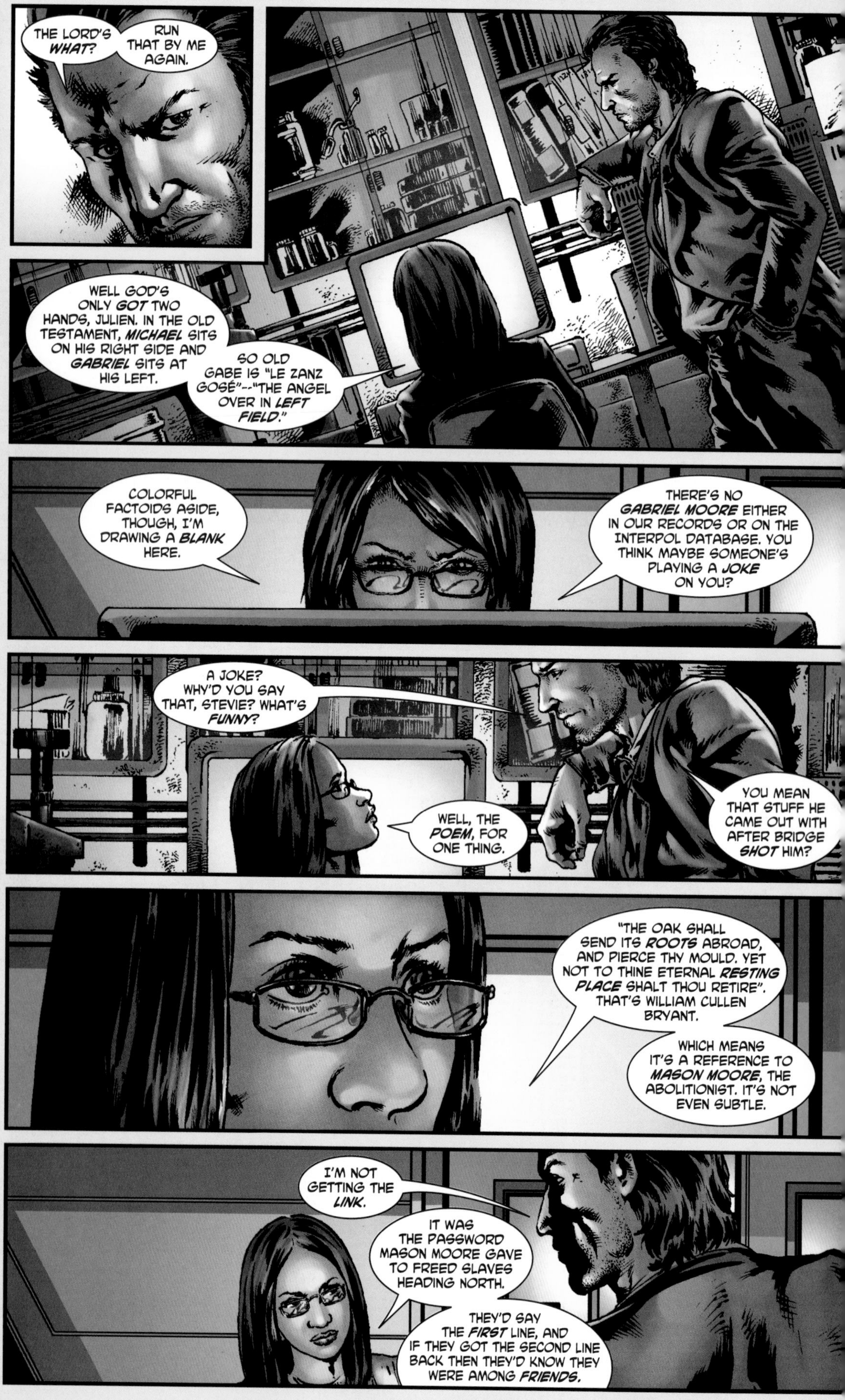
THE LORD'S *WHAT?*
RUN THAT BY ME AGAIN.
WELL GOD'S ONLY *GOT* TWO HANDS, JULIEN. IN THE OLD TESTAMENT, *MICHAEL* SITS ON HIS RIGHT SIDE AND *GABRIEL* SITS AT HIS LEFT.
SO OLD GABE IS "LE ZANZ GOSÉ"--"THE ANGEL OVER IN *LEFT FIELD.*"
COLORFUL FACTOIDS ASIDE, THOUGH, I'M DRAWING A *BLANK* HERE.
THERE'S NO *GABRIEL MOORE* EITHER IN OUR RECORDS OR ON THE INTERPOL DATABASE. YOU THINK MAYBE SOMEONE'S PLAYING A *JOKE* ON YOU?
A JOKE? WHY'D YOU SAY THAT, STEVIE? WHAT'S *FUNNY?*
WELL, THE *POEM*, FOR ONE THING.
YOU MEAN THAT STUFF HE CAME OUT WITH AFTER BRIDGE *SHOT* HIM?
"THE OAK SHALL SEND ITS *ROOTS* ABROAD, AND PIERCE THY MOULD. YET NOT TO THINE ETERNAL *RESTING PLACE* SHALT THOU RETIRE". THAT'S WILLIAM CULLEN BRYANT.
WHICH MEANS IT'S A REFERENCE TO *MASON MOORE*, THE ABOLITIONIST. IT'S NOT EVEN SUBTLE.
I'M NOT GETTING THE *LINK*.
IT WAS THE PASSWORD MASON MOORE GAVE TO FREED SLAVES HEADING NORTH.
THEY'D SAY THE *FIRST* LINE, AND IF THEY GOT THE SECOND LINE BACK THEN THEY'D KNOW THEY WERE AMONG *FRIENDS.*

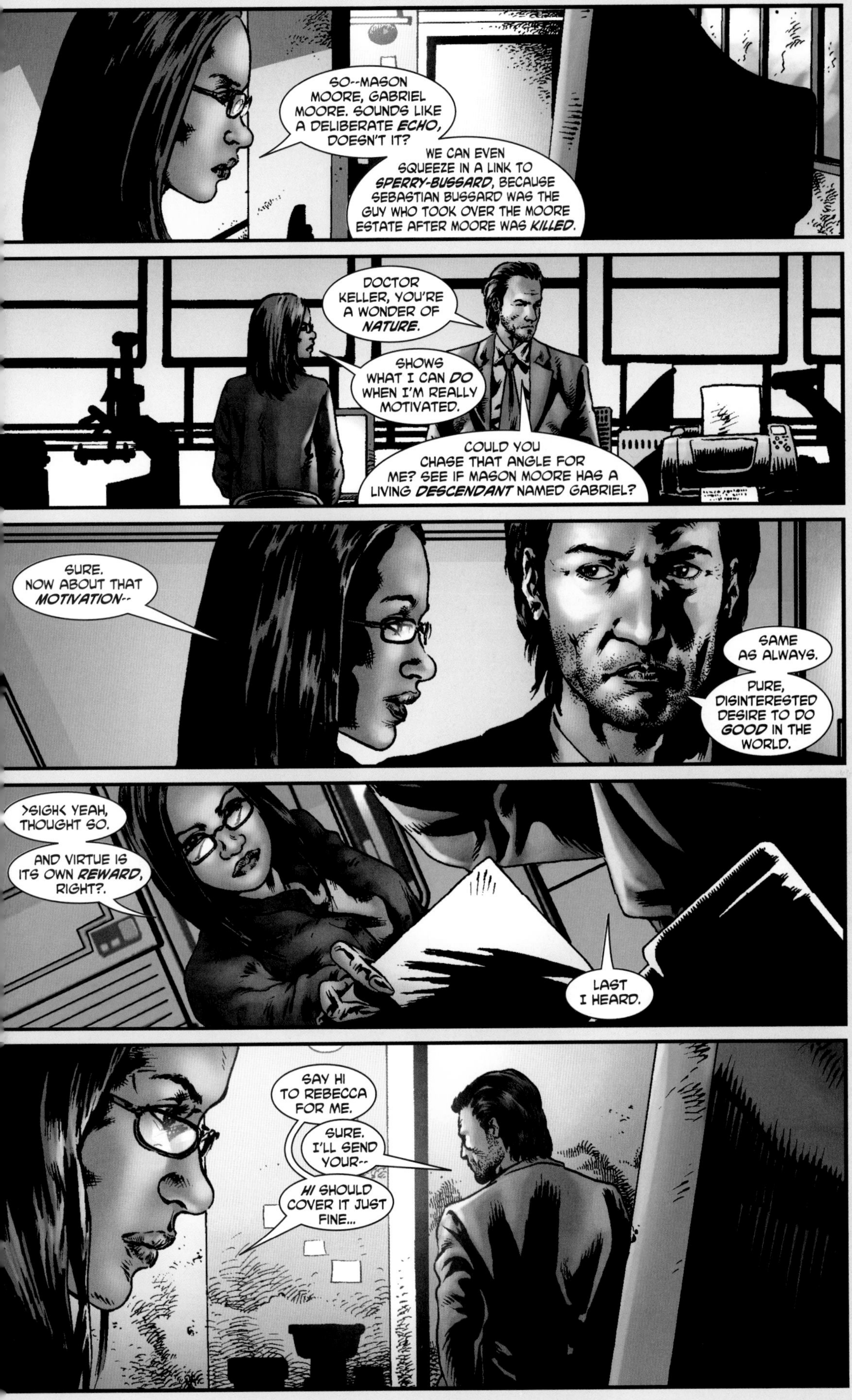
SO--MASON MOORE, GABRIEL MOORE. SOUNDS LIKE A DELIBERATE *ECHO*, DOESN'T IT?
WE CAN EVEN SQUEEZE IN A LINK TO *SPERRY-BUSSARD*, BECAUSE SEBASTIAN BUSSARD WAS THE GUY WHO TOOK OVER THE MOORE ESTATE AFTER MOORE WAS *KILLED*.
DOCTOR KELLER, YOU'RE A WONDER OF *NATURE*.
SHOWS WHAT I CAN *DO* WHEN I'M REALLY MOTIVATED.
COULD YOU CHASE THAT ANGLE FOR ME? SEE IF MASON MOORE HAS A LIVING *DESCENDANT* NAMED GABRIEL?
SURE. NOW ABOUT THAT *MOTIVATION*--
SAME AS ALWAYS.
PURE, DISINTERESTED DESIRE TO DO *GOOD* IN THE WORLD.
>SIGH< YEAH, THOUGHT SO.
AND VIRTUE IS ITS OWN *REWARD*, RIGHT?.
LAST I HEARD.
SAY HI TO REBECCA FOR ME.
SURE. I'LL SEND YOUR--
HI SHOULD COVER IT JUST FINE...

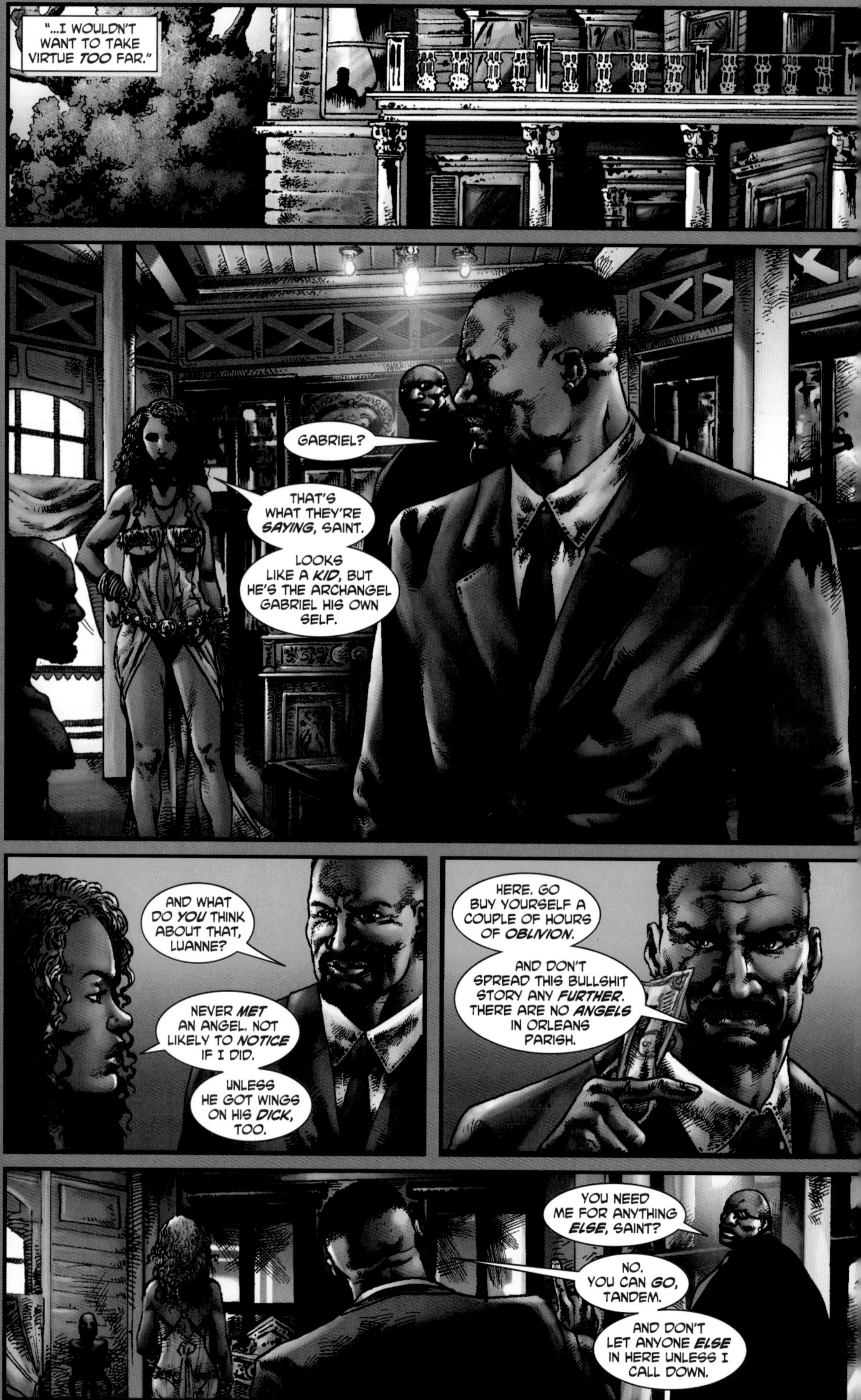
"...I WOULDN'T WANT TO TAKE VIRTUE *TOO* FAR."
GABRIEL?
THAT'S WHAT THEY'RE *SAYING*, SAINT.
LOOKS LIKE A *KID*, BUT HE'S THE ARCHANGEL GABRIEL HIS OWN SELF.
AND WHAT DO *YOU* THINK ABOUT THAT, LUANNE?
NEVER *MET* AN ANGEL. NOT LIKELY TO *NOTICE* IF I DID.
UNLESS HE GOT WINGS ON HIS *DICK*, TOO.
HERE. GO BUY YOURSELF A COUPLE OF HOURS OF *OBLIVION*.
AND DON'T SPREAD THIS BULLSHIT STORY ANY *FURTHER*. THERE ARE NO *ANGELS* IN ORLEANS PARISH.
YOU NEED ME FOR ANYTHING *ELSE*, SAINT?
NO. YOU CAN *GO*, TANDEM.
AND DON'T LET ANYONE *ELSE* IN HERE UNLESS I CALL DOWN.

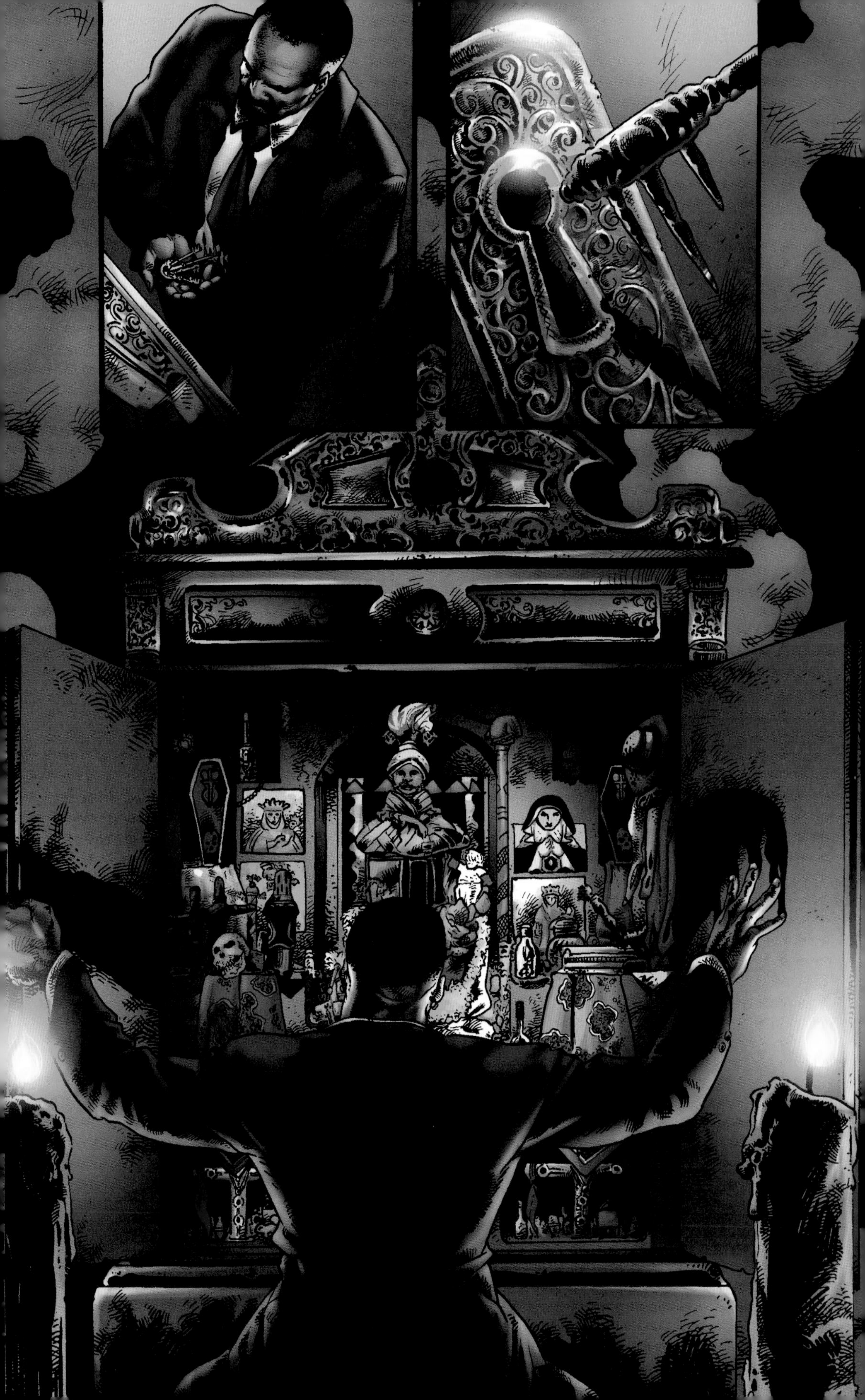

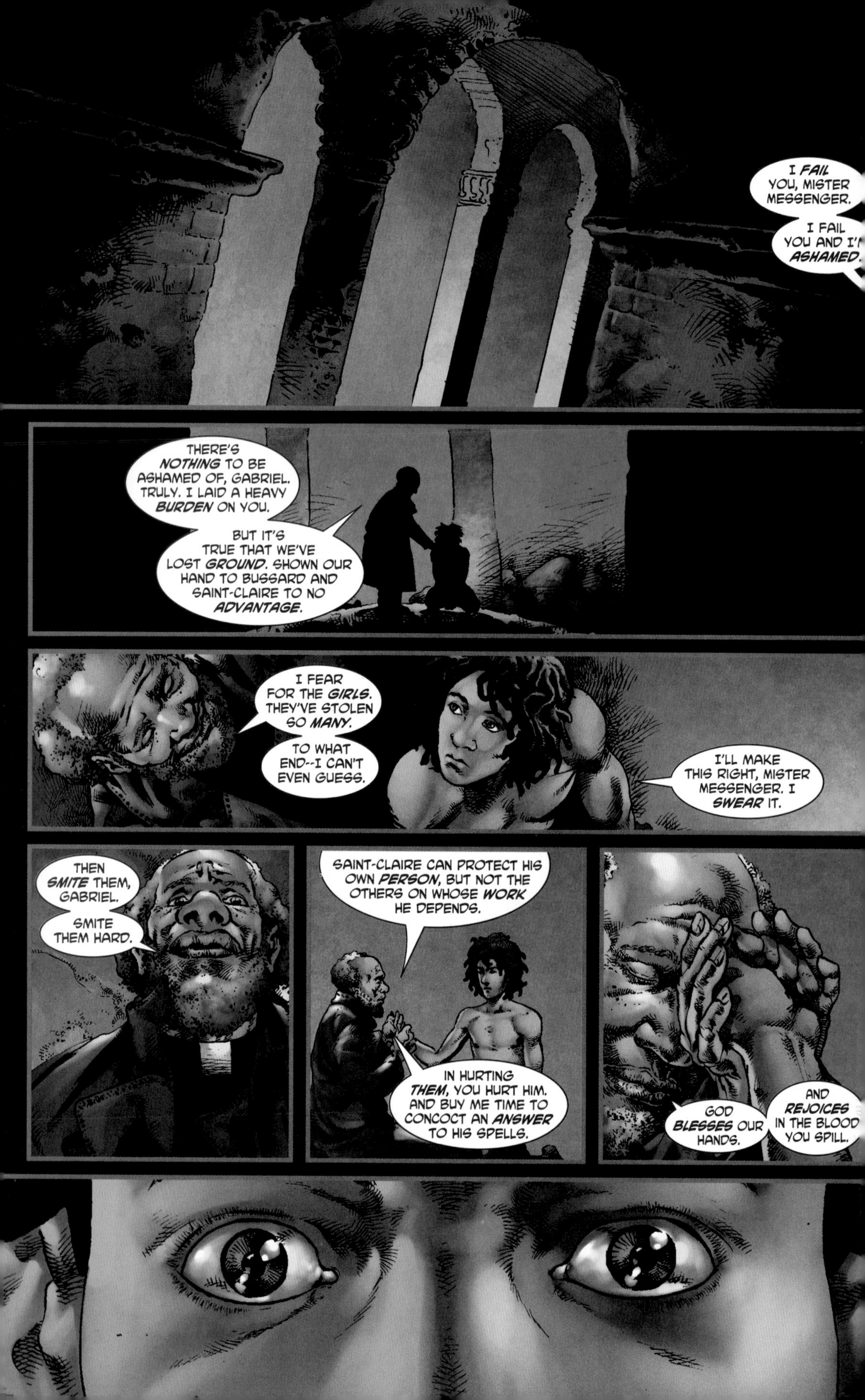
I FAIL YOU, MISTER MESSENGER.
I FAIL YOU AND I'M ASHAMED.
THERE'S NOTHING TO BE ASHAMED OF, GABRIEL. TRULY. I LAID A HEAVY BURDEN ON YOU.
BUT IT'S TRUE THAT WE'VE LOST GROUND. SHOWN OUR HAND TO BUSSARD AND SAINT-CLAIRE TO NO ADVANTAGE.
I FEAR FOR THE GIRLS. THEY'VE STOLEN SO MANY.
TO WHAT END--I CAN'T EVEN GUESS.
I'LL MAKE THIS RIGHT, MISTER MESSENGER. I SWEAR IT.
THEN SMITE THEM, GABRIEL.
SMITE THEM HARD.
SAINT-CLAIRE CAN PROTECT HIS OWN PERSON, BUT NOT THE OTHERS ON WHOSE WORK HE DEPENDS.
IN HURTING THEM, YOU HURT HIM. AND BUY ME TIME TO CONCOCT AN ANSWER TO HIS SPELLS.
GOD BLESSES OUR HANDS.
AND REJOICES IN THE BLOOD YOU SPILL.

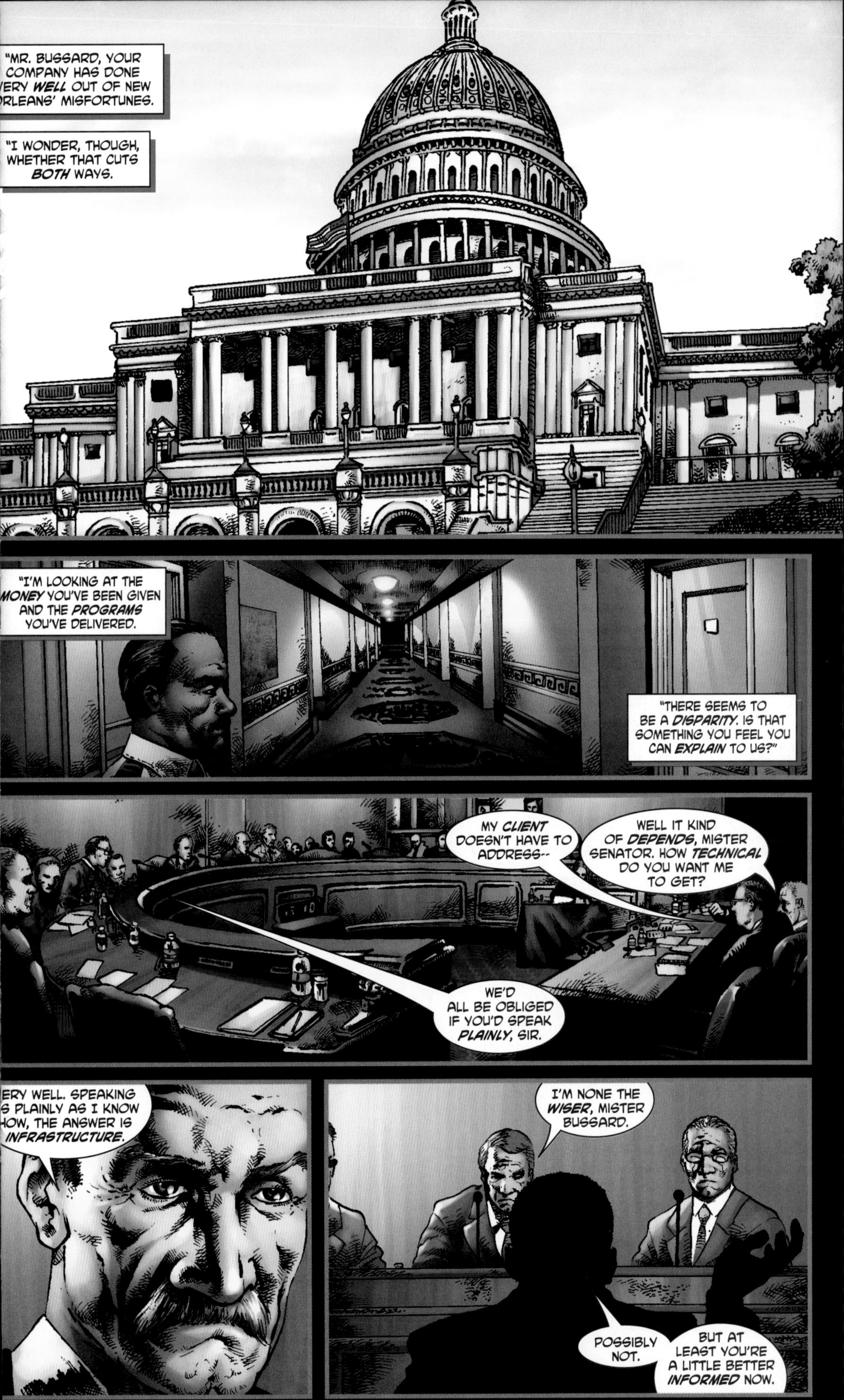
"MR. BUSSARD, YOUR COMPANY HAS DONE VERY WELL OUT OF NEW ORLEANS' MISFORTUNES.
"I WONDER, THOUGH, WHETHER THAT CUTS BOTH WAYS.
"I'M LOOKING AT THE MONEY YOU'VE BEEN GIVEN AND THE PROGRAMS YOU'VE DELIVERED.
"THERE SEEMS TO BE A DISPARITY. IS THAT SOMETHING YOU FEEL YOU CAN EXPLAIN TO US?"
MY CLIENT DOESN'T HAVE TO ADDRESS--
WE'D ALL BE OBLIGED IF YOU'D SPEAK PLAINLY, SIR.
WELL IT KIND OF DEPENDS, MISTER SENATOR. HOW TECHNICAL DO YOU WANT ME TO GET?
ERY WELL. SPEAKING S PLAINLY AS I KNOW HOW, THE ANSWER IS INFRASTRUCTURE.
I'M NONE THE WISER, MISTER BUSSARD.
POSSIBLY NOT.
BUT AT LEAST YOU'RE A LITTLE BETTER INFORMED NOW.

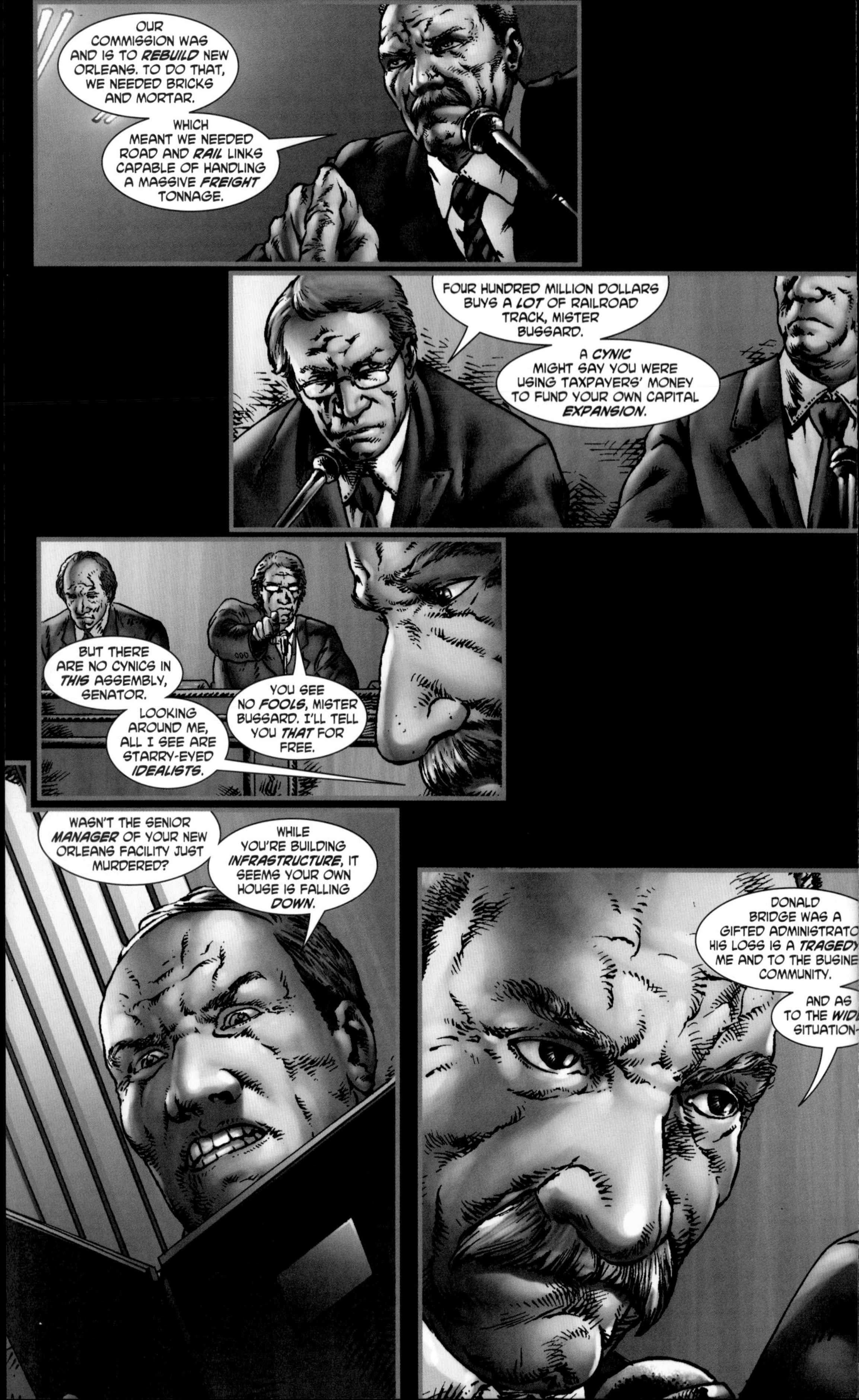
OUR COMMISSION WAS AND IS TO *REBUILD* NEW ORLEANS. TO DO THAT, WE NEEDED BRICKS AND MORTAR.
WHICH MEANT WE NEEDED ROAD AND *RAIL* LINKS CAPABLE OF HANDLING A MASSIVE *FREIGHT* TONNAGE.
FOUR HUNDRED MILLION DOLLARS BUYS A *LOT* OF RAILROAD TRACK, MISTER BUSSARD.
A *CYNIC* MIGHT SAY YOU WERE USING TAXPAYERS' MONEY TO FUND YOUR OWN CAPITAL *EXPANSION*.
BUT THERE ARE NO CYNICS IN *THIS* ASSEMBLY, SENATOR.
LOOKING AROUND ME, ALL I SEE ARE STARRY-EYED *IDEALISTS*.
YOU SEE NO *FOOLS*, MISTER BUSSARD. I'LL TELL YOU *THAT* FOR FREE.
WASN'T THE SENIOR *MANAGER* OF YOUR NEW ORLEANS FACILITY JUST MURDERED?
WHILE YOU'RE BUILDING *INFRASTRUCTURE*, IT SEEMS YOUR OWN HOUSE IS FALLING *DOWN*.
DONALD BRIDGE WAS A GIFTED ADMINISTRATO HIS LOSS IS A *TRAGED* ME AND TO THE BUSINE COMMUNITY.
AND AS TO THE *WID* SITUATION-

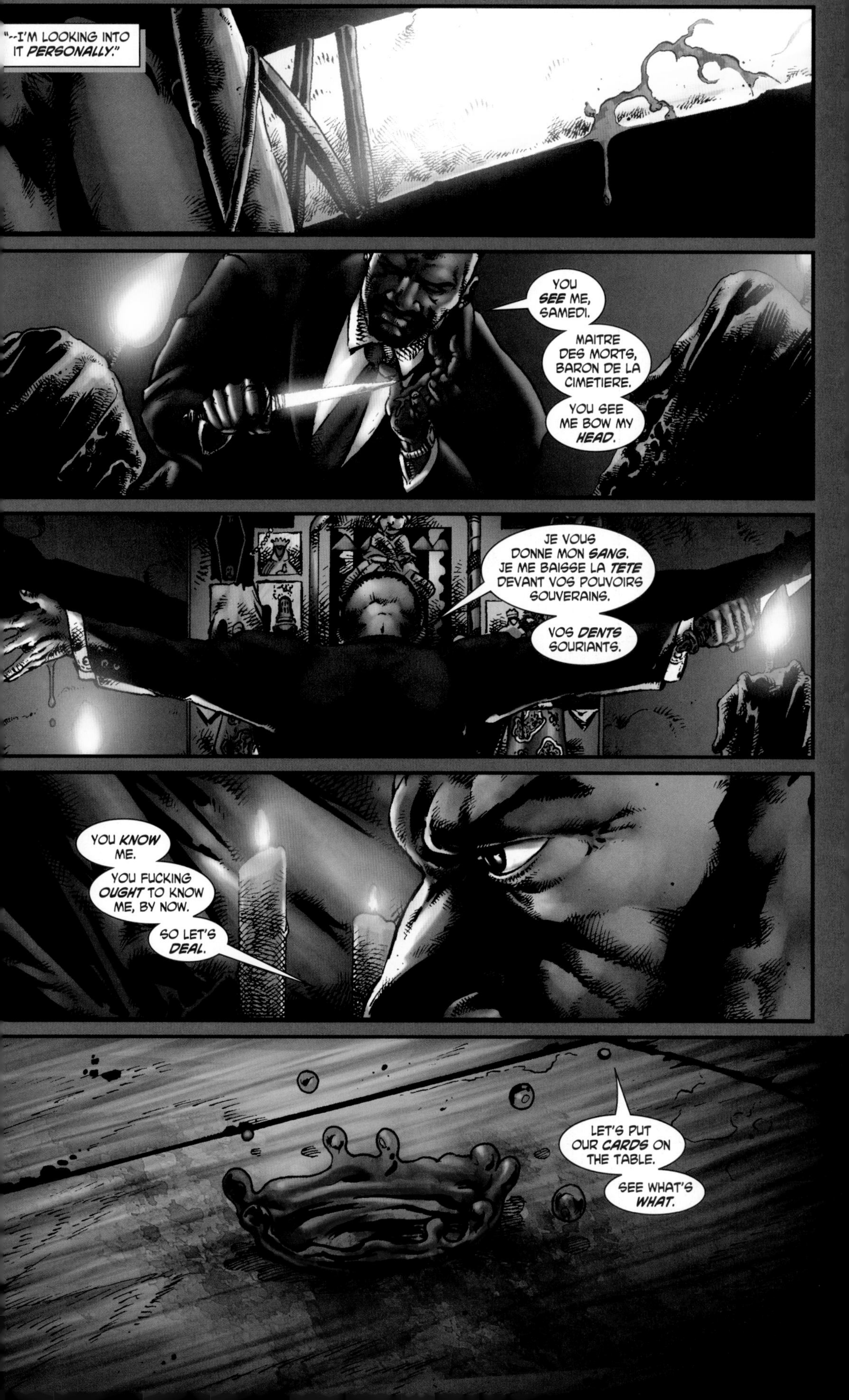
"--I'M LOOKING INTO IT PERSONALLY."
YOU SEE ME, SAMEDI.
MAITRE DES MORTS, BARON DE LA CIMETIERE.
YOU SEE ME BOW MY HEAD.
JE VOUS DONNE MON SANG. JE ME BAISSE LA TETE DEVANT VOS POUVOIRS SOUVERAINS.
VOS DENTS SOURIANTS.
YOU KNOW ME.
YOU FUCKING OUGHT TO KNOW ME, BY NOW.
SO LET'S DEAL.
LET'S PUT OUR CARDS ON THE TABLE.
SEE WHAT'S WHAT.

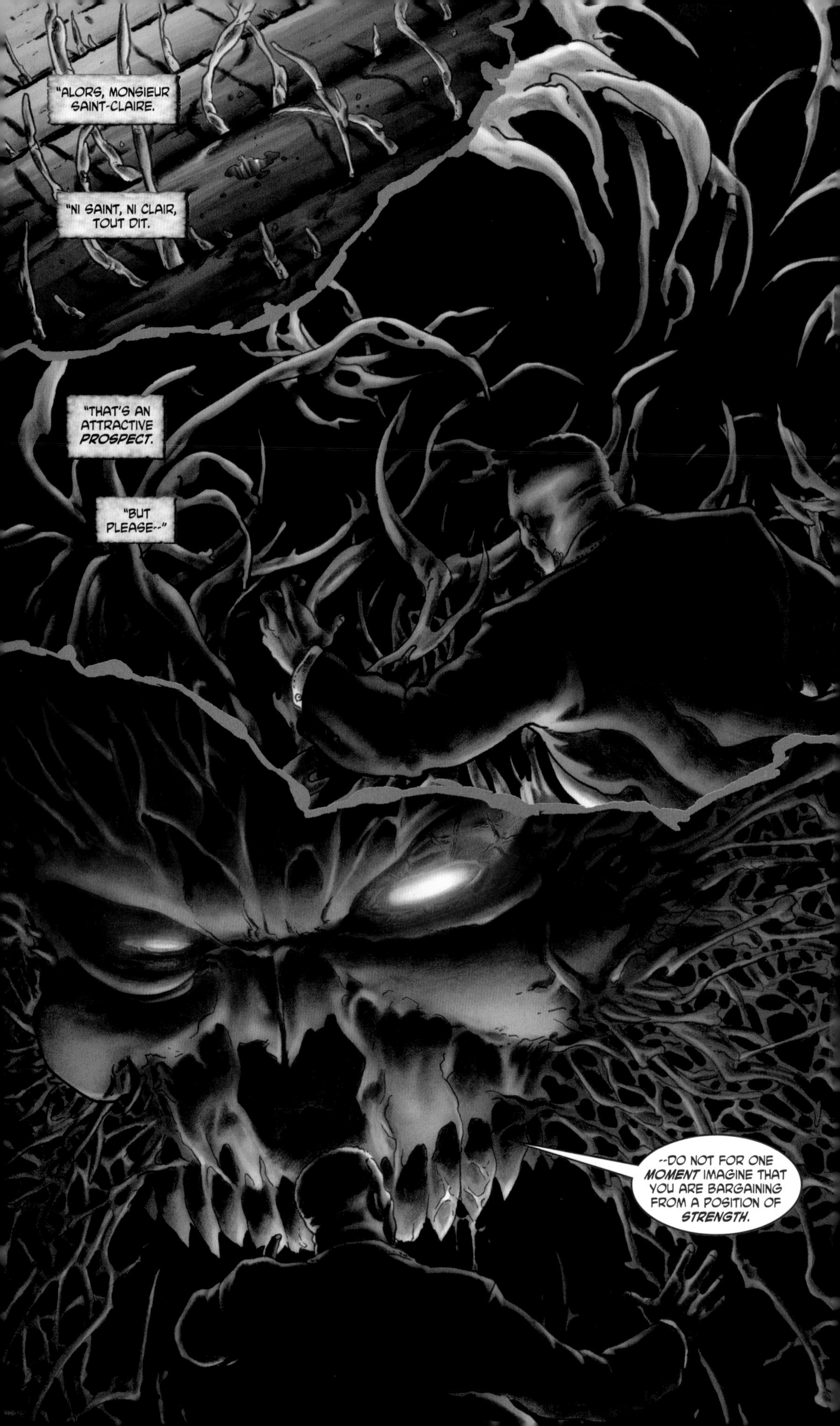
"ALORS, MONSIEUR SAINT-CLAIRE.
"NI SAINT, NI CLAIR, TOUT DIT.
"THAT'S AN ATTRACTIVE *PROSPECT*.
"BUT PLEASE--"
--DO NOT FOR ONE *MOMENT* IMAGINE THAT YOU ARE BARGAINING FROM A POSITION OF *STRENGTH*.

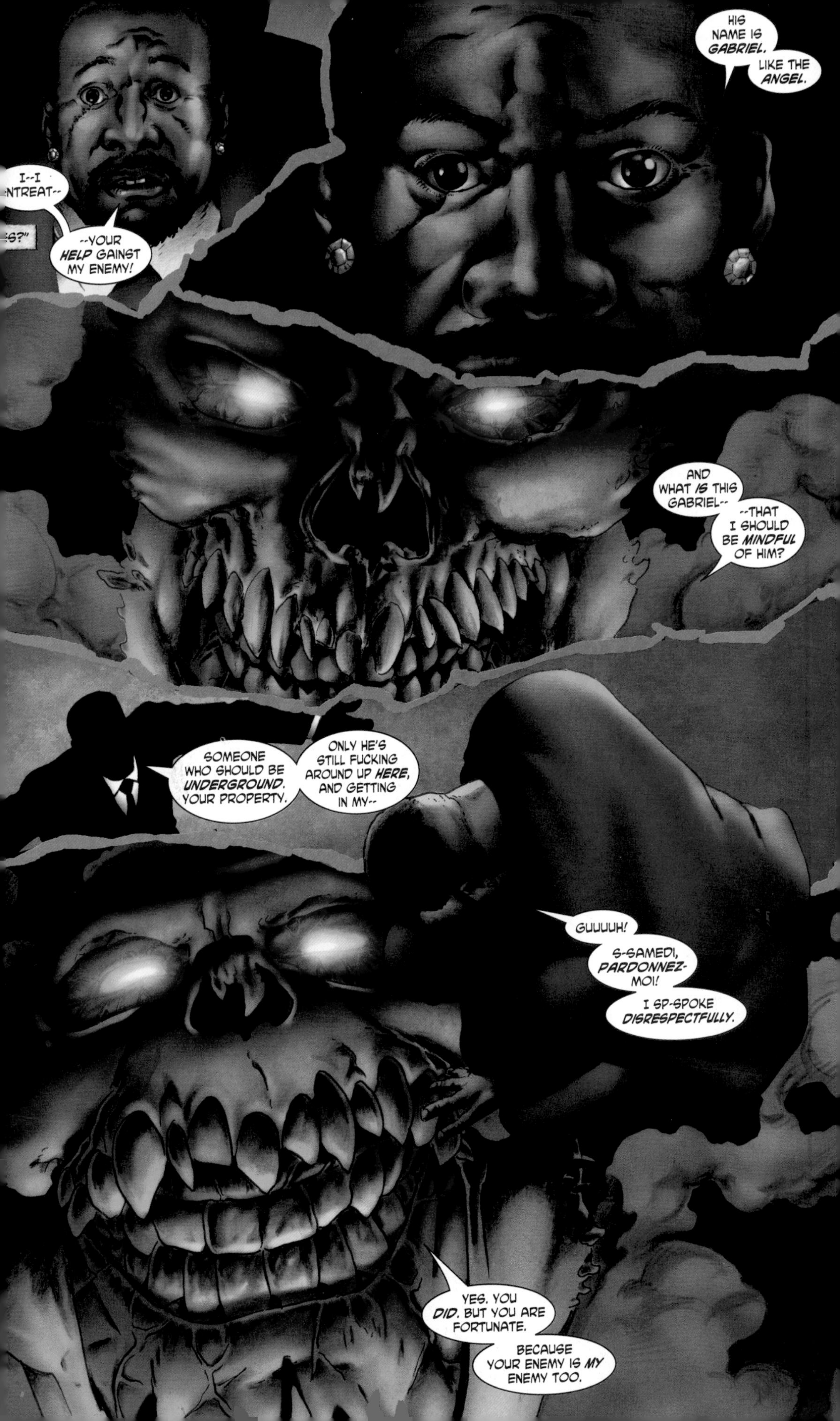
HIS NAME IS GABRIEL.
LIKE THE ANGEL.
I--I ENTREAT--
--YOUR HELP GAINST MY ENEMY!
AND WHAT IS THIS GABRIEL--
--THAT I SHOULD BE MINDFUL OF HIM?
SOMEONE WHO SHOULD BE UNDERGROUND. YOUR PROPERTY.
ONLY HE'S STILL FUCKING AROUND UP HERE, AND GETTING IN MY--
GUUUUH!
S-SAMEDI, PARDONNEZ-MOI!
I SP-SPOKE DISRESPECTFULLY.
YES. YOU DID. BUT YOU ARE FORTUNATE.
BECAUSE YOUR ENEMY IS MY ENEMY TOO.

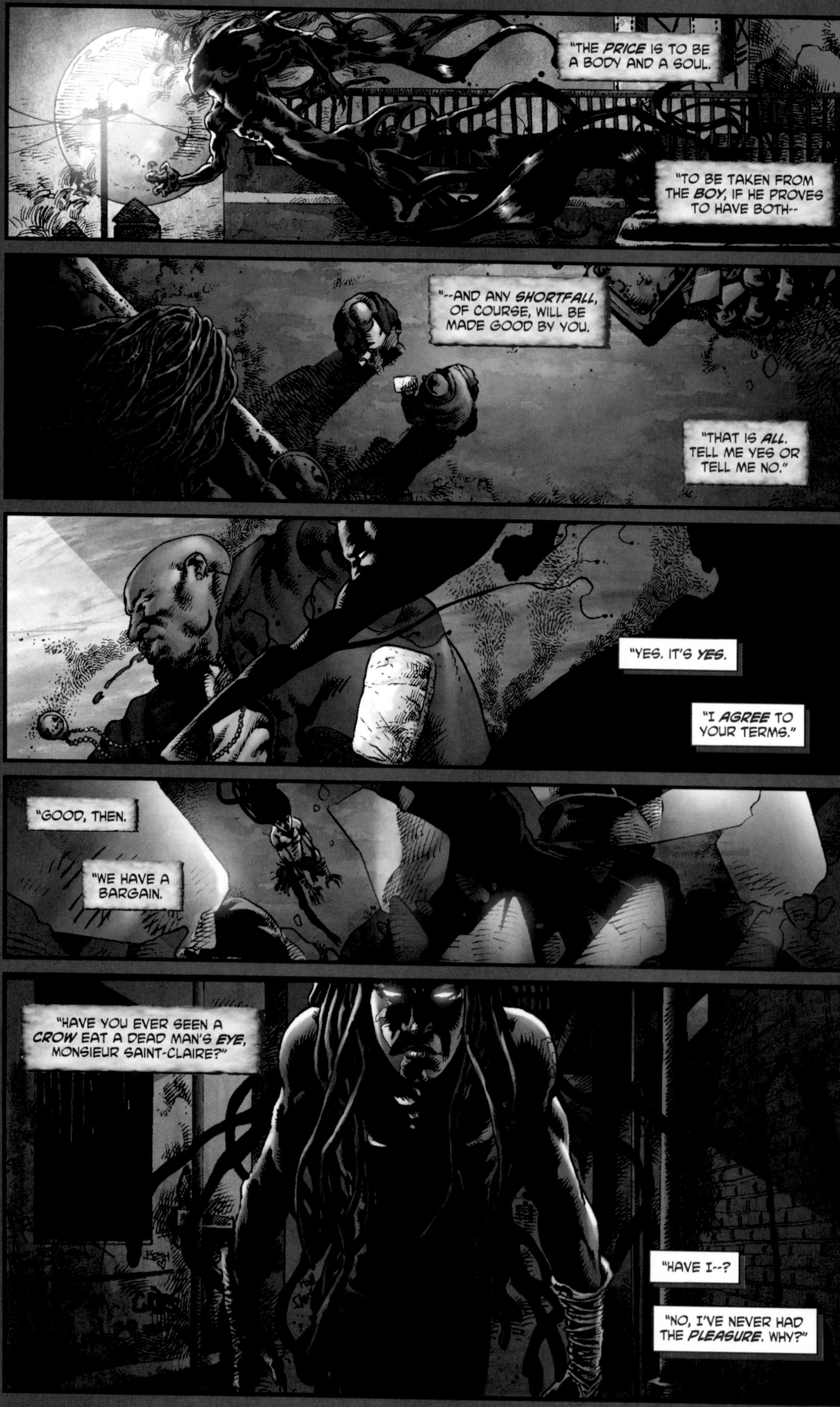
"THE PRICE IS TO BE A BODY AND A SOUL.
"TO BE TAKEN FROM THE BOY, IF HE PROVES TO HAVE BOTH--
"--AND ANY SHORTFALL, OF COURSE, WILL BE MADE GOOD BY YOU.
"THAT IS ALL. TELL ME YES OR TELL ME NO."
"YES. IT'S YES.
"I AGREE TO YOUR TERMS."
"GOOD, THEN.
"WE HAVE A BARGAIN.
"HAVE YOU EVER SEEN A CROW EAT A DEAD MAN'S EYE, MONSIEUR SAINT-CLAIRE?"
"HAVE I--?
"NO, I'VE NEVER HAD THE PLEASURE. WHY?"

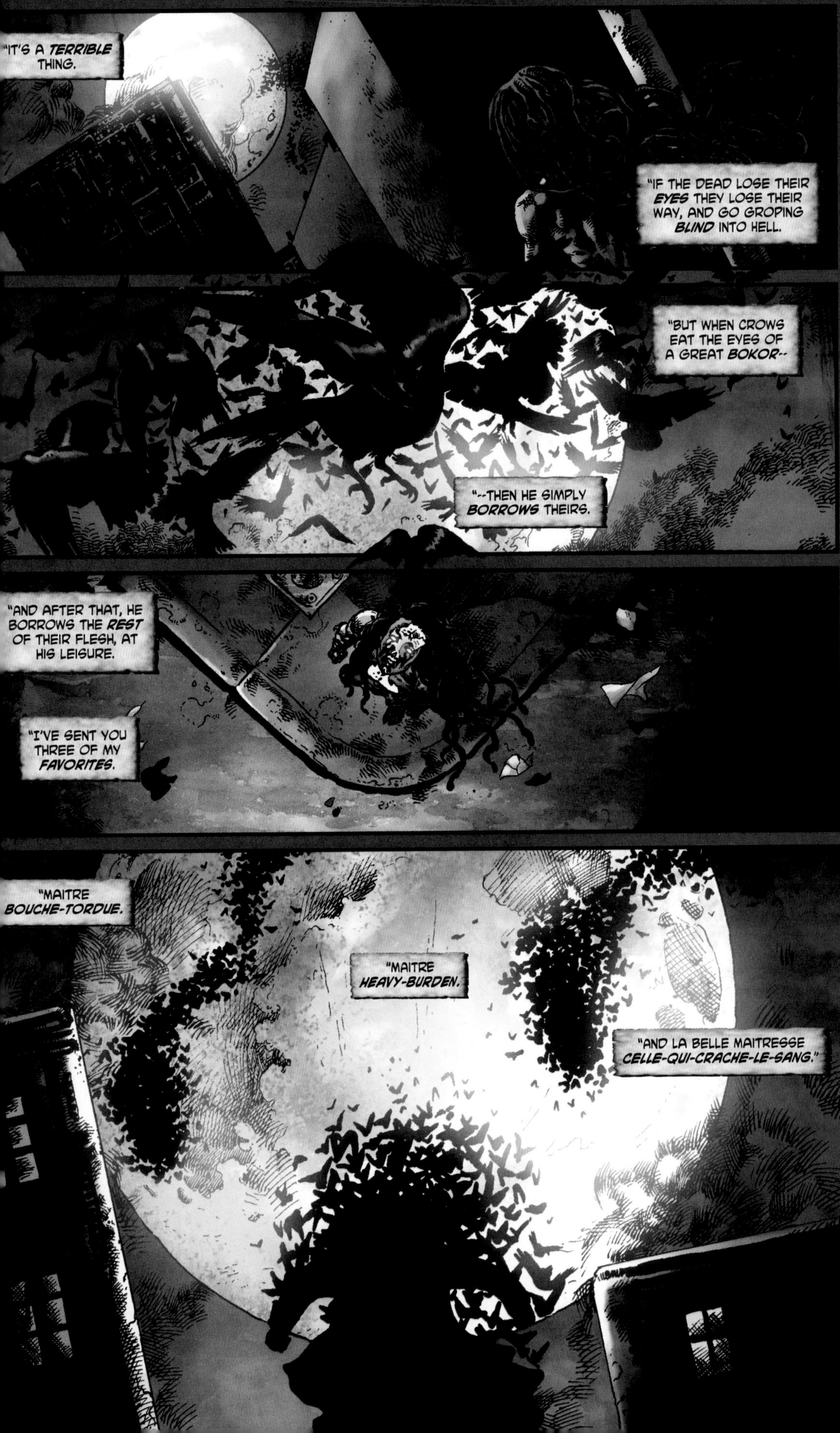
"IT'S A TERRIBLE THING.
"IF THE DEAD LOSE THEIR EYES THEY LOSE THEIR WAY, AND GO GROPING BLIND INTO HELL.
"BUT WHEN CROWS EAT THE EYES OF A GREAT BOKOR--
"--THEN HE SIMPLY BORROWS THEIRS.
"AND AFTER THAT, HE BORROWS THE REST OF THEIR FLESH, AT HIS LEISURE.
"I'VE SENT YOU THREE OF MY FAVORITES.
"MAITRE BOUCHE-TORDUE.
"MAITRE HEAVY-BURDEN.
"AND LA BELLE MAITRESSE CELLE-QUI-CRACHE-LE-SANG."

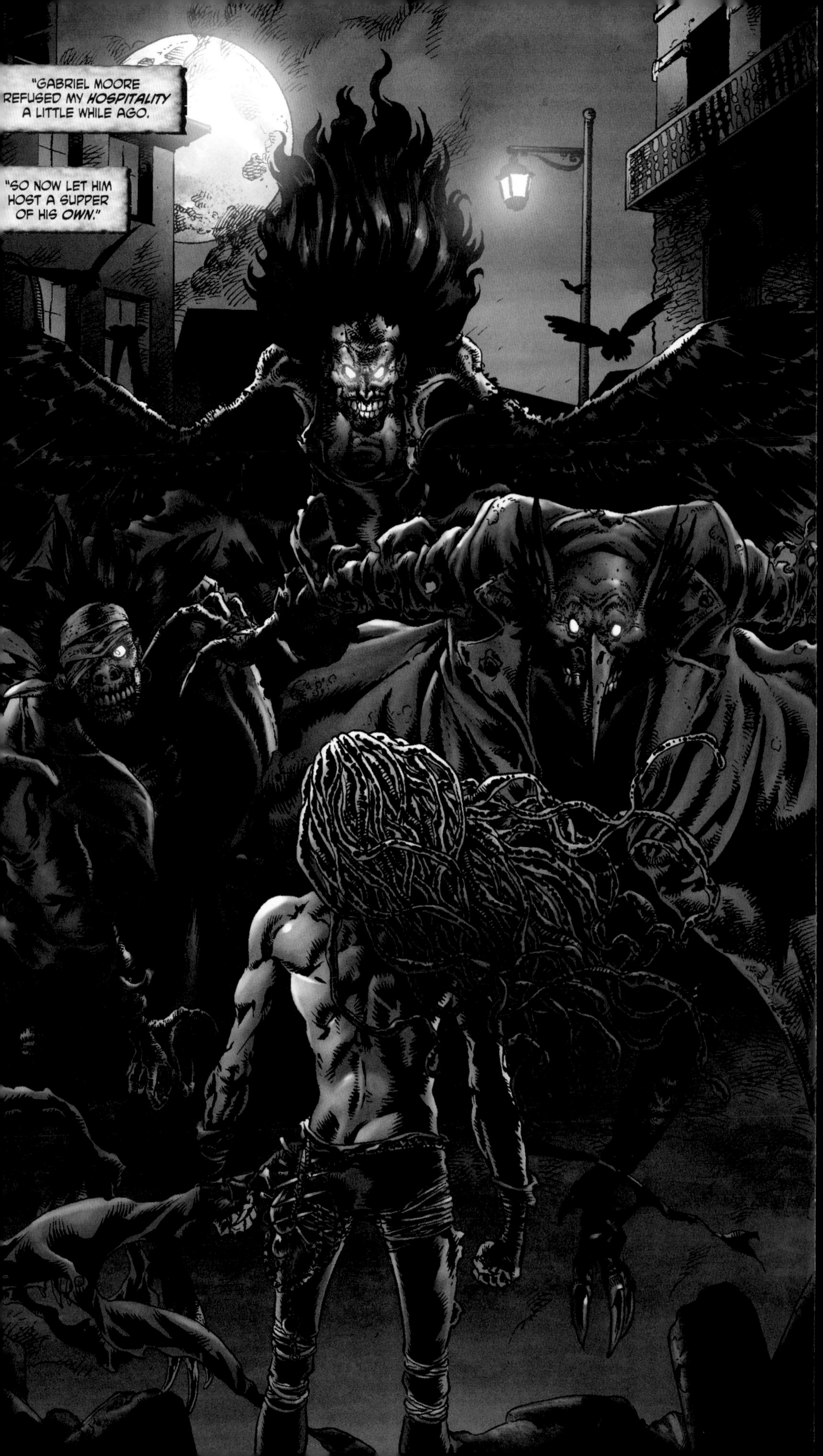
"GABRIEL MOORE REFUSED MY HOSPITALITY A LITTLE WHILE AGO.
"SO NOW LET HIM HOST A SUPPER OF HIS OWN."

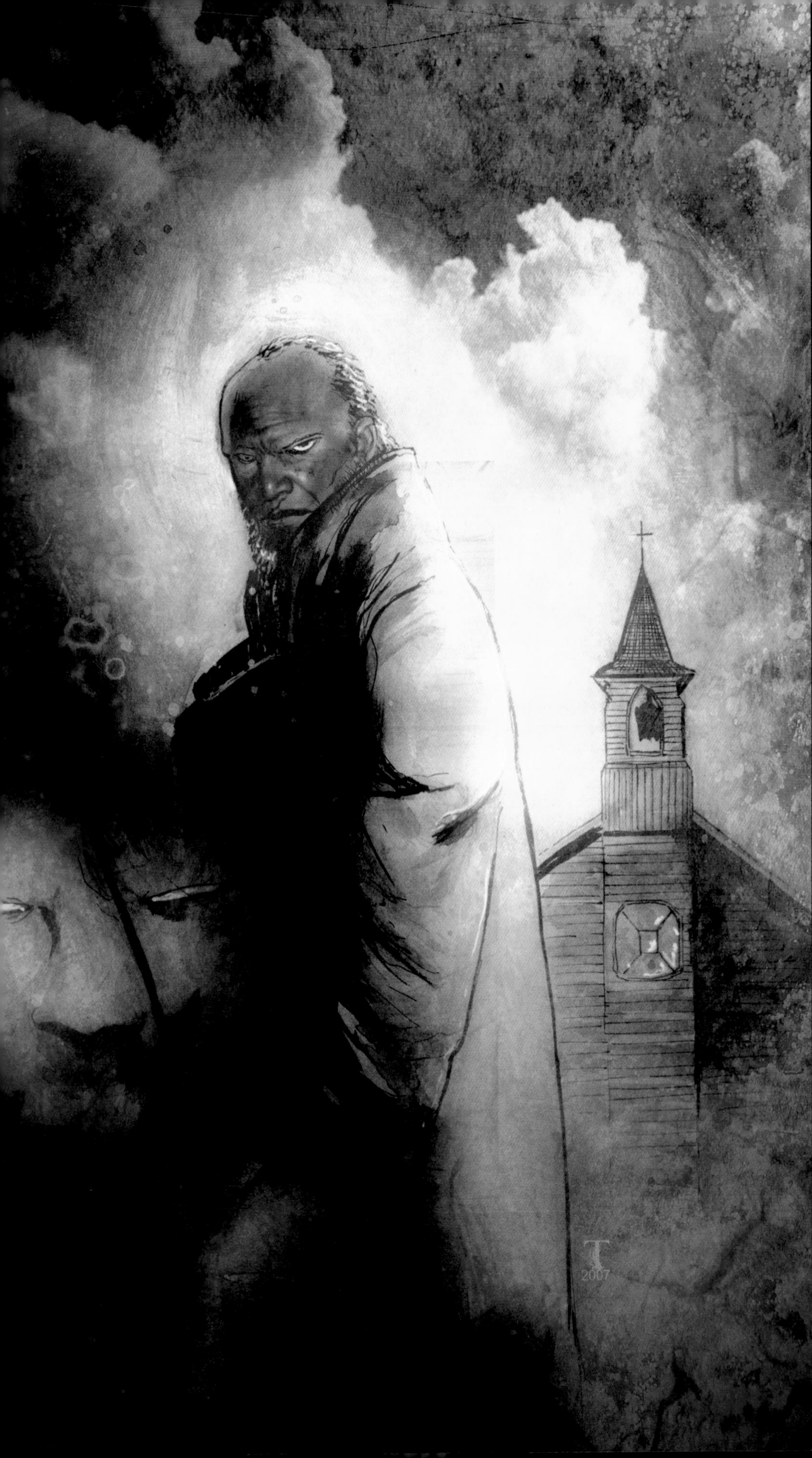

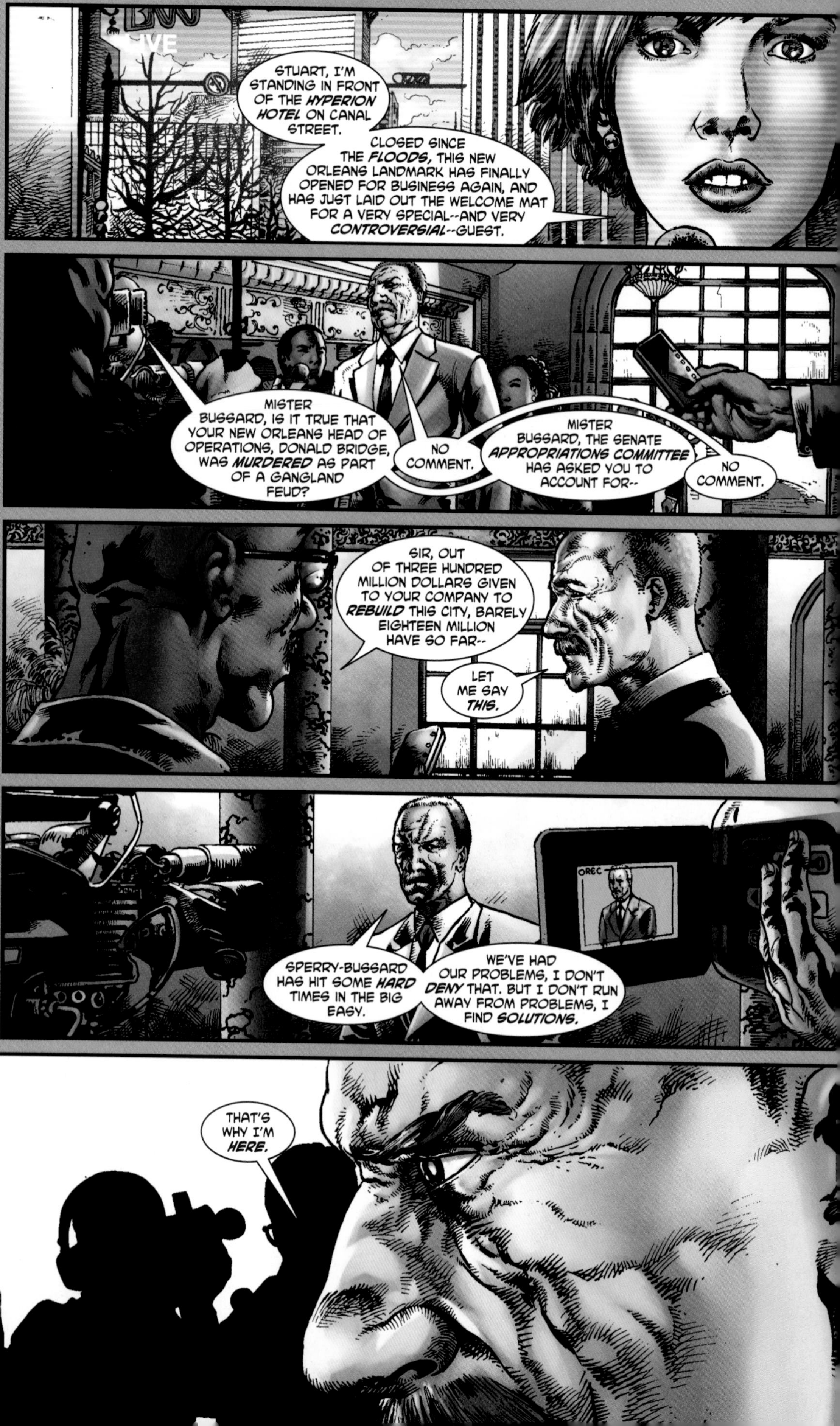
LIVE
STUART, I'M STANDING IN FRONT OF THE HYPERION HOTEL ON CANAL STREET.
CLOSED SINCE THE FLOODS, THIS NEW ORLEANS LANDMARK HAS FINALLY OPENED FOR BUSINESS AGAIN, AND HAS JUST LAID OUT THE WELCOME MAT FOR A VERY SPECIAL--AND VERY CONTROVERSIAL--GUEST.
MISTER BUSSARD, IS IT TRUE THAT YOUR NEW ORLEANS HEAD OF OPERATIONS, DONALD BRIDGE, WAS MURDERED AS PART OF A GANGLAND FEUD?
NO COMMENT.
MISTER BUSSARD, THE SENATE APPROPRIATIONS COMMITTEE HAS ASKED YOU TO ACCOUNT FOR--
NO COMMENT.
SIR, OUT OF THREE HUNDRED MILLION DOLLARS GIVEN TO YOUR COMPANY TO REBUILD THIS CITY, BARELY EIGHTEEN MILLION HAVE SO FAR--
LET ME SAY THIS.
REC
SPERRY-BUSSARD HAS HIT SOME HARD TIMES IN THE BIG EASY.
WE'VE HAD OUR PROBLEMS, I DON'T DENY THAT. BUT I DON'T RUN AWAY FROM PROBLEMS, I FIND SOLUTIONS.
THAT'S WHY I'M HERE.

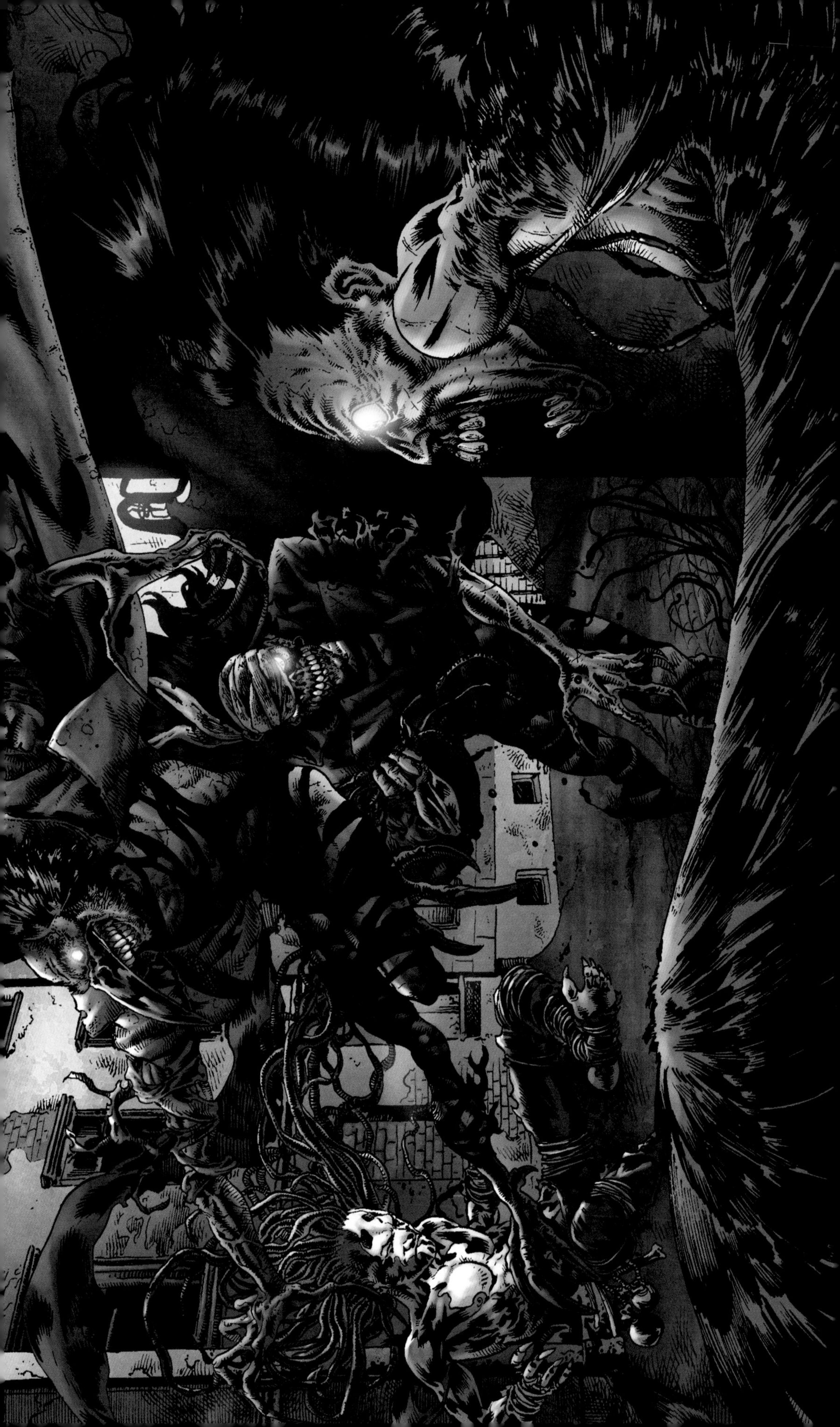

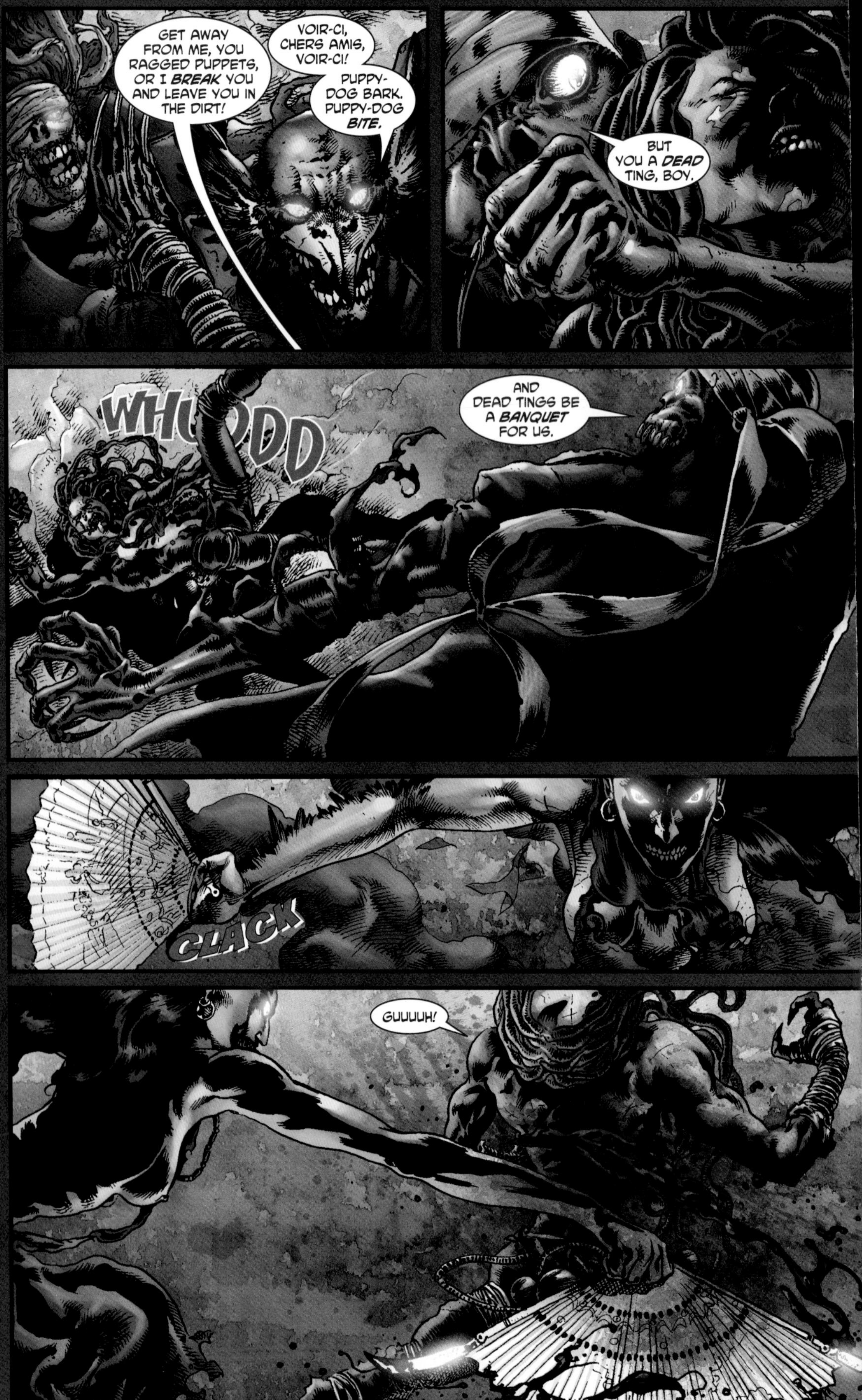
GET AWAY FROM ME, YOU RAGGED PUPPETS, OR I BREAK YOU AND LEAVE YOU IN THE DIRT!
VOIR-CI, CHERS AMIS, VOIR-CI!
PUPPY-DOG BARK. PUPPY-DOG BITE.
BUT YOU A DEAD TING, BOY.
WHUDDD
AND DEAD TINGS BE A BANQUET FOR US.
CLACK
GUUUUH!

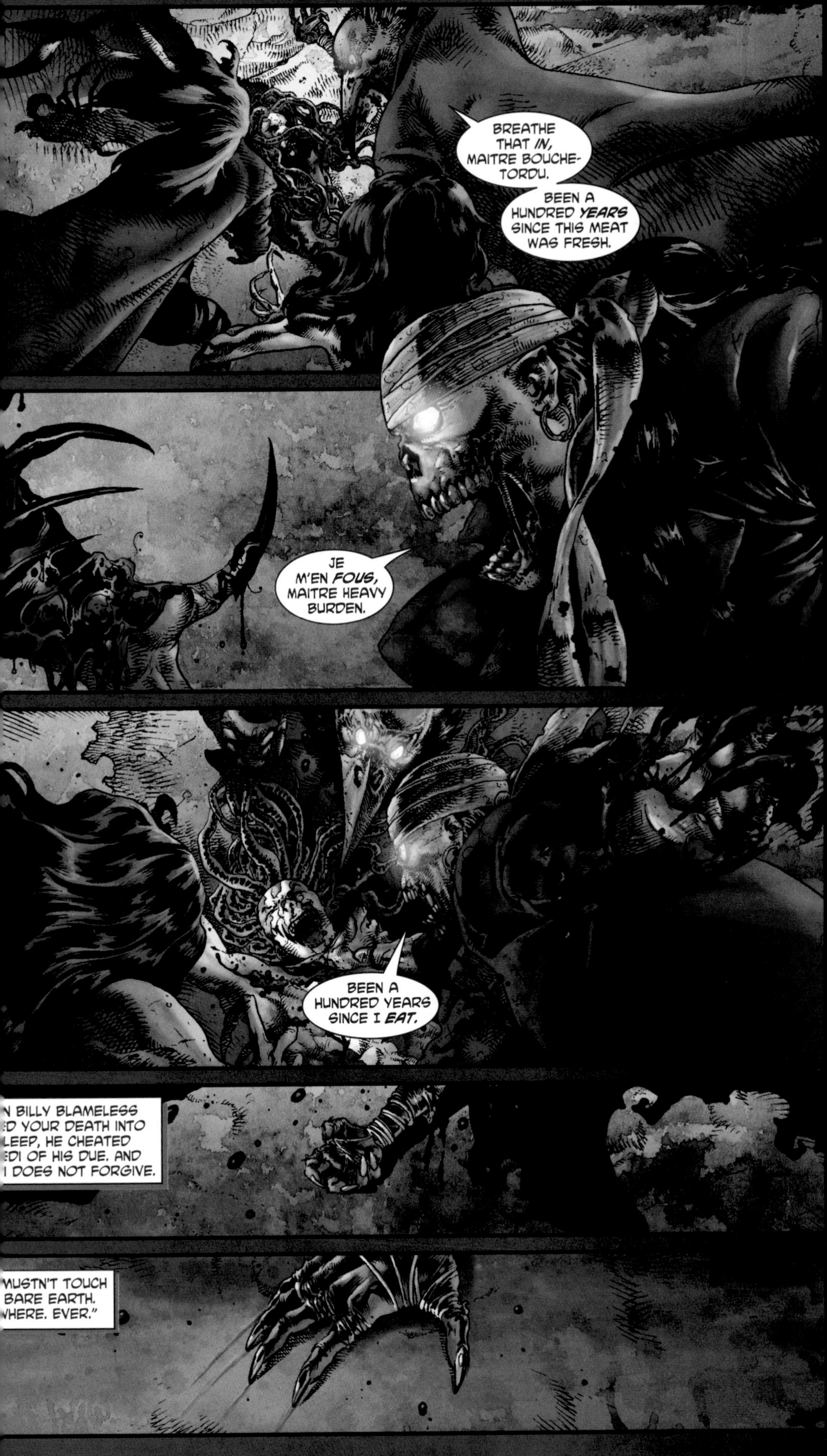
BREATHE THAT IN, MAITRE BOUCHE-TORDU.
BEEN A HUNDRED YEARS SINCE THIS MEAT WAS FRESH.
JE M'EN FOUS, MAITRE HEAVY BURDEN.
BEEN A HUNDRED YEARS SINCE I EAT.
N BILLY BLAMELESS
ED YOUR DEATH INTO
LEEP, HE CHEATED
EDI OF HIS DUE. AND
I DOES NOT FORGIVE.
MUSTN'T TOUCH
BARE EARTH.
WHERE. EVER."

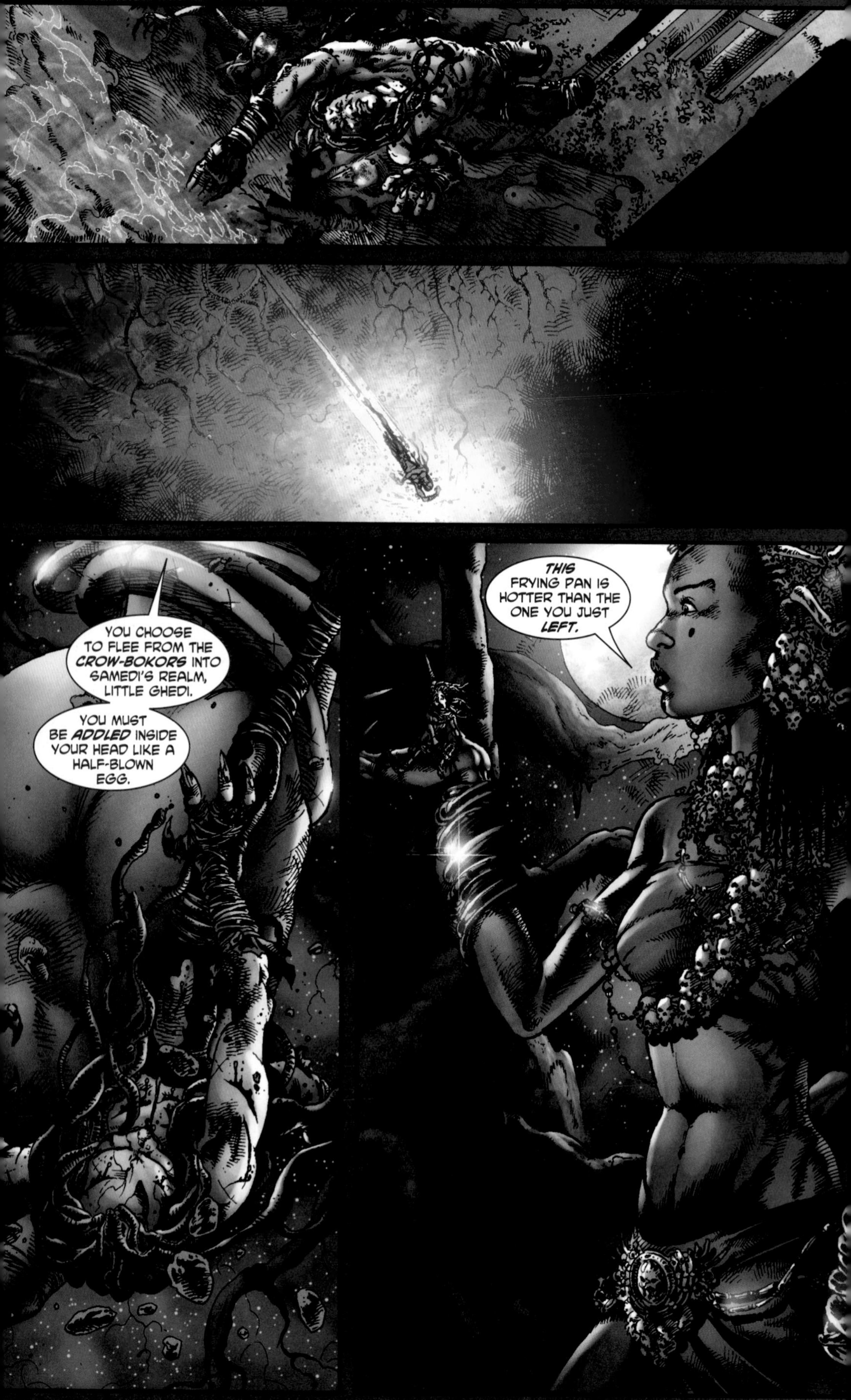

YOU CHOOSE TO FLEE FROM THE CROW-BOKORS INTO SAMEDI'S REALM, LITTLE GHEDI.
YOU MUST BE ADDLED INSIDE YOUR HEAD LIKE A HALF-BLOWN EGG.
THIS FRYING PAN IS HOTTER THAN THE ONE YOU JUST LEFT.

POLICE HEADQUARTERS, NEW ORLEANS' NINTH WARD.

--BELEAGUERED CEO *MARTIN BUSSARD* PROMISED THAT HE WON'T RUN FROM HIS COMPANY'S PROBLEMS, HE'LL FIND--

PRRT
PRRT
PRRT

LAND.

HEY, CHÈRE. YOU *WATCHING* THIS SHIT?

HEARING IT. JULIEN, WHERE THE HELL *ARE* YOU?

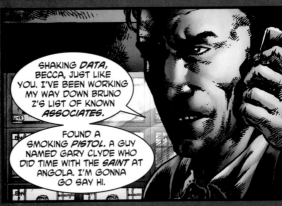

SHAKING *DATA*, BECCA, JUST LIKE YOU. I'VE BEEN WORKING MY WAY DOWN BRUNO Z'S LIST OF KNOWN *ASSOCIATES.*

FOUND A SMOKING *PISTOL.* A GUY NAMED GARY CLYDE WHO DID TIME WITH THE *SAINT* AT ANGOLA. I'M GONNA GO SAY HI.

FINE. BUT WHY DID YOU HAVE TO DROP *STEVIE KELLER* IN MY LAP?

SHE'S DOODLING ON MY *FILES* WITH A GREEN FUCKING FELT PEN.

SHE'S GOT A GOOD MIND. MAYBE SHE'LL PICK UP ON SOMETHING WE *MISSED.*

A GOOD MIND?

YEAH. YOU KNOW, SUPPLE. FULLY *ROUNDED.* INVITINGLY OPEN.

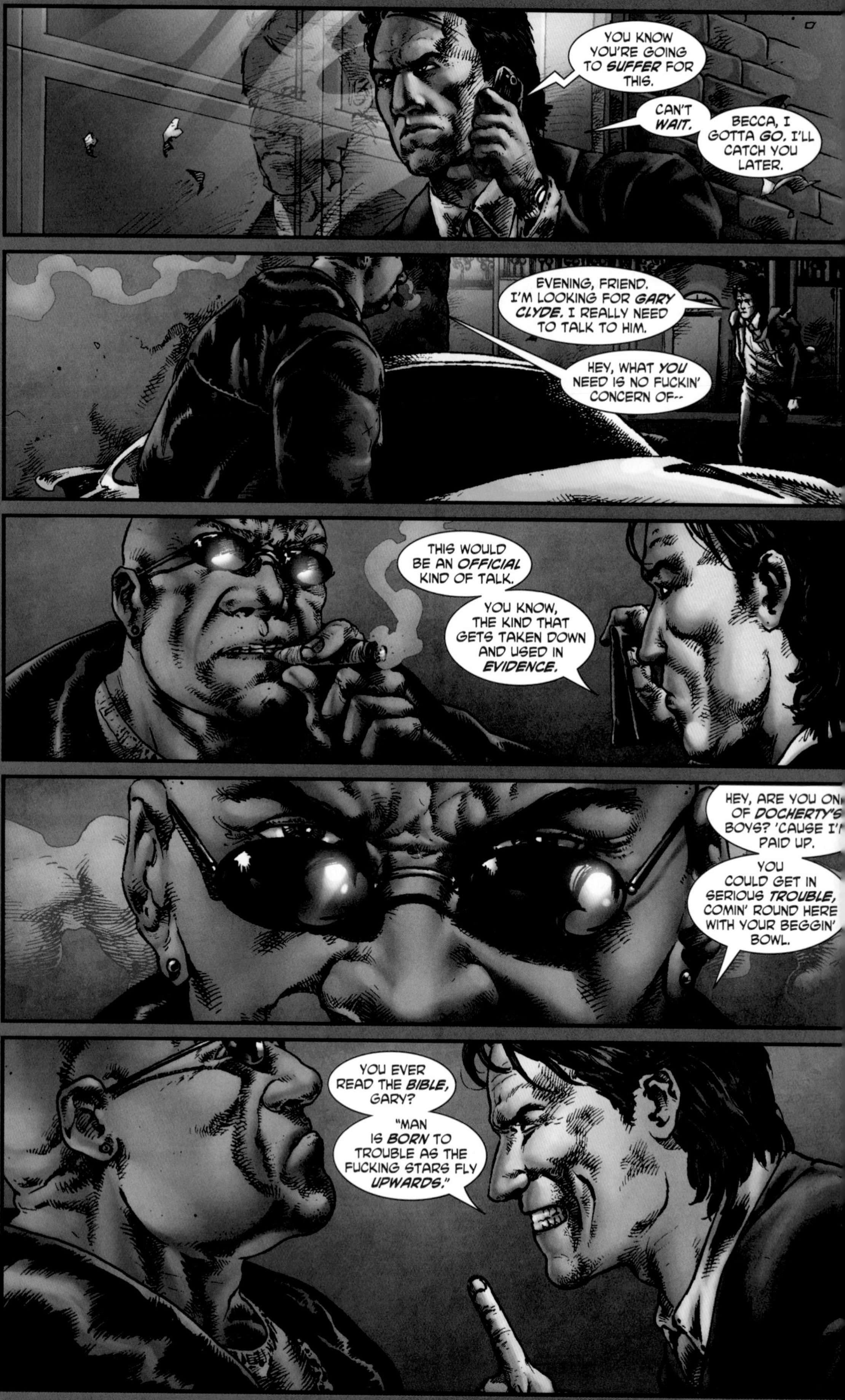
YOU KNOW YOU'RE GOING TO SUFFER FOR THIS.
CAN'T WAIT.
BECCA, I GOTTA GO. I'LL CATCH YOU LATER.
EVENING, FRIEND. I'M LOOKING FOR GARY CLYDE. I REALLY NEED TO TALK TO HIM.
HEY, WHAT YOU NEED IS NO FUCKIN' CONCERN OF--
THIS WOULD BE AN OFFICIAL KIND OF TALK.
YOU KNOW, THE KIND THAT GETS TAKEN DOWN AND USED IN EVIDENCE.
HEY, ARE YOU ON OF DOCHERTY'S BOYS? 'CAUSE I' PAID UP.
YOU COULD GET IN SERIOUS TROUBLE, COMIN' ROUND HERE WITH YOUR BEGGIN' BOWL.
YOU EVER READ THE BIBLE, GARY?
"MAN IS BORN TO TROUBLE AS THE FUCKING STARS FLY UPWARDS."

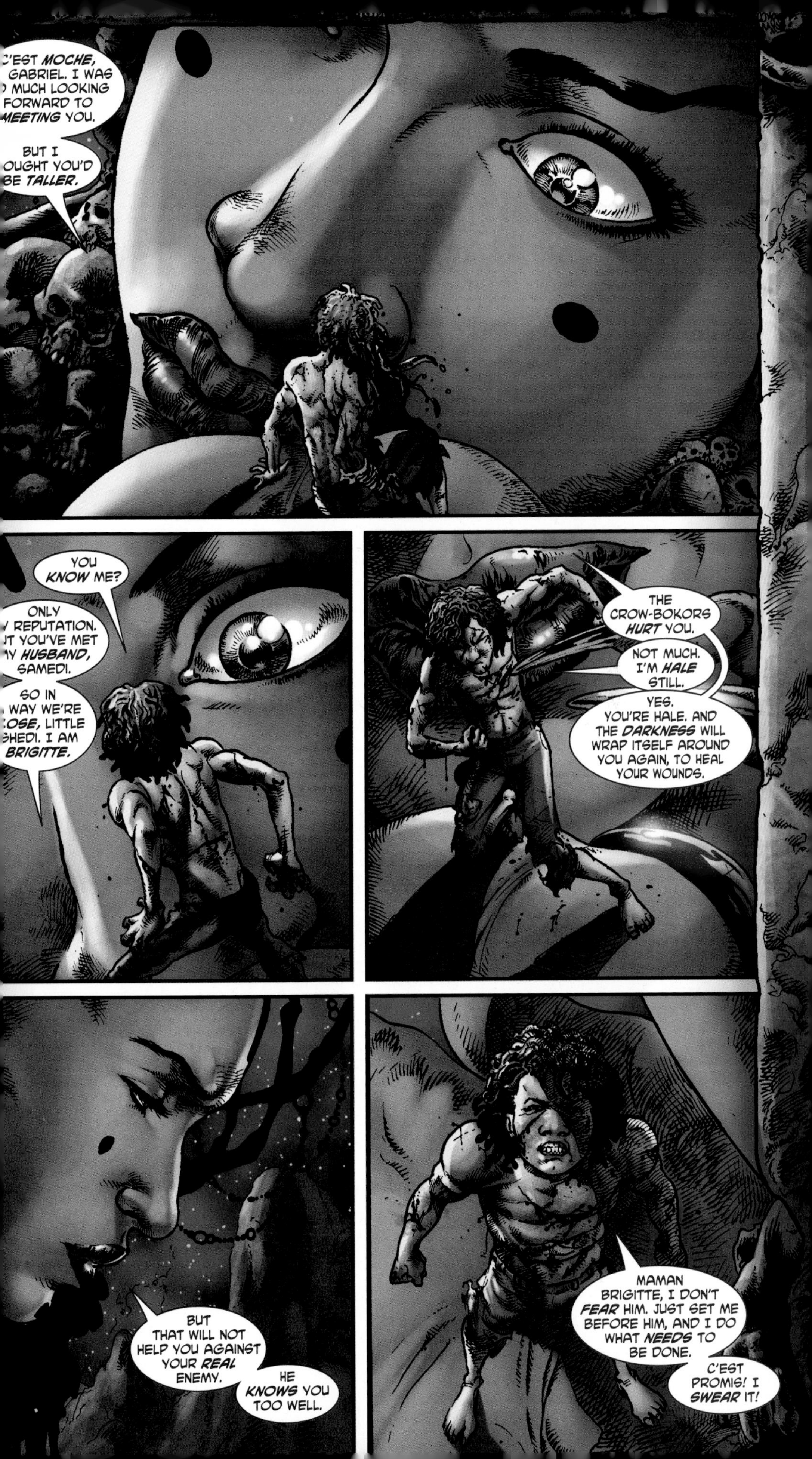
C'EST MOCHE, GABRIEL. I WAS O MUCH LOOKING FORWARD TO MEETING YOU.
BUT I OUGHT YOU'D BE TALLER.
YOU KNOW ME?
ONLY Y REPUTATION. T YOU'VE MET Y HUSBAND, SAMEDI.
SO IN WAY WE'RE OSE, LITTLE HEDI. I AM BRIGITTE.
THE CROW-BOKORS HURT YOU.
NOT MUCH. I'M HALE STILL.
YES. YOU'RE HALE. AND THE DARKNESS WILL WRAP ITSELF AROUND YOU AGAIN, TO HEAL YOUR WOUNDS.
BUT THAT WILL NOT HELP YOU AGAINST YOUR REAL ENEMY.
HE KNOWS YOU TOO WELL.
MAMAN BRIGITTE, I DON'T FEAR HIM. JUST SET ME BEFORE HIM, AND I DO WHAT NEEDS TO BE DONE.
C'EST PROMIS! I SWEAR IT!

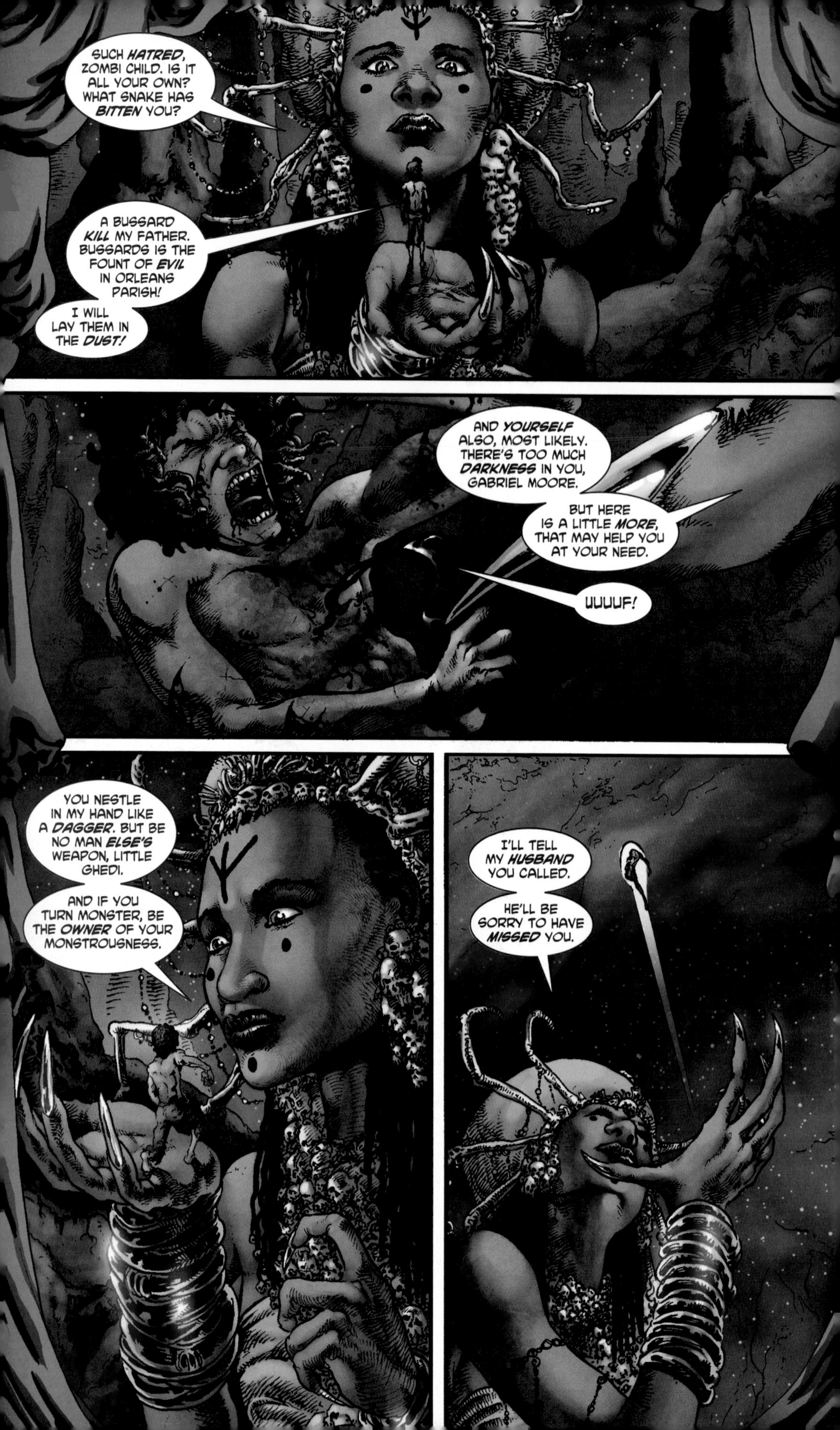
SUCH HATRED, ZOMBI CHILD. IS IT ALL YOUR OWN? WHAT SNAKE HAS BITTEN YOU?
A BUSSARD KILL MY FATHER. BUSSARDS IS THE FOUNT OF EVIL IN ORLEANS PARISH!
I WILL LAY THEM IN THE DUST!
AND YOURSELF ALSO, MOST LIKELY. THERE'S TOO MUCH DARKNESS IN YOU, GABRIEL MOORE.
BUT HERE IS A LITTLE MORE, THAT MAY HELP YOU AT YOUR NEED.
UUUUF!
YOU NESTLE IN MY HAND LIKE A DAGGER. BUT BE NO MAN ELSE'S WEAPON, LITTLE GHEDI.
AND IF YOU TURN MONSTER, BE THE OWNER OF YOUR MONSTROUSNESS.
I'LL TELL MY HUSBAND YOU CALLED.
HE'LL BE SORRY TO HAVE MISSED YOU.

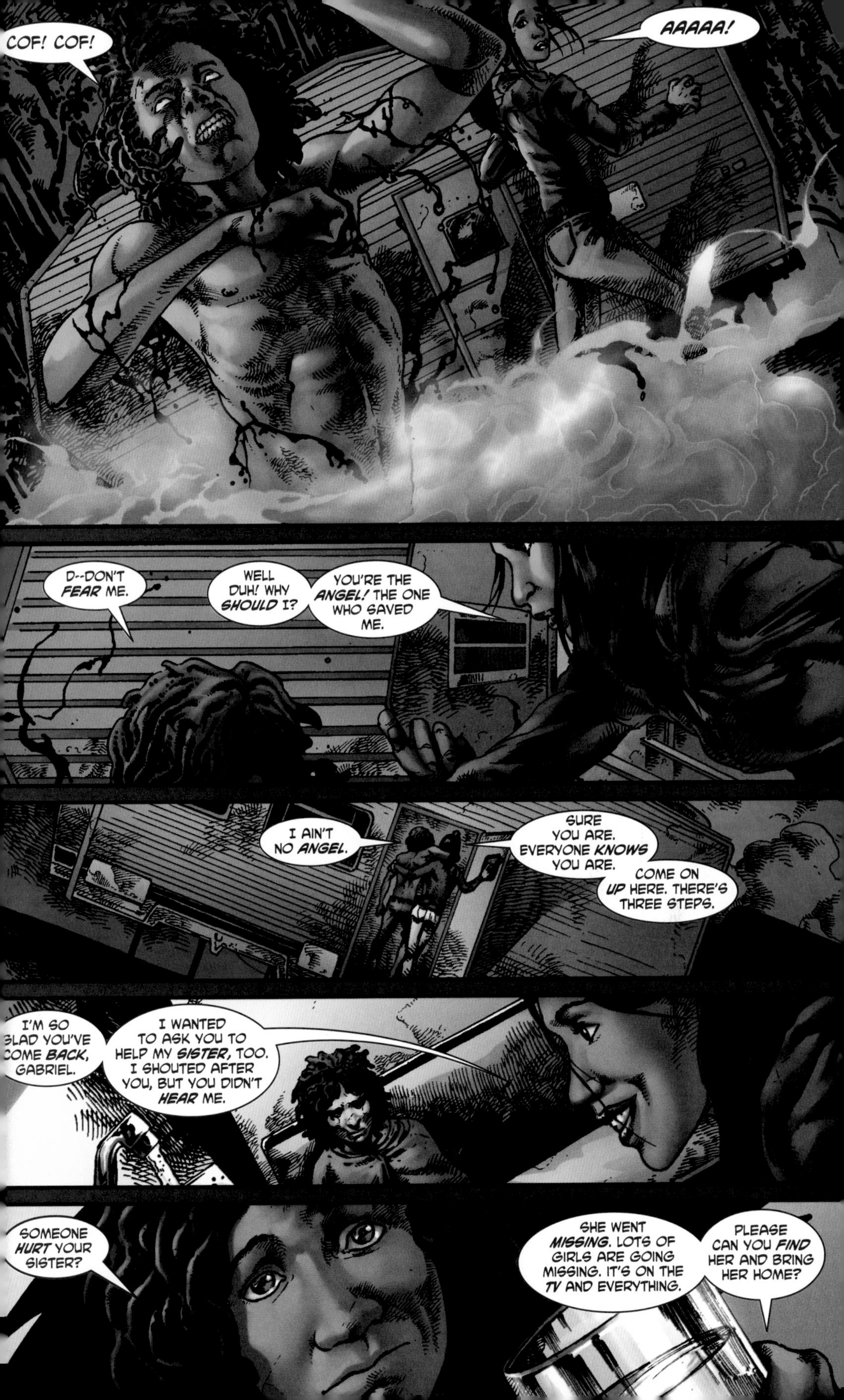
COF! COF!
AAAAA!
D--DON'T FEAR ME.
WELL DUH! WHY SHOULD I?
YOU'RE THE ANGEL! THE ONE WHO SAVED ME.
I AIN'T NO ANGEL.
SURE YOU ARE. EVERYONE KNOWS YOU ARE.
COME ON UP HERE. THERE'S THREE STEPS.
I'M SO GLAD YOU'VE COME BACK, GABRIEL.
I WANTED TO ASK YOU TO HELP MY SISTER, TOO. I SHOUTED AFTER YOU, BUT YOU DIDN'T HEAR ME.
SOMEONE HURT YOUR SISTER?
SHE WENT MISSING. LOTS OF GIRLS ARE GOING MISSING. IT'S ON THE TV AND EVERYTHING.
PLEASE CAN YOU FIND HER AND BRING HER HOME?

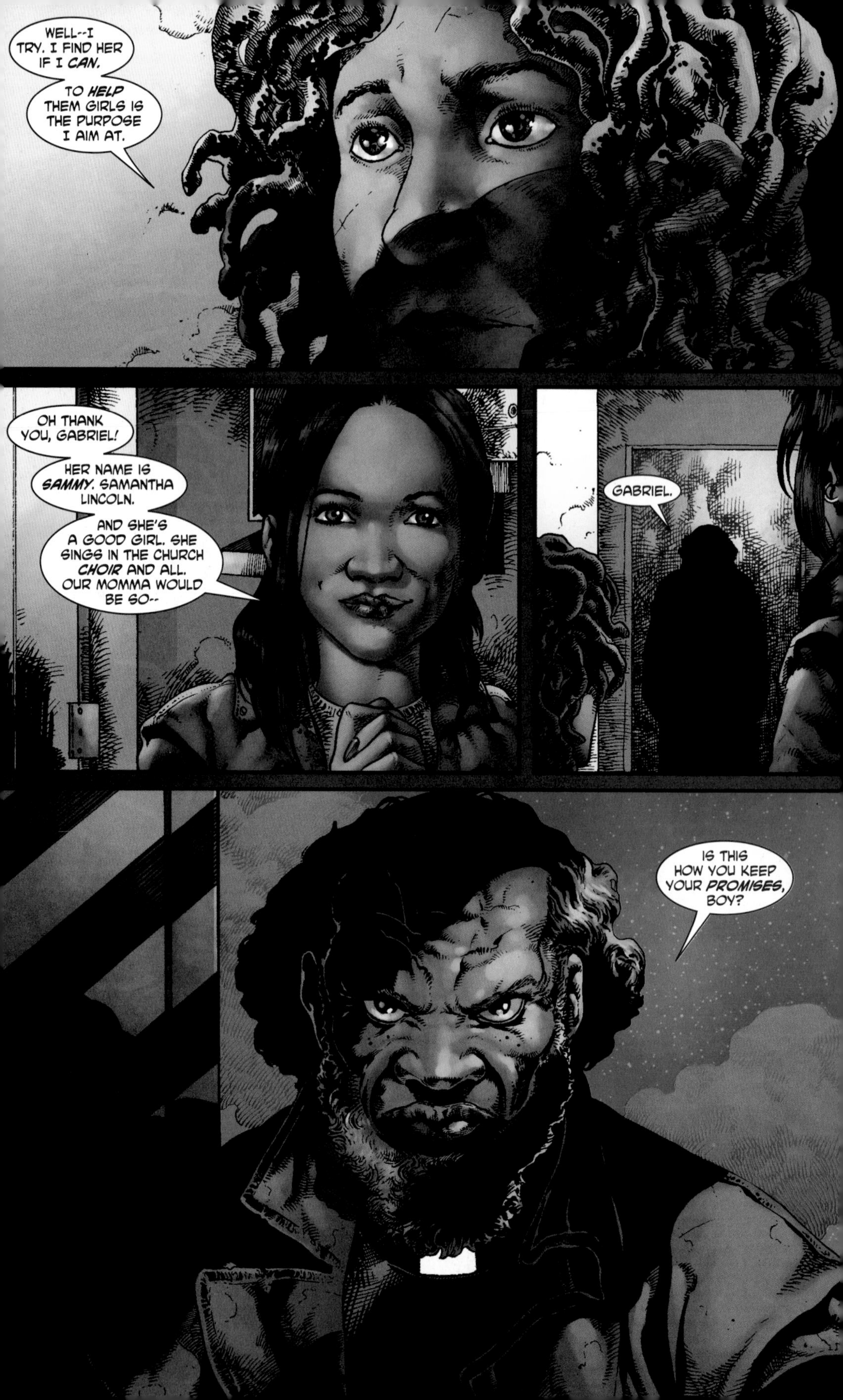
WELL--I TRY. I FIND HER IF I *CAN.*
TO ***HELP*** THEM GIRLS IS THE PURPOSE I AIM AT.
OH THANK YOU, GABRIEL!
HER NAME IS ***SAMMY.*** SAMANTHA LINCOLN.
AND SHE'S A GOOD GIRL. SHE SINGS IN THE CHURCH ***CHOIR*** AND ALL. OUR MOMMA WOULD BE SO--
GABRIEL.
IS THIS HOW YOU KEEP YOUR ***PROMISES,*** BOY?

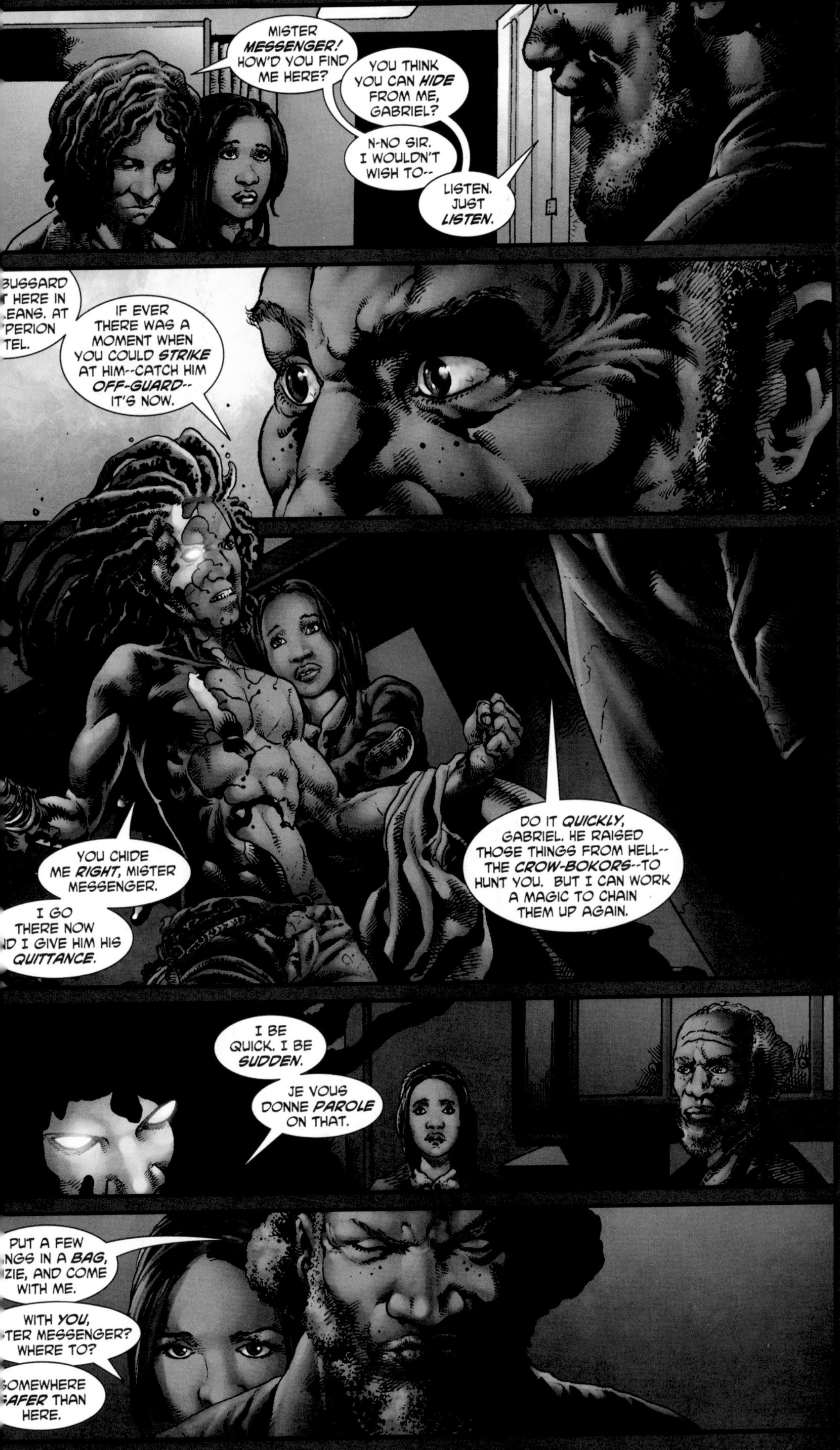
MISTER MESSENGER! HOW'D YOU FIND ME HERE?
YOU THINK YOU CAN HIDE FROM ME, GABRIEL?
N-NO SIR. I WOULDN'T WISH TO--
LISTEN. JUST LISTEN.
BUSSARD HERE IN EANS. AT PERION TEL.
IF EVER THERE WAS A MOMENT WHEN YOU COULD STRIKE AT HIM--CATCH HIM OFF-GUARD--IT'S NOW.
DO IT QUICKLY, GABRIEL. HE RAISED THOSE THINGS FROM HELL--THE CROW-BOKORS--TO HUNT YOU. BUT I CAN WORK A MAGIC TO CHAIN THEM UP AGAIN.
YOU CHIDE ME RIGHT, MISTER MESSENGER.
I GO THERE NOW ND I GIVE HIM HIS QUITTANCE.
I BE QUICK. I BE SUDDEN.
JE VOUS DONNE PAROLE ON THAT.
PUT A FEW NGS IN A BAG, ZIE, AND COME WITH ME.
WITH YOU, TER MESSENGER? WHERE TO?
OMEWHERE AFER THAN HERE.

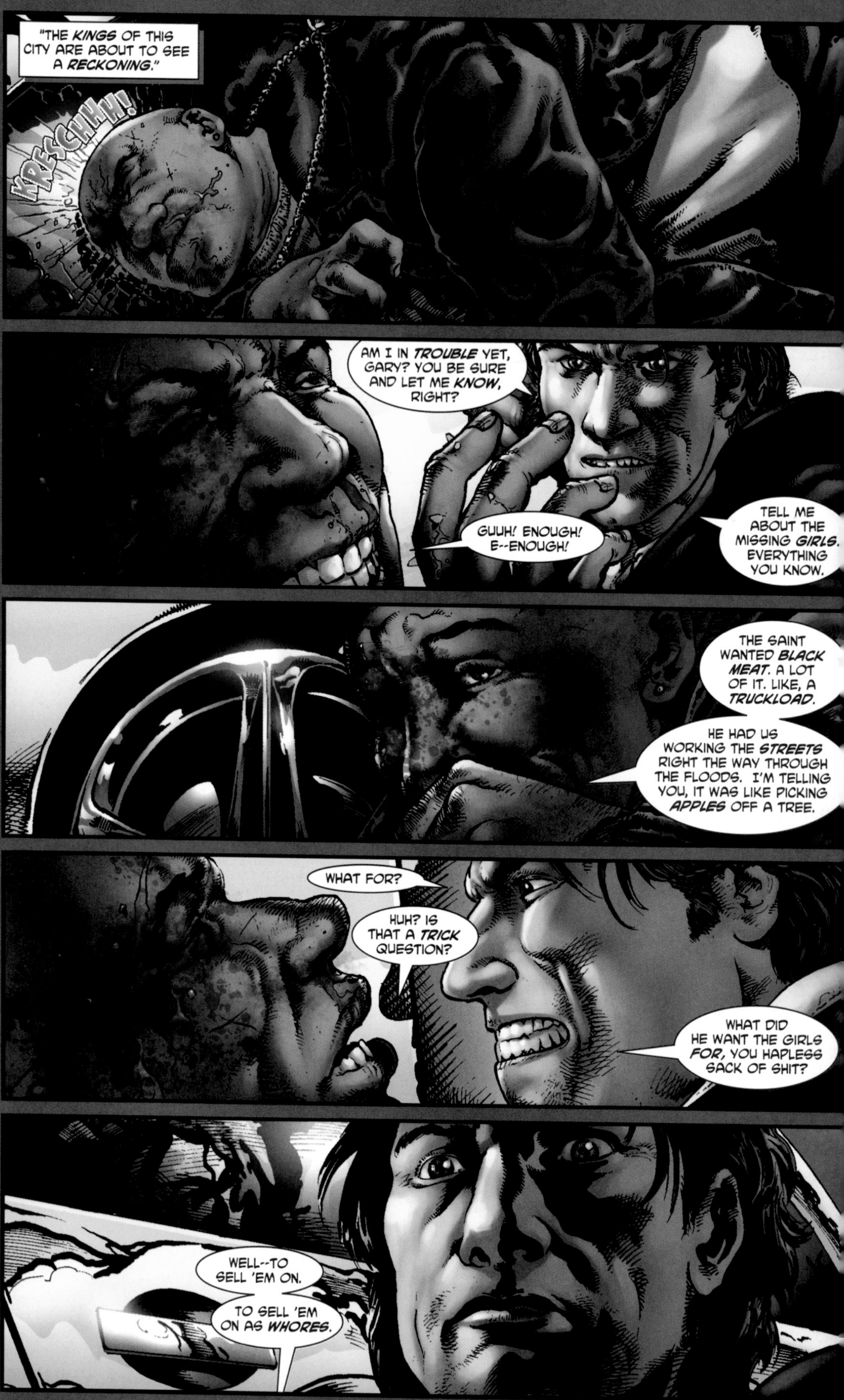
"THE KINGS OF THIS CITY ARE ABOUT TO SEE A RECKONING."
KRESCHHH!
AM I IN TROUBLE YET, GARY? YOU BE SURE AND LET ME KNOW, RIGHT?
GUUH! ENOUGH! E--ENOUGH!
TELL ME ABOUT THE MISSING GIRLS. EVERYTHING YOU KNOW.
THE SAINT WANTED BLACK MEAT. A LOT OF IT. LIKE, A TRUCKLOAD.
HE HAD US WORKING THE STREETS RIGHT THE WAY THROUGH THE FLOODS. I'M TELLING YOU, IT WAS LIKE PICKING APPLES OFF A TREE.
WHAT FOR?
HUH? IS THAT A TRICK QUESTION?
WHAT DID HE WANT THE GIRLS FOR, YOU HAPLESS SACK OF SHIT?
WELL--TO SELL 'EM ON.
TO SELL 'EM ON AS WHORES.

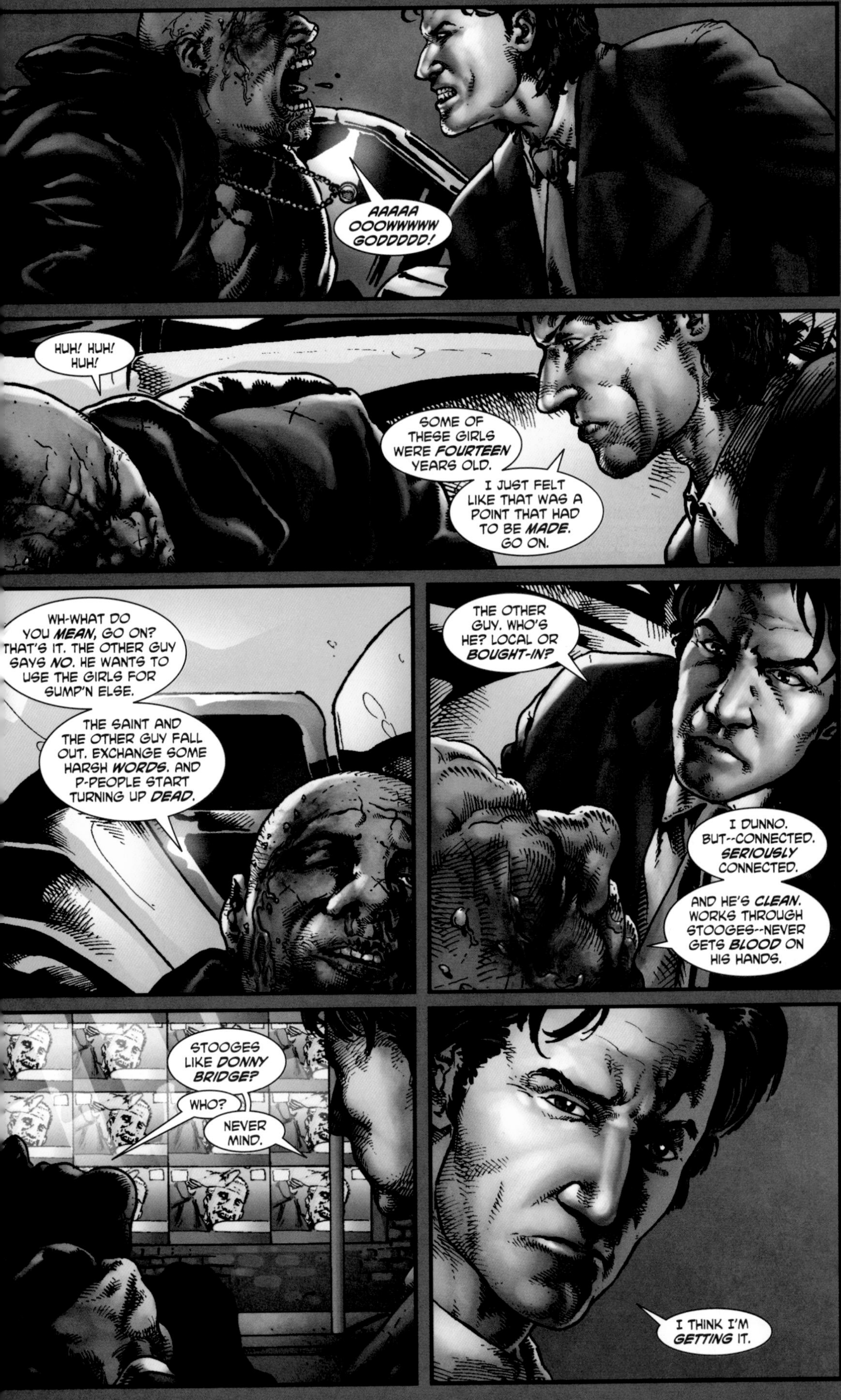
AAAAA OOOWWWWW GODDDDD!
HUH! HUH! HUH!
SOME OF THESE GIRLS WERE FOURTEEN YEARS OLD.
I JUST FELT LIKE THAT WAS A POINT THAT HAD TO BE MADE. GO ON.
WH-WHAT DO YOU MEAN, GO ON? THAT'S IT. THE OTHER GUY SAYS NO. HE WANTS TO USE THE GIRLS FOR SUMP'N ELSE.
THE SAINT AND THE OTHER GUY FALL OUT. EXCHANGE SOME HARSH WORDS. AND P-PEOPLE START TURNING UP DEAD.
THE OTHER GUY. WHO'S HE? LOCAL OR BOUGHT-IN?
I DUNNO. BUT--CONNECTED. SERIOUSLY CONNECTED.
AND HE'S CLEAN. WORKS THROUGH STOOGES--NEVER GETS BLOOD ON HIS HANDS.
STOOGES LIKE DONNY BRIDGE?
WHO?
NEVER MIND.
I THINK I'M GETTING IT.

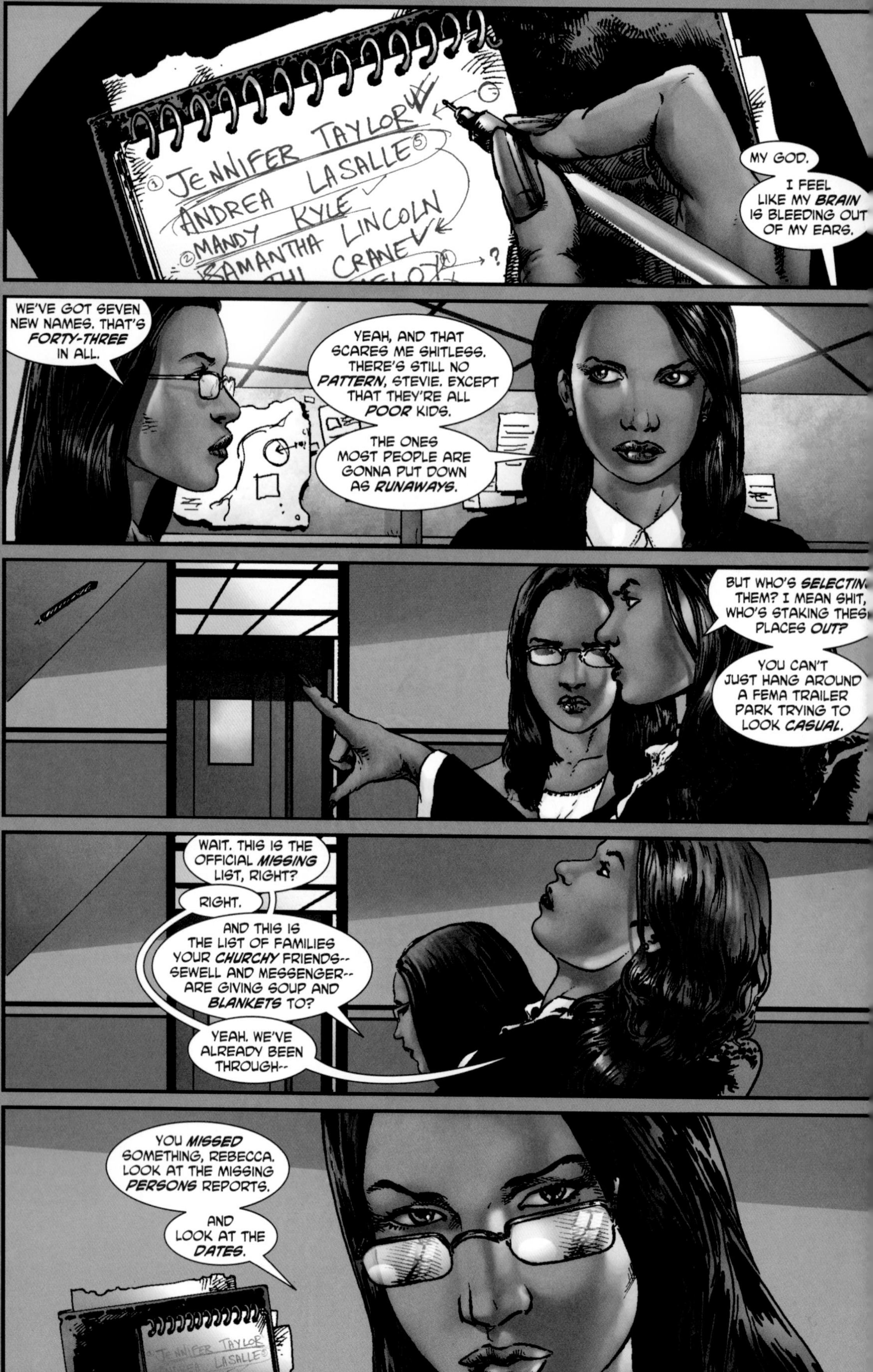
JENNIFER TAYLOR
ANDREA LASALLE
MANDY KYLE
SAMANTHA LINCOLN
CRANE
MY GOD.
I FEEL LIKE MY BRAIN IS BLEEDING OUT OF MY EARS.
WE'VE GOT SEVEN NEW NAMES. THAT'S FORTY-THREE IN ALL.
YEAH, AND THAT SCARES ME SHITLESS. THERE'S STILL NO PATTERN, STEVIE. EXCEPT THAT THEY'RE ALL POOR KIDS.
THE ONES MOST PEOPLE ARE GONNA PUT DOWN AS RUNAWAYS.
BUT WHO'S SELECTIN THEM? I MEAN SHIT, WHO'S STAKING THES PLACES OUT?
YOU CAN'T JUST HANG AROUND A FEMA TRAILER PARK TRYING TO LOOK CASUAL.
WAIT. THIS IS THE OFFICIAL MISSING LIST, RIGHT?
RIGHT.
AND THIS IS THE LIST OF FAMILIES YOUR CHURCHY FRIENDS-- SEWELL AND MESSENGER-- ARE GIVING SOUP AND BLANKETS TO?
YEAH. WE'VE ALREADY BEEN THROUGH--
YOU MISSED SOMETHING, REBECCA. LOOK AT THE MISSING PERSONS REPORTS.
AND LOOK AT THE DATES.

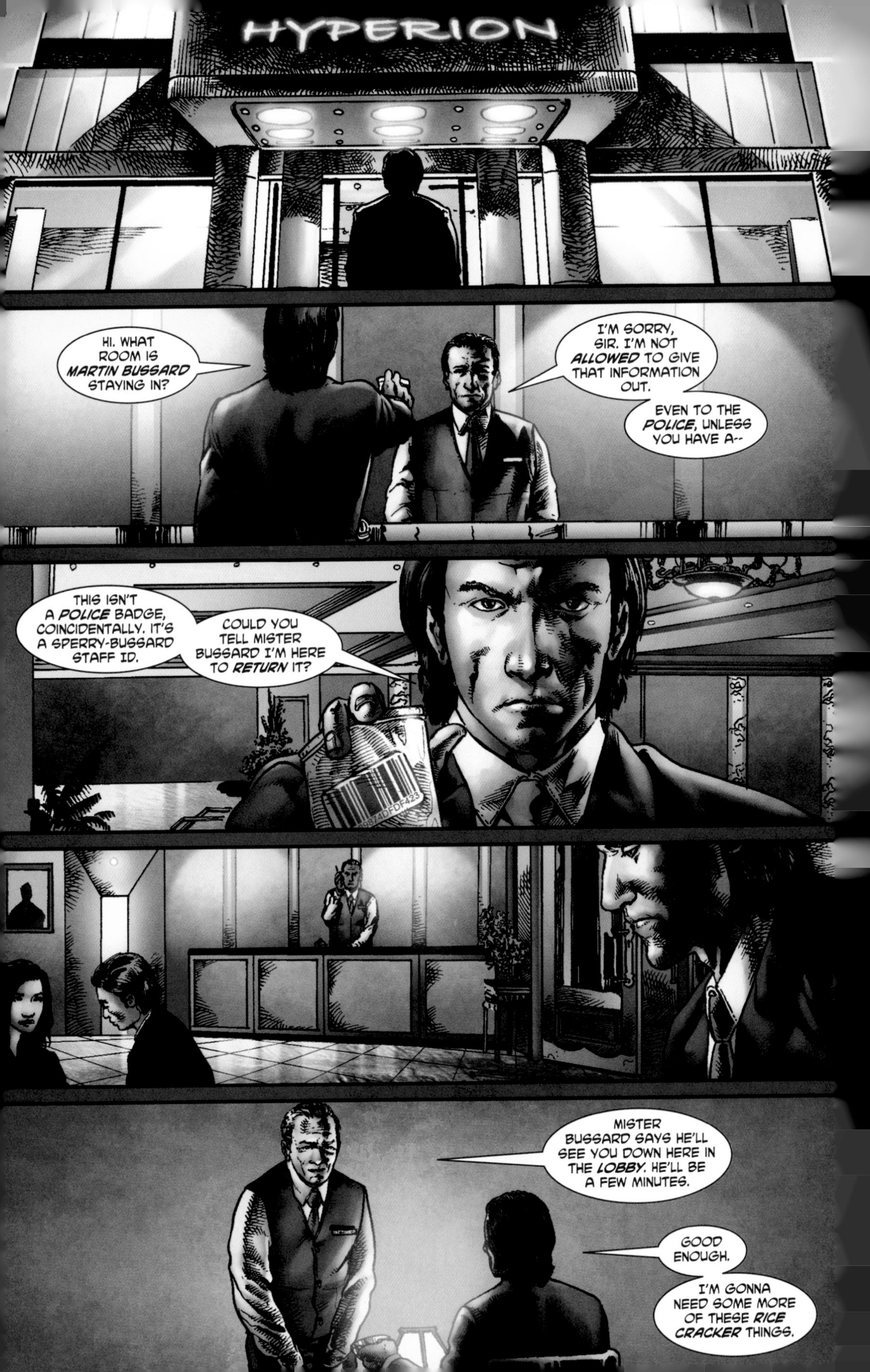
HYPERION
HI. WHAT ROOM IS MARTIN BUSSARD STAYING IN?
I'M SORRY, SIR. I'M NOT ALLOWED TO GIVE THAT INFORMATION OUT.
EVEN TO THE POLICE, UNLESS YOU HAVE A--
THIS ISN'T A POLICE BADGE, COINCIDENTALLY. IT'S A SPERRY-BUSSARD STAFF ID.
COULD YOU TELL MISTER BUSSARD I'M HERE TO RETURN IT?
MISTER BUSSARD SAYS HE'LL SEE YOU DOWN HERE IN THE LOBBY. HE'LL BE A FEW MINUTES.
GOOD ENOUGH.
I'M GONNA NEED SOME MORE OF THESE RICE CRACKER THINGS.

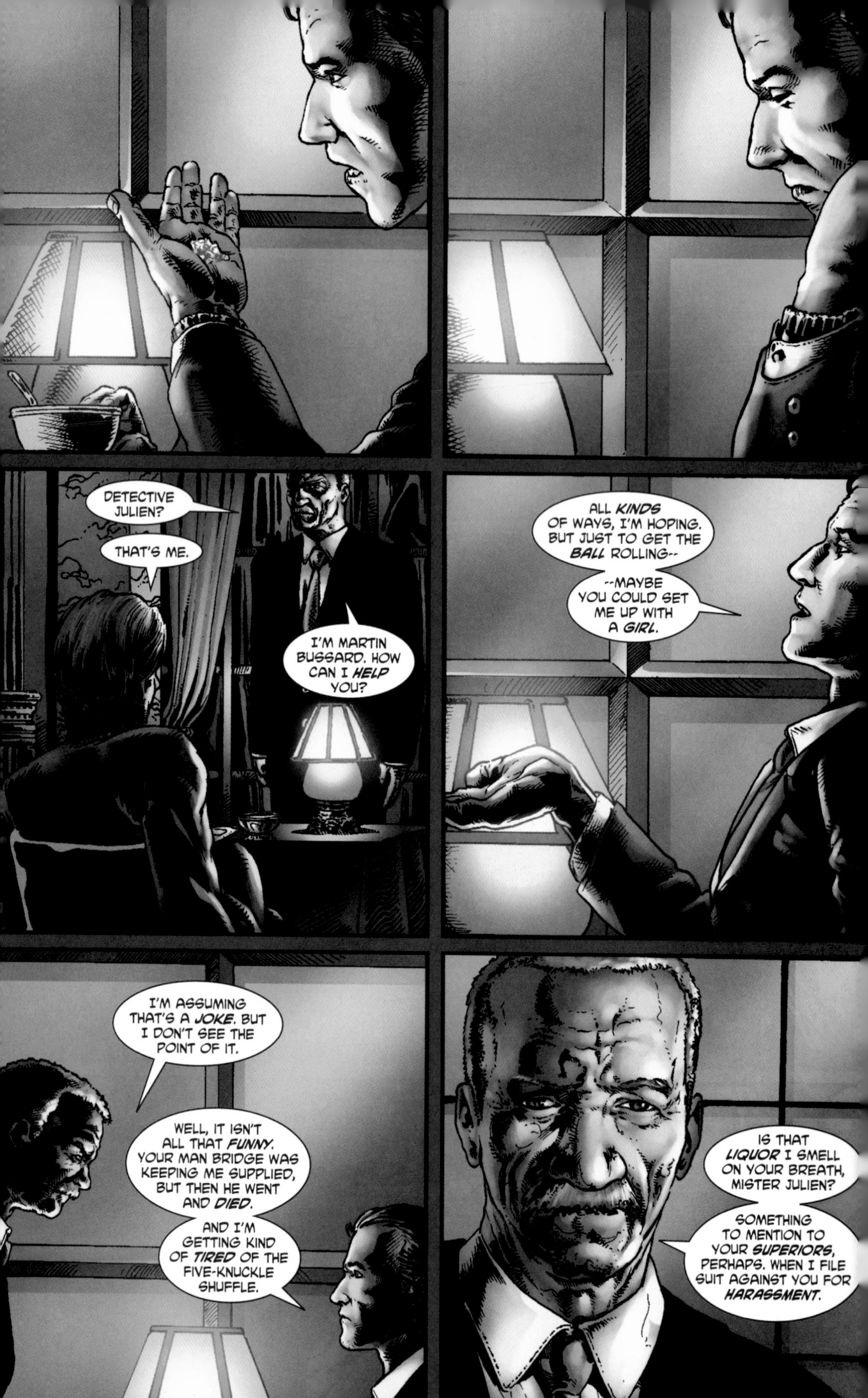
DETECTIVE JULIEN?
THAT'S ME.
I'M MARTIN BUSSARD. HOW CAN I *HELP* YOU?
ALL *KINDS* OF WAYS, I'M HOPING. BUT JUST TO GET THE *BALL* ROLLING--
--MAYBE YOU COULD SET ME UP WITH A *GIRL*.
I'M ASSUMING THAT'S A *JOKE*. BUT I DON'T SEE THE POINT OF IT.
WELL, IT ISN'T ALL THAT *FUNNY*. YOUR MAN BRIDGE WAS KEEPING ME SUPPLIED, BUT THEN HE WENT AND *DIED*.
AND I'M GETTING KIND OF *TIRED* OF THE FIVE-KNUCKLE SHUFFLE.
IS THAT *LIQUOR* I SMELL ON YOUR BREATH, MISTER JULIEN?
SOMETHING TO MENTION TO YOUR *SUPERIORS*, PERHAPS. WHEN I FILE SUIT AGAINST YOU FOR *HARASSMENT*.

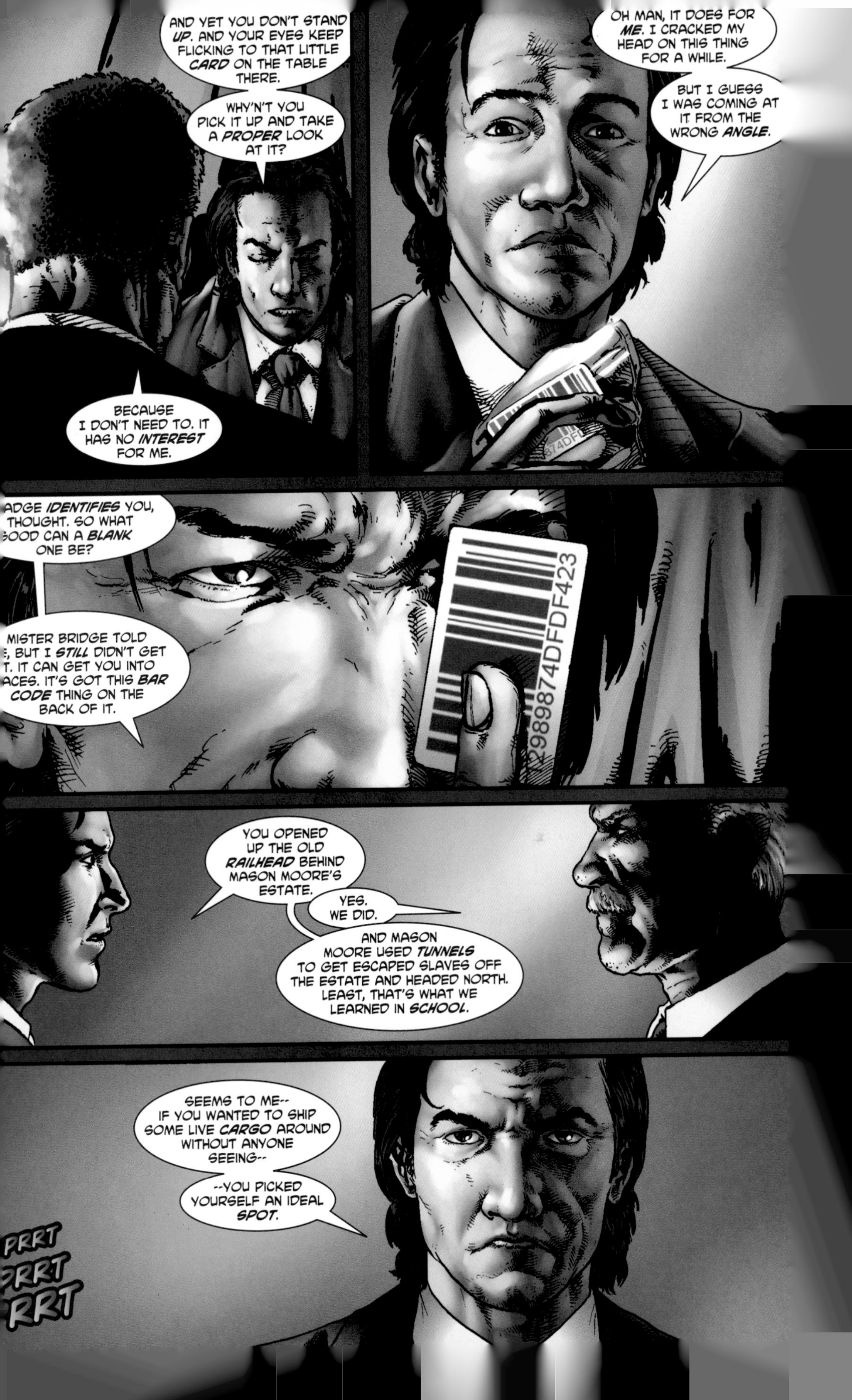
AND YET YOU DON'T STAND UP. AND YOUR EYES KEEP FLICKING TO THAT LITTLE CARD ON THE TABLE THERE.
WHY'N'T YOU PICK IT UP AND TAKE A PROPER LOOK AT IT?
BECAUSE I DON'T NEED TO. IT HAS NO INTEREST FOR ME.
OH MAN, IT DOES FOR ME. I CRACKED MY HEAD ON THIS THING FOR A WHILE.
BUT I GUESS I WAS COMING AT IT FROM THE WRONG ANGLE.
ADGE IDENTIFIES YOU, THOUGHT. SO WHAT GOOD CAN A BLANK ONE BE?
MISTER BRIDGE TOLD , BUT I STILL DIDN'T GET T. IT CAN GET YOU INTO ACES. IT'S GOT THIS BAR CODE THING ON THE BACK OF IT.
YOU OPENED UP THE OLD RAILHEAD BEHIND MASON MOORE'S ESTATE.
YES. WE DID.
AND MASON MOORE USED TUNNELS TO GET ESCAPED SLAVES OFF THE ESTATE AND HEADED NORTH. LEAST, THAT'S WHAT WE LEARNED IN SCHOOL.
SEEMS TO ME-- IF YOU WANTED TO SHIP SOME LIVE CARGO AROUND WITHOUT ANYONE SEEING--
--YOU PICKED YOURSELF AN IDEAL SPOT.
PRRT
PRRT
RRT

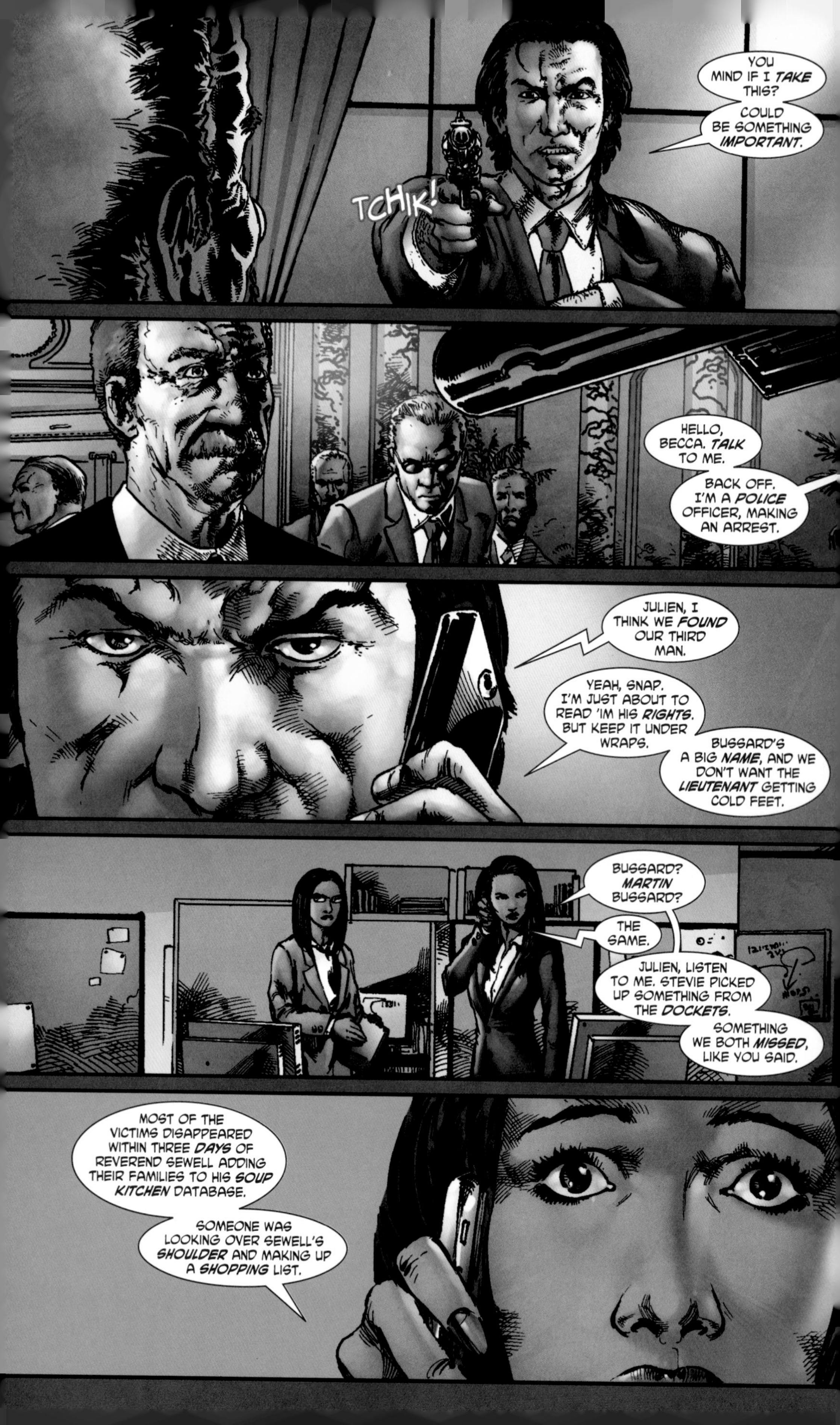

YOU MIND IF I *TAKE* THIS?
COULD BE SOMETHING *IMPORTANT*.
TCHIK!
HELLO, BECCA. *TALK* TO ME.
BACK OFF. I'M A *POLICE* OFFICER, MAKING AN ARREST.
JULIEN, I THINK WE *FOUND* OUR THIRD MAN.
YEAH, SNAP. I'M JUST ABOUT TO READ 'IM HIS *RIGHTS*. BUT KEEP IT UNDER WRAPS.
BUSSARD'S A BIG *NAME*, AND WE DON'T WANT THE *LIEUTENANT* GETTING COLD FEET.
BUSSARD? *MARTIN* BUSSARD?
THE SAME.
JULIEN, LISTEN TO ME. STEVIE PICKED UP SOMETHING FROM THE *DOCKETS*.
SOMETHING WE BOTH *MISSED*, LIKE YOU SAID.
MOST OF THE VICTIMS DISAPPEARED WITHIN THREE *DAYS* OF REVEREND SEWELL ADDING THEIR FAMILIES TO HIS *SOUP KITCHEN* DATABASE.
SOMEONE WAS LOOKING OVER SEWELL'S *SHOULDER* AND MAKING UP A *SHOPPING* LIST.

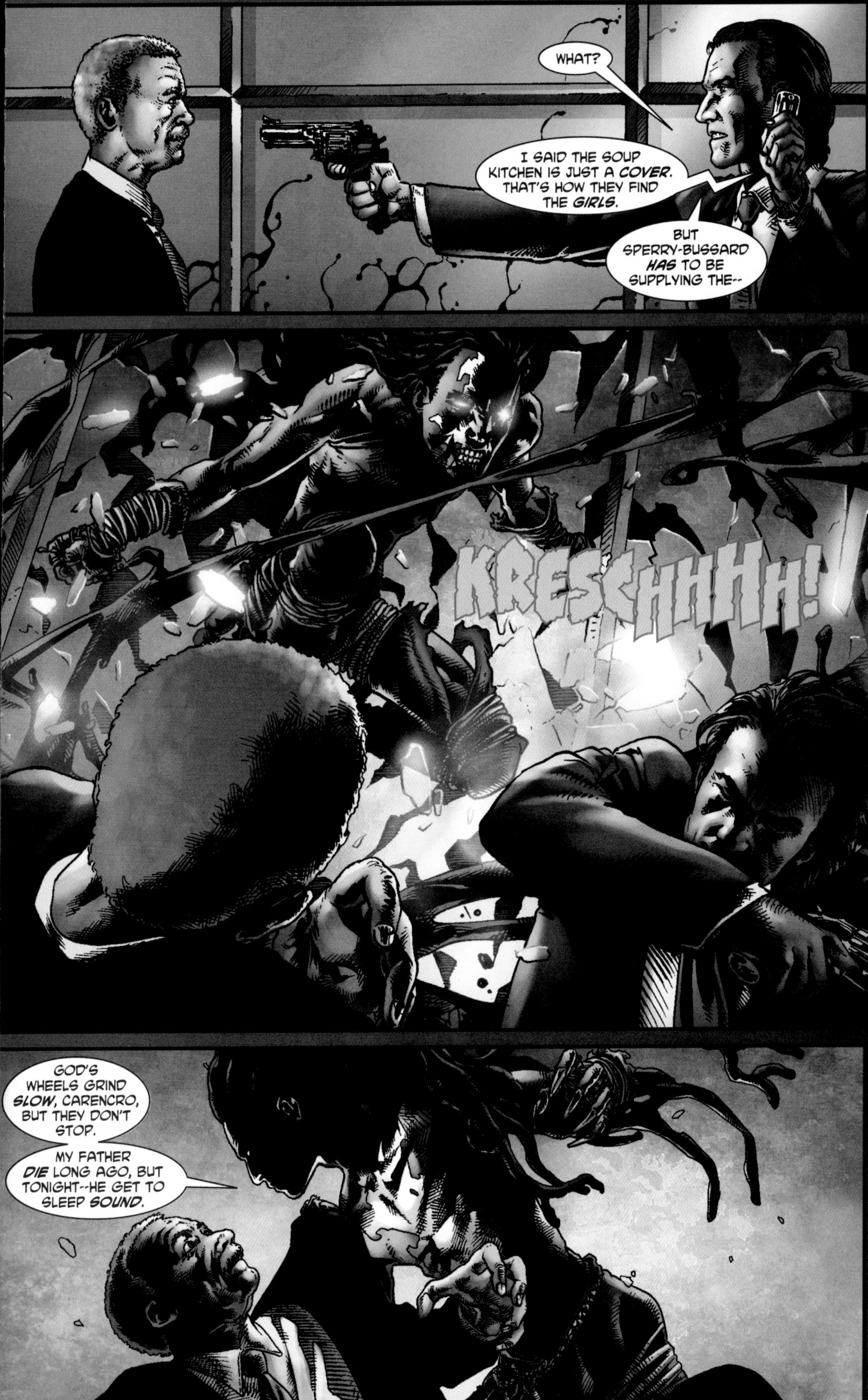
WHAT?
I SAID THE SOUP KITCHEN IS JUST A COVER. THAT'S HOW THEY FIND THE GIRLS.
BUT SPERRY-BUSSARD HAS TO BE SUPPLYING THE--
KRESCHHHH!
GOD'S WHEELS GRIND SLOW, CARENCRO, BUT THEY DON'T STOP.
MY FATHER DIE LONG AGO, BUT TONIGHT--HE GET TO SLEEP SOUND.

"SO THERE YOU GO, YOU CREEPY LITTLE FUCKER.

"IT IS WHAT IT IS."

Le Chateau Suspendu

ANOTHER TIME, WHEN YOU WANT TO MAKE MISCHIEF--

--MAYBE YOU'LL GIVE THE SAINT A MISS.

CRRRKKKK!

SAMEDI? C'EST CONCLU?

IS IT DONE?

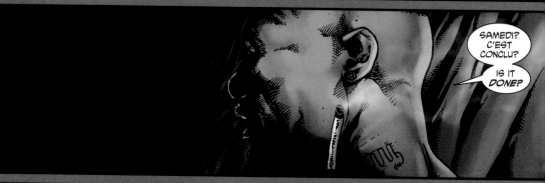

NO, SAINT-CLAIRE. IT'S NOT. I WARNED YOU NOT TO CROSS ME.

NOW YOU WENT AND MADE A DEAL FOR A BODY AND A SOUL. AND YOU DIDN'T DELIVER.

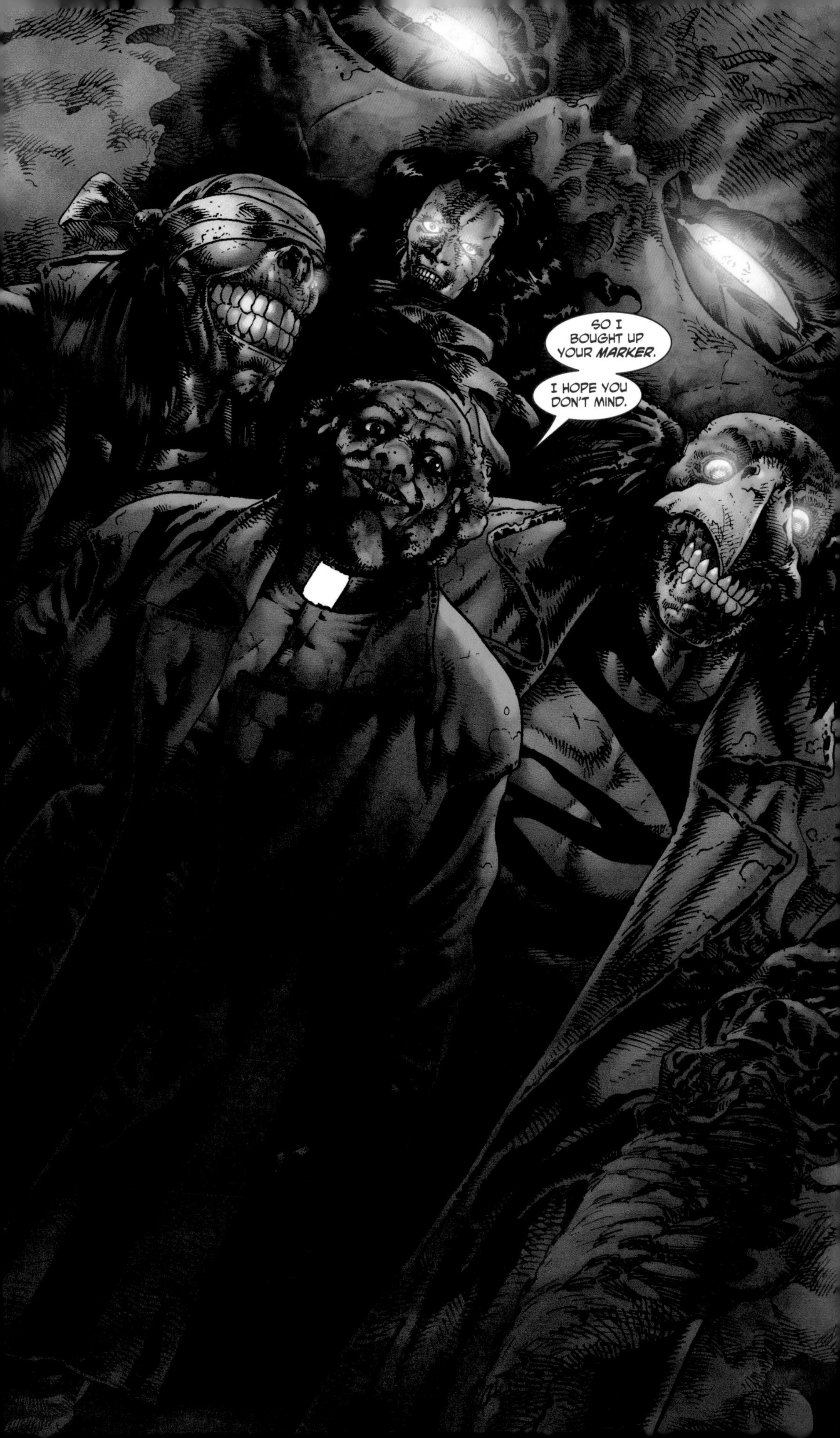
SO I BOUGHT UP YOUR *MARKER*.
I HOPE YOU DON'T MIND.

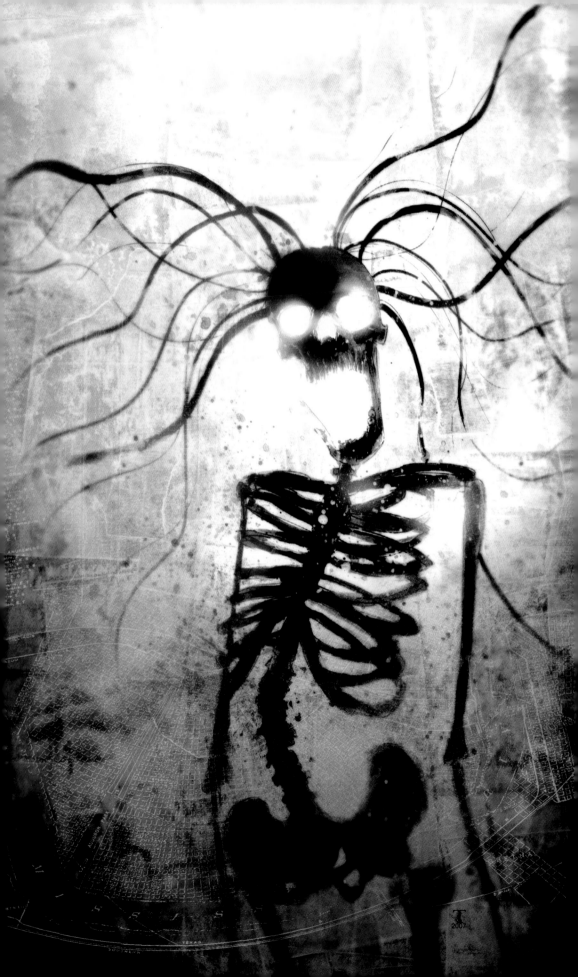

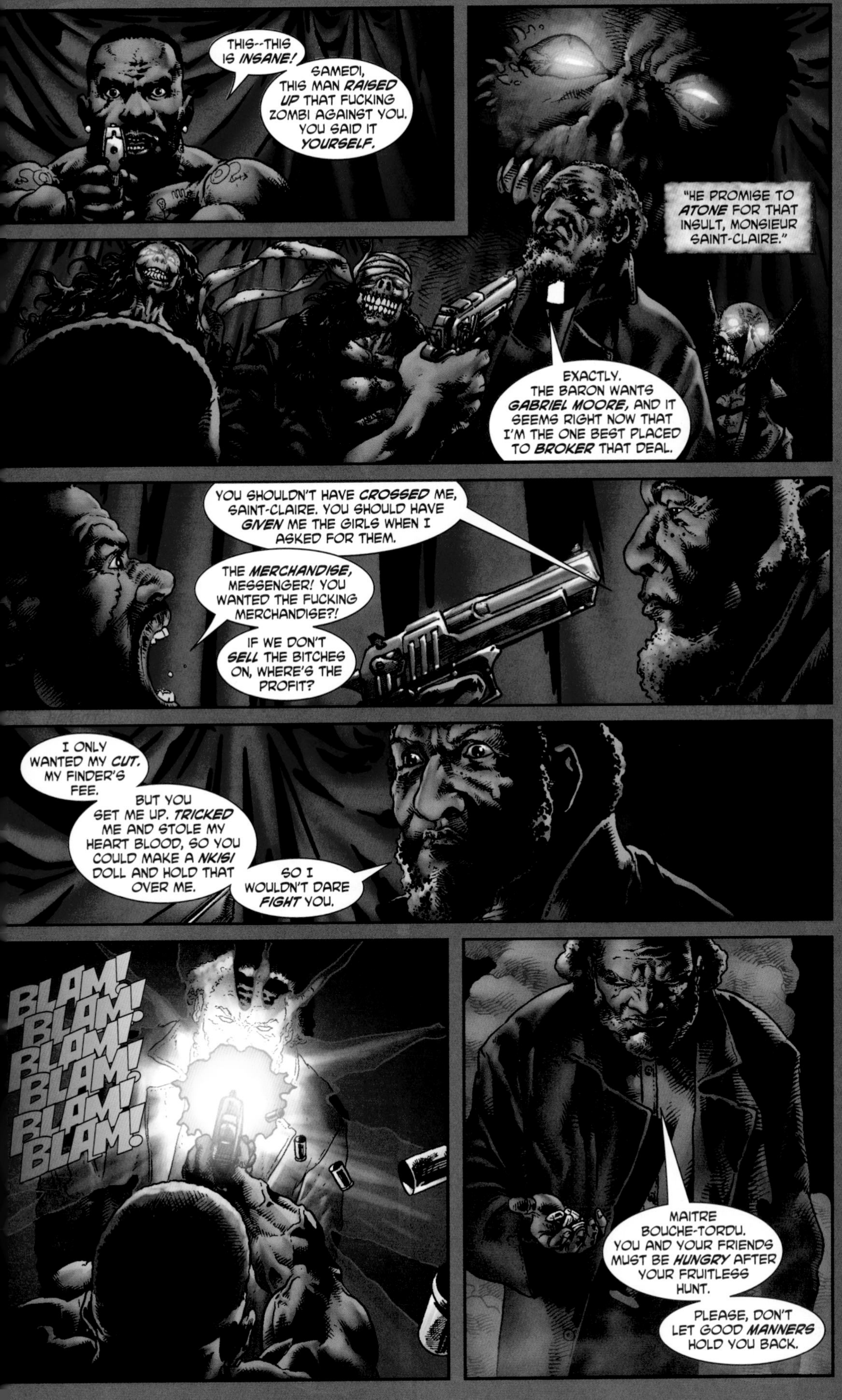
THIS--THIS IS INSANE!
SAMEDI, THIS MAN RAISED UP THAT FUCKING ZOMBI AGAINST YOU. YOU SAID IT YOURSELF.
"HE PROMISE TO ATONE FOR THAT INSULT, MONSIEUR SAINT-CLAIRE."
EXACTLY. THE BARON WANTS GABRIEL MOORE, AND IT SEEMS RIGHT NOW THAT I'M THE ONE BEST PLACED TO BROKER THAT DEAL.
YOU SHOULDN'T HAVE CROSSED ME, SAINT-CLAIRE. YOU SHOULD HAVE GIVEN ME THE GIRLS WHEN I ASKED FOR THEM.
THE MERCHANDISE, MESSENGER! YOU WANTED THE FUCKING MERCHANDISE?!
IF WE DON'T SELL THE BITCHES ON, WHERE'S THE PROFIT?
I ONLY WANTED MY CUT. MY FINDER'S FEE.
BUT YOU SET ME UP. TRICKED ME AND STOLE MY HEART BLOOD, SO YOU COULD MAKE A NKISI DOLL AND HOLD THAT OVER ME.
SO I WOULDN'T DARE FIGHT YOU.
BLAM! BLAM! BLAM! BLAM! BLAM! BLAM! BLAM!
MAITRE BOUCHE-TORDU. YOU AND YOUR FRIENDS MUST BE HUNGRY AFTER YOUR FRUITLESS HUNT.
PLEASE, DON'T LET GOOD MANNERS HOLD YOU BACK.

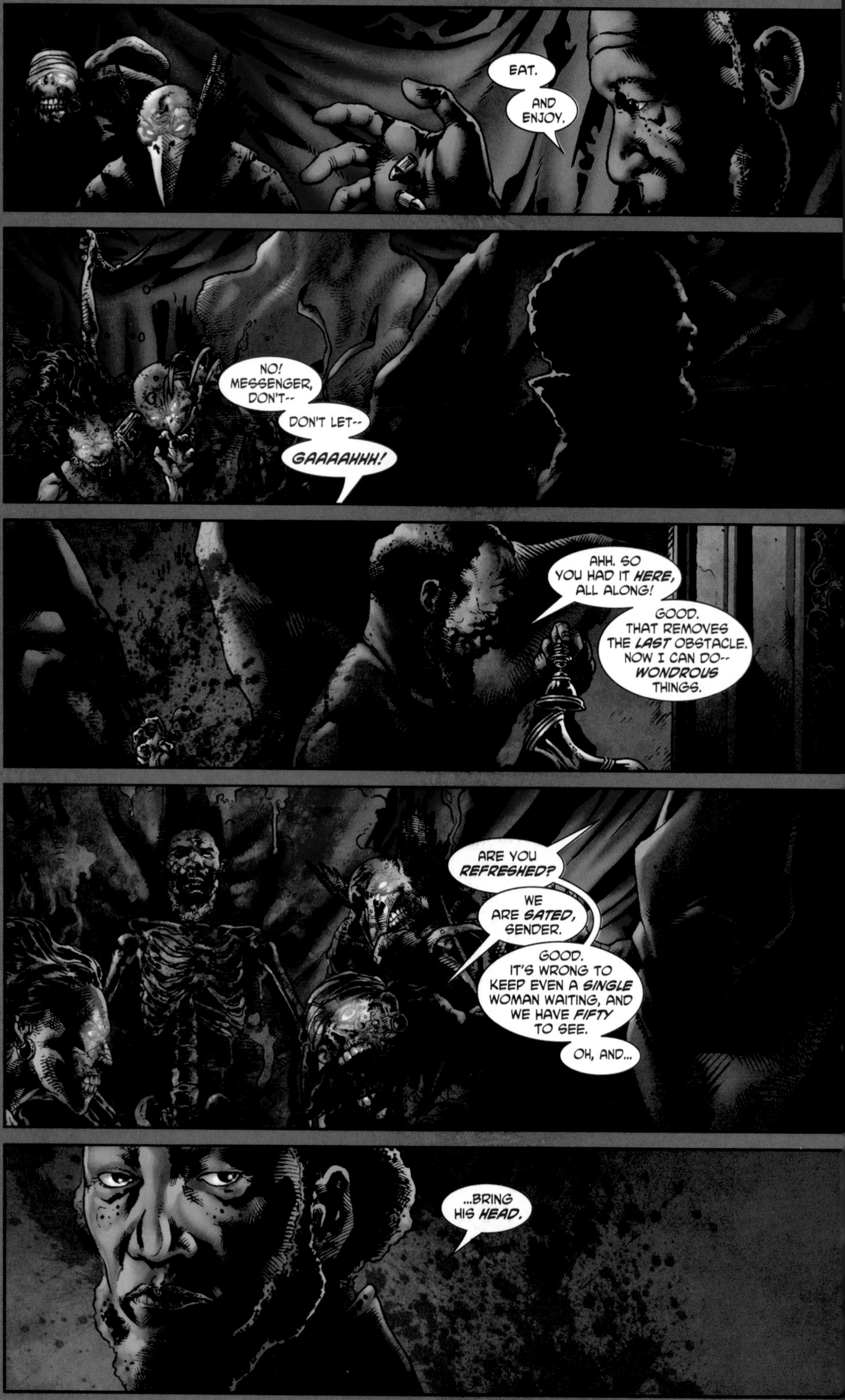
EAT.
AND ENJOY.
NO! MESSENGER, DON'T--
DON'T LET--
GAAAAHHH!
AHH. SO YOU HAD IT HERE, ALL ALONG!
GOOD. THAT REMOVES THE LAST OBSTACLE. NOW I CAN DO-- WONDROUS THINGS.
ARE YOU REFRESHED?
WE ARE SATED, SENDER.
GOOD. IT'S WRONG TO KEEP EVEN A SINGLE WOMAN WAITING, AND WE HAVE FIFTY TO SEE.
OH, AND...
...BRING HIS HEAD.

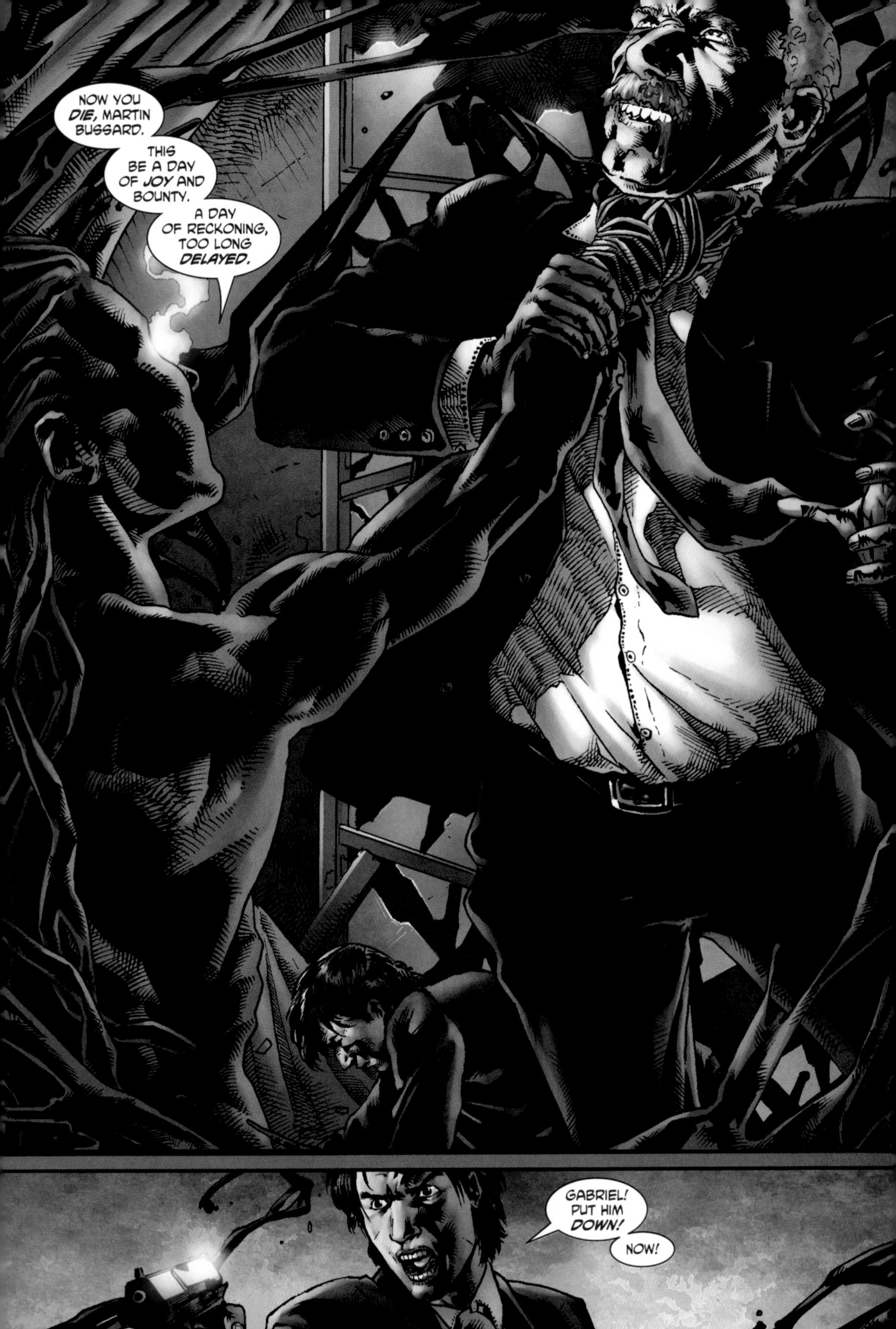
NOW YOU DIE, MARTIN BUSSARD.
THIS BE A DAY OF JOY AND BOUNTY.
A DAY OF RECKONING, TOO LONG DELAYED.

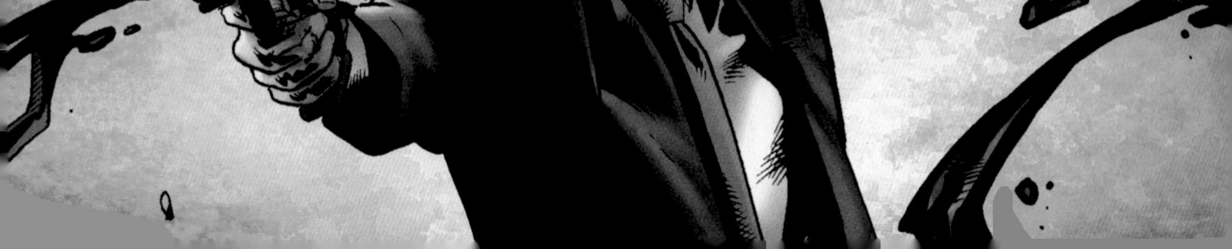
GABRIEL! PUT HIM DOWN!
NOW!

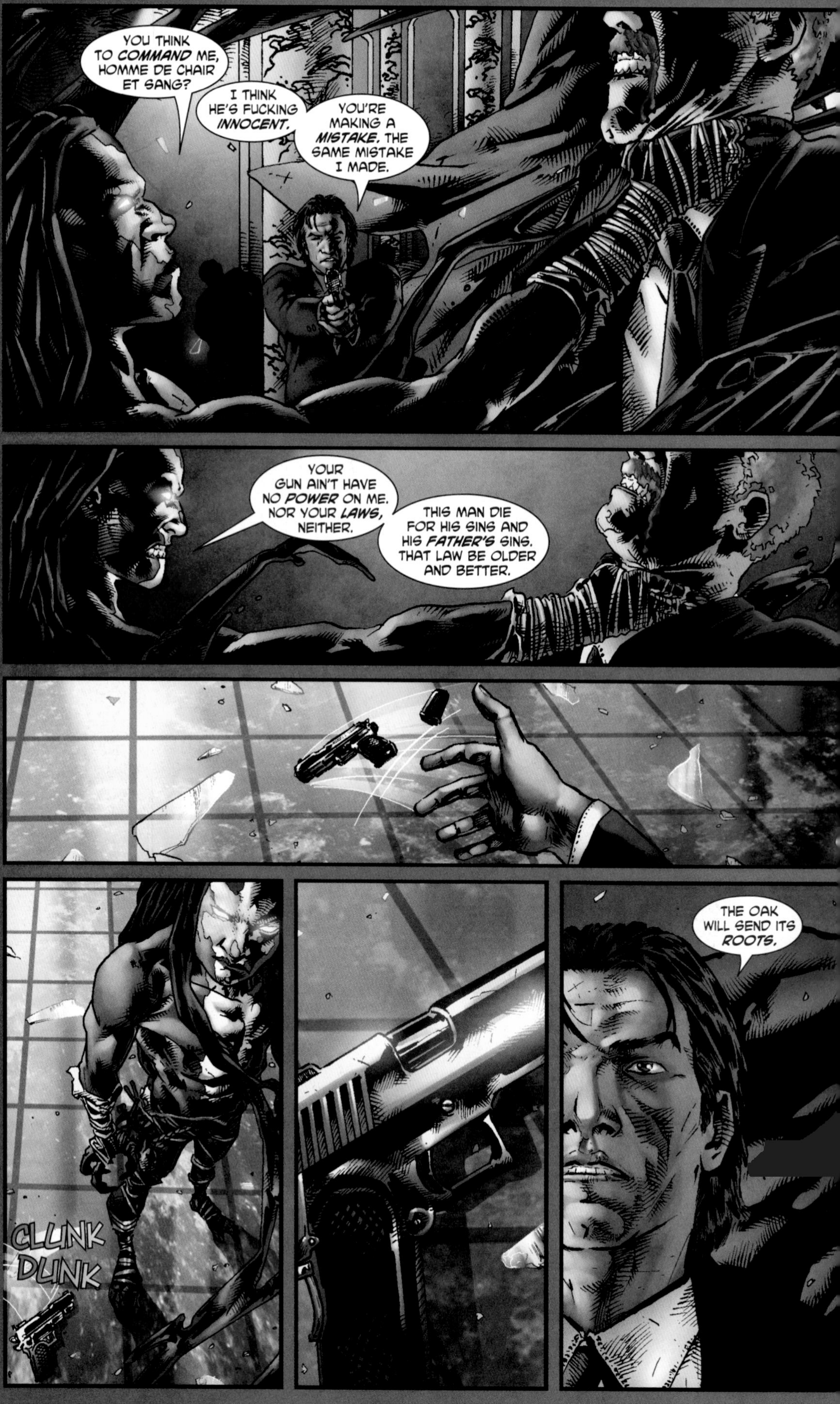
YOU THINK TO COMMAND ME, HOMME DE CHAIR ET SANG?
I THINK HE'S FUCKING INNOCENT.
YOU'RE MAKING A MISTAKE. THE SAME MISTAKE I MADE.
YOUR GUN AIN'T HAVE NO POWER ON ME. NOR YOUR LAWS, NEITHER.
THIS MAN DIE FOR HIS SINS AND HIS FATHER'S SINS. THAT LAW BE OLDER AND BETTER.
CLUNK DUNK
THE OAK WILL SEND ITS ROOTS.

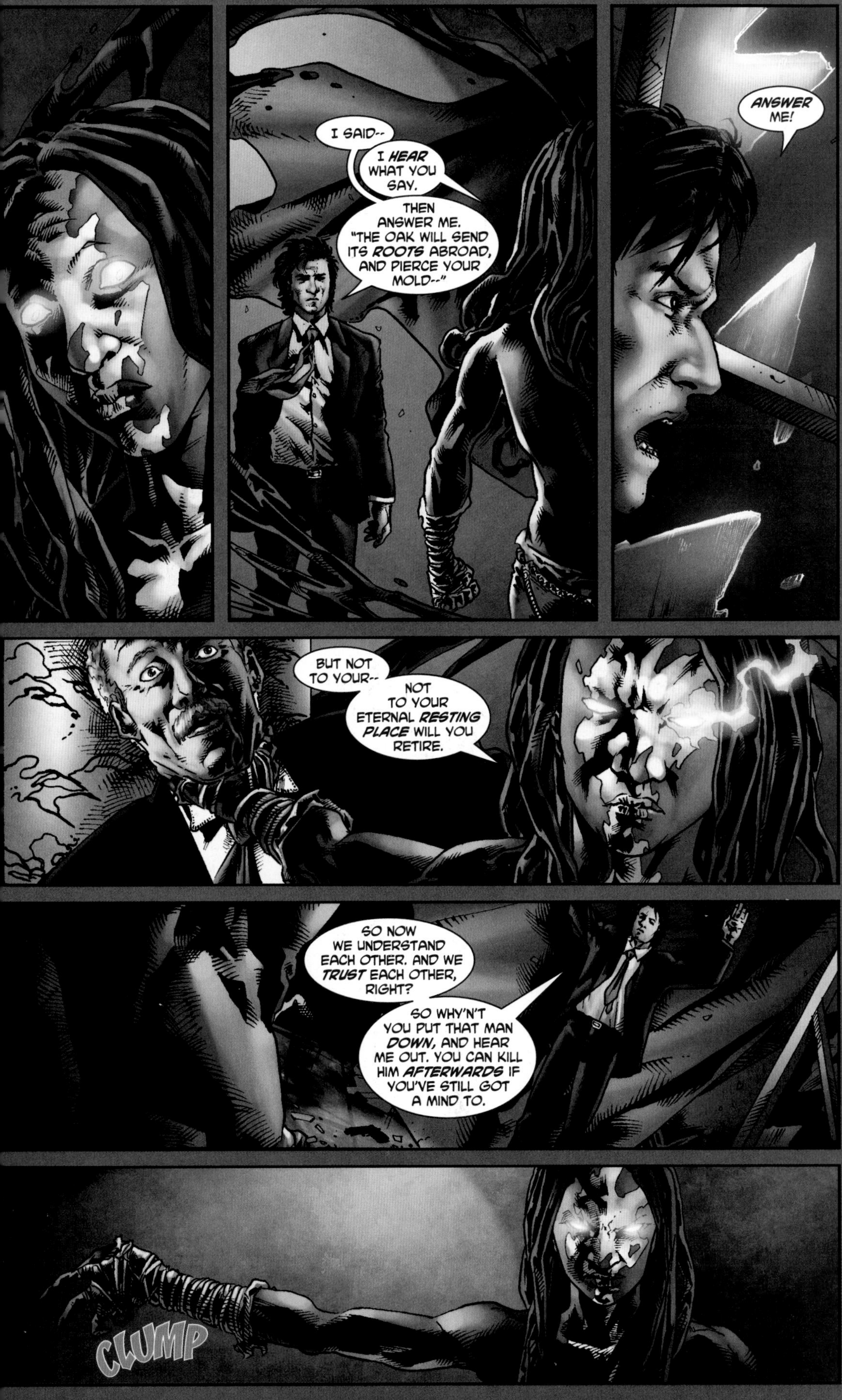
I SAID--
I HEAR WHAT YOU SAY.
THEN ANSWER ME. "THE OAK WILL SEND ITS ROOTS ABROAD, AND PIERCE YOUR MOLD--"
ANSWER ME!
BUT NOT TO YOUR--
NOT TO YOUR ETERNAL RESTING PLACE WILL YOU RETIRE.
SO NOW WE UNDERSTAND EACH OTHER. AND WE TRUST EACH OTHER, RIGHT?
SO WHY'N'T YOU PUT THAT MAN DOWN, AND HEAR ME OUT. YOU CAN KILL HIM AFTERWARDS IF YOU'VE STILL GOT A MIND TO.
CLUMP

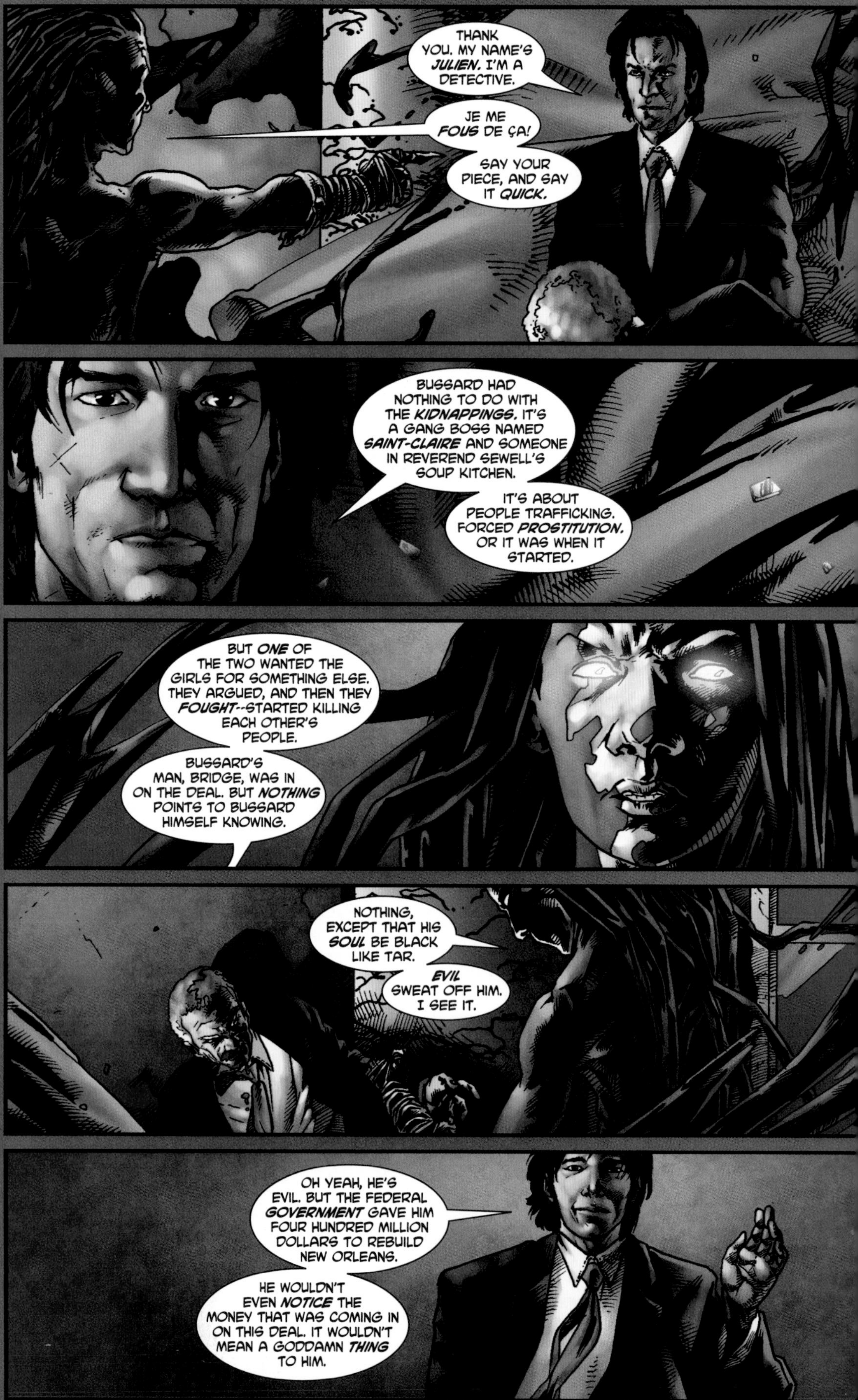
THANK YOU. MY NAME'S JULIEN. I'M A DETECTIVE.
JE ME FOUS DE ÇA!
SAY YOUR PIECE, AND SAY IT QUICK.
BUSSARD HAD NOTHING TO DO WITH THE KIDNAPPINGS. IT'S A GANG BOSS NAMED SAINT-CLAIRE AND SOMEONE IN REVEREND SEWELL'S SOUP KITCHEN.
IT'S ABOUT PEOPLE TRAFFICKING. FORCED PROSTITUTION. OR IT WAS WHEN IT STARTED.
BUT ONE OF THE TWO WANTED THE GIRLS FOR SOMETHING ELSE. THEY ARGUED, AND THEN THEY FOUGHT--STARTED KILLING EACH OTHER'S PEOPLE.
BUSSARD'S MAN, BRIDGE, WAS IN ON THE DEAL. BUT NOTHING POINTS TO BUSSARD HIMSELF KNOWING.
NOTHING, EXCEPT THAT HIS SOUL BE BLACK LIKE TAR.
EVIL SWEAT OFF HIM. I SEE IT.
OH YEAH, HE'S EVIL. BUT THE FEDERAL GOVERNMENT GAVE HIM FOUR HUNDRED MILLION DOLLARS TO REBUILD NEW ORLEANS.
HE WOULDN'T EVEN NOTICE THE MONEY THAT WAS COMING IN ON THIS DEAL. IT WOULDN'T MEAN A GODDAMN THING TO HIM.

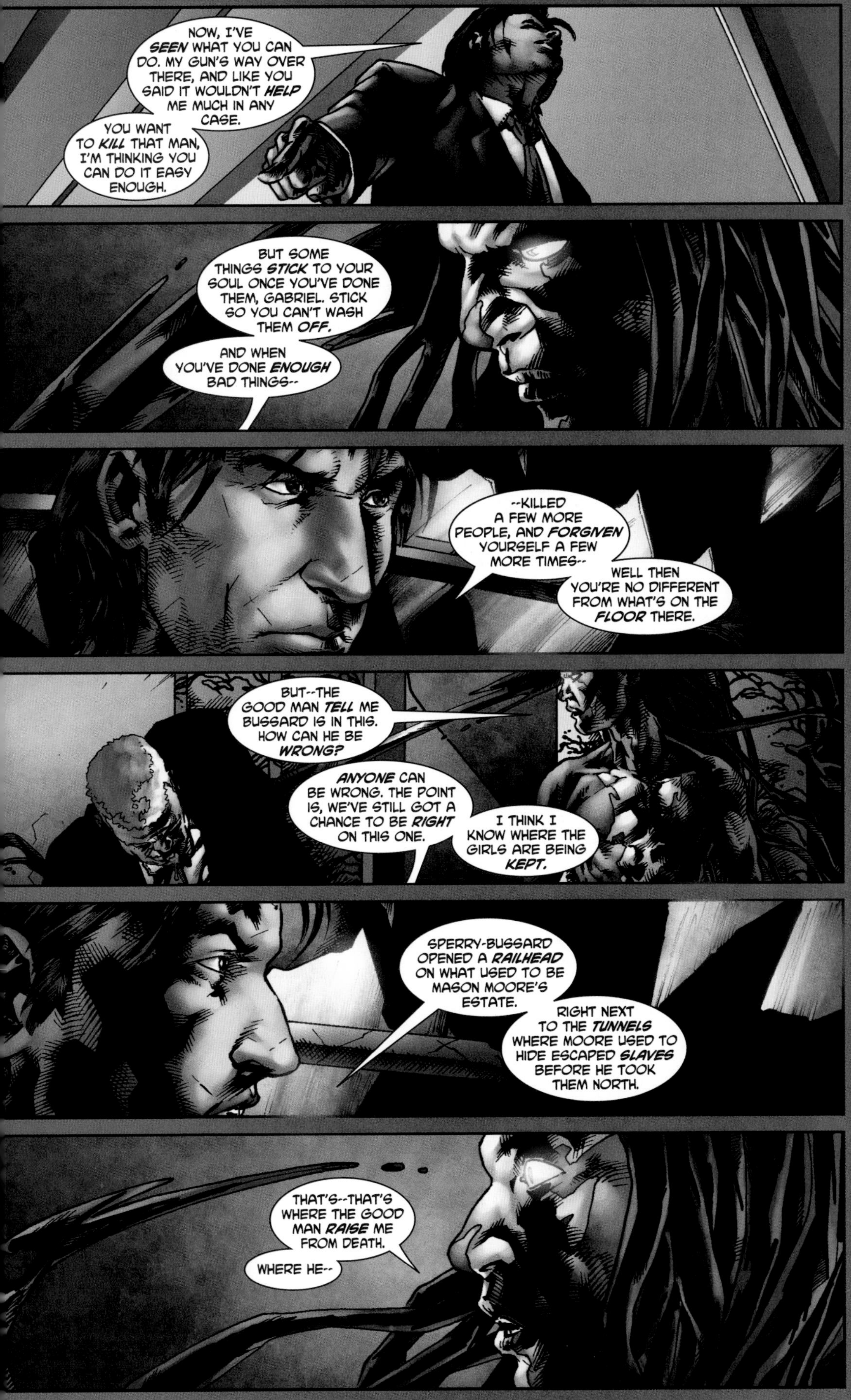
NOW, I'VE SEEN WHAT YOU CAN DO. MY GUN'S WAY OVER THERE, AND LIKE YOU SAID IT WOULDN'T HELP ME MUCH IN ANY CASE.
YOU WANT TO KILL THAT MAN, I'M THINKING YOU CAN DO IT EASY ENOUGH.
BUT SOME THINGS STICK TO YOUR SOUL ONCE YOU'VE DONE THEM, GABRIEL. STICK SO YOU CAN'T WASH THEM OFF.
AND WHEN YOU'VE DONE ENOUGH BAD THINGS--
--KILLED A FEW MORE PEOPLE, AND FORGIVEN YOURSELF A FEW MORE TIMES--
WELL THEN YOU'RE NO DIFFERENT FROM WHAT'S ON THE FLOOR THERE.
BUT--THE GOOD MAN TELL ME BUSSARD IS IN THIS. HOW CAN HE BE WRONG?
ANYONE CAN BE WRONG. THE POINT IS, WE'VE STILL GOT A CHANCE TO BE RIGHT ON THIS ONE.
I THINK I KNOW WHERE THE GIRLS ARE BEING KEPT.
SPERRY-BUSSARD OPENED A RAILHEAD ON WHAT USED TO BE MASON MOORE'S ESTATE.
RIGHT NEXT TO THE TUNNELS WHERE MOORE USED TO HIDE ESCAPED SLAVES BEFORE HE TOOK THEM NORTH.
THAT'S--THAT'S WHERE THE GOOD MAN RAISE ME FROM DEATH.
WHERE HE--

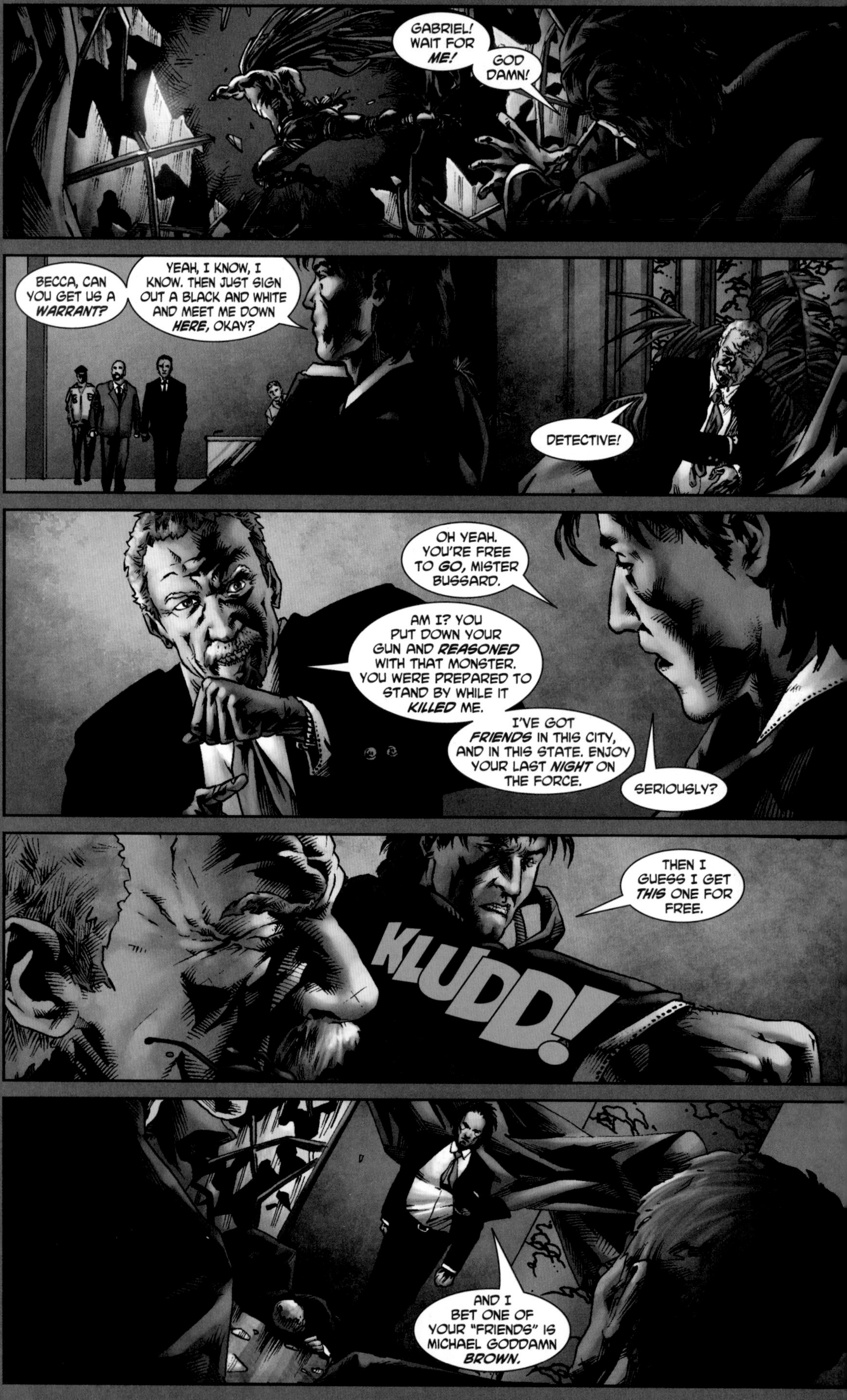
GABRIEL! WAIT FOR ME!
GOD DAMN!
BECCA, CAN YOU GET US A WARRANT?
YEAH, I KNOW, I KNOW. THEN JUST SIGN OUT A BLACK AND WHITE AND MEET ME DOWN HERE, OKAY?
DETECTIVE!
OH YEAH. YOU'RE FREE TO GO, MISTER BUSSARD.
AM I? YOU PUT DOWN YOUR GUN AND REASONED WITH THAT MONSTER. YOU WERE PREPARED TO STAND BY WHILE IT KILLED ME.
I'VE GOT FRIENDS IN THIS CITY, AND IN THIS STATE. ENJOY YOUR LAST NIGHT ON THE FORCE.
SERIOUSLY?
THEN I GUESS I GET THIS ONE FOR FREE.
KLUDD!
AND I BET ONE OF YOUR "FRIENDS" IS MICHAEL GODDAMN BROWN.

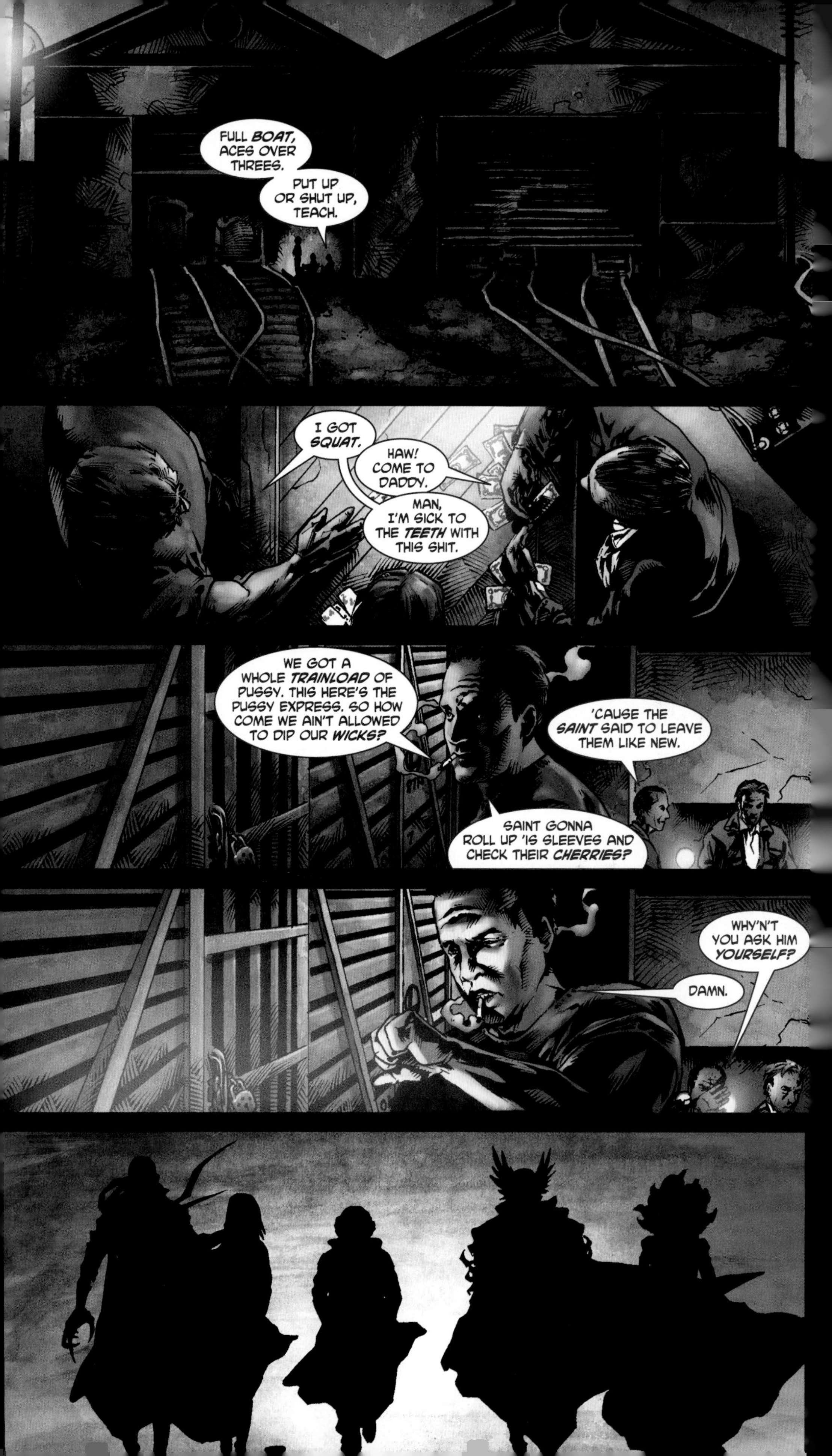
FULL BOAT, ACES OVER THREES.
PUT UP OR SHUT UP, TEACH.
I GOT SQUAT.
HAW! COME TO DADDY.
MAN, I'M SICK TO THE TEETH WITH THIS SHIT.
WE GOT A WHOLE TRAINLOAD OF PUSSY. THIS HERE'S THE PUSSY EXPRESS. SO HOW COME WE AIN'T ALLOWED TO DIP OUR WICKS?
'CAUSE THE SAINT SAID TO LEAVE THEM LIKE NEW.
SAINT GONNA ROLL UP 'IS SLEEVES AND CHECK THEIR CHERRIES?
WHY'N'T YOU ASK HIM YOURSELF?
DAMN.

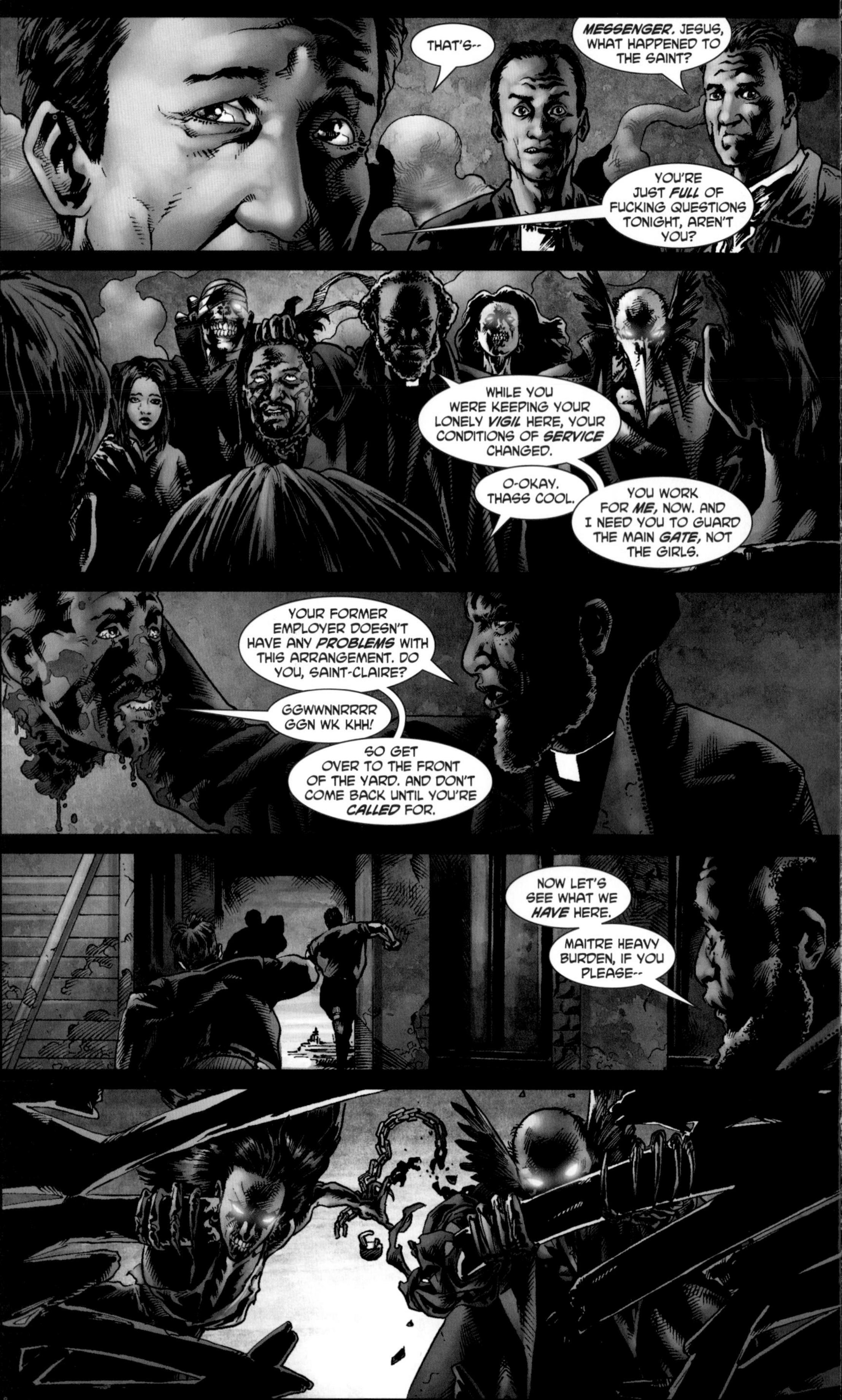
THAT'S--
MESSENGER. JESUS, WHAT HAPPENED TO THE SAINT?
YOU'RE JUST FULL OF FUCKING QUESTIONS TONIGHT, AREN'T YOU?
WHILE YOU WERE KEEPING YOUR LONELY VIGIL HERE, YOUR CONDITIONS OF SERVICE CHANGED.
O-OKAY. THASS COOL.
YOU WORK FOR ME, NOW. AND I NEED YOU TO GUARD THE MAIN GATE, NOT THE GIRLS.
YOUR FORMER EMPLOYER DOESN'T HAVE ANY PROBLEMS WITH THIS ARRANGEMENT. DO YOU, SAINT-CLAIRE?
GGWWNNRRRR GGN WK KHH!
SO GET OVER TO THE FRONT OF THE YARD. AND DON'T COME BACK UNTIL YOU'RE CALLED FOR.
NOW LET'S SEE WHAT WE HAVE HERE.
MAITRE HEAVY BURDEN, IF YOU PLEASE--

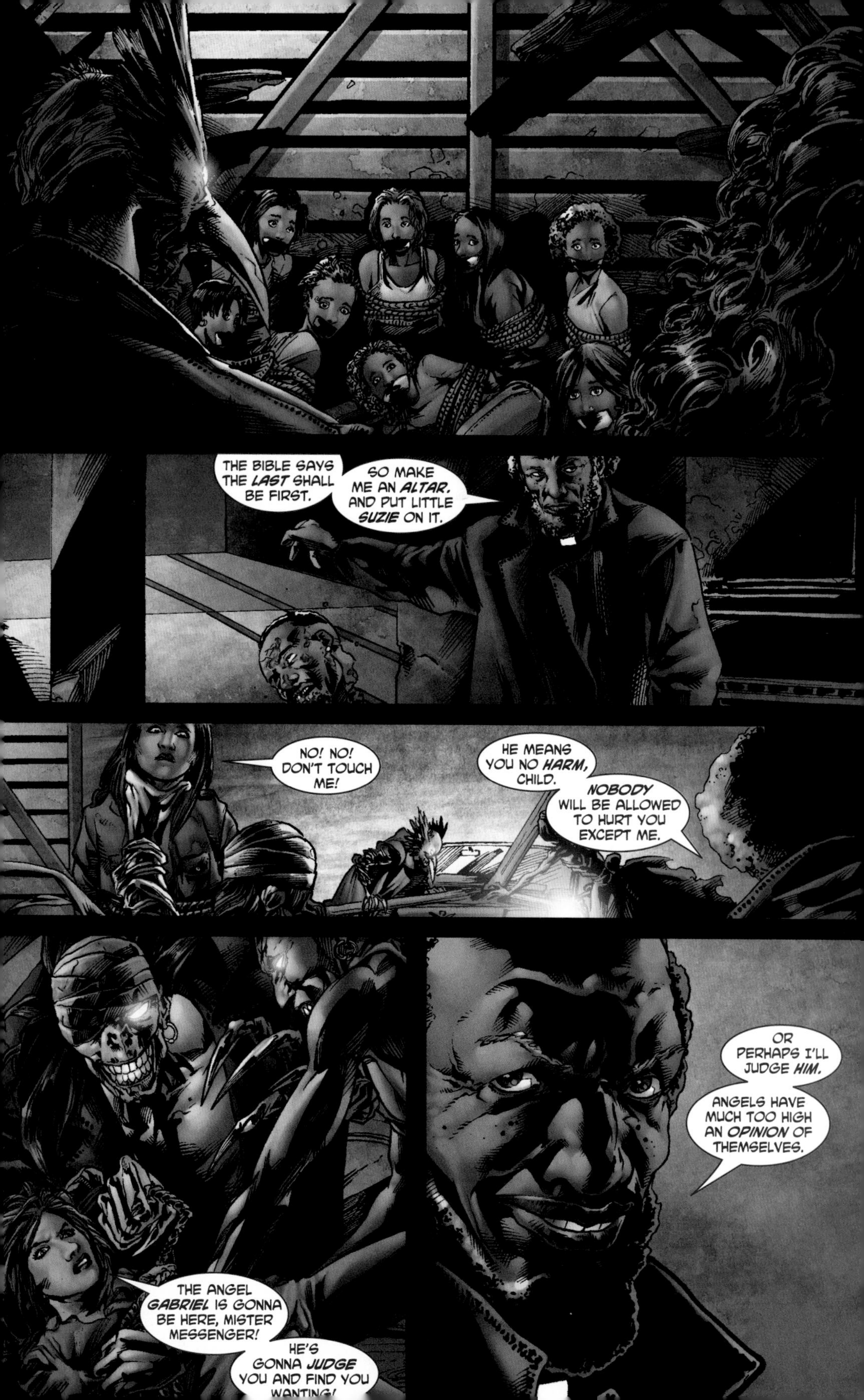
THE BIBLE SAYS THE *LAST* SHALL BE FIRST.
SO MAKE ME AN *ALTAR*, AND PUT LITTLE *SUZIE* ON IT.
NO! NO! DON'T TOUCH ME!
HE MEANS YOU NO *HARM*, CHILD.
NOBODY WILL BE ALLOWED TO HURT YOU EXCEPT ME.
THE ANGEL *GABRIEL* IS GONNA BE HERE, MISTER MESSENGER!
HE'S GONNA *JUDGE* YOU AND FIND YOU WANTING!
OR PERHAPS I'LL JUDGE *HIM*.
ANGELS HAVE MUCH TOO HIGH AN *OPINION* OF THEMSELVES.

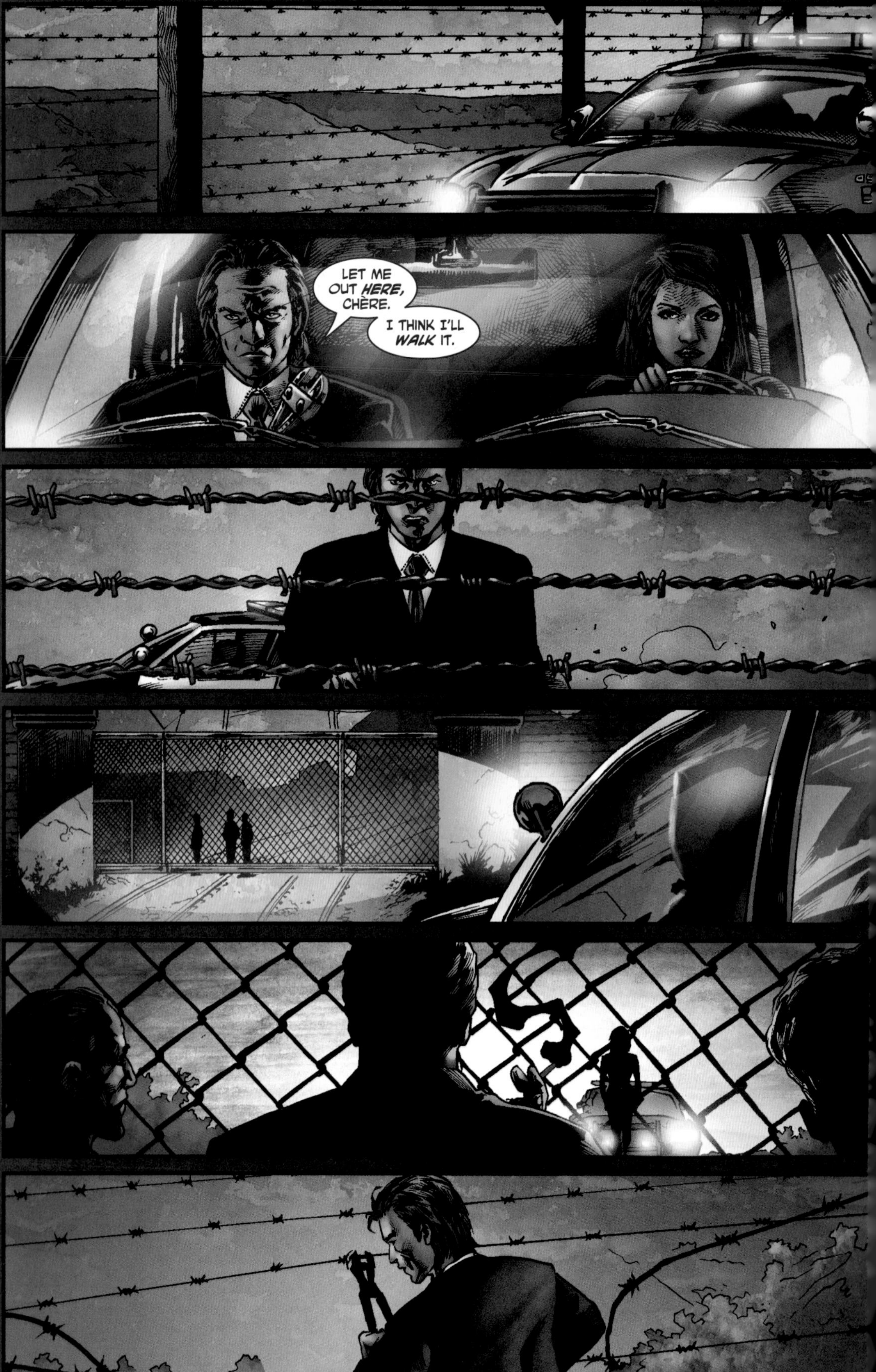
LET ME OUT *HERE*, CHÈRE.
I THINK I'LL *WALK* IT.

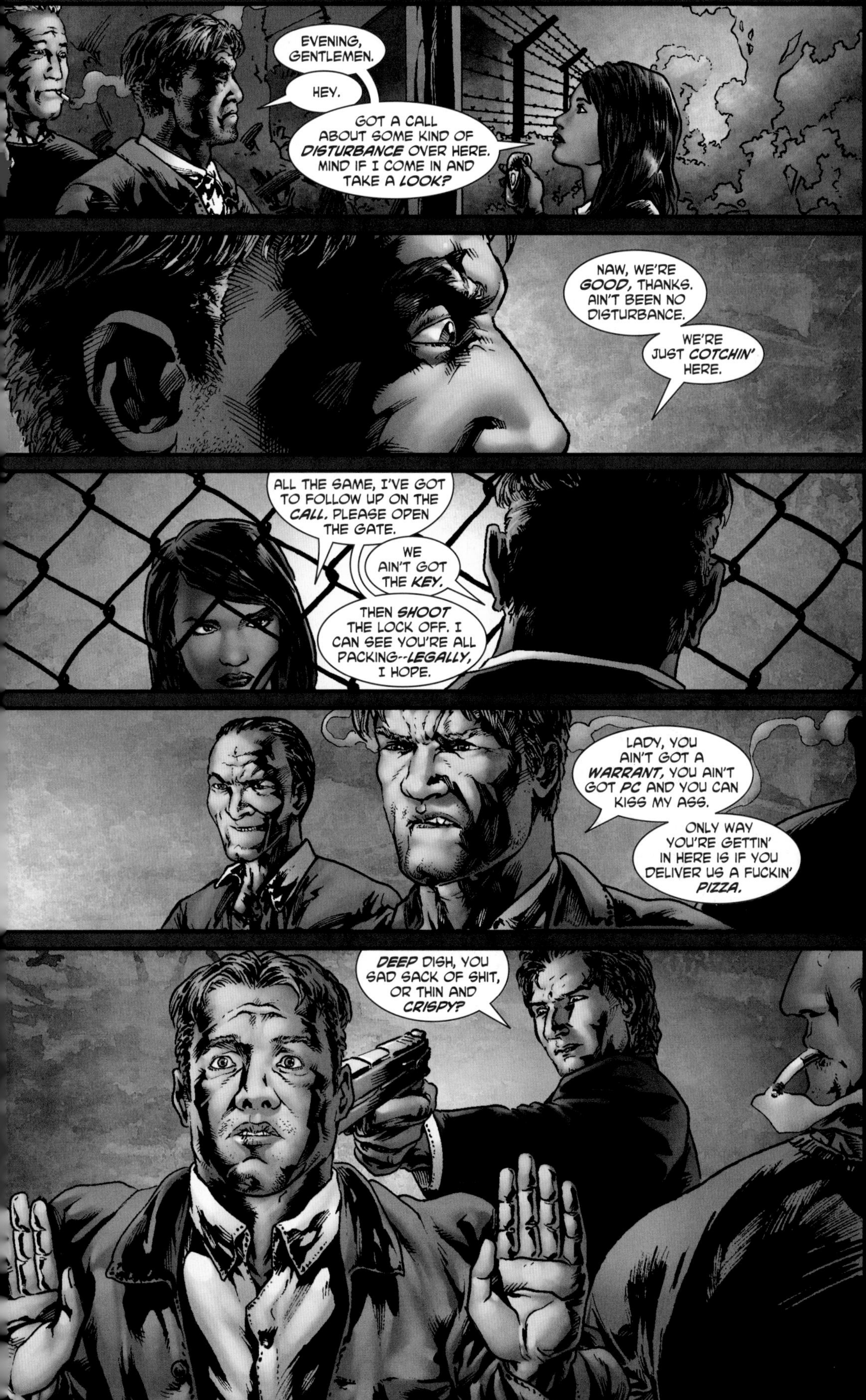

EVENING, GENTLEMEN.
HEY.
GOT A CALL ABOUT SOME KIND OF *DISTURBANCE* OVER HERE. MIND IF I COME IN AND TAKE A *LOOK?*
NAW, WE'RE *GOOD,* THANKS. AIN'T BEEN NO DISTURBANCE.
WE'RE JUST *COTCHIN'* HERE.
ALL THE SAME, I'VE GOT TO FOLLOW UP ON THE *CALL.* PLEASE OPEN THE GATE.
WE AIN'T GOT THE *KEY.*
THEN *SHOOT* THE LOCK OFF. I CAN SEE YOU'RE ALL PACKING--*LEGALLY,* I HOPE.
LADY, YOU AIN'T GOT A *WARRANT,* YOU AIN'T GOT *PC* AND YOU CAN KISS MY ASS.
ONLY WAY YOU'RE GETTIN' IN HERE IS IF YOU DELIVER US A FUCKIN' *PIZZA.*
DEEP DISH, YOU SAD SACK OF SHIT, OR THIN AND *CRISPY?*

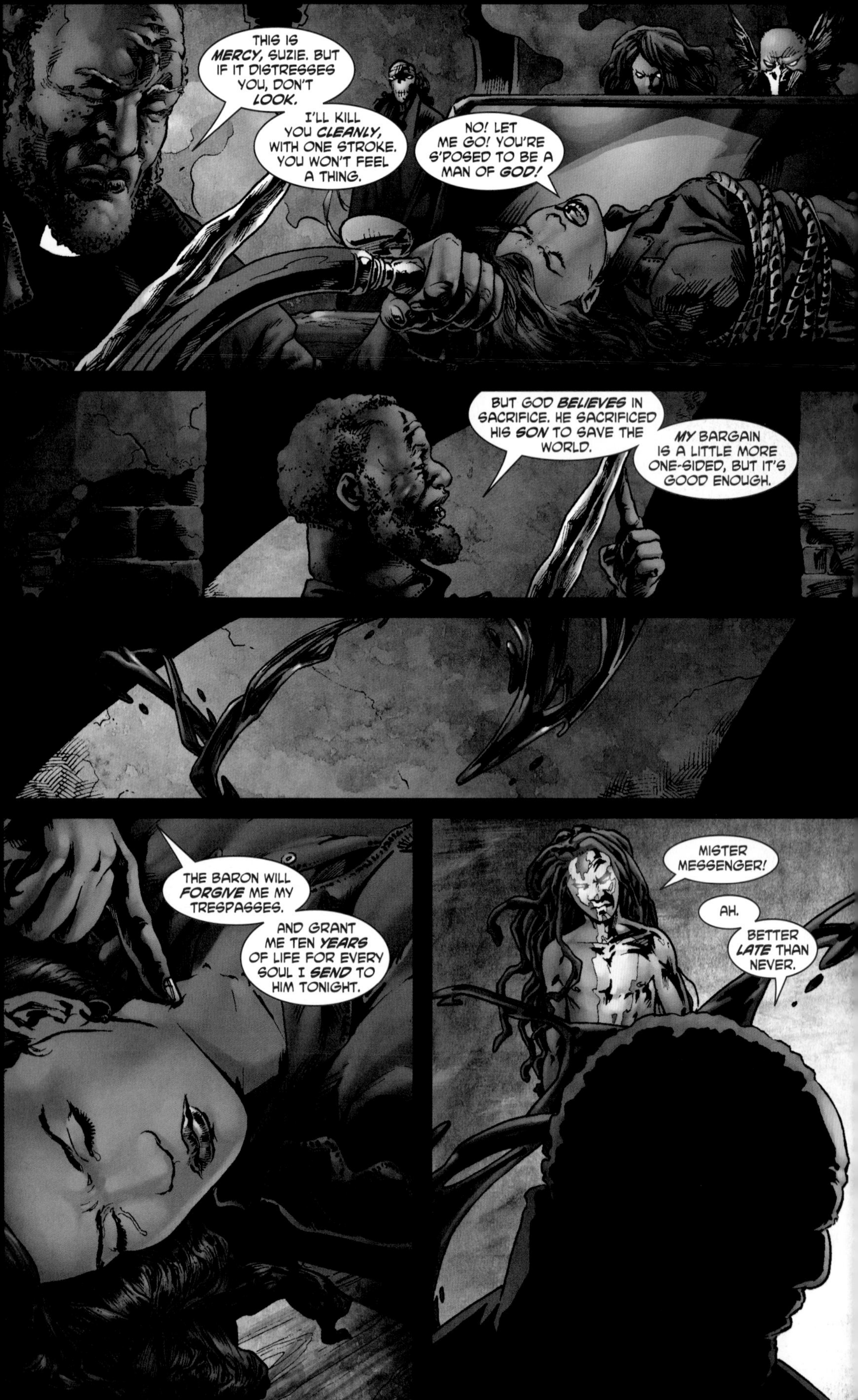
THIS IS MERCY, SUZIE. BUT IF IT DISTRESSES YOU, DON'T LOOK.
I'LL KILL YOU CLEANLY, WITH ONE STROKE. YOU WON'T FEEL A THING.
NO! LET ME GO! YOU'RE S'POSED TO BE A MAN OF GOD!
BUT GOD BELIEVES IN SACRIFICE. HE SACRIFICED HIS SON TO SAVE THE WORLD.
MY BARGAIN IS A LITTLE MORE ONE-SIDED, BUT IT'S GOOD ENOUGH.
THE BARON WILL FORGIVE ME MY TRESPASSES.
AND GRANT ME TEN YEARS OF LIFE FOR EVERY SOUL I SEND TO HIM TONIGHT.
MISTER MESSENGER!
AH.
BETTER LATE THAN NEVER.

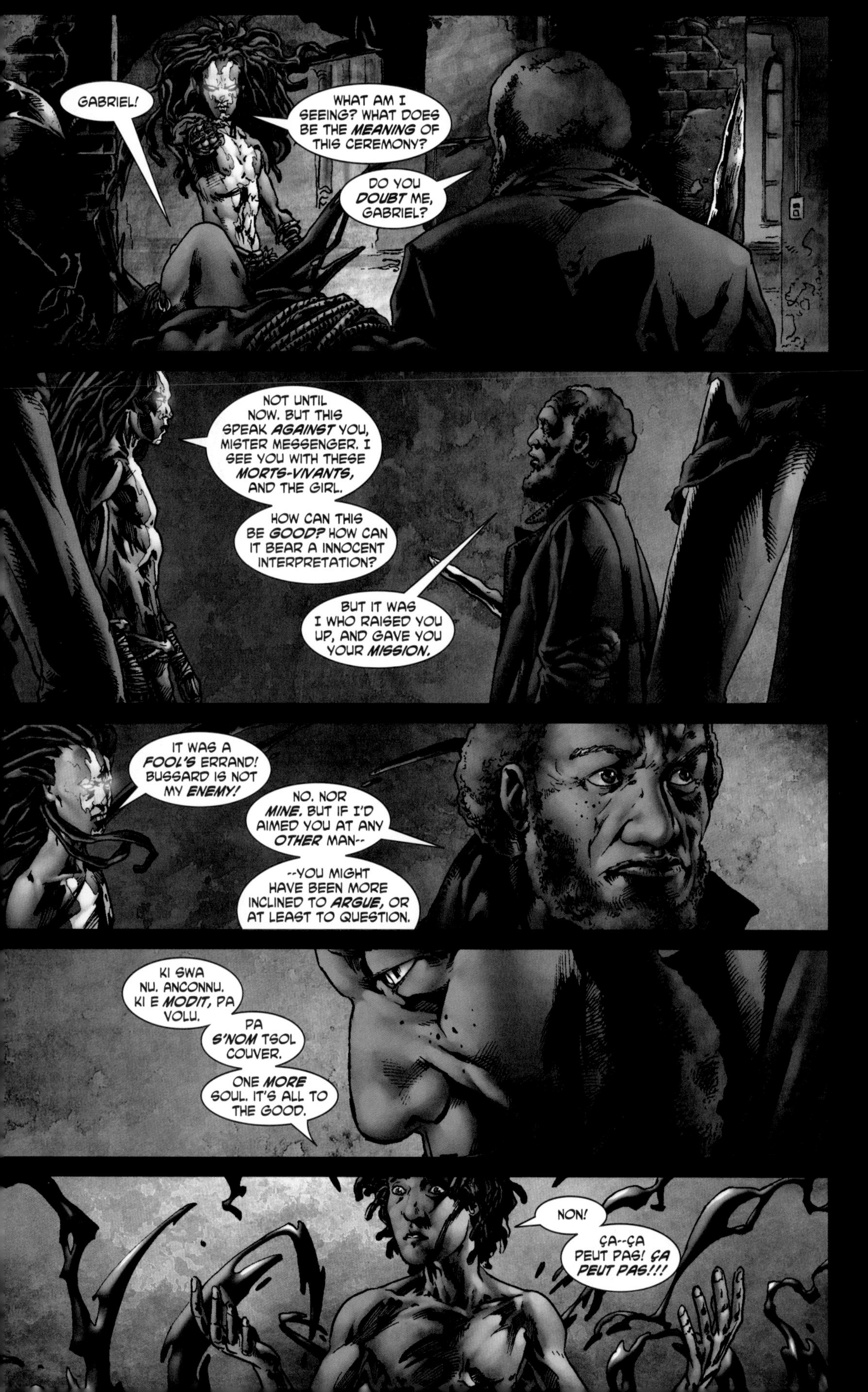
GABRIEL!
WHAT AM I SEEING? WHAT DOES BE THE *MEANING* OF THIS CEREMONY?
DO YOU *DOUBT* ME, GABRIEL?
NOT UNTIL NOW. BUT THIS SPEAK *AGAINST* YOU, MISTER MESSENGER. I SEE YOU WITH THESE *MORTS-VIVANTS,* AND THE GIRL.
HOW CAN THIS BE *GOOD?* HOW CAN IT BEAR A INNOCENT INTERPRETATION?
BUT IT WAS I WHO RAISED YOU UP, AND GAVE YOU YOUR *MISSION.*
IT WAS A *FOOL'S* ERRAND! BUSSARD IS NOT MY *ENEMY!*
NO. NOR *MINE.* BUT IF I'D AIMED YOU AT ANY *OTHER* MAN--
--YOU MIGHT HAVE BEEN MORE INCLINED TO *ARGUE,* OR AT LEAST TO QUESTION.
KI SWA NU. ANCONNU. KI E *MODIT,* PA VOLU.
PA *S'NOM* TSOL COUVER.
ONE *MORE* SOUL. IT'S ALL TO THE GOOD.
NON!
ÇA--ÇA PEUT PAS! *ÇA PEUT PAS!!!*

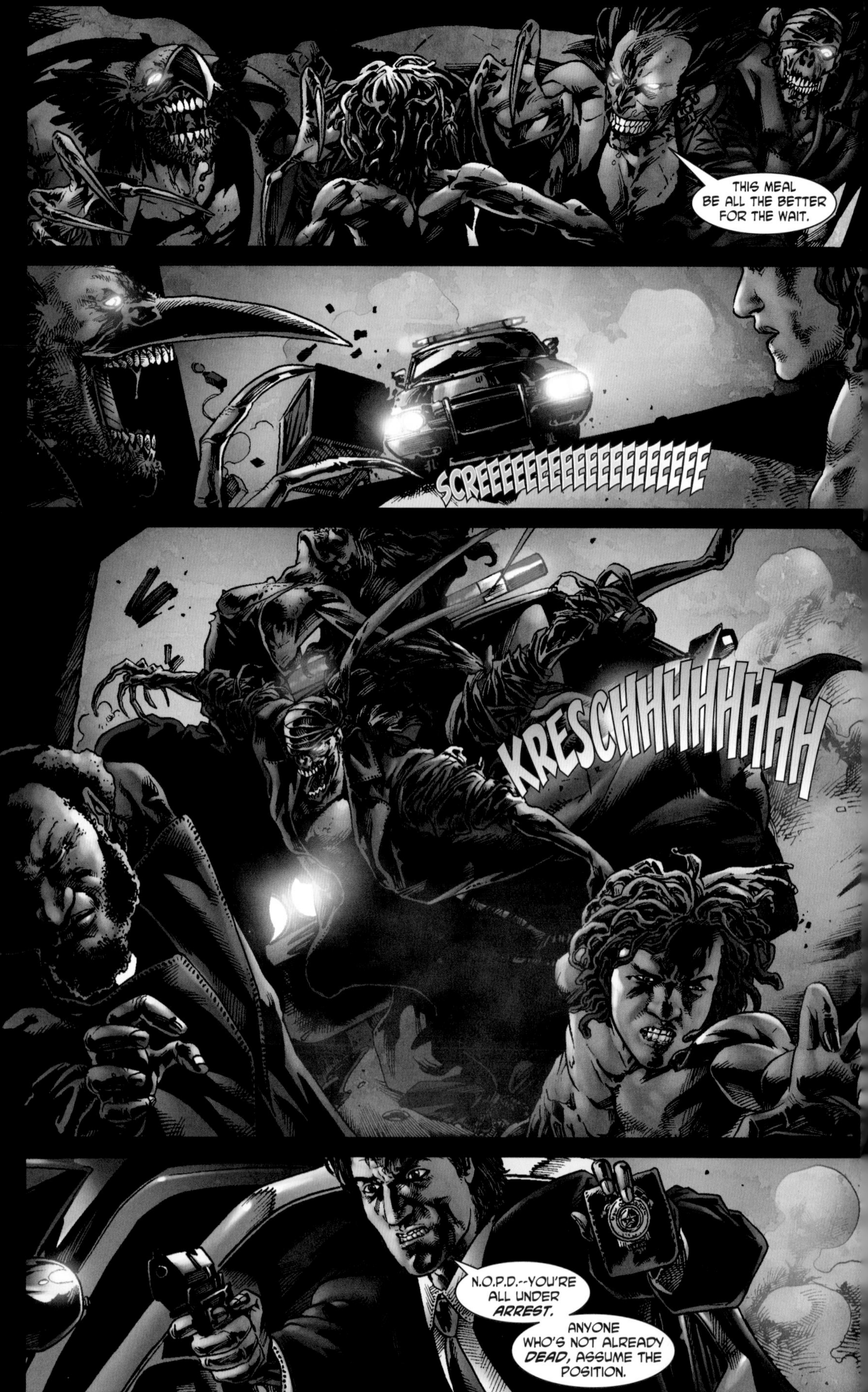
THIS MEAL BE ALL THE BETTER FOR THE WAIT.
SCREEEEEEEEEEEEEEEEEE
KRESCHHHHHHHHH
N.O.P.D.--YOU'RE ALL UNDER *ARREST.*
ANYONE WHO'S NOT ALREADY *DEAD,* ASSUME THE POSITION.

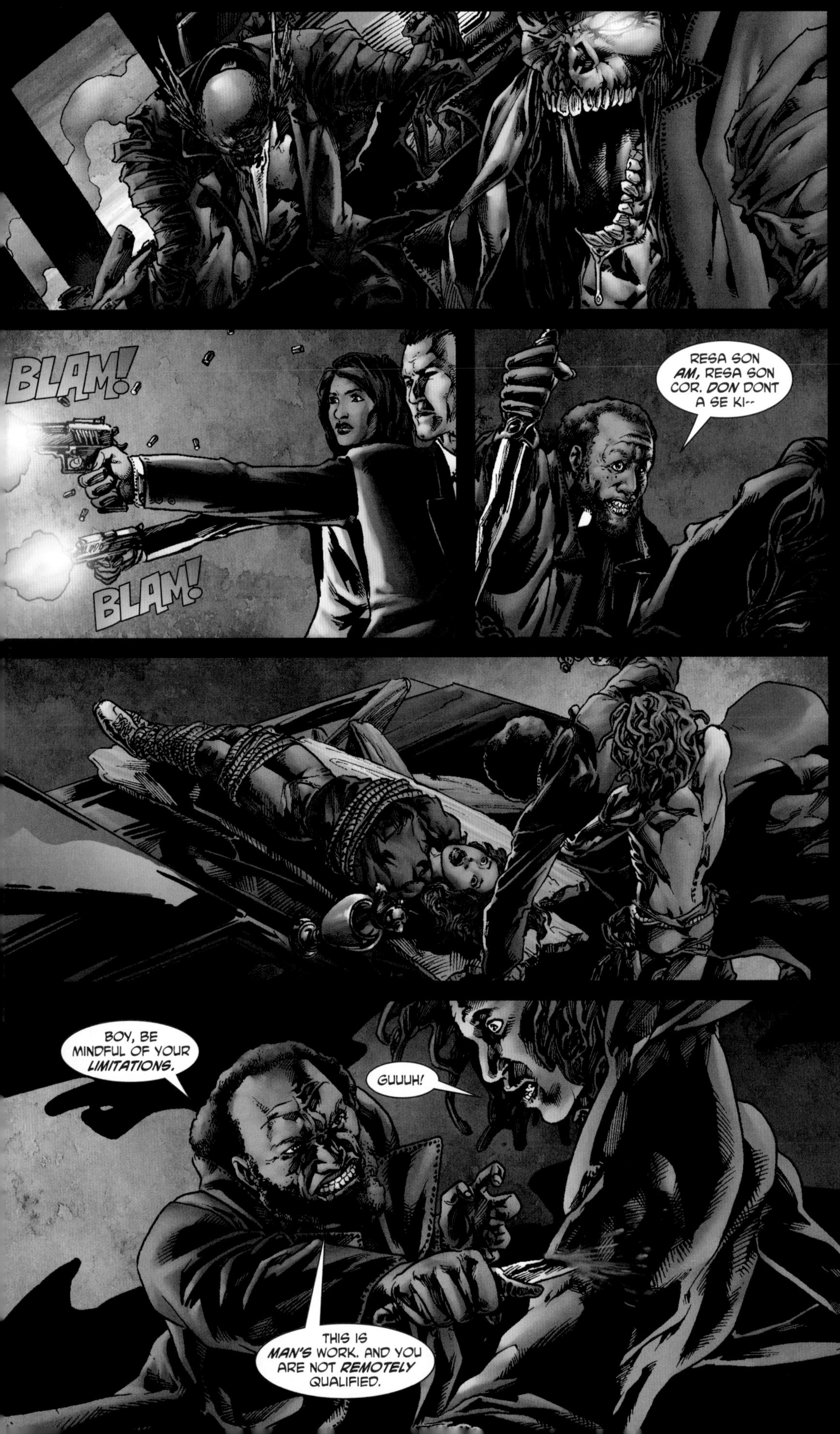
BLAM!
BLAM!
RESA SON AM, RESA SON COR. DON DONT A SE KI--
BOY, BE MINDFUL OF YOUR LIMITATIONS.
GUUUH!
THIS IS MAN'S WORK. AND YOU ARE NOT REMOTELY QUALIFIED.

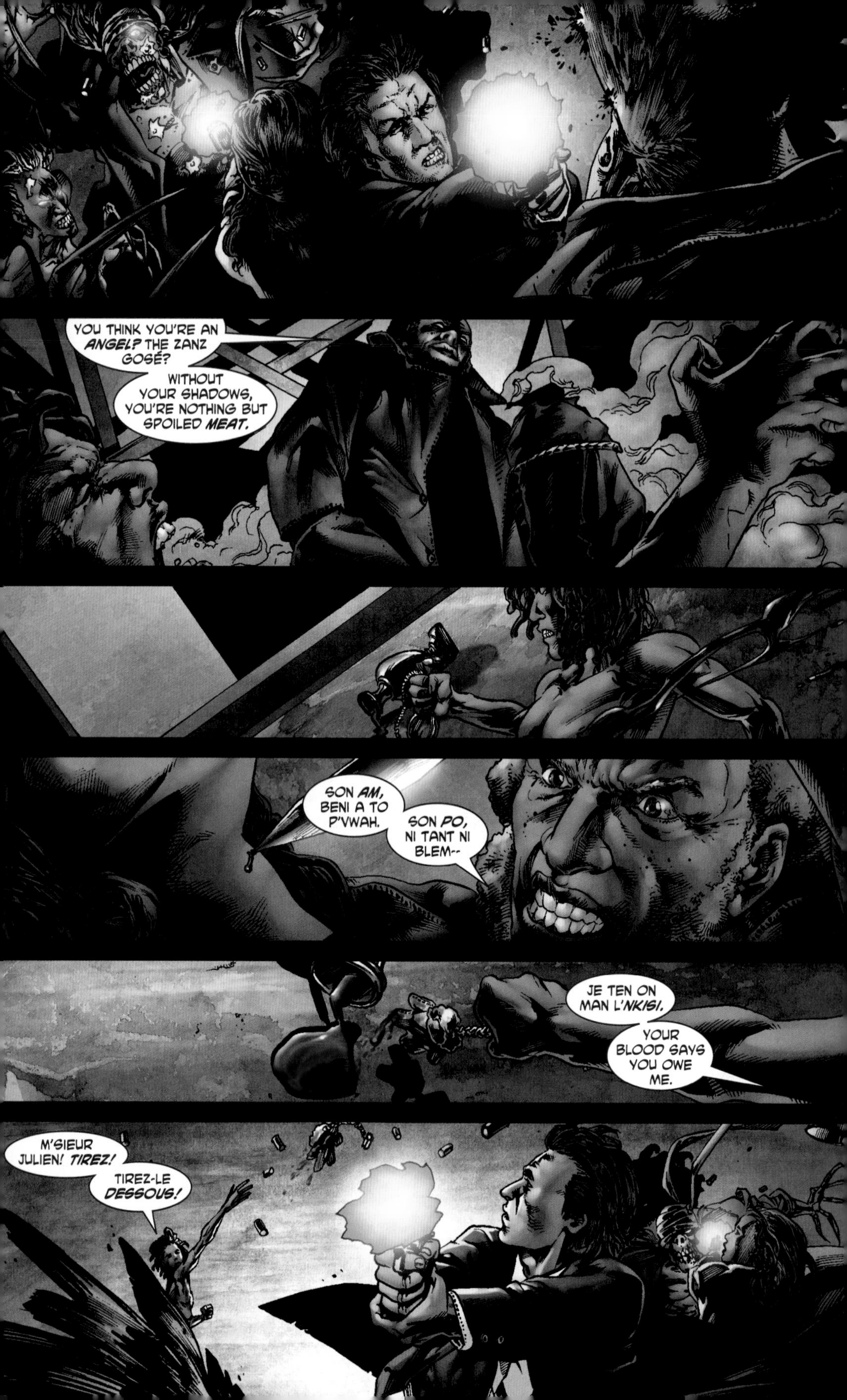
YOU THINK YOU'RE AN ANGEL? THE ZANZ GOSÉ?
WITHOUT YOUR SHADOWS, YOU'RE NOTHING BUT SPOILED MEAT.
SON AM, BENI A TO P'VWAH.
SON PO, NI TANT NI BLEM--
JE TEN ON MAN L'NKISI.
YOUR BLOOD SAYS YOU OWE ME.
M'SIEUR JULIEN! TIREZ!
TIREZ-LE DESSOUS!

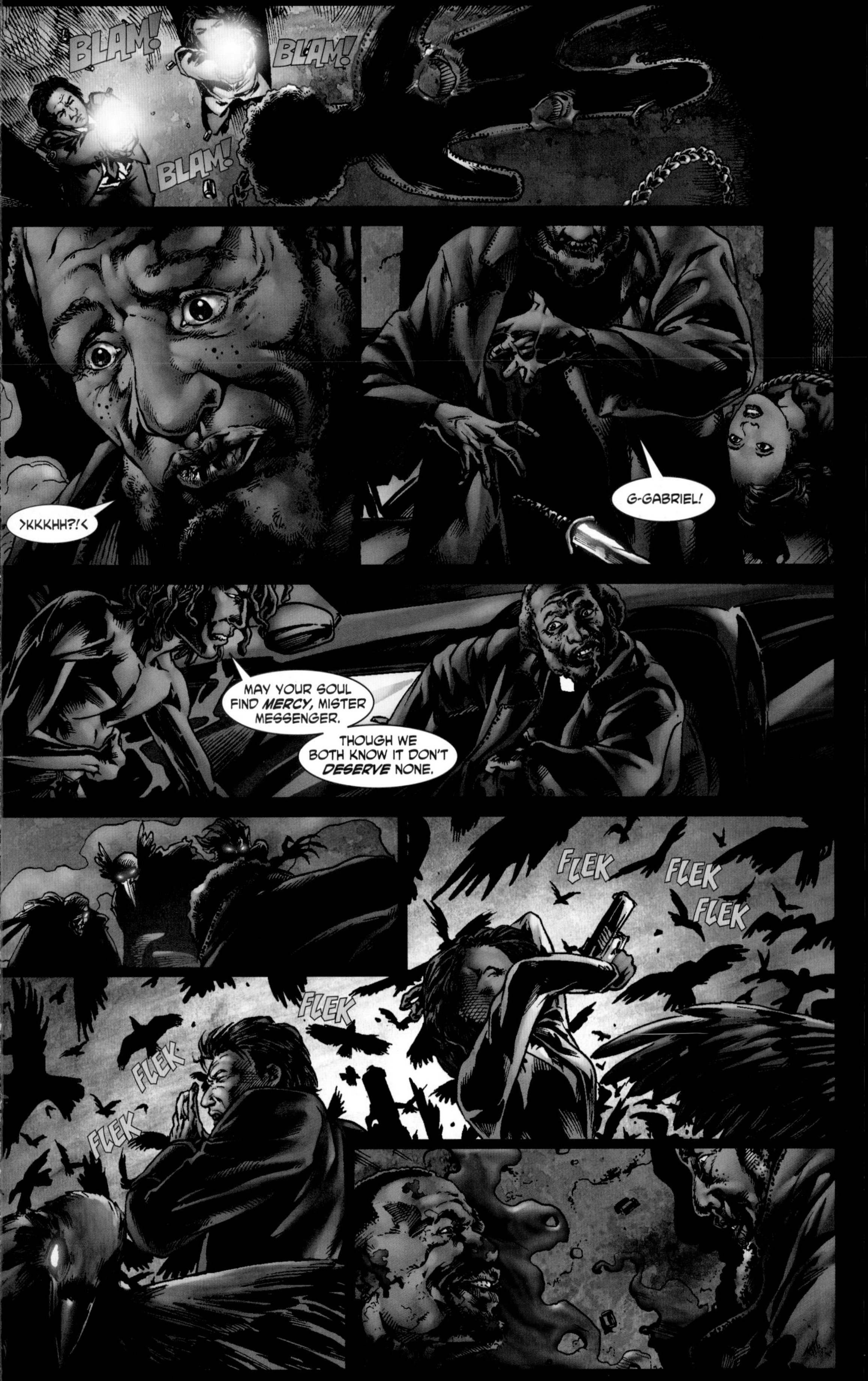
BLAM!
BLAM!
BLAM!
>KKKHH?!<
G-GABRIEL!
MAY YOUR SOUL FIND MERCY, MISTER MESSENGER.
THOUGH WE BOTH KNOW IT DON'T DESERVE NONE.
FLEK
FLEK
FLEK
FLEK
FLEK
FLEK

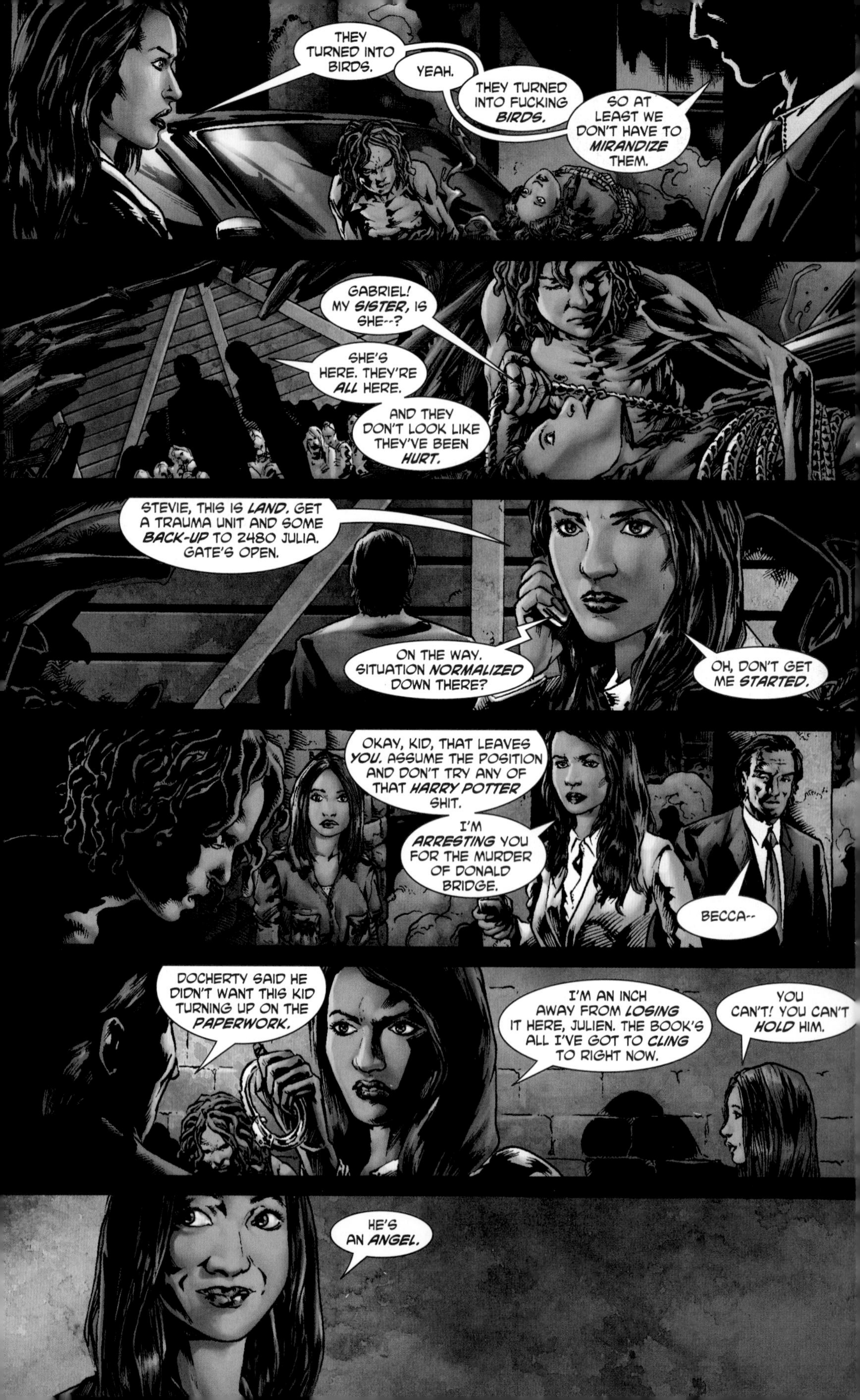
THEY TURNED INTO BIRDS.
YEAH.
THEY TURNED INTO FUCKING *BIRDS.*
SO AT LEAST WE DON'T HAVE TO *MIRANDIZE* THEM.
GABRIEL! MY *SISTER,* IS SHE--?
SHE'S HERE. THEY'RE *ALL* HERE.
AND THEY DON'T LOOK LIKE THEY'VE BEEN *HURT.*
STEVIE, THIS IS *LAND.* GET A TRAUMA UNIT AND SOME *BACK-UP* TO 2480 JULIA. GATE'S OPEN.
ON THE WAY. SITUATION *NORMALIZED* DOWN THERE?
OH, DON'T GET ME *STARTED.*
OKAY, KID, THAT LEAVES *YOU.* ASSUME THE POSITION AND DON'T TRY ANY OF THAT *HARRY POTTER* SHIT.
I'M *ARRESTING* YOU FOR THE MURDER OF DONALD BRIDGE.
BECCA--
DOCHERTY SAID HE DIDN'T WANT THIS KID TURNING UP ON THE *PAPERWORK.*
I'M AN INCH AWAY FROM *LOSING* IT HERE, JULIEN. THE BOOK'S ALL I'VE GOT TO *CLING* TO RIGHT NOW.
YOU CAN'T! YOU CAN'T *HOLD* HIM.
HE'S AN *ANGEL.*

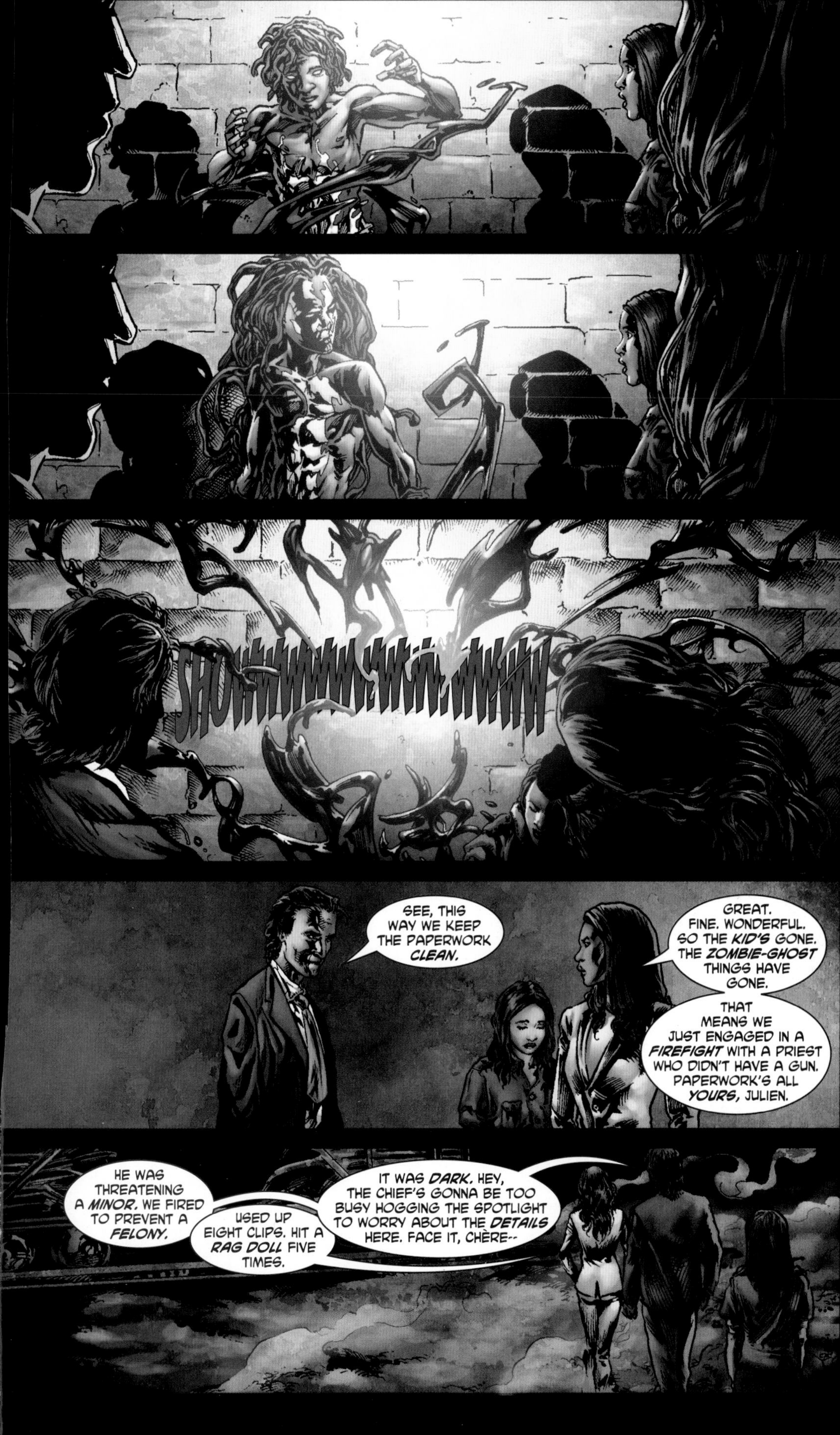

SHOWWWWWWWWWWW
SEE, THIS WAY WE KEEP THE PAPERWORK CLEAN.
GREAT. FINE. WONDERFUL. SO THE KID'S GONE. THE ZOMBIE-GHOST THINGS HAVE GONE.
THAT MEANS WE JUST ENGAGED IN A FIREFIGHT WITH A PRIEST WHO DIDN'T HAVE A GUN. PAPERWORK'S ALL YOURS, JULIEN.
HE WAS THREATENING A MINOR. WE FIRED TO PREVENT A FELONY.
USED UP EIGHT CLIPS. HIT A RAG DOLL FIVE TIMES.
IT WAS DARK. HEY, THE CHIEF'S GONNA BE TOO BUSY HOGGING THE SPOTLIGHT TO WORRY ABOUT THE DETAILS HERE. FACE IT, CHÈRE--

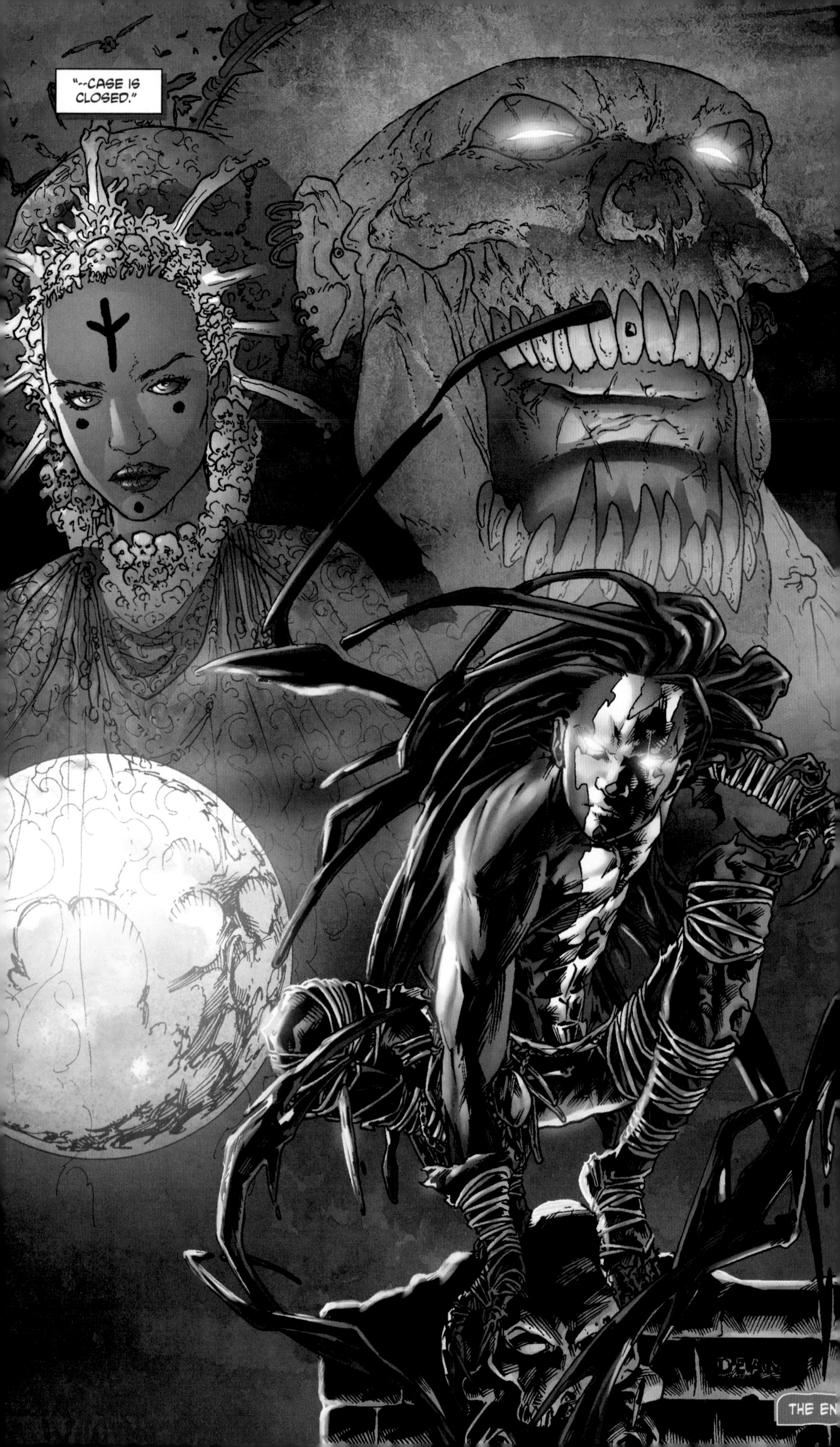
"--CASE IS CLOSED."
DEAN
THE EN

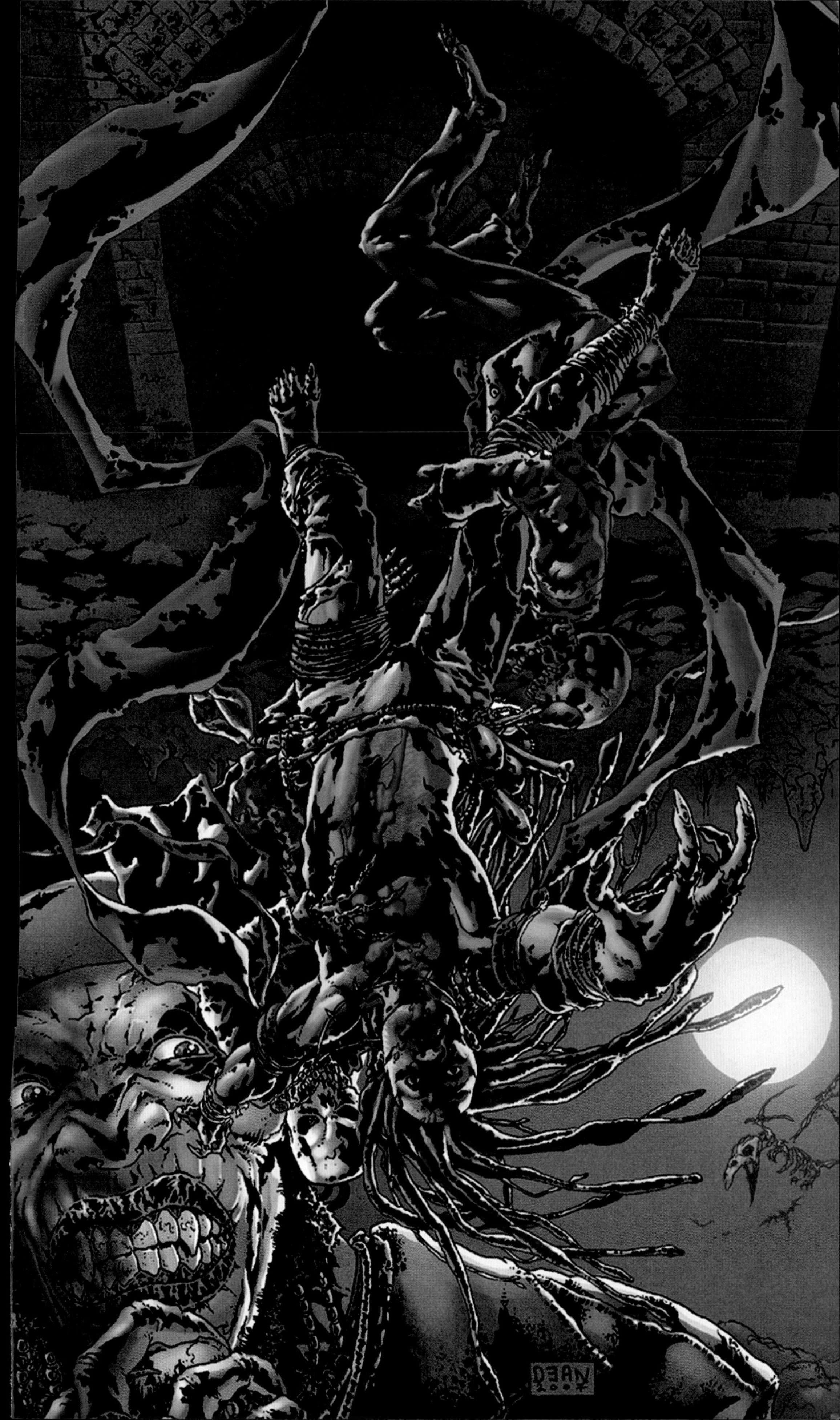

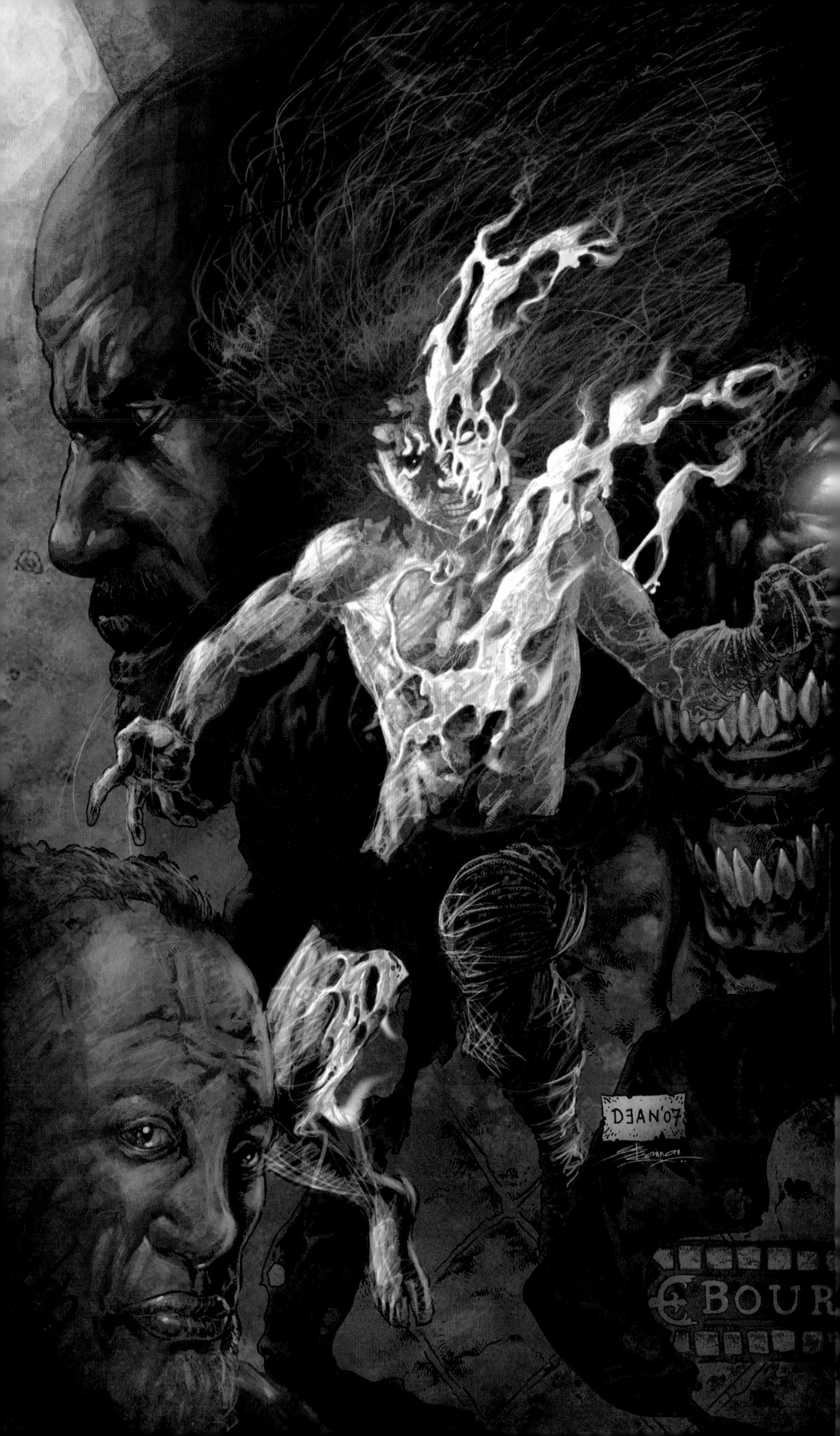
DEAN'07
BOUR

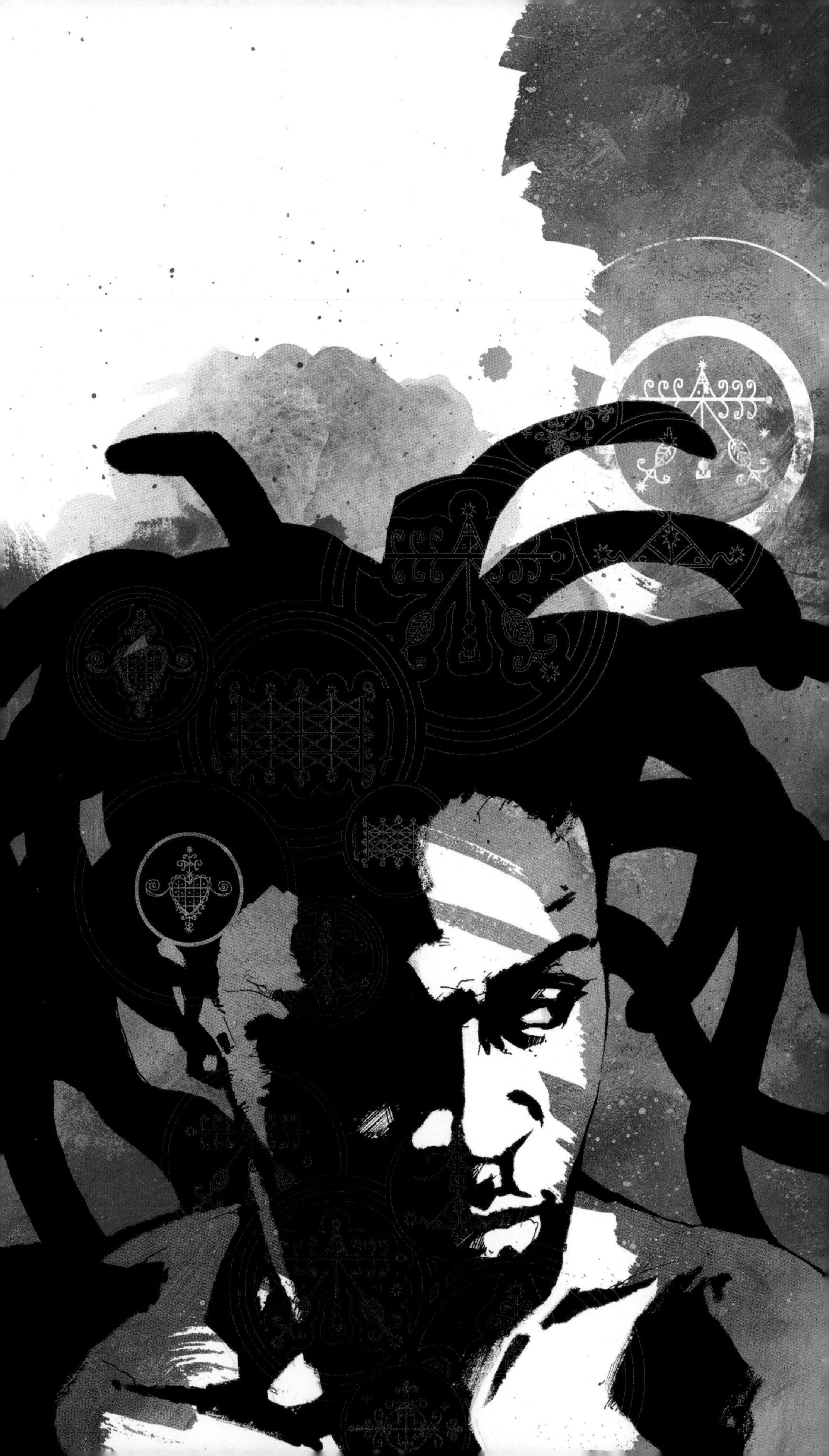

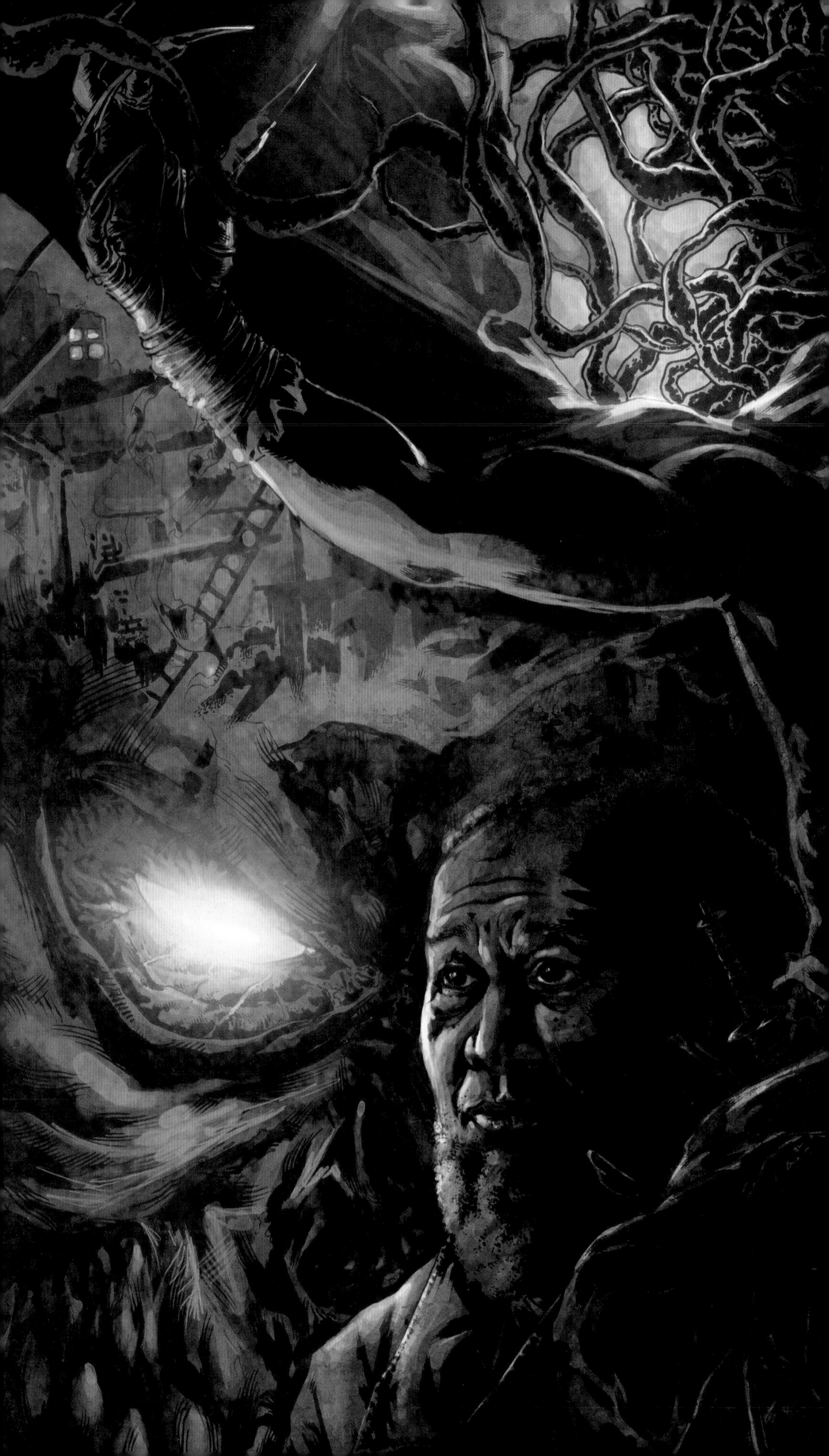

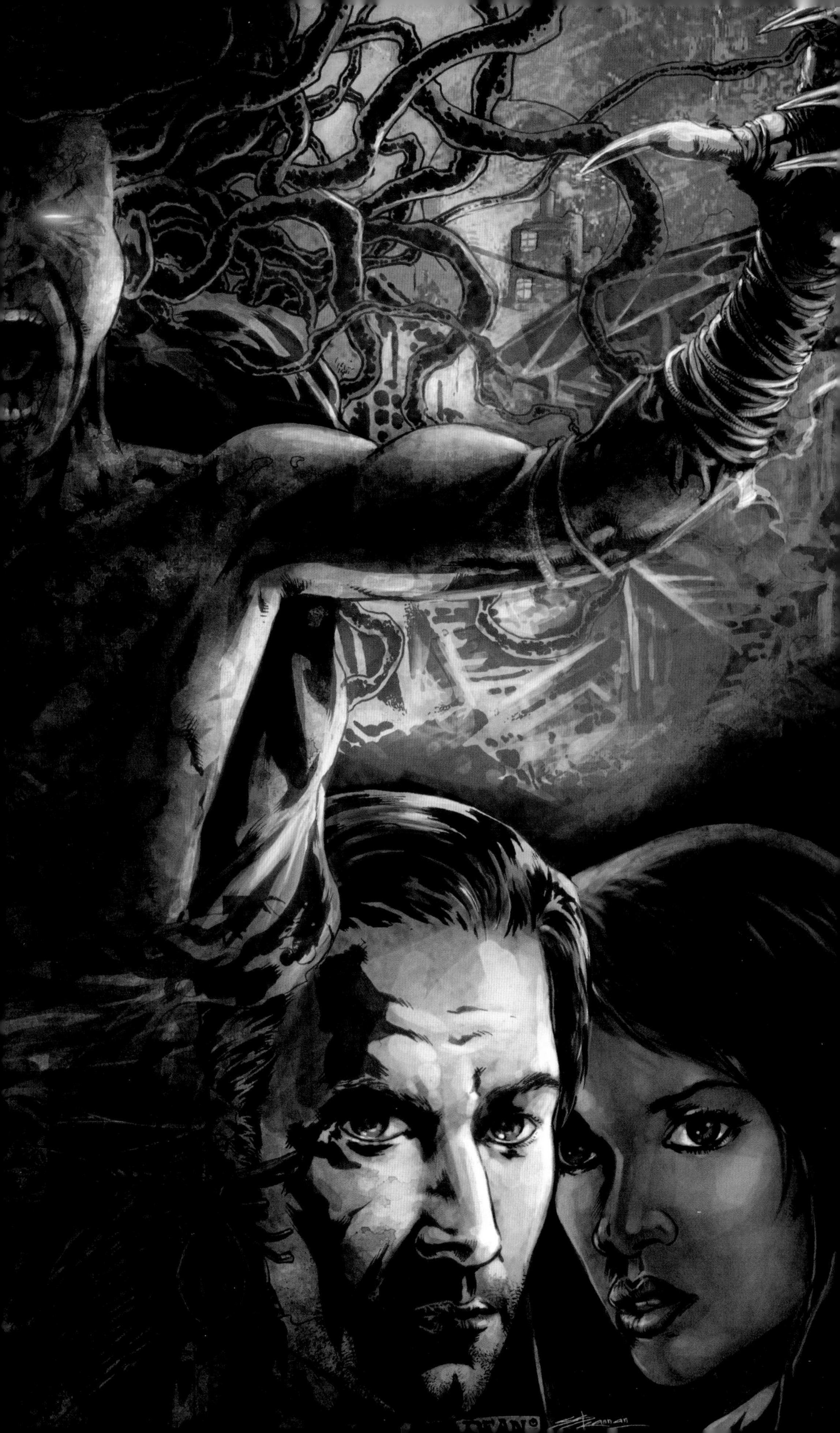

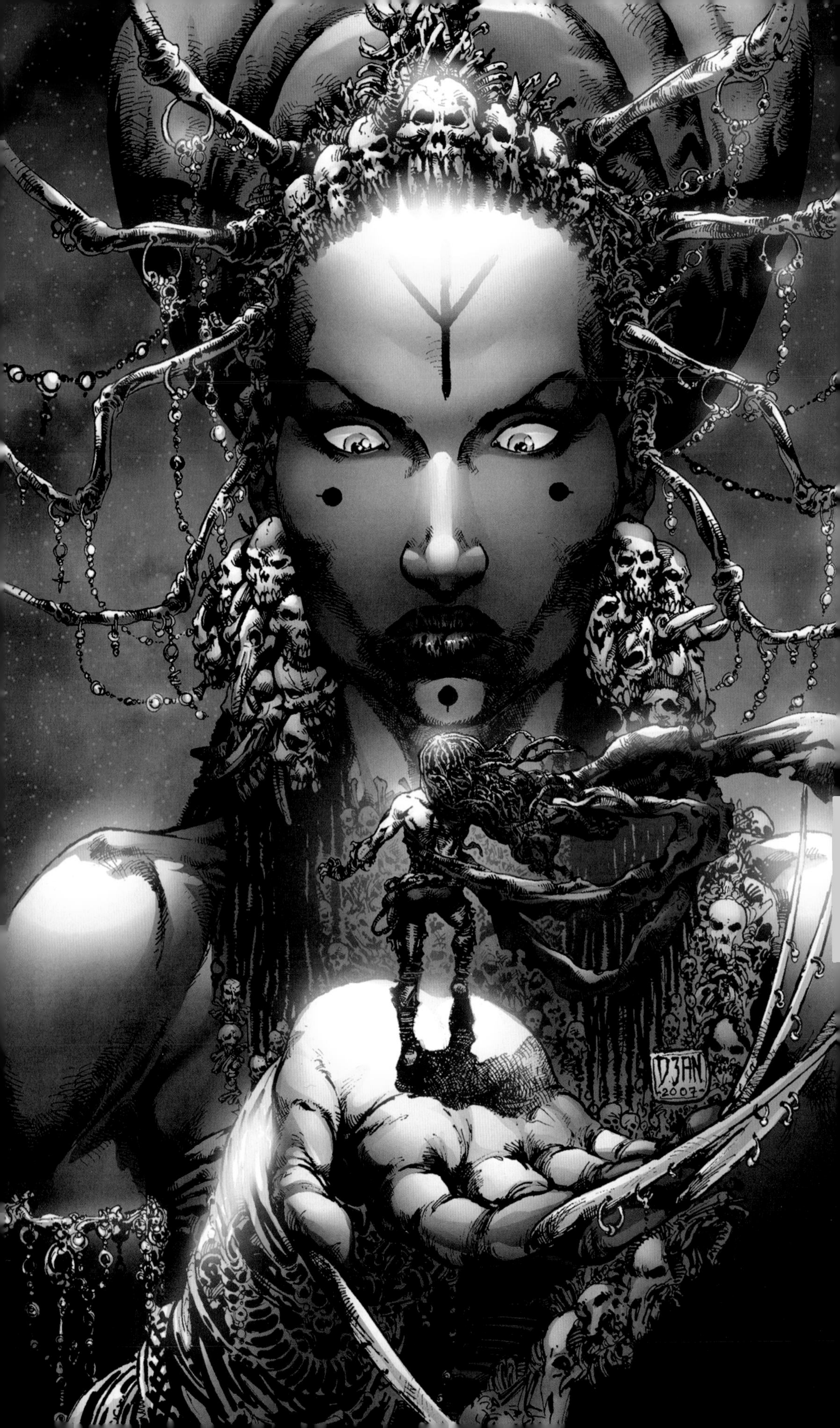